Federal Tax Policy

Studies of Government Finance

Federal Tax Policy

JOSEPH A. PECHMAN

THIRD EDITION

Studies of Government Finance

THE BROOKINGS INSTITUTION

WASHINGTON, D.C.

Library of Congress Cataloging in Publication Data:

Pechman, Joseph A   1918–
  Federal tax policy.
  (Studies of government finance: Second series)
  Bibliography: p .
  Includes index.
  1. Final policy—United States.   2. Taxation—
United States.   I. Title.   II. Series.
HJ257.2.P4   1977   336.2′00973   76-54901
ISBN 0-8157-6978-4
ISBN 0-8157-6977-6 pbk.

9 8 7 6 5 4 3 2 1

THE BROOKINGS INSTITUTION is an independent organization devoted to nonpartisan research, education, and publication in economics, government, foreign policy, and the social sciences generally. Its principal purposes are to aid in the development of sound public policies and to promote public understanding of issues of national importance.

The Institution was founded on December 8, 1927, to merge the activities of the Institute for Government Research, founded in 1916, the Institute of Economics, founded in 1922, and the Robert Brookings Graduate School of Economics and Government, founded in 1924.

The Board of Trustees is responsible for the general administration of the Institution, while the immediate direction of the policies, program, and staff is vested in the President, assisted by an advisory committee of the officers and staff. The bylaws of the Institution state: "It is the function of the Trustees to make possible the conduct of scientific research, and publication, under the most favorable conditions, and to safeguard the independence of the research staff in the pursuit of their studies and in the publication of the results of such studies. It is not a part of their function to determine, control, or influence the conduct of particular investigations or the conclusions reached."

The President bears final responsibility for the decision to publish a manuscript as a Brookings book. In reaching his judgment on the competence, accuracy, and objectivity of each study, the President is advised by the director of the appropriate research program and weighs the views of a panel of expert outside readers who report to him in confidence on the quality of the work. Publication of a work signifies that it is deemed a competent treatment worthy of public consideration but does not imply endorsement of conclusions or recommendations.

The Institution maintains its position of neutrality on issues of public policy in order to safeguard the intellectual freedom of the staff. Hence interpretations or conclusions in Brookings publications should be understood to be solely those of the authors and should not be attributed to the Institution, to its trustees, officers, or other staff members, or to the organizations that support its research.

Foreword

IN THE PAST fifteen years the federal government has enacted nine major tax laws. Some of them were primarily intended to raise or lower revenues so as to stabilize the economy, others were intended to improve the structure of the tax system and to promote particular economic objectives, and still others were designed to combine stabilization and structural objectives. All of them were controversial; each was considered and debated at length by the public and Congress. But many believe that the nation's system continues to need substantial change.

The purpose of this third edition, like its predecessors, is to explain the intricacies of the tax system so that the interested citizen may better understand and contribute to the public discussion and to the resolution of the main issues. This edition reflects tax developments between 1970 and 1976. It emphasizes the newer issues, including the effects of the Tax Reform Act of 1976 on the taxation of income, estates, and gifts; inflation adjustments for income tax purposes; the relation between the corporation and individual income taxes; the relative merits of graduated income and expenditure taxes; and the plight of the cities.

The reader should note that this book is one economist's interpretation of professional opinion in this difficult and controversial area of public policy. Conflicting points of view are presented, but their proponents will not necessarily agree with the author's interpretation and evaluation. Moreover, in the interest of brevity, the discussion sometimes omits details that others might regard as important. For further information and different points of view, the reader should refer to the extensive literature cited in the bibliographical notes.

Joseph A. Pechman, director of Economic Studies at the Brookings Institution, has had long experience in tax research and in research on the tax legislative process. He acknowledges once again his gratitude for editorial assistance on the earlier editions from Charles B. Saunders, Jr., and Virginia C. Haaga, and research assistance from Andrew T. Williams and John Yinger. He also acknowledges again the constructive review and comments on the earlier editions by Boris I. Bittker, Charles F. Conlon, L. Laszlo Ecker-Racz, Richard Goode, Arnold C. Harberger, and Richard Slitor.

In preparing this edition, he received valuable suggestions from Henry J. Aaron, Michael J. Boskin, E. C. Halbach, Jr., Gerald R. Jantscher, Will S. Meyers, Joseph J. Minarik, Richard P. Nathan, Eytan Sheshinsky, John B. Shoven, Emil M. Sunley, Jr., Stanley S. Surrey, and Bernard Wolfman. Todd Easton and Robin M. Donaldson programmed the calculations of the effects of the income taxes presented in chapters 4 and 5.

Elizabeth H. Cross edited this edition. Evelyn P. Fisher reviewed the manuscript for accuracy and consistency, as she did the manuscripts of both previous editions. Kathleen Kane and Thang Long Ton That assisted Mrs. Fisher in verifying factual data. Fred Powell prepared the figures and Florence Robinson the index.

The volume is the fifth publication in the Brookings Studies of Government Finance second series, which is devoted to examining issues in taxation and public expenditure policy. Research on the revenue and distributional implications of the structural features of the income taxes was supported by a grant from the RANN program of the National Science Foundation. The author is indebted to the Center for Advanced Study in the Behavioral Sciences for providing a congenial and stimulating atmosphere in the academic year 1975–76, during which he prepared this revision.

The author's views are his own, and should not be ascribed to the officers, trustees, or other staff members of the Brookings Institution, to the National Science Foundation, or to the Center for Advanced Study in the Behavioral Sciences.

November 1976   GILBERT Y. STEINER
Washington, D.C.   *Acting President*

Contents

Text Tables

Appendix Tables

Figures

CHAPTER ONE

Introduction

FEDERAL, state, and local government receipts now amount to almost one-third of the gross national product. They come from a variety of taxes, as well as from fees, charges, and other miscellaneous sources. The taxes cover almost the entire spectrum: income taxes, general and selective consumption taxes, payroll taxes, estate and gift taxes, and property taxes.

Despite the large amount of money collected—$445 billion in 1975—U.S. taxes are by no means the heaviest in the world. Most advanced European countries impose relatively higher taxes. In 1973, for example, taxes ranged between 35 and 46 percent of the gross national product in Austria, France, Germany, the Netherlands, and Norway, but were 28 percent in the United States (appendix table C-5).

Features of the U.S. Tax System

The most distinctive feature of the U.S. tax system is that it places great weight on the individual and corporation income taxes. These account for 43 percent of the total revenues (including receipts from social insurance taxes) of all levels of government. At the federal level, they account for 59 percent (table 1-1).

A second distinction is that it is a federal system (figure 1-1): the national and state governments have independent taxing powers, and

1

Table 1-1. Federal and State and Local Taxes and Other Revenues, by Major Source, 1975

Major source	*Revenues*[a]	
	Amount (billions of dollars)	*Percentage of total*
Federal		
Individual income	120.7	43.3
Corporation income	42.6	15.3
Excises	16.4	5.9
Estate and gift	4.9	1.8
Payroll	86.5	31.0
Other	7.7	2.7
Total	278.7	100.0
State and local		
Individual income	22.8	13.7
Corporation income	6.7	4.0
Sales	51.6	31.0
Estate and gift	1.6	0.9
Payroll	1.8	1.1
Property	53.7	32.3
Other	28.2	16.9
Total	166.3	100.0
All levels		
Individual income	143.6	32.3
Corporation income	49.2	11.1
Sales and excises	68.0	15.3
Estate and gift	6.5	1.5
Payroll	88.3	19.8
Property	53.7	12.1
Other	35.8	8.0
Total	445.1	100.0

Source: *Survey of Current Business*, vol. 56 (July 1976), tables 3.2, 3.4, 3.11. Figures are rounded.
a. Revenues are defined as receipts in the national income accounts less contributions for social insurance other than federal payroll taxes. Federal grants-in-aid are not included in state-local receipts.

the local governments derive their taxing powers from the state governments. There is duplication among the tax sources of the three governmental levels, especially between the federal government and state governments, but the tax structures differ markedly. The federal government relies primarily on income taxes, the states on consumption taxes, and the localities on real property taxes.

Two-thirds of all taxes are collected by the federal government, but state and local taxes have been rising at a much more rapid rate during the past three decades because of the rapid growth in demand

Figure 1-1. Receipts of Federal and State and Local Governments, 1946–75

Billions of dollars (ratio scale)

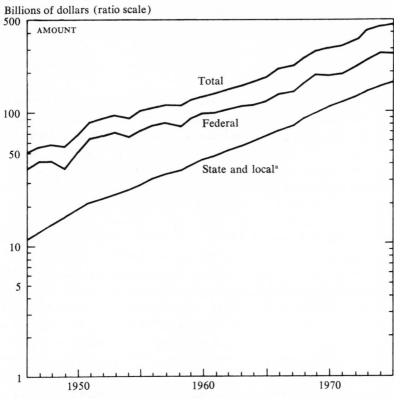

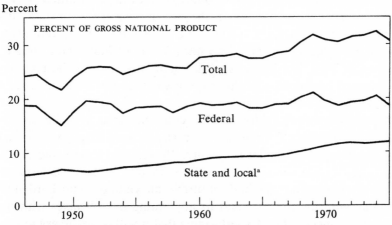

Source: Appendix table C-3. Receipts are on a national income accounts basis.
a. State and local receipts have been adjusted to exclude federal grants-in-aid.

for the public services that are operated and administered primarily by state and local governments. Although all governments finance most of their revenue needs from their own taxes, there is a well-developed system of intergovernmental assistance, which transfers funds from higher to lower levels of government. Such transfers have risen rapidly in recent years.

The broad outlines of the tax system have remained about the same since the Second World War, when the federal government greatly expanded the coverage of the individual income tax and substantially increased corporation tax rates. Nevertheless, the structure has not been static—during the past fifteen years, great changes have occurred at all levels of government. Federal income tax rates have been reduced substantially; increases in the personal exemption and the adoption of a low-income allowance have eliminated from the income tax rolls virtually all individuals and families officially classified as poor; depreciation allowances have been liberalized, and an investment credit has been in effect since 1962, except for five months in 1966–67 and twenty-eight months in 1969–71 when it was suspended for stabilization reasons; practically all selective excise taxes other than the taxes on liquor and tobacco and highway and airway user taxes have been reduced or eliminated; payroll taxes have been raised; and numerous revisions have been made in the income tax bases. At the state and local levels, tax rates have risen steadily. Traditional opposition to state income and sales taxes has broken down; three-quarters of the states now have both. To alleviate the burden of sales and property taxes on the poor, the idea of a tax credit for state sales and local property taxes against state income taxes (with refunds to those not subject to income tax) has taken hold. State and local governments have also been improving administration of the property tax, which continues to be the major revenue source for local governments.

These developments foreshadow continued change and evolution in the years ahead. Tax rates will be raised or lowered as domestic and international circumstances require. Reforms in federal individual and corporation income taxes will continue to be made. Consideration is being given to methods of further alleviating the tax burden on people with low incomes and to integrating payroll taxes with the individual income tax. Experts agree that it will be necessary to perfect the 1976 revisions of the federal estate and gift taxes. State and local finance and intergovernmental fiscal relations will continue to be a major concern of policymakers at all levels of government.

The purpose of this book is to explain these and other issues in federal taxation and to discuss alternative solutions. Chapter 2 examines the relation of taxation to economic growth and stability and of tax policy to overall economic policy. Chapter 3 describes the tax legislative process, discusses its weaknesses, and suggests ways to improve it. Chapters 4 through 8 are devoted to the major federal tax categories: the individual income tax, the corporation income tax, consumption taxes, payroll taxes, and estate and gift taxes. Each chapter describes the basic features of the tax under review, recent changes in the law, and the problems yet unsolved. Chapter 9 analyzes the issues in state-local taxation that are relevant to federal policy.

Goals of Taxation

Taxation is a major instrument of social and economic policy. It has three goals: to transfer resources from the private to the public sector; to distribute the cost of government fairly by income classes (vertical equity) and among people in approximately the same economic circumstances (horizontal equity); and to promote economic growth, stability, and efficiency. From these standpoints, the U.S. tax system is both a source of satisfaction and an object of criticism. The federal part of the system is progressive, thus placing a proportionately heavier burden on those who have greater ability to pay. It is also responsive to changes in business activity and therefore automatically cushions the effect of changes in private incomes on spending. The state-local part of the system is neither progressive nor responsive to changes in income, and it is responsible for many of the fiscal crises that have occurred at the state-local level throughout the country.

The U.S. tax system as a whole is either proportional to income or slightly progressive, depending on who bears the major taxes (figure 1-2). Some say the system is not progressive enough; others believe that the burdens at the top of the income scale, which are mainly due to the taxes on property incomes, are too heavy. But there is a consensus in favor of at least *some* progression in the overall tax burden. Some believe that special provisions go too far in attempting to promote economic incentives; others believe they do not go far enough. Nonetheless, tax policy is generally regarded as a legitimate and use-

Figure 1-2. Effective Rates of Federal, State, and Local Taxes under the Most Progressive and Least Progressive Sets of Incidence Assumptions, by Population Percentile,[a] 1970

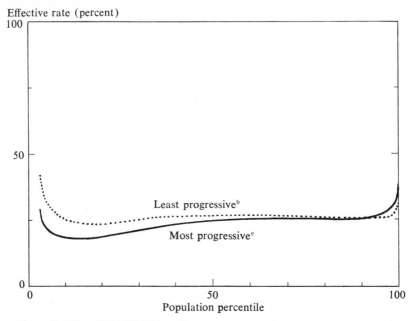

Effective rate (percent)

Least progressive[b]

Most progressive[c]

Population percentile

Source: Brookings 1970 MERGE data file.

a. Population percentiles are ranked in order of comprehensive income, from low to high.

b. Assumes that one-quarter of the corporation income tax is borne by consumers, one-quarter by wage earners, and one-half by shareholders.

c. Assumes that half the corporation income tax is borne by shareholders and half by owners of capital in general.

ful device for promoting economic growth and stability, provided the particular measures chosen are effective means of accomplishing their objectives. Within these broad areas of government, there is considerable controversy about the relative emphasis that should be placed on equity and economic objectives.

These issues involve difficult, technical questions of law, accounting, and economics. They are often obscured by misunderstanding, lack of information, and even misrepresentation. Yet they have important implications for the welfare of every citizen and for the vitality of the economy. This volume attempts to provide factual and analytical information that will help the reader make up his or her own mind. It was prepared in the belief that tax policy is too important to be left solely to the experts, and that taxation can and should be understood by the interested citizen.

CHAPTER TWO

Taxes and Economic Policy

DURING most of the nation's history, federal budget policy was based on the rule that tax receipts should be roughly equal to annual government expenditures. Declining receipts during a business contraction called for an increase in taxes or a reduction in expenditures, while surpluses that developed during periods of prosperity called for lowered tax rates or increased expenditures. This policy reduced private incomes when they were falling and raised them when they were rising. By aggravating fluctuations in purchasing power, the policy of annually balanced budgets accentuated economic instability.

In the 1930s new concepts of budget policy emerged that emphasized the relation of the federal budget to the performance of the economy. Adjustments in federal expenditures and taxes were to be made to reduce unemployment or to check inflation. Budget surpluses were to be used to restrain private spending during prosperity, deficits to stimulate spending during recessions. But variations in government expenditures were expected to play a more active role than tax rate variations in counteracting fluctuations in private demand.

The view prevailing today is that private demand can be stimulated or restrained by tax as well as expenditure changes. Higher taxes and lower government expenditures help fight inflation by restraining private demand; lower taxes and higher expenditures help fight recession by stimulating private demand. Fiscal policy has been actively used since the early 1960s to promote economic stability, with good results on some occasions (for example, when taxes were cut in 1964, 1971, and 1975) and disappointing results in others (for example, when the Vietnam War surtax was imposed in 1968).

The purpose of this chapter is to explain how the fiscal actions of the government, including changes in expenditures and taxes, affect the level of economic activity and the rate of economic growth. Taxes will be emphasized because the focus of this volume is on taxation. But changes in government spending cannot be ignored, as the rapid increase in expenditures for the Vietnam War clearly showed in the latter part of the 1960s. That experience and the vicissitudes of the 1970s also demonstrated that the growth and stability of the economy depend not only on fiscal decisions, but on many other government decisions—particularly those concerning monetary policy—which are outside the scope of this book.

Fiscal economics is based on national income analysis as it has developed over the past forty years. The essence of this analysis is that the level of expenditures depends on total output or gross national product, which in turn depends on the total spending of consumers, business, and government. At any given time, there is a level of output that is consistent with full employment of the nation's supply of labor (except for seasonal, and a small amount of frictional, unemployment). This level is called *potential* or *full employment GNP* (figure 2-1). The major objectives of fiscal policy are to stabilize the economy at full employment, maintain price stability, and promote economic growth and efficiency.

Stabilization Policy

The federal government exerts great influence on total spending, and hence on output, through its expenditure and tax policies. It alters total spending directly by varying its own spending and indirectly by raising or lowering taxes. If expenditures are increased or taxes lowered, the spending of higher incomes by the recipients requires additional output, which in turn generates still more income and spending; and the cycle repeats itself. The cumulative increase in GNP is therefore a multiple of the initial increase in government expenditures or reduction in taxes. Correspondingly, reductions in expenditures or increases in taxes reduce GNP by a multiple of the initial action.

**Figure 2-1. Gross National Product, Actual and Potential, and Unemployment
Rate, by Quarter, 1955–75**
Billions of 1972 dollars

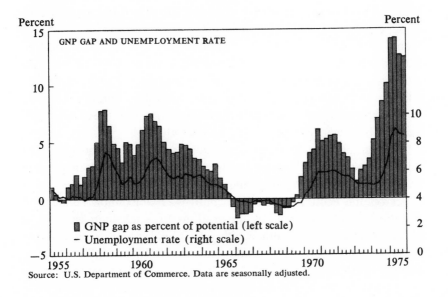

Source: U.S. Department of Commerce. Data are seasonally adjusted.

Impact of Expenditure and Tax Changes

The process of income and output creation through fiscal policy may be illustrated by the following hypothetical examples. Assume that out of each dollar of GNP 25 cents is taken in federal taxes and the remaining 75 cents goes to consumers and business. Assume also that consumers and business together spend 80 percent of any additional income they receive after taxes.

If the government increased its purchases by $10 billion, private income before tax would initially rise by the same amount. Tax revenues would be $2.5 billion higher, and private disposable income would rise $7.5 billion, of which consumers and business would spend $6 billion. This additional spending would generate another increase in income, with $1.5 billion going to taxes and the remaining $4.5 billion to consumers and business. Of the latter amount, consumers and business would spend $3.6 billion, which would generate still another round of rising income and spending, and so on. The total increase in GNP (including the initial $10 billion of government purchases) would amount to $25 billion ($10 + 6 + 3.6 + ...$). This is a multiplier of 2.5 times the original increase in spending.

Consider what would happen if, instead of increasing expenditures, the government reduced taxes by $10 billion. Consumers and business would again spend 80 percent of the higher after-tax incomes, or $8 billion. This would generate the same amount of additional private income, of which consumers and business would receive $6 billion and spend $4.8 billion, and so on. The total increase in GNP would be $20 billion ($8 + 4.8 + ...$), or two times the original tax cut. The difference between the multipliers in the two illustrations reflects the differences in first-round effects of the expenditure and tax changes: in this round output is raised by the entire amount of the expenditure increase but by only 80 percent of the tax reduction.

If expenditures and taxes were increased simultaneously by the same amount, the effects of the two actions would not cancel one another because, dollar for dollar, expenditures have a more potent effect on the economy than tax changes. For example, under the assumptions in the previous illustrations, if a tax increase of $10 billion were enacted together with a $10 billion increase in government spending, the former would reduce GNP by $20 billion and the latter would stimulate a $25 billion increase, leaving a net increase of

$5 billion. In other words, an increase in expenditures that is fully financed by an increase in taxes will on balance increase the GNP. (This theorem assumes that the change in spending resulting from an increase or decrease in private disposable income will be the same regardless of the source of the income change and that investment and other economic behavior will not be influenced by the government's action. The multipliers used are illustrative only; estimates of the multipliers vary greatly.)

The effect of changes in government expenditures and taxes on the size of the government's deficit depends on the increase in GNP generated by the fiscal stimulus and on tax rates. In the previous examples, federal taxes were assumed to account for 25 percent of any increment to GNP. Thus the increase in GNP would raise tax receipts by $6.25 billion if expenditures were increased by $10 billion (0.25 × $25 billion), causing an increased deficit (or a reduced surplus) of $3.75 billion. If taxes were reduced by $10 billion, the increase in GNP would raise tax receipts by $5 billion (0.25 × $20 billion), causing a $5 billion increase in the deficit. If expenditures and taxes were raised simultaneously by $10 billion, the increase in GNP would raise tax receipts by $1.25 billion (0.25 × $5 billion) and *reduce* the deficit (or increase the surplus) by that amount.

Monetary policy also plays an important role in stabilization policy. Suppose the federal government increased expenditures or reduced taxes. As GNP increased, individuals and business firms would need more money to conduct their business affairs. If the money supply did not increase, the greater demand for money would drive up interest rates. The higher interest rates would tend to reduce residential construction, business investment, and state-local construction, thus offsetting at least some of the effect of the initial increase in spending. Fiscal policy thus requires an accommodating monetary policy if it is to be fully effective, but the precise combination of monetary and fiscal measures necessary to obtain any desired response is not known.

Built-in Stabilizers

In addition to discretionary changes in taxes and expenditures (that is, deliberate government actions to vary taxes or the rate of expenditures), the fiscal system itself contributes to stabilization by generating automatic tax and expenditure adjustments that cushion the effect of changes in GNP. These *built-in stabilizers* moderate the fall in private income and spending when GNP declines and restrain private income and spending when GNP rises. They are automatic in the sense that they respond to changes in GNP without any action on the part of the government.

The two major groups of built-in fiscal stabilizers are taxes, in particular the income taxes, and transfers, such as unemployment compensation and welfare payments.

Among taxes, the federal individual income tax is the leading stabilizer. When incomes fall, many people who were formerly taxable drop below the taxable level; others are pushed down into lower tax brackets. Conversely, when incomes rise, people who were formerly not taxed become taxable, and others are pushed into higher tax brackets. Under the rates in effect in 1977, federal individual income tax receipts automatically increase or decrease by about 15 percent for every 10 percent increase or decrease in personal income. Since consumption depends on disposable personal income, automatic changes in receipts from the individual income tax keep consumption more stable than it otherwise would be.

Variations in receipts from the corporation income tax are proportionately larger than variations in individual income tax receipts because profits fluctuate widely over a business cycle. The variation in corporate profits is a major nonfiscal stabilizer in the economic system. When economic activity slows down, profits fall both in absolute terms and as a percentage of GNP, absorbing much of the impact of the reduction in incomes. During a cyclical recovery, profits rise much faster than other kinds of income. Corporation taxes vary directly with profits and absorb the impact of declining corporate earnings during the downswing. During the upswing, rising tax liabilities tend to restrain the growth of corporation incomes. The effect of variations in corporation tax liabilities on dividends is relatively small because corporate managers try to keep dividends in line with long-term earnings. Fluctuations in investment are probably reduced to some extent, but the precise effect is unknown.

The yield of a general consumption tax (such as a general sales tax) responds about in proportion to changes in income, but a consumption tax is less effective as an automatic stabilizer than the individual income tax, which responds more than in proportion to income. The federal government relies on specific excise taxes, which are even less effective automatic stabilizers than a general consumption tax because they are levied on the number of units rather than the value of purchases (for example, cents per gallon) and thus do not increase as prices increase.

On the expenditure side, the major built-in stabilizer is unemployment compensation. Insured workers who become unemployed are entitled to benefits for up to twenty-six weeks in most states. Benefits for an additional thirteen weeks are paid throughout the nation when the national unemployment rate is 4.5 percent or more for three consecutive months, and in any state when the state unemployment rate has increased by 20 percent over the average of the two preceding years and is at least 4 percent. During recessions, eligibility for benefits is extended for periods of up to sixty-five weeks. These payments help maintain consumption as output and employment fall. As incomes go up and employment increases, unemployment compensation declines. Other transfer payments (social security, public assistance) have strong upward trends, but the amounts usually rise faster during recessions and more slowly during expansions.

The effect of built-in stabilizers on the federal surplus, as distinct from the discretionary actions of the government, can be calculated. Because of the built-in stabilizers, the actual surplus or deficit reflects the prevailing levels of income and employment, as well as the government's fiscal policy. Figure 2-2 shows how the effect of the built-in stabilizers may be separated from the discretionary changes.

Each line in the figure shows the surplus or deficit that would be realized at various levels of employment under two different budget programs, A and B. For simplicity, it is assumed that the tax system is the same, but that expenditures are $4 billion higher under program B. (The surplus is therefore $4 billion lower or the deficit $4 billion higher.) The lines slope upward, indicating that as employment and income increase tax revenues increase and the deficits become smaller or the surpluses larger. The effect of the built-in stabilizers is given by the slope of each line: the greater the slope, the larger the impact of the built-in stabilizers on the surplus or deficit. In figure 2-2, both programs have the same built-in stability features because the tax systems are identical. However, an actual deficit of $3 billion is realized when employment is at 94 percent of the labor force under program A and 95 percent under program B. Clearly, program B is more expansionary than program A. Differences between programs

Figure 2-2. Effect of Level of Activity on Federal Surplus or Deficit

Surplus or deficit (billions of dollars)

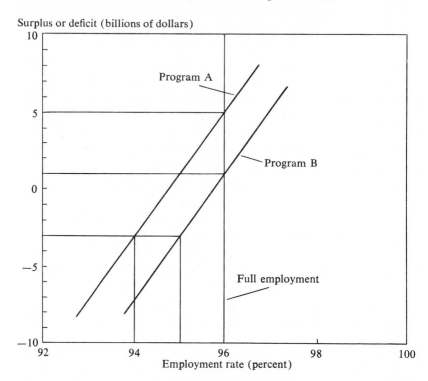

Employment rate (percent)

will also be due in practice to differences in tax rates; in such cases, the lines would not be parallel, but the slope of each line would still measure the built-in flexibility of each program.

The Full Employment Surplus

The degree of stimulation provided by fiscal policy is popularly regarded as a function of the *current* budget surplus or deficit (that is, the budget is considered to be restrictive when it is running a surplus and expansionary when it is in deficit). It should be clear from figure 2-2 that actual surpluses or deficits are poor guides for evaluating fiscal policy because they include the effects of both automatic and discretionary fiscal actions.

The economic effects of two fiscal programs may be compared by examining the surplus or deficit at any given level of employment. By convention, the comparison is made at full employment (traditionally, when 96 percent of the labor force is employed). Defined in this way, the "full employment surplus" is $5 billion under program A in figure 2-2 and $1 billion under program B. The difference of $4 billion reflects the assumed difference in expenditures. In practice, the differences are due to differences in taxes as well as expenditures.

There are two types of budget statements in current use—the official *unified budget* and the *national income accounts budget*. The full employment surplus is usually computed on a national income accounts basis, but it can be adjusted to the definitions in the unified budget (see page 16).

The budget program that is appropriate at a given time depends on the strength of private demand for consumption and investment goods. When private demand is high, a large full employment surplus is called for; when private demand is weak, a small full employment surplus, or even a full employment deficit, is required. Efforts to achieve a larger surplus or a lower deficit than is consistent with full employment would depress employment and incomes. If the budget called for too small a full employment surplus, total demand would be too high and prices would rise.

Another characteristic of the full employment surplus is its tendency to increase with the passage of time. As the economy grows, individual and business incomes increase and potential federal receipts rise. Inflation raises receipts even more as money incomes are adjusted to compensate for the rise in prices. At 1976 income levels and tax rates and on the assumption of 96 percent employment and inflation of 5 percent, federal receipts increase by about $43 billion a year, or 2.2 percent of potential GNP. Thus the full employment surplus would rise each year by about $43 billion, less any increase in expenditures the government decided to make. With 10 percent inflation the rise in federal receipts would be close to $70 billion a year, or 3.7 percent of potential GNP.

This upward creep in the full employment surplus has been called the *fiscal dividend* or the *fiscal drag*. It is identified as a *dividend* when used to describe the leeway available in the federal budget to finance higher federal expenditures without raising tax rates. During the early 1960s the fiscal dividend was large enough to finance tax rate reductions as well as expenditure increases. More recently, with continued high commitments for defense, the fiscal dividend has not been sufficient to provide fully for needed domestic social programs.

The automatic increase in federal receipts that accompanies the

The Two Budgets

The official budget statement of the federal government is the *unified budget,* which is an instrument of management and control of federal activities financed with federally owned funds. This budget includes cash flows to and from the public resulting from all federal fiscal activity, including the trust funds, and the net lending of government-owned enterprises. Thus the unified budget provides a comprehensive picture of the financial impact of federal programs, but it does not measure their contribution to the current income and output of the nation. For this purpose, economists make use of the statement of receipts and expenditures in the official national income accounts, often called the *national income accounts budget.*

Like the unified budget, the national income accounts budget includes the activities of trust funds and excludes purely intragovernmental transactions (for example, interest on federal bonds owned by federal agencies) that do not affect the general public. But there are significant differences between the two in timing and coverage. The national income accounts budget includes receipts and expenditures when they affect private incomes, which is not necessarily when the federal government receives cash or pays it out. This adjustment involves putting receipts (except those from personal taxes) on an accrual basis and counting expenditures when goods are delivered rather than when payment is made. The adjustment for coverage excludes purely financial transactions because these represent an exchange of assets or claims and not a direct addition to income or production.

There are some differences in the size of surpluses or deficits between the two accounts, and even in their movements (figure 2-3).

Figure 2-3. Federal Surpluses and Deficits, Two Budget Concepts, Fiscal Years 1954–76

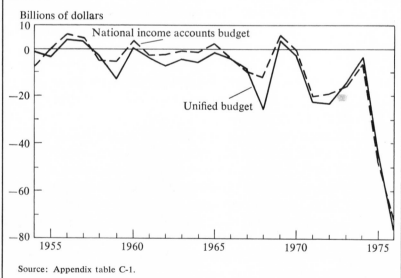

Billions of dollars

Source: Appendix table C-1.

Figure 2-4. Full Employment Surplus as a Percentage of Potential Gross National Product, National Income Accounts Basis, 1955–75

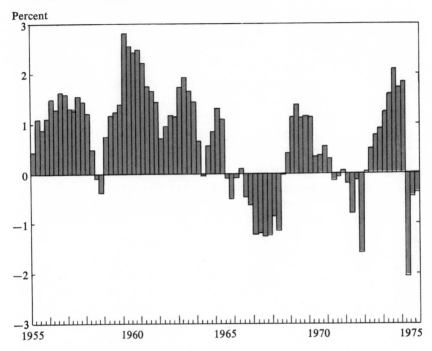

Source: Council of Economic Advisers.

increase in incomes resulting from real growth or inflation is also called the *fiscal drag* because it acts as a retarding influence on the economy unless it is offset by rising expenditures or tax reductions. This terminology becomes fashionable—in periods such as the early 1960s and the mid-1970s—when government expenditures do not rise fast enough to absorb the automatic growth in tax receipts.

According to current estimates, except for the years 1965–68, when Vietnam War expenditures grew rapidly, and 1971–72 and 1975, when antirecession tax cuts were made, the federal budget would have been in surplus or close to balance in every quarter between 1955 and 1975 had full employment been maintained (figure 2-4). However, the actual budget showed a deficit during most of the period because of the disappointing performance of the economy. In 1964, 1971, and 1975, the full employment surplus was sharply reduced by tax reductions to stimulate the economy. In each instance, employment began to move upward as soon as, or shortly after, the tax cuts went into effect, and the budget deficits declined. These experiences illustrate the principle that, in slack periods, temporarily enlarged deficits help improve both the condition of the economy and the federal budget.

On the other hand, planning for a larger surplus, without regard to the strength of private demand, may produce unsatisfactory rates of employment and output and create budget deficits besides. The sharp increases in the full employment surplus in 1959, 1969, and 1973 clearly helped bring about the recessions of 1960–61, 1970–71, and 1974–75.

Fiscal policy has erred on the side of ease as well as restraint. The rapid buildup of military expenditures for the Vietnam War wiped out the full employment surplus beginning in mid-1965, the full employment deficit averaging 0.3 percent of potential GNP in 1966, 1.2 percent in 1967, and 0.4 percent in 1968. This created an inflation from which the economy is yet to recover.

Although it is the most convenient single measure of restrictiveness or ease in the federal budget, the full employment surplus must be used with considerable care. In the first place, the degree of fiscal restraint needed at any given time depends on the strength of private demand. The full employment surplus appropriate for one period may not be appropriate for another. Second, differences in the level and composition of expenditures and taxes have an important bearing on the significance of the full employment surplus. For example, an increase in the full employment surplus resulting from a reduction in government expenditures on goods and services would be more restrictive than that resulting from a tax increase of the same amount. Third, the restrictiveness of a given *amount* of surplus, say, $10 billion, would be much greater in a $1,000 billion economy than in a $2,000 billion economy. In making comparisons over time, the full employment surplus should be expressed as a percentage of potential GNP (see figure 2-4). Finally, there is no simple way to adjust the full employment surplus for the effect of price increases. Most calculations of the full employment surplus remove the effect of the built-in response of the federal budget to a business recession but do not remove the built-in response of the budget to inflation. For these reasons, the meaning of the full employment surplus is likely to be unambiguous only during relatively short periods when changes in expenditures and taxes, and in the rate of growth of prices, are relatively small. Analysis of the fiscal impact of the budget over long periods requires more detailed information than the full employment surplus provides by itself.

Expenditure versus Tax Adjustments to Promote Stability

Both expenditure and tax rate changes can be used for stabilization purposes. Although expenditure changes have somewhat larger multiplier effects, they are not necessarily preferable to changes in tax rates. In the first place, government expenditures should be determined by long-run national needs and not by short-run cyclical considerations. The controlling principle is that government outlays should not exceed the level at which the benefit to the nation's citizens of an additional dollar of expenditures would be the same in public and private use. This level is unlikely to rise or fall sharply during such short periods as a business contraction or expansion. Second, considerations of economic efficiency argue against large short-run variations in expenditures. For example, it would be wasteful to slow down construction of a road or hydroelectric plant, once construction had begun, in the interest of reducing aggregate spending. Third, there might be a long delay between a decision to undertake an expenditure and its effect on output and employment. When recessions are relatively brief—as they have been since the end of World War II—the impact of a decision to make an expenditure change often is not felt until recovery is under way. But during periods of rapidly rising defense expenditures, such as occurred during the Korean and Vietnam wars, a slowing down or deferment of some government programs usually becomes necessary to keep total demand from outstripping the productive potential of the economy.

Of the various taxes, the individual income tax is the most suitable for stabilization purposes. Under the withholding system for wages and salaries, changes in tax rates can be made effective in a matter of days and can also be terminated quickly. In most cases, the effect of a tax change on a worker's take-home pay is indistinguishable from the effect of a change in the gross weekly wage. Corporation income tax changes are not likely to have significant effects on investment if it is known, or expected, that they will be of short duration. Consumption tax changes may have a perverse effect in the short run; the expectation of a reduction may delay spending, and the expectation of an increase may accelerate spending. Nevertheless, once they become effective, consumption tax changes are at least as powerful as income tax changes in stimulating or restraining consumer demand.

Some economists believe that consumption depends on income that is expected to be received regularly and is not much affected by temporary changes in income. On this hypothesis, temporary income tax changes would have relatively little impact on consumption. Most economists believe that a temporary income tax change would have some effect on consumer spending, although they agree that it would be less powerful than a permanent tax change. Income tax changes also operate with a lag, because consumers do not alter their spending immediately in response to changes in disposable income.

Tax changes are often assumed to have the greatest effect on consumption if they are confined to the lower income classes. This view presupposes that the poor spend proportionately more out of any additional dollars they may receive than the rich. There is no evidence to confirm or deny this assumption. For policy purposes, it is probably satisfactory to assume that the incremental consumption rate is fairly high throughout most of the income distribution. This would suggest that, if the distribution of the tax burden is considered equitable by the large majority of taxpayers, tax rates could be moved up or down uniformly for stabilization purposes under a simple formula, such as an equal percentage-point change in the rates for all brackets.

Tax rate changes are sometimes criticized on the ground that they are too small to exert a significant economic effect. With seventy million taxpayers, a $21 billion individual income tax cut would be equivalent to an average increase in take-home pay of less than $6 a week per taxpayer, a negligible amount in comparison with a total GNP of $2,000 billion. The comparison is erroneous, however, because it compares weekly and annual income flows. A $21 billion tax cut would amount to more than 1 percent of the GNP, whether expressed on a weekly, monthly, or annual basis. Because tax changes have a multiplier effect, a tax cut of this magnitude would give a substantial stimulus to the economy. The deviation from full employment GNP, which tax cuts are intended to narrow, is usually less than 10 percent.

Tax adjustments can be used to restrain as well as to stimulate demand and are therefore important policy instruments for counter-acting inflation. It may be impractical, if not impossible, to cut back government expenditures when inflation threatens. About 40 percent of federal expenditures are for defense, foreign aid, education, and research and development, which should not be altered for short-run reasons. Much of the remainder of the federal budget provides assistance to low-income people, who are particularly hard-pressed during an inflation. If the inflationary pressure is the direct result of an increase in government spending for defense or war purposes, tax increases must be used to withdraw excess purchasing power from the income stream.

The time required to complete the legislative process is the major obstacle to the prompt use of tax changes for stabilization purposes. Congressional consideration of major tax legislation may take eighteen months or more. Proposals have been made to give the President authority to make temporary changes in individual income tax rates or to speed up congressional procedures for action on presidential recommendations. However, Congress has not seriously considered such plans (see pages 49–50).

Automatic Budget Rules

It is now widely understood that following a policy of annually balanced budgets would accentuate business fluctuations. But many people continue to believe it unwise to rely exclusively on discretion to guide budget decisions. Discretionary policy depends heavily on forecasting techniques that are still subject to error. It is also feared that removing budgetary restraint would lead to excessive federal expenditures. To avoid these pitfalls, attempts have been made to formulate rules that would reduce the element of judgment in budget decisions without impairing economic growth and stability.

The best-known plan is the *stabilizing budget policy* of the Committee for Economic Development, a nonprofit organization of influential businessmen and educators. Under this policy, tax rates would be set to balance the budget or yield a small surplus at full employment. The rates would remain unchanged until there was a major change in the level of expenditures. Reliance would be placed on the built-in stabilizers to moderate fluctuations in private demand.

The CED plan would operate successfully only if full employment could be achieved with a balance or a small surplus in the federal budget. Nor does it offer a systematic method for raising additional revenues should federal expenditures rise by more than the amount of the automatic growth in tax receipts, or for lowering taxes should federal expenditures rise by less than the amount of the automatic growth in tax receipts. With federal expenditure needs rising rapidly and recession still a considerable threat to economic stability, it would be both hazardous and unwise to keep tax rates unchanged for long periods.

A second type of plan—aimed at helping to solve the fiscal drag problem—would reduce individual income tax rates each year by a given amount, say, 2 percentage points (which would reduce income tax receipts by about $13 billion a year at 1976 income levels), with the $30 billion remaining from the fiscal dividend of approximately $43 billion to be used for increasing federal expenditures. Presumably, the plan would begin with a surplus or deficit consistent with full employment. The drawback of this approach is that it would freeze the allocation of increased federal receipts between tax reduction and increased expenditures. Periods when it would have been desirable to cut tax rates by a fixed amount or a fixed percentage each year have been rare in the nation's history.

A third approach to an automatic budget policy would be to build into the budget a formula that would trigger upward or downward changes in tax rates when certain predetermined economic indexes were reached. For example, legislation might provide for a 1-percentage-point reduction in income tax rates for every increase of 0.5 percent in unemployment above 4.5 percent of the labor force, or an increase of 1 percentage point for every rise of 2 points in a general price index such as the consumer or the wholesale price index. While this type of formula would add to the effectiveness of the built-in stabilizers if the changes were correctly timed, no one index or set of indexes could be used with confidence to signal an economic movement justifying tax action.

Clearly, budget policy cannot be based on a rigid set of rules. Nevertheless, the search for budget rules has improved public understanding of the elements of fiscal policy. Great emphasis is placed on the automatic stabilizers for their cushioning effect on private disposable incomes and spending. Recognition of the capacity of the federal tax system to generate rising revenues has alerted policymakers to the need for making positive decisions to determine the relative social priorities of public and private expenditures, so that the appropriate amounts can be allocated to tax reduction and to higher government expenditures. In practice, the political advantages of an immediate tax reduction are frequently more attractive than the long-run benefits of new or improved government programs. Thus tax rate reductions or other revenue-losing tax provisions were enacted in 1962, 1964, 1969, 1971, and 1975 to offset the fiscal drag or to stimulate the economy, and the ratio of federal expenditures to GNP has remained roughly the same for the last two decades.

Policies to Promote Economic Growth

Fiscal policies are useful in promoting long-run economic growth as well as short-run stability. The objective of growth policy is to provide both relatively full employment for the labor force and industrial capacity, at stable prices. Growth may be disappointing for two reasons: the resources of the economy may not be employed to their full potential because the economy is in recession or is being deliberately held down to combat inflationary pressures, or the rate of growth of potential output at full employment may be too low. The policies required under these circumstances differ, although they are often confused.

Achieving Full Employment and Stable Prices

The major contribution that fiscal policy can make to economic growth is to help keep total demand roughly in line with the productive potential of the economy. An economy operating at less than full employment is one in which potential GNP is larger than the total of actual spending by consumers, business, and government. The remedy is to increase private or public spending through fiscal and monetary stimulation. Conversely, when total demand exceeds the capacity of the economy to produce goods and services, the remedy is to curtail private or public spending through fiscal and monetary restraint.

Although the basic principles of stabilization policy are clear, they have been difficult to apply in practice. Failure to absorb the normal growth in revenues will produce successively higher full employment surpluses, which may hold actual output below the economic potential of the economy. The high levels of unemployment and the large gap between potential and actual GNP in 1958–61, 1970–71, and 1974–75 (see figure 2-1) were caused largely by excessively restrictive fiscal policies that arose in this way. On the other hand, too large a growth in government expenditures relative to normal revenue growth may produce excess demand, which in turn leads to rising prices. The inflation that began in mid-1965 was triggered by the jump in Vietnam War expenditures, which were superimposed on an economy already operating at close to full employment. A temporary 10 percent surtax on individual and corporation income taxes was enacted in the summer of 1968, but this was about three years after the decision to escalate the war had been made.

It now seems clear that it will always be difficult to maintain full employment in a modern industrial economy and keep price increases within acceptable limits. Since the end of the Second World War, prices have shown a tendency to rise in the United States and other industrial countries, even when total spending has been below potential GNP. Many economists believe this can be resolved only by supplementing fiscal and monetary policies with some form of wage-price or "incomes" policy to keep wage increases roughly in line with the average growth in productivity of the economy as a whole and to prevent price increases not justified by cost increases. Under such a policy, prices would decline in industries with above-average productivity increases and rise in industries with below-average productivity increases, but the average of all prices would be stable. These principles were established by the Council of Economic Advisers in 1962 as voluntary "guideposts" for wage and price behavior. The guideposts had the strong backing of Presidents Kennedy and Johnson and appeared to have some effect in restraining wage and price increases (a judgment that some professional economists dispute) until mid-1965, when the rapid buildup of military expenditures for the Vietnam War upset the balance between supply and demand. Mandatory price and wage controls were imposed at the request of the Nixon administration between August 1971 and April 1974. These controls seemed to moderate the rise in prices, but they were allowed to lapse after food and fuel price increases generated a double-digit inflation that could not be contained by controls. No country has yet devised a workable incomes policy under conditions of high employment, and the search continues.

Experience has shown that the major effect of inflation on growth is felt when the attempt is made to restore balance in the economy. Inflation distorts the distribution of the national income among different groups. Each group tries to protect itself against erosion of its share through wage or price increases or government transfer payments. Such pressures continue to be felt long after excess demand has been removed by fiscal and monetary restraint and tend to prolong the inflationary episode. Thus, without an effective incomes policy, it may be possible to halt inflation only at the cost of high unemployment and slow growth for relatively long periods. It is, of course, much less costly in social and economic terms to avoid inflation in the first place.

Raising the Growth Rate

If full employment is maintained, the rate of economic growth will depend on the ability of the economy to raise the rate of growth of potential output. The factors affecting potential output are the size of the labor force, the length of the average workweek and workyear, and productivity (output per man-hour). Productivity depends on the size of the capital stock, the quality of human resources, the attitudes and skills of management, the efficiency of resource use, and the amount of technological progress. Most of these factors are influenced to some extent by government expenditure and tax policy, but the influence is most direct and quantitatively most important on the rate of national investment in both physical and human resources.

To increase the rate of growth, the rate of national investment must be raised to a higher level and held there for a long time. The federal government can contribute to increasing the investment rate through fiscal policy in three ways: it can adopt a policy of budget surpluses when the economy is operating at full employment; it can increase investment in physical and human capital directly through its own expenditures; and it can adopt tax measures that provide incentives for private saving and investment.

SAVING THROUGH BUDGET SURPLUSES. The key to understanding growth policy is the relation between saving and investment. Measured statistically, national saving is the difference between national output and the amounts spent by consumers and government; private investment is also that part of the national product not consumed or used for government purposes. Thus national saving is equal to private investment. In effect, through saving, the nation sets aside the resources needed for private investment purposes; otherwise the resources would be used to produce goods and services for consumers and government.

When the federal government runs a budget surplus, it adds its own saving to that generated by the private economy. When the budget is in deficit, national saving is reduced. Since increased saving and investment are needed to raise the growth rate, the federal government can stimulate a higher growth rate by running budget surpluses at full employment. And the larger the full employment surplus is, the larger the potential contribution to growth.

This growth strategy can be implemented only if there is sufficient investment demand in the private economy to use up the saving generated in the federal budget. If private demand for investment is too low, the federal surplus will generate unemployment rather than more growth. In other words, the full employment surplus must be just large enough to offset the deficiency in private saving. If there is more than enough private saving for the existing investment demand, the budget should be in deficit even at full employment.

An important ingredient of any strategy to increase the rate of private investment is monetary policy. Easy money provides ready access to credit and lowers the cost of borrowing for investment purposes by reducing interest rates. Tight money restrains the growth of credit and raises interest rates. Therefore, the best policy to promote private investment would combine a budget surplus with easy money. In implementing such a policy, it is important to avoid taxes that impair investment incentives.

In practice, the extent of monetary ease that a nation can afford is limited by balance-of-payments considerations. If interest rates are driven down too far, private capital will leave the country to take advantage of higher interest rates abroad. Under the system of floating exchange rates now in effect for the world's major currency blocs, the outflow of funds will lead to a devaluation of the national currency, thus restoring international equilibrium. When interest rates must be kept up for balance-of-payments reasons, fiscal policy must be easier (that is, the surplus must be lower or the deficit higher) to prevent a drop in demand and employment.

INCREASING INVESTMENT DIRECTLY. It is not generally realized that investment is undertaken by government as well as by private firms. Outlays for education, training of manpower, health, research

and development, roads, and other public facilities are essential elements of national investment. Such outlays are not substitutable for
private investment, or vice versa. Education and research expenditures are perhaps the most important components of national investment, yet most of these expenditures are paid for by government
(primarily state and local in the case of education, and primarily
federal in the case of research). There is no basis for prejudging how
total investment should be distributed between the public and private
sectors, and it is important to avoid doctrinaire positions about one
or the other. Both types of investment contribute to the nation's
economic growth.

Public investment is financed directly by government through the
tax system. If private demand is strong, the appropriate policy for
growth would be to raise enough tax revenues to pay for needed government investment as well as to leave an additional margin of saving
for private investment.

INCREASING SAVING AND INVESTMENT INCENTIVES. Given the
aggregate level of taxation, the tax structure can be an important
independent factor in determining the growth potential of the economy. The tax structure may encourage consumption or saving, help
raise or lower private investment in general or in particular industries, stimulate or restrain the outflow of investment funds to foreign
countries, and subsidize or discourage particular expenditures by
individuals and business firms. Most tax systems, including that of
the United States, have numerous features that promote saving and
investment. For example, the federal income taxes provide liberal
depreciation allowances, an investment credit, offsets for business
losses against other income over a period of eleven years, averaging
of individual income for tax purposes over a period of five years, and
preferential treatment of capital gains and income from mining.
These and other provisions will be discussed in later chapters.

The "Debt Burden"

Effective use of fiscal policy to promote the full employment and
growth objectives is hindered by public concern over the growth of
the national debt. It is widely feared that a long succession of annual
deficits and a resulting rise in the national debt will impose danger-
ously heavy burdens on later generations. There is also concern about
the economic burden of interest payments.

Growth of the national debt can impose a burden on future generations if it crowds out private capital formation. In this respect, there is a difference between debt created under conditions of excessive unemployment and debt created under conditions of full employment.

In a situation of substantial unemployment, an increase in the public debt can finance deficits that government uses to purchase goods and services directly or to make transfer payments. Since there are unemployed resources, the goods and services acquired by government or by the recipients of transfer payments do not take the place of goods and services that might otherwise have been produced. If accompanied by the appropriate monetary policy, the debt increase can be absorbed without impeding the flow of funds into private capital formation. In fact, a higher level of economic activity will stimulate private investment. The community is better off when the expenditures are made; and later generations will also benefit to the extent that the expenditures increase private and public investment in human or physical capital that will yield future services.

The situation is more complicated if the economy is at full employment. Then an increase in government expenditures that leads to a deficit (or reduces a surplus) in the federal budget cannot increase total output. This means either that prices will rise or that offsetting tax increases or monetary restraint will be required. If inflation is to be avoided, the necessary restraint must reduce consumption or investment. If the impact is on consumption, taxpayers will have in effect exchanged a collective good or service for current consumption. If the impact is on private or public investment, later generations will be worse off to the extent that the rate of growth of productive capacity has been reduced.

Since the federal government usually runs surpluses when the economy is at full employment (see figure 2-4), there is little likelihood that the federal debt added in peacetime will be burdensome in an economic sense. Deficits incurred to restore or maintain full employment raise output and employment and actually increase the resources available to current and later generations.

The existence of the national debt does mean that interest must be paid to holders of the debt, and tax rates are therefore higher than they would be without the debt. The transfer of interest from general taxpayers to bondholders is a burden on the economy if the taxes levied to pay interest on the debt reduce saving or lower economic

Figure 2-5. Relation of Net Federal Debt and Net Interest on Debt to the Gross National Product, Fiscal Years 1942–75[a]

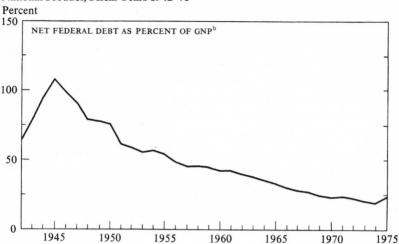

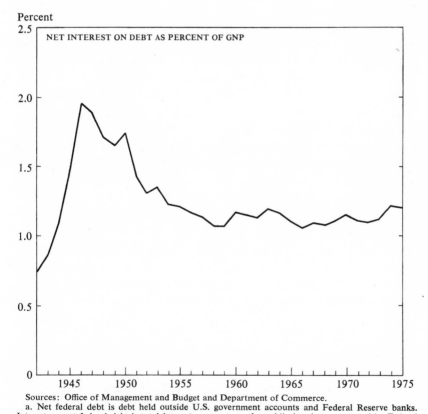

Sources: Office of Management and Budget and Department of Commerce.
a. Net federal debt is debt held outside U.S. government accounts and Federal Reserve banks. Interest on net federal debt is total interest payments to the public less interest earned by Federal Reserve banks.
b. Net federal debt at the end of calendar years as percent of fiscal year GNP.

efficiency. (If the government debt is paid back by a per capita tax—which has no effect on economic incentives—and the market for bonds is competitive, the debt is exactly equivalent to the tax receipts and therefore will not burden future generations.) In any case, the debt burden in the United States must be light because net interest payments represent a small proportion of federal expenditures (less than 10 percent in 1976). Moreover, the ratio of net federal debt to the gross national product has been declining since the end of World War II (figure 2-5), and interest payments on the net debt, which fell markedly in the early postwar years, have amounted to only slightly more than 1 percent of GNP since the early 1950s. The growth of the economy over this period has kept the burden of the debt in relation to total production from rising, even though the interest rates at which debt can be issued have increased sharply.

Summary

The strength of the economy depends heavily on the fiscal policies pursued by the federal government. These policies involve the use of tax and expenditure changes to promote full employment, economic growth, and price stability. The fiscal system itself generates automatic tax and expenditure changes that help dampen fluctuations in private disposable income and spending. Although they are extremely important, the built-in stabilizers can only moderate downward and upward movements in business activity. To halt and reverse such movements, the built-in stabilizers must be supplemented by discretionary changes in government expenditures or tax rates.

There is no basis for making a priori judgments regarding the relative merits of tax and expenditure changes. At any given level of government expenditures, the level of economic activity depends on the *ratio* of tax receipts to expenditures. When private demand is low and the economy is operating below capacity, taxes are too high relative to expenditures. In these circumstances, the ratio should be reduced—by cutting taxes, by raising expenditures, or both. Conversely, when demand is too high, taxes should be raised or expenditures reduced, or both. The appropriate action at any particular time depends on the relative need for private and for public expenditures.

It is impossible to predict whether stabilization policy will require surpluses or deficits in the federal budget. If private demand is weak, full employment may not be possible without federal deficits. If private demand is strong, surpluses will be needed to prevent prices from rising. On the basis of the past record, there is little reason to expect that the U.S. economy will need the stimulus of sustained deficits to remain at full employment.

The first step toward a policy to promote economic growth is to maintain full employment of resources. This requires avoidance of both inflation and recession. Inflation cannot be halted without interrupting the growth of the economy, sometimes for long periods. Recession not only wastes human and physical resources but also leaves a legacy of inadequate investment, which retards the growth of productivity.

After full employment has been achieved, the growth rate can be increased only by raising the rate of growth of potential output. This will require more saving and more investment. The best strategy for increasing saving and investment would be to combine a large budget surplus with an easy money policy. The surplus would increase national saving; easy money would increase private investment by making credit more readily available and by reducing interest rates. Saving and investment incentives may also be improved through higher depreciation allowances, investment credits, and other structural tax provisions.

CHAPTER THREE

The Tax Legislative Process

THE PROCESS of decisionmaking in tax policy is one of the most interesting, puzzling, and controversial features of the federal legislative process. It can be speedy and effective or slow and ponderous. A small army of people participate, but only a few key figures are familiar to the public. The process has been criticized by many, but attempts to alter it even in minor ways have been unavailing.

Basic to an understanding of how the process works is the stipulation in Article I, Section 8, of the Constitution that "Congress shall have power to lay and collect taxes." Congress has always guarded its taxing power jealously. Presidents can recommend changes, but only Congress has the power to translate these recommendations into law. Practically every major presidential tax proposal is thoroughly revised by Congress, and not a few are rejected outright.

A tax law is always a compromise among the views of powerful individuals and groups. The President, the secretary of the treasury, and members of the two congressional tax committees—the House Committee on Ways and Means and the Senate Committee on Finance—are subject to great pressure from the numerous political, economic, and social groups affected by the bill or attempting to have it changed to their advantage. Substantial delays in enactment of tax legislation occur when the participants have difficulty finding a formula to reconcile major opposing interests.

The tax legislative machinery is backed by competent staffs of experts in both the legislative and executive branches of the federal government. Taxation is one of five major policy areas considered important enough to warrant a joint congressional committee (atomic energy, defense production, economic policy, and government operations are the other four). Established in 1926, the Joint Committee on Internal Revenue Taxation consists of five ranking members each from the House Ways and Means Committee and the Senate Finance Committee, with three from the majority party and two from the minority party. Its official functions are to review large refunds proposed by the commissioner of internal revenue and to make studies for the two tax committees. The Joint Committee itself does not participate in the legislative process. In practice, its major function is to provide a technical staff of about thirty-five lawyers and economists to prepare tax legislation for the committees. Additional help is furnished by the committees themselves and by the legislative counsels of the House and Senate, who do the actual drafting. Treasury experts are also available for assistance during the legislative process. Through long and intimate association, the committees have learned to rely on the various staffs for background information needed to help formulate a consensus and to assist in translating committee decisions into legislative language.

The present tax structure is an outgrowth of legislation dating back to the beginning of the Republic. The laws were first assembled and codified in the Internal Revenue Code of 1939, which was completely revised and superseded by the Internal Revenue Code of 1954. Changes in the tax laws have since been enacted as amendments to the 1954 code.

The code is a technical and complex legal document. Many of its sections reflect years of study and analysis by government and nongovernment tax experts. Few people have mastered its technicalities and nuances. Nevertheless, it is the vehicle through which the federal government now collects over $300 billion of internal revenues annually. It is also the basis on which each year over 125 million tax returns are filed, 60 million refunds are paid, 3 million delinquent notices are served to taxpayers, and more than 1,000 people are convicted of tax crimes.

Between 1948 and 1976 Congress enacted sixteen major tax bills and dozens of lesser bills. Each bill required months of preparation

Table 3-1. Legislative History of Major Federal Tax Bills Enacted, and Revenue Gain or Loss, 1948–76

Title of act	Date of President's message	Date of House passage	Date of Senate passage	Date of enactment	Time between initiation and enact- ment (months)	Full-year revenue gain (+) or loss (−) (billions of dollars)
Revenue Act of 1948	a	2/2/48	3/22/48	4/2/48[b]	3[c]	−5.0
Revenue Act of 1950	1/23/50	6/29/50	9/1/50	9/23/50	8	+4.6
Excess Profits Tax Act of 1950	d	12/5/50	12/20/50	1/3/51	3	+3.3
Revenue Act of 1951	2/2/51	6/22/51	9/28/51	10/20/51	8	+5.7
Internal Revenue Code of 1954	1/21/54[e]	3/18/54	7/2/54	8/16/54	7	−1.4
Excise Tax Reduction Act of 1954	a	3/10/54	3/25/54	3/31/54	2[c]	−1.0
Federal-Aid Highway Act of 1956	2/22/55	4/27/56	5/29/56	6/29/56	16	+2.5
Revenue Act of 1962	4/20/61[f]	3/29/62	9/6/62	10/16/62	18	−0.2[g]
Revenue Act of 1964	1/24/63	9/25/63	2/7/64	2/26/64	13	−11.4
Excise Tax Reduction Act of 1965	5/17/65[f]	6/2/65	6/15/65	6/21/65	1	−4.7
Tax Adjustment Act of 1966	1/24/66[e]	2/23/66	3/9/66	3/15/66	2	h
Revenue and Expenditure Control Act of 1968	8/3/67	2/29/68	4/2/68	6/28/68	11	+10.2
Tax Reform Act of 1969	4/21/69	8/7/69	12/11/69	12/30/69	8	−2.5
Revenue Act of 1971	8/15/71	10/6/71	11/22/71	12/10/71	4	−8.0
Tax Reduction Act of 1975	1/15/75	2/27/75	3/22/75	3/29/75	2	−22.8[i]
Tax Reform Act of 1976	a	12/4/75	8/6/76	10/4/76	44[c]	+1.6[j]

Sources: *Congressional Record, Congressional Quarterly, Annual Reports of the Secretary of the Treasury.*
a. Not recommended by the President.
b. Passed by Congress over the President's veto.
c. Time elapsed from date of first consideration by House Ways and Means Committee.
d. Revenue Act of 1950 directed the House and Senate tax committees to report to their respective houses on excess profits tax bill retroactive to July 1 or October 1, 1950. No special message by the President.
e. Recommended by the President in his budget message.
f. Recommended initially in the budget message transmitted in January of the year indicated.
g. Net after offsetting revenue increases of about $800 million.
h. Bill introduced graduated withholding for individual income tax purposes and accelerated corporation income tax payments, but did not alter tax liabilities.
i. Includes $8.1 billion rebate on 1974 individual income taxes.
j. Does not include the effect of estate and gift tax revisions, which will reduce revenues by $728 million in fiscal 1978 and by increasing amounts to $1.4 billion in fiscal 1981.

before the President made his recommendation, and from one to forty-four months before it was passed by Congress. The two tax committees listened to hundreds of witnesses present thousands of pages of testimony. The final bills ranged in size from a few pages to a peak of 984 pages in 1954, when the code was recodified. Six of the major bills increased taxes on balance, nine reduced them, and in one tax liabilities remained unchanged; the amounts involved ranged from a net increase of $10.2 billion in 1968 to a net reduction of $22.8 billion in 1975 (table 3-1).

The tax system cannot be understood without an appreciation of the personalities, pressures, forces, and conflicts that come into play in making the many difficult decisions that shape a tax bill. This chapter describes the manner in which Congress considers and enacts tax legislation and also describes some of the key people in the process. It is concerned only with tax legislation; tax administration and enforcement, which are extremely important in the overall tax process from the standpoint of the individual taxpayer, fall outside the scope of this book.

Executive Preparation of a Tax Bill

The Treasury Department has primary responsibility for the vast amount of work that goes into preparation of the President's tax recommendations. The work is supervised by the assistant secretary for tax policy (or occasionally by the under secretary). He has at his disposal two staffs: an Office of Tax Analysis, consisting of twenty-five to thirty economists and statisticians who provide the economic analysis of tax problems, estimates of the revenue effects of tax changes, and revenue projections for the budget; and an Office of the Tax Legislative Counsel, consisting of about twenty tax attorneys and an expert in accounting who are responsible for legal and accounting analyses of tax problems, drafting of tax legislation, and review and approval of tax regulations. The assistant secretary calls on the technical, legal, and statistical facilities of the Internal Revenue Service for assistance as needed. He may also seek advice or assistance from consultants in academic, business, and professional fields or in other government agencies.

It is difficult to pinpoint how and when the decision is made to study a particular tax or set of taxes. The impetus often comes from outside groups and experts after considerable public discussion, agitation, and pressure. Occasionally the congressional committees request assurances that certain matters will be taken up in the next tax bill. Or the President, after formal or informal consultation with his advisers, may signal a new departure in tax policy in a speech or news conference. For example, the first official word that President Kennedy was considering a large tax reduction came in a news conference on June 7, 1962; and an aborted plan by President Ford to reduce expenditures and taxes by $28 billion was announced in a news conference on October 6, 1975.

Studies of possible tax legislation are constantly in progress at the Treasury. Intensive work on a particular measure may begin after a decision is made by the President on the advice of responsible officials in his administration. The Council of Economic Advisers and the Office of Management and Budget (formerly the Bureau of the Budget) are equal partners in making decisions on fiscal policy, and they participate in decisions on major features of the tax bill. Decisions on technical tax questions in proposed legislation are usually made within the Treasury (subject, of course, to the approval of the President).

Materials prepared by the Treasury on the various aspects of the tax program include economic, legal, and accounting memorandums discussing each problem from almost every angle. The analysis reviews the history of the problem, evaluates its impact on particular groups and industries and on the economy as a whole, and presents the equity, economic, revenue, and administrative arguments for and against various solutions. Lawyers, accountants, economists, and statisticians participate in this evaluation. Task forces, committees, or informal working groups consisting of representatives of the Treasury and other federal agencies may be organized to consider alternative solutions. Most of the work is done within the executive branch, frequently in cooperation with the staff of the Joint Committee on Internal Revenue Taxation, which plays a crucial role in the tax legislative process. Discussions are also held by senior staff members of the Treasury with industry and labor representatives, officials of business corporations, professional groups, the academic community, and other knowledgeable people.

Work on a major tax bill begins months before the administration's recommendations are transmitted to the Congress; in some cases, the lead time may be as much as a year or longer. The information amassed during these months of research and analysis is funneled through the assistant secretary for tax policy. He may initiate new studies, suggest other approaches, and ask for still more information. He also consults the various experts individually or in groups to narrow the range of alternatives. The secretary of the treasury keeps in touch with the work at all stages and makes the final decision on the program that is submitted to the President, often after consulting other government officials and members of the White House staff.

In a typical year the main features of the tax bill are completed by mid-December. At this time, the President reviews the proposal and approves or modifies it. Final revenue figures are estimated by the Treasury on the basis of an economic projection prepared by the Council of Economic Advisers in consultation with other federal agencies. Drafts of sections to be included in the budget message and the economic report are prepared, and a start is made on the materials to be submitted for congressional consideration.

The President sometimes mentions the broad outlines of his tax program in the State of the Union message. Further elaboration is given in the budget message, which must be transmitted fifteen days after Congress convenes, and the broad economic justification is presented in the economic report, which is due on or before January 20. (In practice, there is some slippage in these dates, and with the consent of Congress the messages may be transmitted one or two weeks after they are legally due.) When the program covers a broad field or is particularly complicated, or when the President wishes to emphasize the importance of his recommendations, he transmits a special tax message to Congress, usually at the end of January or in February; occasionally, when circumstances require new tax legislation, a special tax message is transmitted later in the year.

Disclosure of a major tax program signals the beginning of public debate. Representatives of business, farm, labor, and other groups begin to make pronouncements about the wisdom of the program. National organizations like the Committee for Economic Development, the U.S. Chamber of Commerce, the National Association of Manufacturers, the AFL-CIO, the major international labor unions, trade associations, and citizens' committees scrutinize the program carefully from the standpoint of their own interests and what they regard as the public interest. Major aspects of the program are discussed in newspapers and periodicals, on radio and television.

By the time the House Ways and Means Committee opens public hearings on the bill (usually in February or March), the lines of support and opposition are drawn. At this point Congress takes over.

The Bill in Congress

Article I, Section 7, of the Constitution states: "All bills for raising revenue shall originate in the House of Representatives." Accordingly, a tax bill begins its legislative history in the House and is transmitted to the Senate after the House has completed action. In every other way the Senate is an equal partner in the tax legislative process and frequently makes extensive and fundamental changes in the House version.

The Ways and Means Committee

The tax legislative process begins in the Committee on Ways and Means of the House of Representatives. The committee consists of thirty-seven members divided between majority and minority parties in approximate proportion to their representation in the House. It has responsibility for revenue, debt, customs, trade, and social security legislation—which makes it the most powerful committee in the House.

The committee begins its study by scheduling public hearings for persons who request an opportunity to testify. The Ways and Means Committee room, which seats more than a thousand people, is usually filled to capacity for the first witness, the secretary of the treasury. His testimony typically begins with a long, carefully prepared statement, which gives the full rationale for the administration's position. For example, Secretary Douglas Dillon's presentation on the 1964 bill in January 1963 lasted two days and totaled 643 closely printed pages, including a main oral statement of 31 pages and 612 pages of supplementary tables, legal and technical explanations, and memorandums of analysis.

The secretary ordinarily reads his statement without interruption. The chairman then opens the interrogation and turns the questioning over to each member of the committee, alternating between majority and minority party members in order of seniority. Committee members may take this opportunity to make a public record of the positions they expect to take. Sympathetic members ask questions to buttress the administration's position or to help prepare the way for suitable compromises on difficult issues; those who are opposed attempt to trap the secretary into making untenable, erroneous, and inconsistent statements so as to discredit the tax proposals. Key committee members have a detailed knowledge of the tax law and the intricacies of the new tax bill. The secretary, in turn, is usually well briefed and handles most of the questions himself, turning to an associate for assistance only in connection with technical matters. Occasionally, he handles a question by promising a written reply to be included in the printed record.

After the secretary's testimony, the committee may hear witnesses from other executive agencies. For example, in 1975 the director of the Office of Management and Budget and the chairmen of the Council of Economic Advisers and the Federal Reserve Board appeared before the committee. Testimony is then heard from bankers, businessmen, lawyers, economists, and others representing the interests of private groups (and sometimes of individual clients). Except when the administration's witnesses testify, the broader "public interest" is not well represented. In recent years, representatives of public-interest organizations have begun to appear, and in a few instances the committee has invited professional economists and tax lawyers to testify as experts, but the preponderance of the testimony is from special interest groups.

Meanwhile, the committee members are besieged in private by large numbers of people seeking changes in the bill. Through these contacts, the committee evaluates the strength of the forces aligned for and against each provision of the bill.

The hearings continue until all interested parties have testified. The length of the hearings depends on the importance of the bill, the controversy it has aroused, and the positions of the committee chairman and ranking members. If there is considerable opposition, the hearings may continue for months. For example, twelve days of hearings were held in 1964 by the Ways and Means Committee on what eventually became the Excise Tax Reduction Act of 1965, but the

1973 hearings on the bill that ultimately became the Tax Reform Act of 1976 lasted about three months.

After concluding the hearings, the committee goes into executive session (though since 1974 the public has been allowed to attend). These sessions are conducted in an informal, seminar type of atmosphere. Members of the committee discuss the bill freely, calling on the staffs of the Joint Internal Revenue Committee and the Treasury for information, advice, and assistance as needed. Each proposal is carefully explained by Treasury officials and staff members, and the relevant information and opinions assembled during the hearings are summarized. Votes are taken only after members are satisfied that they have all the information needed to make up their minds.

Several people play a major role in the process of negotiation and compromise that takes place in executive sessions. The most important is the chairman of the Ways and Means Committee, who is not only the presiding officer but also the chief moderator. The ranking spokesman for the minority also exercises substantial influence, particularly if he can persuade a few members of the majority to side with him. The chief of staff of the Joint Internal Revenue Committee supervises the large secretariat that assists the Ways and Means Committee in its deliberations. He attends all sessions, joins in negotiations on the bill, and helps shape the compromise proposed by the chairman and other committee members. The assistant secretary of the treasury acts as chief negotiator for the administration (under instructions from the President and the secretary of the treasury). The secretary often participates in the executive sessions when important issues are discussed.

As tentative decisions are reached, they are translated into legislative language. Preparation of the legislative draft is the responsibility of the legislative counsel of the House of Representatives, but the staffs of the Joint Internal Revenue Committee and the Treasury are regularly called on for assistance. The drafting process is usually slow and time-consuming as the draft must make the intent of the committee as explicit and the provisions of the bill as unambiguous as possible. Considering the pressure on the draftsmen and the complexity of the material, remarkably few errors are made in the process, which is usually completed for quick final action by the committee shortly after the last tentative decision has been made.

At this time, work begins on the committee's report under the direction of the chief of staff of the Joint Internal Revenue Committee. The report, frequently several hundred pages in length, contains a detailed statement of the committee's rationale for recommending the bill, estimates of its effect on revenues, and a section-by-section analysis of its provisions. It also contains the minority views of committee members who disapprove of the bill. As the only written record of the reasons for the committee's actions, the report serves to inform members of the House and provides a basis for later interpretation of the legislation by the Internal Revenue Service and the courts.

When the report is completed, the Ways and Means Committee approves it and instructs the chairman to send the bill to the House.

House Approval

According to the rules of the House of Representatives, revenue legislation is "privileged" business, which is given priority consideration on the floor. In practice, however, the approval of the Rules Committee is sought before the bill is placed on the calendar for floor action. This is done so that the tax bill can be debated under a "closed rule," which requires the House to accept or reject the entire bill except for amendments approved by the Ways and Means Committee.

Because it is conducted under a closed rule, debate on the tax bill in the House is brief, lasting usually only two or three days. The Ways and Means Committee chairman acts as floor manager and chief proponent. Other members of the majority are assigned to defend particular aspects of the bill. The opposition, usually led by the ranking minority member of the committee, may attack the bill with vigor and predict great harm to the nation if it is enacted. But the chairman and ranking minority member of the committee work closely together on every bill and often join in pushing a tax bill through the House.

At the end of the debate, a motion is presented to recommit the bill to the Ways and Means Committee with instructions to report it back with one or more specified amendments. This motion, which constitutes the test vote on the most controversial aspects of the bill, enables its opponents to obtain a vote on a modified version without having to reject the bill altogether. Then there is a final vote on the bill itself. Only on rare occasions has a major tax bill reported by the Ways and Means Committee been rejected by the House.

The Senate Finance Committee

After House passage, the bill is sent to the Senate, where it is immediately referred to the Committee on Finance. This committee of eighteen senior and influential senators has jurisdiction over tax, trade, and social security legislation, veterans' affairs, and other financial matters. Its organization and operations are similar to those of the Ways and Means Committee.

The Finance Committee begins by holding public hearings, and the secretary of the treasury is again the first witness. His appearance here is no less an ordeal than his appearance before the Ways and Means Committee. He may largely repeat his arguments, though focusing his testimony on the House version of the bill. He may ask the committee to modify or reject certain provisions that are unacceptable to the administration; or he may accept the House modifications with only a slight demurrer. The secretary is followed by much the same parade of witnesses that appeared before the Ways and Means Committee, in many instances repeating their earlier statements.

In executive session, most of the cast of characters that assisted on the House side now appear on the Senate side. The Finance Committee usually starts with the first section of the bill and considers amendments proposed by the members in order. On rare occasions the committee approves a substantially unamended version of the bill, but typically the bill is changed significantly before it is reported to the Senate. For example, the Senate Finance Committee reports on the 1976 tax bill listed over sixty major amendments to the House bill and converted the revenue gained from tax reform to a large revenue loss.

When the Finance Committee has agreed on a bill, the staff prepares the committee report, which covers the same ground as the Ways and Means Committee report (often in identical language) and explains the reasons for the Finance Committee amendments.

The Senate Debate

Unlike the House, the Senate places no limit on debate or amendments. Many amendments are offered on the floor. Some of them are intended to change the entire character of the bill, and some are completely unrelated to its subject matter. Administration officers are usually very active at this stage. The President's aides and Senate leaders of his party work together to defeat amendments that are unacceptable to the administration or to restore provisions deleted by the Finance Committee.

Senate discussion of a tax bill is longer and more colorful than that in the House. Individual senators take the occasion not only to go on record but also to try to persuade their colleagues. The debate usually concerns features of the bill that directly affect the pocketbooks of particular groups and individuals and is often highly technical. The debates on many of the tax bills (for example, on the 1951, 1962, 1964, 1969, and 1976 acts) are among the most informed discussions held on the Senate floor.

Most of the amendments proposed on the floor are opposed by the administration or the Finance Committee and are rejected; but the Senate has been known to act against the wishes of both the administration and the committee majority. On the other hand, the Senate debate is the only stage in the entire legislative process when the administration may successfully exercise pressure against the wishes of the powerful committee chairman and ranking committee members. Such pressure is used sparingly and only when needed on major issues.

After the bill has been debated and amended to the satisfaction of the Senate, it is brought to a vote. If it fails to pass, the legislation is abandoned. If the Senate passes the House bill without amendments, it is sent directly to the President. If the Senate amends the bill—and this is the rule rather than the exception—further congressional action is necessary. (During the twenty-five days of Senate debate on the Tax Reform Act of 1976, 209 amendments were proposed, of which 143 were accepted and made part of the Senate version of the bill.) The House generally adopts a motion to disagree with the Senate amendments, thus calling for appointment of a conference committee to adjust the differences between the two versions.

The Bill in Conference

The Committee of Conference is appointed by the speaker of the House and the president of the Senate. Each usually appoints three from the majority and two from the minority. On occasion, there is a difference in the number of conferees from the two chambers, but this has no bearing on the final decision reached by the committee, since each chamber votes as a unit with a majority controlling each group.

The members of the committee are normally the senior members of the two tax committees, unless they elect not to serve.

Conferences may last from a day or two to a week or more, depending on the number of amendments, differences between the two versions, and the complexity of the bill under consideration. Joint Committee and Treasury staff members are often called upon to explain the issues, evaluate the feasibility of suggested compromises, and provide revenue estimates. The bill remains in conference until all differences between the House and Senate versions have been reconciled. High officials of the administration, including the secretary of the treasury and the President, follow the deliberations of the committee carefully and may intervene (directly or through subordinates) with individual conferees to obtain support for the administration's position.

The conference report lists the amendments accepted by each house and gives a highly technical explanation of the changes. Floor statements explaining how the two bills were reconciled provide the essential information necessary for interpreting the legislation.

After approval of the conference report by both houses, the bill is sent to the White House.

Presidential Action

As is the case in all legislation, the President has ten days to consider the bill. During this period, the various government departments analyze the bill and submit their views in the form of written memorandums to the Office of Management and Budget. The major issues are then summarized by the office, and the President makes his final decision, often after hours of consultation and soul-searching with key officials and White House staff members.

By the time the bill reaches the President's desk, administration forces in Congress have tried every legislative device to modify it to meet his requirements. For this reason, the President rarely vetoes a tax bill, even though few of them satisfy him in every detail. In the past thirty-five years, only three important bills—the Revenue Act of 1943, the Revenue Act of 1948, and the Revenue Adjustment Act of 1975—have been vetoed: the 1943 bill by President Roosevelt, the 1948 bill on three occasions in 1947 and 1948 by President Truman, and the 1975 bill by President Ford. Congress passed the 1943 and

1948 bills over the Presidents' vetoes by the necessary two-thirds majority. (The 1943 veto led to the temporary resignation of Senator Alben Barkley from his position as majority leader.) The Tax Reduction Act of 1975, which extended the 1975 tax cuts to 1976, was signed by the President after it was revised to include compromise language expressing the intention of Congress to combine further tax reductions with corresponding expenditure reductions.

The President usually issues a statement when he has acted on the bill. If he has approved it, the statement is brief and expresses pleasure at its enactment. Occasionally he takes exception to some of its provisions, even though he has signed it. If he has vetoed the bill, he issues a longer statement or message explaining why it is unacceptable.

A tax bill may stipulate that the rates take effect within a few days after its final approval. For example, the lower withholding rates provided by the 1964 act became effective eight days after the President signed it. Some of the excise tax reductions of 1965 were put into effect the day following enactment. The withholding rates for 1976 were not enacted until December 23, 1975. Some tax bills have been retroactive, reducing or increasing tax liabilities from the beginning of the calendar year, fiscal year, or quarter in which the bill was finally approved. Others have taken effect at the end of the year.

After the President has signed the bill, the Treasury issues regulations to explain its interpretation of the new law, and the Internal Revenue Service prepares to administer it by issuing new tax forms, advice to taxpayers, revised instructions to withholding agents, and so on. The issuance of regulations may itself be a lengthy process, sometimes requiring over a year if the legislation is particularly complex. Long before these tasks have been completed, a new tax bill may be under way, and the same harassed officials who are responsible for implementing the old law begin the new tax legislative cycle.

Improving the Process

The tax legislative process has been examined by numerous congressional committees, political scientists, students of taxation, citizen and professional committees, and other groups. Opinion is generally critical: tax laws are unnecessarily detailed and complicated and divert attention from the major policy issues; the committees and other members of Congress are said to be unnecessarily influenced by interest groups who do not speak in the national interest; and the slowness of the legislative process restricts the possibilities of prompt tax action for stabilization or other reasons. These criticisms have some validity, but practical solutions are hard to devise. Until recently, Congress had no opportunity to make decisions on the government's overall fiscal policy or to weigh the needs for public services against tax costs. However, new procedures were enacted in 1974 for congressional consideration of the budget, and the initial experience suggests that the process may be effective in coordinating overall tax and expenditure policies.

Simplifying the Tax Law

Almost every bill dealing with the structural provisions of the tax system contains a mass of detailed amendments to the Internal Revenue Code that deal with complicated, sometimes esoteric matters and are written in language that few people can understand. The committee reports on such bills, which are intended to explain the legislation to congressmen and members of the public who have no expertise in taxation, are also lengthy and difficult to understand. For example, the report of the Senate Finance Committee on the 1976 tax reform bill consisted of 606 closely packed pages of technical language plus a supplemental report of 95 pages. For anyone but the expert it is virtually impossible to distinguish the major issues from the minor in such a report, let alone to decide how they should be resolved.

When tax bills are finally brought to the floor of the House or Senate, few representatives or senators are familiar enough with the fine points to understand the implications of the legislation and to debate them with the committee chairmen, who have expert staff assistance to help them cope with the technicalities. Fewer still have the necessary skill and experience to introduce amendments on their own and to persuade the House or the Senate to overrule their tax committees. The emphasis on detail obscures the major policy issues, conceals large tax benefits that may be slipped in by influential committee members on behalf of special interest groups, and slows down the pace of congressional action on tax reform.

The practice of legislating every detail of the tax structure arose partly because Congress has not been willing to leave the details of the tax law to the interpretation of the tax administrator and partly because the courts have not consistently construed the Code on the basis of underlying theme and congressional purpose. To break this practice, Congress would have to declare its intention to make general tax policy and to leave the details to be worked out by the Treasury Department through its regulations. The specific language of the regulations might be subject to review and comment by the staff of the Joint Internal Revenue Committee. When there are differences of opinion, the issues might be brought to the attention of the Joint Committee itself, which could consider remedial legislation if it concluded that the proposed regulations would not carry out the congressional intent. Many tax experts believe that the tax legislative and administrative processes would be much more effective and less vulnerable to the quiet influence of lobbyists under such a procedure.

Representation of the Public Interest

Individuals who appear before the two tax committees hardly represent a cross section of opinion on tax matters. The committees generally permit anyone to testify; expert testimony comes only from administration officials and, on occasion, a few invited economists and tax lawyers. The result is that, day after day, the committees are subject to a drumfire of complaints against the tax system, arguments against the elimination of special tax advantages, and reasons for additional preferences.

In such an atmosphere, the secretary of the treasury assumes the role of defender of the national interest. He spends much of his time fighting off new tax advantages and is only moderately successful in eliminating old ones. Whether taxes are to be raised or lowered, most of the witnesses find good reasons for favoring the groups or individuals they represent. The secretary takes a broader, national view and tries to strike a balance among competing claims. Since the stakes are high and there are no generally accepted criteria for evaluating questions of tax policy, his decisions may be regarded as arbitrary or contrary to the public interest by some groups and be vigorously opposed in open hearings or in behind-the-scenes lobbying. Occasionally, he is supported by some of the national citizens' organizations, but testimony from them—although more frequent in recent years—is still the exception rather than the rule.

Fortunately, the committee members are not neophytes in the legislative process. Most of them have the capacity to detect a self-serving witness. Furthermore, they have an excellent opportunity to check the merits of the public testimony in executive session or in private with the staffs of the Joint Internal Revenue Committee and the Treasury and with outside experts. When the issues are particularly significant and complicated, the staffs prepare summaries of the pros and cons of the various positions. (In 1975 twenty-seven pamphlets on specific tax reform issues were prepared for the Ways and Means Committee.) Through such methods, individual committee members familiarize themselves with the major issues and evaluate the mass of information hurled at them.

It would nevertheless be helpful to give the public, congressmen, and committee members easier access to impartial analysis and expert opinion on tax matters. Two things can be done to improve consideration of tax legislation.

First, the Joint Internal Revenue Committee or the two separate committees might provide background materials *before* a tax issue is put on the legislative calendar. It should be possible to divide the entire field of taxation into several categories and to hold periodic hearings on each category to keep the subject continually under review and to solicit new ideas. The procedures might follow the pattern set by the Ways and Means Committee's famous 1959 *Tax Revision Compendium,* a three-volume collection of articles by leading tax experts, which has greatly influenced all tax legislation since its publication.

Second, the Joint Committee might organize expert commissions or task forces once every five years to review the major problems in taxation and to make recommendations for legislative action. This type of advisory council was set up to consider social security matters once every four years by the Social Security Act; these councils have had a significant impact on the development of the social security system.

But procedural changes by themselves will not greatly improve the results of the tax legislative process. Powerful forces are arrayed against major changes in the tax structure, while there is no effective lobby for the general public. The key may be to reform the campaign financing laws so that congressmen will not be dependent on the financial support of powerful lobbies for their election. Until the people elect representatives and senators who are able to resist pressure from special interest groups, progress in reforming the tax system will continue to be slow.

Accelerating Tax Action

A serious drawback of the tax legislative process is that it cannot be used to raise or lower taxes quickly. The President has no practical method for obtaining immediate congressional consideration of a new tax proposal, since tradition dictates that all tax changes must be carefully considered by the Ways and Means Committee and the Finance Committee. The delay in enactment of the Vietnam War surtax prevented timely action to control the inflation that was already under way. To combat recessions, reliance is often placed on expenditure changes, which have two shortcomings. They create inefficiencies in the conduct of government programs that should not be turned on and off for short-run economic reasons. They also tend to have a delayed impact on the economy because of the long lead time generally required to put them into effect.

Many tax experts and national citizens' organizations have recommended that the President be authorized to make temporary increases or reductions in tax rates. This approach would emphasize changes that are neutral in their impact on the existing tax structure, as opposed to changes that would alter the distribution of the tax burden. More fundamental reforms would be reserved for long-run revisions of the tax structure, which necessarily entail lengthy and searching debate.

In general, the proposals would permit the President to make a uniform change—up or down—in individual income tax rates of a maximum percent or a maximum number of percentage points for a period of six months, with the authority to renew the change for additional six-month periods as conditions required. The change would take effect thirty or sixty days after submission to Congress, unless it were rejected by a joint resolution. President Kennedy made such a recommendation (but limited it to changes in a downward direction) in 1962 and 1963, and President Johnson renewed it in 1964; but the tax committees showed no interest in this approach and did not even bring it up for discussion.

President Johnson modified the proposal in his 1965 economic report to allay suspicion that he sought to preempt congressional authority over tax rates. He suggested that Congress merely alter its procedures to permit rapid action on temporary income tax cuts proposed by the President to combat recession. (Tax increases were not mentioned.) Because of congressional sensitivity, the President did not fill in the details, preferring to let Congress make the decision. After Congress acted swiftly on excise tax legislation in 1965, President Johnson modified his position still further. His 1966 economic report simply stressed the need for background studies to establish guidelines for temporary tax changes.

As a result of the frequent long delays in the enactment of tax legislation, experts believe that the only practical way to speed congressional action on changes in tax rates is for the President to establish the practice of formally recommending a tax change, if it is needed, at the beginning of each year. If Congress acted promptly on this recommendation, other tax changes would be needed during the year only in wartime or other emergencies. The 1975 tax cut, which was recommended by President Ford (in different form) on January 15, 1975, was enacted in ten weeks. Continuation of this practice would go a long way toward increasing the speed and flexibility of the tax legislative process.

Consideration of Overall Fiscal Policies

Legislative control over the fiscal policies of the federal government was at one time divided between the appropriations committees and the tax committees. The appropriations committees, which act through a large number of subcommittees working on individual agency appropriations, view their role as primarily that of watchdog over the efficiency of government operations rather than of general policymaker; and the tax committees tend to be conservative about changing the level of taxes, particularly in the upward direction.

Fiscal policy planning and guidance by the President are undertaken primarily through his annual budget messages and economic reports. These are reviewed and considered by the Joint Economic Committee, which was created by the Employment Act of 1946. Its hearings, which are usually brief but structured to bring out opposing views, and its report on the President's economic report have improved public and congressional understanding of economic policy problems. However, the Joint Economic Committee does not have authority to propose or initiate legislation.

A Joint Committee on the Legislative Budget was created by Congress in 1947 to improve its consideration of fiscal policy, but the results were disappointing. The committee did not have enough information to make judgments regarding overall fiscal policy, and its recommendations were not binding on the appropriations and tax committees. As a result, the committee resolutions were political and served little purpose. The effort was abandoned after both houses ignored the resolutions in two successive years.

The Revenue and Expenditure Control Act of 1968 imposed a limit on some government expenditures at the insistence of the chairman of the Ways and Means Committee, who viewed the growth of government expenditures with alarm. Whether this attempt to legislate the level of total expenditures in a tax bill did very much good is still the subject of debate. But it is clear that control of expenditures can hardly be exercised in a responsible manner through the tax process.

A major impetus to reforming the congressional budget process was provided by President Nixon, who in 1973 attempted to impound appropriations previously approved by Congress and the President. Congress realized that it had no mechanism to prevent such action or even to consider it in relation to the budget as a whole. To establish an orderly process for budget planning, the Congressional Budget and Impoundment Control Act of 1974 was enacted. This act set up new procedures to prevent a President from impounding previously approved appropriations without congressional approval and also to deal with the inadequacies of the congressional budget process.

The legislation requires the President to notify Congress when he intends to impound any appropriations. The impoundments are allowed to take effect unless they are disapproved by both houses of Congress within forty-five days after the President's notification. During fiscal 1976 the President proposed the impoundment of appropriations of $3.3 billion, but Congress agreed to only $138 million.

The act also requires Congress to approve two concurrent resolutions that will provide the basis for congressional consideration of taxes in relation to expenditures. The first resolution, which must be enacted by both houses by May 15 of each year, specifies levels of budget outlays and budget authority for the next fiscal year (which begins on October 1), the surplus or deficit that is "appropriate in the light of economic conditions," the recommended level of taxation, and the appropriate statutory debt limit. This resolution is intended to provide guidance to the committees that are responsible for decisions on appropriations and taxes. A second concurrent resolution reaffirming or revising the level of expenditures, appropriations, receipts, and the debt limit of the first resolution must be passed by September 15.

Any differences between the amounts specified in the resolution and the actions of the appropriations and tax committees must be reconciled with the resolution by September 25. The concurrent resolutions are not subject to approval by the President, but Congress cannot adjourn for the year until action on the second resolution is completed and the appropriation and tax actions are reconciled with it.

The legislation set up the Congressional Budget Office to provide expert staff support for Congress in evaluating the budget. The new office, which is the congressional counterpart of the Office of Management and Budget in the executive branch, must prepare a report on the choices in the President's budget by April 1 of each year that includes budget projections for each of the next five fiscal years as well. The office is also directed to estimate five-year costs of all bills reported out by congressional committees and projections of revenue losses through special tax provisions, called "tax expenditures" in the legislation (see chapter 4). The budget committees in both houses also have professional staffs to help them evaluate budget policies and to decide on the appropriate level of expenditures and revenues in the concurrent resolutions.

Congress followed the new procedures during 1975 and 1976 with good results. The resolutions were seriously debated in the committees and on the floor of each house. The final totals, which provided for deficits of $74 billion in fiscal 1976 and $51 billion in fiscal 1977, were consistent with the fiscal policy needed to promote recovery from the deep and prolonged 1974–75 recession. After enactment, Congress actually lived up to the guidelines laid down in the resolutions; in several instances, the budget committee chairmen succeeded in cutting appropriations that threatened to raise expenditures for particular categories above the limits set. The Congressional Budget Office issued numerous useful reports during the two years on the state of the economy and on the relation between the budget and economic developments. While procedures alone cannot ensure good fiscal policies, experience so far suggests that Congress is taking the new legislation seriously and has begun to make decisions on taxes in the light of economic and budgetary needs.

Summary

The tax legislative process begins in the Treasury and other federal agencies where tax problems are analyzed and solutions are proposed for the President's consideration. The President transmits his recommendations to Congress, where they are carefully reviewed by the two powerful tax committees, are revised to compromise the conflicts of major opposing interests, and are sent in turn to the House and Senate floors for approval. Differences between the two bills are settled by a conference committee; the revised version is returned to both houses for approval; and the bill becomes law when the President signs it or when Congress passes it over his veto.

The tax legislative process is unique in several respects. The work concerns a highly complex set of laws, yet all the decisions are made (as they should be) through the political process. Leading roles are played by the President, the secretary of the treasury and his assistant secretary for tax policy, the chairmen of the two tax committees, and the chief of staff of the Joint Internal Revenue Committee. Behind the scenes, competent staffs in both the executive and legislative branches help move the tax bill through its various stages. For all these people, a tax bill is a grueling experience, demanding physical stamina as well as political acumen.

Greater attention is being given in Congress to overall fiscal policies since the enactment of new congressional budget procedures in 1974 and the establishment of the Congressional Budget Office. Reform of the tax process is still needed: first, to permit Congress to concentrate on major policy issues rather than on details of the tax law; second, to give better representation to the public interest in the deliberations of the Ways and Means Committee and the Finance Committee; and third, to accelerate action on tax changes to combat inflation or recession.

Some believe that the federal tax legislative process impedes progress toward a better tax system, but this is probably an unfair assessment of the work of the congressional tax committees and an unrealistic appraisal of the balance of forces for and against tax reform. While many questionable provisions have crept into the U.S. tax laws, erosion of the tax base has been halted in recent years, and some steps have been taken to reverse it. Moreover, the overall distribution of federal taxes continues to be progressive despite the strong interests arrayed against progression and equitable taxation. More progress will be made along these lines only when sufficient political power is mobilized to persuade the tax committees, and Congress as a whole, that tax reform has widespread and determined popular support.

CHAPTER FOUR

The Individual Income Tax

ANY SURVEY of tax sources should begin with the nation's fairest and most productive source of revenue, the individual income tax. All advanced industrial countries levy a direct tax on individual incomes, but nowhere is this tax as important as in the United States. In recent years, 44 percent of federal budget receipts have come from this source.

The individual income tax is uniquely suited to raising revenue in a democratic country, where the distribution of income, and thus of ability to pay, is unequal. Theoreticians may disagree about the meaning of the term "ability to pay," but the close association between a person's income and his or her taxpaying ability is commonly accepted. The idea that the income tax should be progressive is also generally accepted.

The individual income tax has still another attractive feature. Income alone does not determine a person's ability to pay; family responsibilities are also important. A single person may be able to get along on an income of $5,000 a year, but a married man with two children would have great difficulty in making ends meet on that income. The individual income tax takes such differences into account by allowing personal exemptions and deductions, which are subtracted from an individual's total income to arrive at the income subject to tax.

For almost thirty years after its adoption in 1913, the individual income tax applied mainly to a small number of high-income people. Exemptions were high by today's standards, and few incomes were large enough to be subject to tax at the lowest rate, let alone the higher graduated rates. In the national effort to raise needed revenue during the Second World War, exemptions were drastically reduced. They have been raised several times since the war, but remain low by prewar standards. Tax rates were also raised in wartime and have remained much higher than in earlier years. At the same time, personal incomes have continued to increase with the growth of the economy and with the inflations associated with the Second World War, the Korean War, and the Vietnam War and its aftermath. The combination of lower exemptions, higher rates, and higher incomes increased the yield of the individual income tax manyfold. In 1939 tax liabilities were about $1 billion; in 1977 they will reach $140 billion.

This tremendous expansion would not have been possible without both ready compliance with income tax laws and effective administration. In many countries where compliance is poor and administration is weak, there is great reluctance to rely heavily on the income tax. In this country, the record of compliance is good—although it could still be improved—and practical methods have been developed for administering a mass income tax, at a cost of only about 0.5 percent of the tax collected. In the early 1940s many people—even highly placed officials of the Bureau of Internal Revenue—doubted that an income tax covering almost everyone could be administered effectively. Although some problems remain, in an advanced country the administrative feasibility of an individual income tax of almost universal coverage is no longer questioned.

There are good economic reasons for using the income tax as a major source of revenue. The automatic flexibility of the tax promotes economic stability, and the progressive rates reduce excessive concentration of economic power and control. Some believe that the income tax is needed also to moderate the growth of private savings, which could hold down private demand for goods and services. Others believe that the income tax impairs work and investment incentives and thereby reduces the nation's economic growth. These are difficult questions, which will be discussed later. Nonetheless, it is correct to say that the modern individual income tax, if carefully designed and well administered, is a powerful and essential economic instrument for a modern industrial economy.

The Structure of the Federal Income Tax

The basic structure of the federal income tax is simple. The taxpayer adds up his income from all taxable sources, subtracts certain allowable deductions and exemptions for himself, his wife, his children, and other dependents, and then applies the tax rates to the remainder. But this procedure has many pitfalls for the taxpayer, and difficult questions of tax policy arise at almost every stage. It is therefore important to understand the main features of the income tax structure.

Adjusted Gross Income and Taxable Income

The two major concepts of income that appear on the tax return are adjusted gross income and taxable income.

Adjusted gross income is the closest approach in tax law to what an economist might call "total income." But it departs from an economic definition of income in important respects. It is the total income from all taxable sources, less moving and certain other expenses incurred by employees in earning that income, payments by the self-employed and employees into retirement plans, and alimony. In general, only *money* income is treated as taxable, but many items of money income are excluded. These include one-half of realized capital gains on assets held for more than one year (more than nine months in 1977), interest on state and local government bonds, all transfer payments (for example, social security benefits and unemployment compensation), some fringe benefits received by employees from their employers (the most important of these are contributions to pension and health plans), and income on savings through life insurance. The emphasis on money income means that unrealized capital gains and such imputed income as the rental value of owner-occupied homes are automatically excluded.

Taxable income is computed by making two sets of deductions from adjusted gross income. The first are those personal expenditures that are allowed as deductions by law—charitable contributions; interest paid; state-local income, general sales, property, and gasoline taxes; medical and dental expenses above 3 percent of adjusted gross income; and losses from casualty or theft above $100 for each loss. In lieu of these deductions, the taxpayer may use the *standard deduction,* which was 10 percent of adjusted gross income (up to a maximum of $1,000) for the period 1944–69 and gradually increased to 16 percent (up to a maximum of $2,400 for single persons and $2,800 for married couples) by 1976. A minimum standard deduction of $200, plus $100 for each exemption, which was in effect from 1964 through 1969, has been replaced by a "low-income allowance," which began at $1,100 in 1970 and reached $1,700 for single persons and $2,100 for married couples in 1976.

When the standard deduction was first adopted in 1944, it was used by over 80 percent of those filing returns. As incomes have risen and deductible expenditures have increased, the percentage using the standard deduction has declined. In 1974 the standard deduction was still used on 53.6 million returns, or almost two-thirds of the 83.3 million filed (appendix table C-6). But the amount of the standard deduction was small compared to the itemized deductions, which have increased with the growth of homeownership, state-local taxes, and use of consumer credit as well as the normal increase in expenditures that occurs as incomes rise. Total deductions reported on all 1974 returns amounted to $196 billion; of this amount, $120 billion were itemized deductions, and $76 billion were standard deductions.

The second set of deductions provides an allowance for personal exemptions. The exemptions for the taxpayer, his spouse, and other dependents are $750 per person. The law also gives one additional exemption each to the husband and wife if they are over sixty-five years of age, and still another exemption to the blind. In addition, beginning in 1975, a credit against the income tax has been allowed in lieu of an increase in exemptions; in 1976 and 1977 the credit is the larger of (1) $35 per person in the family or (2) 2 percent of taxable income up to a maximum of $180.

Figure 4-1 traces the changes in the tax base (that is, taxable income) since the beginning of World War II. In 1947 only about 40 percent of personal income was subject to tax; by 1969 this had risen to 52 percent of personal income. Increases in the exemption have reduced the growth of taxable income since 1969, but taxable income was still close to 50 percent of personal income in 1974 and rising. This increase was caused by one of the two factors mentioned earlier

Figure 4-1. Ratio of Taxable Individual Income to Personal Income, 1947–74

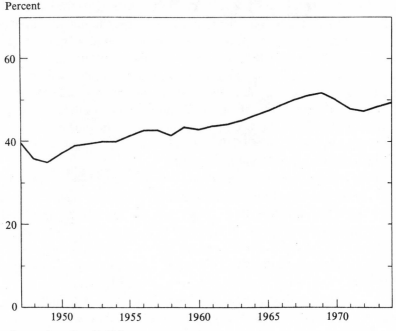

Percent

Source: Appendix table B-5.

—the upward shift in incomes. The rise has been interrupted only when exemptions were increased (1948 and 1970–71), and when nontaxable transfer payments increased during recession years (1949, 1954, 1958, and 1960).

In 1974, 49.6 percent of personal income went into the tax base, 17.2 percent represented differences in definition between personal income and adjusted gross income, 6.5 percent either was not reported on tax returns or was received by persons who were not taxable, 11.8 percent was accounted for by exemptions, and another 14.9 percent by deductions (table 4-1). Stated somewhat differently, about $5 billion out of every $10 billion of personal income went into the tax base.

Tax Rates

The tax rates are graduated by a bracket system (table 4-2). Other methods of graduation have been used elsewhere, but this seems to be

Table 4-1. Derivation of the Federal Individual Income Tax Base from Personal Income, 1974

Derivation of the tax base	Amount (billions of dollars)	Percentage distribution
Personal income	1,153.3	100.0
Conceptual differences between adjusted gross income and personal income[a]	197.8	17.2
Adjusted gross income not reported on tax returns or reported by individuals who were not taxable	75.3	6.5
Personal exemptions on taxable returns	136.6	11.8
Personal deductions on taxable returns	171.4	14.9
Taxable income on taxable returns (tax base)	572.4	49.6

Source: Appendix tables B-2 and B-4. Figures are rounded.
a. For details, see appendix table B-1.

the most practical. Under this system, the income scale is divided into segments, or brackets, and rates are applied only to the income in each bracket. Rates increase by no more than 5 percentage points from one bracket to the next to avoid large and abrupt increases in tax rates as incomes rise. People with taxable incomes of $20,000 or less read their tax liabilities directly from a tax table. Those with incomes above $20,000 calculate their tax liabilities from tax rate schedules.

There are now four separate rate schedules for different categories of taxpayers. The basic rates, which apply to married taxpayers filing separate returns, range from 14 percent on the first $500 of taxable income to 70 percent on the amount of taxable income above $100,000. For married couples filing joint returns, the tax rates are applied to half the taxable income of the couple, and the result is multiplied by two. As table 4-2 shows, this income-splitting feature doubles the width of the brackets for married couples. Single persons have a special rate schedule which ensures that their tax is never more than 120 percent of the tax imposed on joint returns with the same total taxable income. Single persons who are heads of households also use a special rate schedule, with rates that are about halfway between the rates for single persons and the rates for joint returns.

Although the rates are graduated up to $100,000 of taxable income, much of the tax base is concentrated in the lowest brackets.

60   *Federal Tax Policy*

Table 4-2. Federal Individual Income Tax Rates, 1977

Taxable income (dollars)	Married couples (separate returns)	Single persons	Heads of households	Married couples (joint returns)
0–500	14	14	14	14
500–1,000	15	15	14	14
1,000–1,500	16	16	16	15
1,500–2,000	17	17	16	15
2,000–3,000	19	19	18	16
3,000–4,000	19	19	18	17
4,000–6,000	22	21	19	19
6,000–8,000	25	24	22	19
8,000–10,000	28	25	23	22
10,000–12,000	32	27	25	22
12,000–14,000	36	29	27	25
14,000–16,000	39	31	28	25
16,000–18,000	42	34	31	28
18,000–20,000	45	36	32	28
20,000–22,000	48	38	35	32
22,000–24,000	50	40	36	32
24,000–26,000	50	40	38	36
26,000–28,000	53	45	41	36
28,000–32,000	53	45	42	39
32,000–36,000	55	50	45	42
36,000–38,000	55	50	48	45
38,000–40,000	58	55	51	45
40,000–44,000	58	55	52	48
44,000–50,000	60	60	55	50
50,000–52,000	62	62	56	50
52,000–60,000	62	62	58	53
60,000–64,000	64	64	58	53
64,000–70,000	64	64	59	55
70,000–76,000	66	66	61	55
76,000–80,000	66	66	62	58
80,000–88,000	68	68	63	58
88,000–90,000	68	68	64	60
90,000–100,000	69	69	64	60
100,000–120,000	70	70	66	62
120,000–140,000	70	70	67	64
140,000–160,000	70	70	68	66
160,000–180,000	70	70	69	68
180,000–200,000	70	70	70	69
200,000 and over	70	70	70	70

Source: Internal Revenue Code.

In 1973, 62 percent of taxable income was subject to the 14–19 percent rates in the first six brackets, and only 3.6 percent was taxed at rates of 50 percent or more (appendix table B-6).

The tax liabilities computed from the four rate schedules are modified in three ways. First, the first $50,000 of long-term capital gains is subject to a maximum rate of 25 percent. Second, the tax rate on earned income (salaries and professional and self-employment income, deferred compensation, and income from pensions and annuities) is limited to a maximum marginal rate of 50 percent. In effect, the provision slices off the rate schedule for earned incomes at 50 percent. Third, certain "tax preferences" are subject to a separate minimum tax. The base of the minimum tax is computed by subtracting from the total of the statutory tax preferences a $10,000 exemption or half the regular income tax for the year, whichever is higher. The minimum tax rate, initially set at 10 percent in 1969, was raised to 15 percent in 1976.

Methods of Tax Payment

Between 1913 and 1942 federal income taxes were paid in quarterly installments during the year following receipt of income. When the coverage of the income tax was extended to the majority of income recipients during World War II, it was realized that the old system could not operate successfully. People with low and middle incomes tend to use their income as it becomes available. Their future incomes are uncertain, and it is difficult to budget for taxes that do not become due until some time after the income is received. If income stops because of unemployment or sickness, an income tax debt accrued in the prior year may become a serious burden. Even high-income taxpayers find it easier to meet tax payments currently than a year later, particularly when incomes fluctuate. Synchronization of tax payments with receipt of income is also economically desirable to maximize the stabilizing effect of the income tax.

The current payment system, introduced in 1943, is based on the principle that taxes become due when incomes are earned, rather than in the following year when tax returns are filed. In practice, the system remains fully current for most wage and salary earners because their taxes are withheld by their employers. People who receive other types of income estimate their tax and pay it in quarterly installments dur the year in which it is received.

WITHHOLDING. Withholding for income tax purposes applies to all employees except farm workers and domestic servants, at rates ranging from 16 percent of wages and salaries over $108 a month to 36 percent in the top brackets. Employees with additional income that is not subject to withholding may elect to have an extra amount withheld from their wages or salaries in order to reduce or avoid the quarterly installment payments. Withholding is also available for pensions and annuities at the request of the recipient.

The amounts withheld by the employer are remitted to the government quarterly if they total less than $200 a month. Employers withholding between $200 and $2,000 are required to deposit the tax withheld in an authorized bank within fifteen days after the end of the first two months of a quarter and by the last day of the month following the final month of a quarter. Employers withholding more than $2,000 a month are required to make deposits of the amounts withheld four times each month.

The withholding system is the backbone of the individual income tax. In 1973, the latest year for which data are available, the total tax liability amounted to $111.2 billion. Withholding brought in $103.6 billion; payments of estimated tax, $19.6 billion; and final payments on April 15 of the following year, $12.8 billion. These payments exceeded the total tax due by $24.9 billion, which was refunded to the taxpayers (appendix table C-7).

DECLARATION OF ESTIMATED TAX. Since withholding applies only to wages and salaries and the rate cuts off at 36 percent rather than 70 percent, millions of taxpayers do not have their taxes fully withheld; and no tax at all has to be withheld from nonwage sources. The declaration system was devised to take up the slack.

A declaration is required of all persons whose estimated tax exceeds the amount withheld by $100 or more and who have relatively large incomes (more than $500 of nonwage income or a gross wage income of more than $20,000 if they are single, heads of households, or married with a spouse who does not receive wages, more than $10,000 if married and both spouses receive wages, and more than $5,000 if married and filing separate returns). Declarations are filed on or before April 15, and the estimated tax not withheld is payable in installments on April 15, June 15, and September 15 of the current year and January 15 of the following year (January 31 if paid with a final tax return). These requirements were set so that people whose income is not subject to withholding—farmers, businessmen, and recipients of property income—will pay their tax currently, and so that wage and salary earners in the higher brackets will pay on a current basis the part of their tax that is not withheld. Farmers and fishermen may file their declarations on January 15 of the following year or omit them entirely if they file their final returns by March 1.

Taxpayers who do not pay as much as 80 percent of their final tax through withholding and declaration (66⅔ percent in the case of farmers and fishermen) must pay a charge of 7 percent a year for the amount falling short of 80 percent. However, no charge is made for any installment if the tax paid by the date of the installment is based on (a) the previous year's tax; (b) the previous year's income with the current year's rates and exemptions; or (c) 90 percent of the tax on the actual income received before the installment date.

As a result of the progressive withholding rates and the liberal requirements for declaration payments, the sums collected through declarations of estimated tax have been relatively small. Whereas taxes withheld increased from $9.6 billion to $103.6 billion between 1944 and 1973, declaration payments increased from $5.5 billion to only $19.6 billion during the same period (appendix table C-7).

Final Tax Reconciliation

The reconciliation between an individual's final tax liability and his or her prepayments is made on the final tax return, which is filed not later than April 15 (although an extension of two months can be automatically obtained by request). A taxpayer who owes more tax sends the Internal Revenue Service a check for the balance due along with the return; if too much tax has been withheld or paid as estimated tax, the excess is refunded or credited to the next year's tax if the taxpayer so requests.

Few returns have identical prepayments and final liabilities. In 1973 only 2.2 million out of a total of 80.7 million returns showed prepayments exactly equal to final liabilities (including returns of taxpayers who filed but were not subject to any tax). Of the remaining 78.5 million, 64.2 million received a refund check (or chose to credit the overpayment against the estimated tax for the following year), and 14.2 million had a balance of tax due (appendix table C-8).

Refunds greatly outnumbered balances of tax due for several

reasons. (1) Withholding is based on the assumption that the employee works regularly (part time or full time), and thus the total amount of exemptions for the year is apportioned equally among pay periods; but employment is often irregular because of seasonality, changes of jobs, illness, and the like. (2) Employees may claim fewer exemptions for withholding purposes than they are entitled to. (3) The withholding tables allow only for the standard deduction, whereas many employees—particularly those who own homes—have large deductions, which they itemize when filing their returns. To moderate overwithholding on this score, the Tax Adjustment Act of 1966 permits those who have large itemized deductions to claim additional exemptions for withholding purposes.

When the current payment system was adopted, great concern was expressed that overwithholding might be resented by taxpayers. Since the end of World War II, the number of returns with overpayments has never fallen below 30 million in any one year and it reached 64 million in 1973 (appendix table C-8). But there have been few complaints. Apparently people would rather receive a check from the government than pay a tax bill, particularly since most of the refunds are mailed within two months after the tax return is filed.

Possible Modification of the Current Payment System

Proposals have been made to expand the withholding system to include incomes other than wages and salaries. On several occasions Congress has rejected plans for withholding on interest and dividends at a flat rate. A withholding system without exemptions was considered too burdensome for the aged and other nontaxable people; and corporations, banks, and other financial institutions paying interest and dividends argued that it would be too costly to administer a plan involving exemption certificates. In 1962 Congress compromised the issue by requiring payers of interest and dividends to send an information return (with a copy to the government) to all recipients receiving $10 or more of interest or dividends a year. Interest and dividend reporting has greatly improved, but interest underreporting is still heavy. Although it was anticipated that present procedures would be evaluated after a few years of experience, little interest in remedying the situation has been shown by either the executive branch or Congress.

Economic Effects

Three issues are of particular importance in appraising the economic effects of the individual income tax: its role as a stabilizer of consumption expenditures, its effect on saving, and its influence on work and investment incentives.

Role as Stabilizer

Stability of yield was once regarded as a major criterion of a good tax. Today there is general agreement that properly timed changes in tax yields can help increase demand during recessions and restrain the growth of demand during periods of expansion. One of the virtues of the progressive individual income tax is that its yield automatically rises and falls more than in proportion to changes in personal income. Moreover, the system of paying taxes currently has greatly accelerated the reaction of income tax revenues to changes in income. An important by-product of current payment is that changes in tax rates have an almost immediate effect on the disposable income of most taxpayers. These features have made the personal income tax extremely useful for promoting economic stabilization and growth.

The automatic response of the individual income tax—its *built-in flexibility*—can be explained by the following example. Suppose a taxpayer with a wife and two children earns $10,000 a year when he is employed and uses the standard deduction. His taxable income is $4,900 ($10,000 less $2,100 for the low-income allowance and $3,000 for the personal exemptions), and the tax under 1977 rates, exemptions, and per capita credit is $651. The following table shows what the effect on his taxable income and tax would be if his income dropped to $8,000:

Adjusted gross income	$10,000	$8,000
Less exemptions	3,000	3,000
Less low-income allowance	2,100	2,100
Taxable income	4,900	2,900
Tax after credit	651	294
Disposable income	9,349	7,706

Whereas adjusted gross income declined by 20 percent, taxable income was reduced 41 percent and the tax 55 percent.

Such examples are multiplied millions of times during a recession, while the opposite occurs during boom periods. Those with lower or higher incomes find that their tax is reduced or increased proportionately more than their income. As a result, disposable income is more stable than it would be in the absence of the tax. (In the above example, disposable income declined only $1,643 though income before tax dropped $2,000.) Since disposable income is the major determinant of consumption, expenditures of consumers are also more stable than they would be without the tax.

Individual income tax rate or exemption changes are also used to stimulate or restrain the economy. Substantial income tax reductions were made in 1964, 1971, and 1975 to raise consumer expenditures, while a special surtax was enacted during the Vietnam War to moderate the growth in expenditures. All the tax cuts helped stimulate economic recovery, but the surtax did not have a major effect on spending because monetary policy was relaxed prematurely and because expectations of inflation were more pervasive than had been anticipated. Those who believe consumption is determined largely by what individuals regard as their "permanent" income argue that the surtax was not effective because it was a temporary tax change. Nevertheless, most people are persuaded that income tax changes can contribute significantly to regulating the rate of growth of private demand, but that permanent changes are more effective than temporary ones.

Effect on Saving and Consumption

The individual income tax applies to the entire income of an individual whether it is spent or saved. Some have argued that the income tax is unfair to those who save because it applies both to the income that gives rise to the saving and to the income produced by the saving. But almost all economists now agree that, on equity grounds, this double taxation argument does not have much merit. At any time, a person has the option of making a new decision to spend or to save part of the income he or she has after tax. If the decision is to save, a new tax is not necessarily incurred. It is only if the saving is invested in an income-producing asset that new income is generated, and this new income is subject to additional tax.

The individual income tax is often contrasted with a general consumption or expenditure tax, which is an alternative method of taxing people in accordance with "ability to pay." In the case of the income tax, the measure of ability to pay is income; in the case of the expenditure tax, the measure is consumption. The tax on consumption may also be levied at progressive rates. It is theoretically possible (though difficult in practice) to approximate the degree of progression of an income tax by a consumption tax.

The income tax reduces the gain made when an individual saves rather than consumes part of his or her income, while an expenditure tax makes future consumption relatively as attractive as present consumption. Under the income tax, the interest reward for saving and investing is reduced by the tax; under the expenditure tax, the net reward is always equal to the market rate of interest regardless of the tax rate. Thus the consumption tax is neutral with respect to the consumption-saving choice, while the income tax distorts it. This means that an expenditure tax encourages saving more than does an equal-yield income tax that is distributed in the same proportions by income classes. The degree of distortion depends on how sensitive saving is to the interest rate, but the interest elasticity of saving—and hence the magnitude of the distortion—is not known.

It can be shown that a consumption tax is equivalent to an income tax that exempts all property income and applies only to earned income. Aside from the question of equity this raises, it is clear that taxation of consumption alone would permit the accumulation of vast fortunes, which would give the owners the ability to exercise great power over the economic and political life of the nation. To prevent this, the expenditure tax would have to be accompanied by a relatively stiff annual tax on wealth and high death taxes.

Graduated expenditure taxes are often proposed as a method of avoiding or correcting the defects of the income tax base, particularly in the top brackets, where the preferential treatment of capital gains, tax-exempt interest, depletion allowances (see chapter 5), and other favorable provisions permit the accumulation of large fortunes with little or no payment of income tax. An expenditure tax would reach such incomes when they were spent without resort to regressive taxation.

Despite this advantage, the expenditure tax was used only briefly in India and Sri Lanka (it was reintroduced in the latter in 1976). This reflects in part the prevailing view that income is a better index of ability to pay than consumption. Moreover, there are problems with implementing an expenditure tax that its proponents often disregard. To avoid a reduction of progressivity, the expenditure tax rates would have to be much higher than the income tax rates. For example, if in a given taxable income bracket, the income tax rate was 60 percent and the marginal saving rate was 25 percent, the marginal tax rate on income less saving would have to be 80 percent to raise the same revenue from the bracket (if there were no change in the marginal propensity to save). Furthermore, there is no guarantee that the expenditure tax base would not be eroded as much as, or more than, the income tax. Taxation of housing and durable goods at expenditure tax rates would probably be regarded by most people as onerous. Deductions for these and other expenditures that might be regarded as essential would greatly restrict the revenue productivity of an expenditure tax.

An expenditure tax was recommended by the Treasury during World War II, but it was rejected by Congress primarily because of its novelty and complexity. An expenditure tax is more difficult to administer than an income tax, and compliance is more difficult for taxpayers. Although it is hard to imagine total replacement of the income tax by an expenditure tax, the latter might be a useful supplement if it became necessary to discourage consumption. (For further discussion of the expenditure tax, see chapter 6.)

Work and Investment Incentives

The individual income tax affects economic incentives in two different directions. On the one hand, it reduces the financial rewards of greater effort and risk-taking and thus tends to discourage these activities. On the other hand, it may provide a greater incentive to obtain more income because it decreases the income left over for spending. There is no a priori basis for deciding which effect is most important.

Taxation is only one of many factors affecting work and investment incentives. This makes it extremely difficult to interpret the available statistical evidence or the results of direct interviews with taxpayers. The evidence suggests that income taxation does not significantly reduce the amount of labor supplied by workers and managers who are the primary family earners. Work habits are not easily changed, and for most people in a modern industrial society there is little opportunity to vary their hours of work or the intensity of their efforts in response to changes in tax rates. Nearly all people who are asked about income taxation grumble about it, but relatively few say that they work fewer hours or exert less than their best efforts to avoid tax. The maximum 50 percent marginal rate for earned income, which was enacted in 1969, was justified on incentive grounds, but there is no evidence that it has had a significant impact on labor supply and therefore may not be worth the cost (estimated at $500 million in fiscal 1977).

Recent empirical work suggests that female workers, particularly those who are the secondary earners in a family, are affected by the income tax. These workers have a much greater opportunity to vary their work effort than do primary earners, and econometric analyses have shown that they do respond to higher wages by working longer hours. It has been suggested that the effective tax rate on working spouses be lowered as a method of encouraging them to work more. (See the sections on the family and earned income below.)

As for risk-taking, the problem is complicated. In the first place, the tax rates on capital gains are much lower than those on ordinary incomes. Numerous studies have demonstrated that the opportunity to earn income in the form of capital gains stimulates investment and risk-taking. Second, taxpayers may offset business losses against ordinary income not only for the current year but also for three prior years and seven succeeding years; capital losses may similarly be offset against capital gains, and half of these losses (up to $2,000 a year in 1977 and $3,000 a year beginning in 1978) may be offset against ordinary income indefinitely. Such offsets diminish the consequences of loss by the investor. Third, much of the nation's investment is undertaken by large corporations. These firms are generally permitted to retain earnings after paying tax at the corporation rate, which is more moderate than the rates for investors in the top personal income tax brackets. Finally, the law provides incentives to invest through generous depreciation allowances and a 10 percent investment credit. In any case, experience suggests that the major stimulus to investment comes from a healthy and prosperous economy.

The discussion in the next section indicates that much can be done to improve the structure of the income tax. But there is little basis for the assertions made from time to time that the income tax has had an adverse effect on the economy.

Structural Problems

The personal income tax is determined by the definition of income, allowable deductions, personal exemptions, tax rates, and tax credits. These elements can be combined in various ways to produce a given amount of revenue. In recent years, there has been increasing recognition that the definition of taxable income under the U.S. tax law is deficient. Many of the exclusions and deductions are not essential for effective personal income taxation and have cut into the income tax base unnecessarily. This process of "erosion" has been halted in recent years, but only limited progress has been made in reversing it.

Erosion of the income tax base makes higher tax rates necessary. It puts a premium on earning and disposing of incomes in forms that receive preferential treatment, thus often distorting the allocation of resources. Under a progressive tax system, the tax value of any deduction or exclusion increases as the marginal tax rates increase, so that preferences (that are not in the form of tax credits) are most valuable to those with the highest incomes. Erosion also violates the principle that taxpayers with equal incomes should pay the same tax. These departures from vertical and horizontal equity, which often seem arbitrary, contribute to taxpayer dissatisfaction and create pressures for the enactment of additional special benefits—pressures that legislators find difficult to resist.

Most of the special provisions in the tax law are akin to direct government expenditures but are not explicitly included in the federal budget. For this reason they have been called "tax expenditures." In recent years, tax expenditures have amounted to about 25 percent of federal budget outlays. (See appendix tables C-14 and C-15.)

Figure 4-2 shows the practical effect of erosion. If the total income reported by taxpayers were subject to the nominal tax rates without any exemptions, deductions, or other special provisions, effective tax rates would begin at 14 percent and rise to almost 70 percent in the very highest brackets. But nobody pays these rates on his entire income. The effect of all the special provisions rises from 12 to 15 percent of total income below $15,000 to a maximum of 41 percent above $1,000,000. Thus, after allowing for the special provisions, the *maximum average effective rate* for any income class is about 33 percent. Exemptions are most important in the lowest income classes and deductions in the top classes; taken together, the effect of these provisions declines as income rises up to $150,000, then rises somewhat above $150,000. Three sets of provisions—those relating to capital gains, preference items, and the maximum tax on earned income—reduce taxes primarily for those in the top brackets, although only the first has a significant effect. Income splitting, which aids all classes above $5,000, benefits most those with incomes between $25,000 and $150,000. The effective rates shown in figure 4-2 are average rates, and there are wide variations in taxes paid at all income levels.

A personal income tax conforming strictly to the principle of horizontal equity is easily described but difficult to implement. It would include in the tax base all income from whatever source derived, permit deductions for expenses of earning income, and also make an allowance for the taxpayer and his or her dependents through the personal exemptions. "Income" is defined by economists as consumption plus tax payments plus (or minus) the net increase (or decrease) in the value of assets during the taxable period. In practice, this definition is usually modified to exclude gifts and inheritances, which are subject to separate taxes, and, for practical reasons, to include capital gains only when realized or transferred to others through gifts and bequests. In the discussion that follows, this comprehensive definition of income will be used as a basis for evaluating the major features of the income tax and the more important proposals for reform.

Personal Exemptions

The history of personal exemptions under the federal individual income tax in the United States since 1913 is summarized in figure 4-3. In constant dollars, exemptions for single persons and families show an unmistakable downward trend. The value, in 1939 prices, of the 1976 per capita exemption and tax credit was $243 for single persons, $487 for a married couple with no children, and $974 for a married couple with two children.

Between 1964 and 1974 the minimum standard deduction (called the low-income allowance since 1970) was used in lieu of increasing exemptions to adjust the minimum taxable levels as prices increased. In 1975 a nonrefundable per capita tax credit was added to reduce the benefits of an exemption increase in the higher income classes. (The credit is nonrefundable because it is limited to the tax otherwise due; if the excess of the credit over the tax liability is payable to the taxpayer, the credit is called refundable.)

Figure 4-2. Influence of Various Provisions on Effective Rates of Federal Individual Income Tax, 1976

Effective rate (percent)

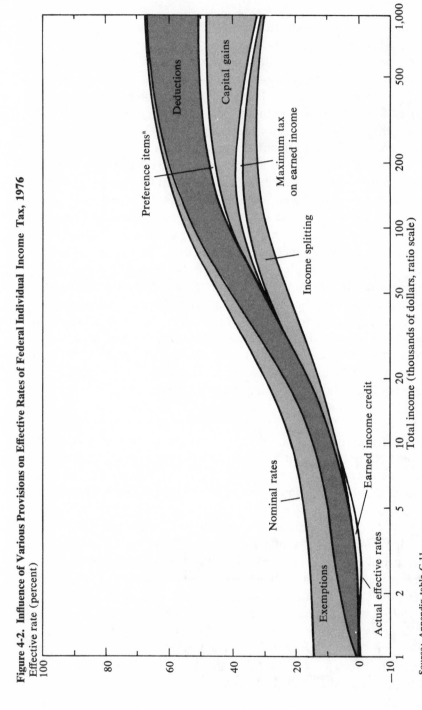

Source: Appendix table C-11.
a. Preference items as defined by the Tax Reform Act of 1969, except excluded net long-term capital gains.

Figure 4-3. History of Federal Individual Income Tax Exemptions in Current and 1939 Prices, 1913–76[a]

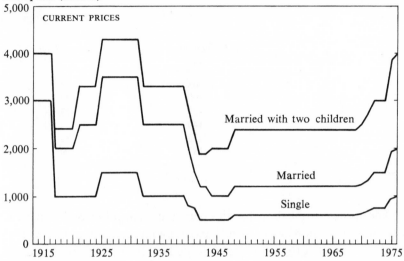

Exemption (dollars)

CURRENT PRICES

Married with two children

Married

Single

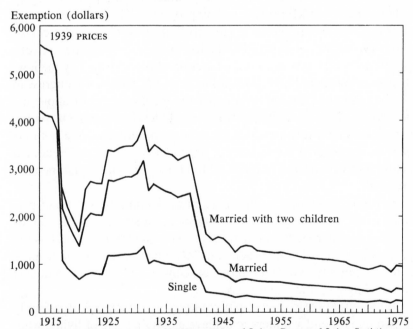

Exemption (dollars)

1939 PRICES

Married with two children

Married

Single

Sources: Appendix table A-1 and U.S. Department of Labor, Bureau of Labor Statistics, consumer price index, all items, series A.

a. For 1944–45 exemptions shown are for surtax purposes only. For 1975 and 1976 figures include the income equivalent of the per capita tax credit.

Table 4-3. Indexes of the Minimum Taxable Level under the Federal Individual Income Tax and Estimated Poverty-Level Budgets for Families of Various Sizes, 1976

Two-person family = 100

	Index	
Size of family	Minimum taxable level	Poverty-level budget
1	66	78
2	100	100
3	124	123
4	149	157
5	173	185
6	197	209

Source: Table 4-4.

The basic justification for the personal exemption is that people with very low incomes have no taxpaying capacity. Taxation below minimum levels of subsistence reduces health and efficiency and results in lower economic vitality, less production, and possibly higher public expenditures for social welfare programs. The personal exemptions contribute to progression (mainly in the lower income brackets) and serve as an administrative device to remove from the tax rolls people with very low incomes, a function also performed by the low-income allowance. Since 1969 it has been the policy of Congress to set the minimum taxable level under the income tax at or above the poverty level as officially defined by the federal government. At the higher income levels, personal exemptions differentiate the tax burdens on the basis of the number of dependents, but the differences in tax for individuals and families of different sizes with equal incomes are small.

Two questions must be discussed in evaluating the system of personal exemptions. First, are the allowances for single persons and for families of different sizes fair relative to one another? Second, is the general level of exemptions adequate? Recent calculations of the incidence of poverty, which are based on concepts of income adequacy, can shed light on these questions.

RELATIVE EXEMPTIONS FOR DIFFERENT FAMILY SIZES. If a family of two must spend x dollars to achieve a certain scale of living, what proportion of x would a single person spend, and how much more than x would families of three, four, five, or more people spend to

Table 4-4. Minimum Taxable Level under the Federal Individual Income Tax and
Estimated Poverty-Level Budgets for Families of Various Sizes, 1976
Dollars

Size of family	Exemptions	Low-income allowance	Tax credit	Minimum taxable level[a]	Poverty-level budget[b]	Difference
1	750	1,700	250	2,700	2,888	−188
2	1,500	2,100	500	4,100	3,717	383
3	2,250	2,100	750	5,100	4,556	544
4	3,000	2,100	1,000	6,100	5,831	269
5	3,750	2,100	1,233	7,083	6,887	196
6	4,500	2,100	1,467	8,067	7,754	313

Sources: Minimum taxable levels are based on exemptions, tax credits, and low-income allowance enacted under the Revenue Adjustment Act of 1975; poverty levels are 1974 data (Bureau of the Census, *Current Population Reports*, P-60 Series, no. 102) projected to 1976 on the basis of the estimated increase in the consumer price index.
 a. Sum of the first three columns.
 b. Poverty-level budgets for 1974 were adjusted for an increase in the consumer price index of 9.2 percent in 1975 and an estimated 6 percent in 1976.

maintain an equivalent standard? Clearly, the answer depends on the criteria used for measuring equivalence. The standard criteria used by the federal government, which are included in the official poverty-line estimates published annually by the Social Security Administration, are based on the amount of income needed to maintain an adequate diet.

As shown in table 4-3, the financial needs of a household do not increase in proportion to the number of people in the household. The relative incomes that would provide roughly equivalent standards of living appear to be in the ratio of 80:100:25 for single, married, and dependent persons, respectively. Income tax exemptions plus the low-income allowance and the per capita tax credit give a ratio of 65: 100:25 for 1976. Although the per capita exemption and credit have been too liberal for dependents and too small for single persons, the addition of the low-income allowance adjusts the ratio approximately to the relative needs of families of different sizes except for single persons who maintain a separate household.

LEVEL OF EXEMPTIONS. The adequacy of the *level* of exemptions may be judged by comparing the incomes needed by families of different sizes with the minimum taxable level (see table 4-4). The minimum taxable levels equal the statutory per capita exemptions plus the income equivalent of the tax credit plus the low-income allowance for 1976. These three elements raised the minimum taxable levels above the poverty lines for all family sizes except single persons in 1976.

It is clear from table 4-4 that the low-income allowance plays a useful role in correcting part of the inadequacy of the per capita exemption. The purpose of the low-income allowance is to augment the regular exemptions at the bottom of the income scale without incurring the heavy cost of raising the exemptions for all taxpayers. On the other hand, the tax credit is virtually equivalent to an increase in the per capita exemption at the minimum taxable level.

TAX CREDITS IN LIEU OF EXEMPTIONS. Before 1975 allowances for taxpayers and dependents were always given in the form of exemptions under the federal income tax. An alternative method, now used in several states, is to convert the allowance to a credit computed by multiplying the value of the exemption by the first-bracket tax rate or some higher rate. With the present 14 percent first-bracket rate, the $750 exemption would be converted to a credit of $105; at a 20 percent rate, the credit would amount to $150; and so on. The credit limits the tax value of the exemption to the same dollar amount for all taxpayers. It would increase the tax liabilities for those with taxable incomes above the bracket chosen to calculate the value of the credit and reduce them for those with taxable incomes below that level. The credit would also narrow the tax differences between families of different sizes above the break-even points and expand them below these points.

In 1975 Congress departed from past practice and provided a relatively small per capita credit ($30) instead of increasing the personal exemptions. In 1976 the per capita credit was increased to $35, but taxpayers were given the option of taking a credit of 2 percent of taxable income (up to $180) if it was higher than $35 for each member of their families. The adoption of a small credit was a compromise between those who wanted to replace the entire exemption with a credit and those who preferred to increase the exemption. The optional credit based on taxable income was intended to extend relatively more tax relief into the middle income class than the flat dollar per capita credit provided.

Carried to the extreme, the logic of the tax credit would lead to an exemption that vanished at some point on the income scale. A vanishing exemption is often supported on the ground that exemptions are not justified for persons with very large incomes, since expenditures for children are not a hardship at these levels. However, few people have seriously recommended a vanishing exemption for the United States.

Complete replacement of the exemption by a credit would be generous for large families in the lowest income classes and would reduce the tax differences by size of family in the higher classes. To avoid this effect, it has been proposed that a tax credit be allowed as an alternative to the exemption rather than as a substitute for it. Low-income taxpayers would use the credit, and those in the higher classes would continue to use the exemptions. But an optional credit would complicate the tax return and be confusing to many taxpayers. More-over, roughly the same effect among income classes could be obtained without narrowing family size tax differences by retaining the exemp-tion and adjusting the tax rates in the higher income classes. But proponents of the credit are not persuaded that the rate adjustments would actually be made.

COST OF EXEMPTION INCREASES. Continued adjustment of the minimum taxable levels to avoid taxing people whose incomes are below the poverty line will be necessary so long as prices continue to increase at high rates. Three alternatives involving changes in the exemption, a supplementary per capita credit, and an optional tax credit are shown in table 4-5. All three alternatives concentrate most of the relief at the lower end of the income scale, but the optional credit is most favorable to the lowest income classes.

The Negative Income Tax

Raising the exemptions or lowering the first-bracket tax rates would do little to alleviate the economic hardship of low-income families. In the first place, when poor families pay any income tax at all, the amount is small; even full relief from income taxation would not help much. Second, families with incomes below the present minimum taxable levels cannot be helped at all by income tax reduc-tion that is confined to those who are taxable.

The traditional method of helping poverty-stricken families has been through public welfare and other direct transfer payments (for example, old age assistance, aid to families with dependent children, medical assistance for the aged, aid to the blind and to disabled persons, and general relief). Most of these programs reach specific

Federal Tax Policy

Table 4-5. Revenue and Distributional Effects of Various Individual Income Tax Exemption and Tax Credit Plans, by Adjusted Gross Income Class, 1976
Income classes in thousands of dollars

Revenue change and adjusted gross income class	$1,050 per capita exemption[a,b]	Raise per capita tax credit from $35 to $70[a,c]	$900 per capita exemption or $240 optional per capita tax credit[a]
Revenue change (billions of dollars)	−3.1	−2.9	−2.9
	Percentage distribution of revenue change		
0–3	0.2	0.6	0.8
3–5	2.9	6.8	12.9
5–10	6.9	20.4	39.7
10–15	10.3	24.5	39.4
15–20	16.9	19.9	9.8
20–25	17.4	12.7	−5.7
25–50	31.0	12.5	−0.9
50–100	11.1	2.1	3.1
100–200	2.7	0.4	0.9
200–500	0.5	...	0.2
500–1,000	0.1	...	...
1,000 and over	...	...	...
All classes	100.0	100.0	100.0
	Percentage change in tax liabilities		
0–3	d	d	d
3–5	−19.5	−43.4	−80.4
5–10	−2.2	−6.2	−11.8
10–15	−1.6	−3.8	−5.9
15–20	−2.2	−2.5	−1.2
20–25	−2.9	−2.1	0.9
25–50	−3.1	−1.2	0.1
50–100	−2.2	−0.4	−0.6
100–200	−1.1	−0.2	−0.3
200–500	−0.4	...	−0.1
500–1,000	−0.2	...	−0.1
1,000 and over	...	...	...
All classes	−2.4	−2.3	−2.2

Source: Brookings 1972 tax file projected to 1976. Figures are rounded.
a. All three plans assume a low-income allowance of $1,700 for single persons and $2,100 for married couples.
b. Assumes elimination of the per capita credit of $35 and the optional credit of 2 percent of taxable income up to a maximum of $180.
c. Assumes elimination of the optional credit of 2 percent of taxable income up to a maximum of $180.
d. Percentages cannot be calculated because present tax liability is negative (as a result of the earned income credit).

categories of the poor; except for general relief, which is inadequate almost everywhere, they provide no assistance to families headed by ablebodied workers who, for reasons of background, training, or temperament, do not participate effectively in the modern industrial economy.

Considerable thought has been given in recent years to the relation between the welfare system and the income tax system. The two developed side by side in response to different pressures, but it is recognized increasingly that one may be regarded as an extension of the other. Direct assistance to low-income people is an extension of progression into the lowest brackets, with negative rather than positive rates. Once this relation is understood, the next natural step is to consider the adoption of a negative income tax.

A negative income tax would provide assistance to families on the basis of how far their income fell below certain minimum standards, without inquiring into the reason for the deficiency. The various welfare programs conducted by government and private nonprofit agencies do not reach all of the poor. The negative income tax is regarded by many as a way to supplement these welfare programs rather than replace them. However, a comprehensive negative income tax could be used to replace the entire categorical welfare system.

BASIC FEATURES. The negative income tax would involve the same computations of taxable income as does the positive income tax. A man, for instance, would add up all his income and subtract his exemptions and deductions. If the result were negative, he would be entitled to a payment *from* the government. The amount of the payment would be computed by applying a new set of tax rates to the negative taxable income. The rates might begin with the first-bracket rate of 14 percent and increase as the amount of negative taxable income increased. But there is not necessarily any relation between the first-bracket rates of the positive and negative parts of the income tax. The rates on negative incomes could begin with, say, 30 percent and go as high as 70, 80, or even 100 percent. However, most negative income tax plans include only one tax rate.

A negative income tax with only one rate would involve a fixed relation among three variables—the basic allowance (A), the break-even level (B), and the tax rate (t) on the family's income—and it would be impossible to change one variable without affecting at least one of the other two. The relation is that the basic allowance is the

Table 4-6. Illustrative Basic Allowances, Tax Rates, and Break-even Levels
under a Negative Income Tax Plan

Basic allowance (A) (dollars)	Tax rate (t) (percent)	Break-even level (B) (dollars)
1,500	33⅓	4,500
2,000	66⅔	3,000
2,000	50	4,000
2,500	50	5,000
3,000	75	4,000
4,000	50	8,000
4,000	66⅔	6,000
5,000	100	5,000

product of the tax rate and the break-even level (or $A = tB$). Thus if
the break-even level is $4,000 and the tax rate is 50 percent, the basic
allowance is $2,000. Conversely, to have a basic allowance of $3,000
and keep the break-even level at $4,000, the tax rate must be 75 per-
cent. Examples of consistent As, Bs, and ts are shown in table 4-6;
there are, of course, many other possibilities.

Because of these relationships, the negative income tax can be
thought of in two ways. It can be regarded as providing a basic allowance to all persons, together with a special tax rate on the incomes of
those who accept the allowance. Or it can be regarded as a payment
that reduces the gap between income and the break-even level by the
same tax rate. The equivalence between these two approaches may be
illustrated with the first combination of A, t, and B in table 4-6. According to the first approach, a family with an income of $2,400
would receive a basic allowance of $1,500 and would pay a tax of
$800 on its income, which would leave it with a disposable income of
$3,100. According to the second, the family would receive a payment
of $700—33⅓ percent of the difference between the $4,500 break-
even level and its income of $2,400—leaving it with the same dis-
posable income of $3,100.

The last entry in table 4-6 shows a basic allowance equal to the
break-even level. This occurs whenever the income recipient must
give up one dollar of the allowance for every dollar of income received: in other words, when the tax rate is 100 percent. The welfare
system in the United States had this feature until the social security
amendments of 1967 required the states to permit recipients to keep

some part of whatever they might earn (this became fully operative in mid-1969).

It might also be noted that there is essentially no difference between a negative income tax and a guaranteed minimum income plan. Under the negative income tax, individuals would receive the basic allowance if they had no other income, and in this sense the basic allowance is a guaranteed minimum. Some guaranteed minimum income plans would impose a tax rate of 100 percent on any income a family might receive, but this is not an essential feature of such plans.

RELATION TO THE POSITIVE INCOME TAX. So long as the break-even levels are no higher than the levels at which the positive income tax begins to apply, the negative income tax can be operated quite independently. However, if the negative income tax is to provide more than a pittance as a basic allowance, the break-even levels may be higher than the levels at which the positive tax takes effect. For example, with a basic allowance of $4,000 and a tax rate of 50 percent, the break-even level would be $8,000 (see table 4-6). The minimum taxable level for a family of four in 1977 amounts to $6,100. Thus the two systems would overlap in the range between $6,100 and $8,000.

The solution to this problem would be to give the family the option of choosing the system under which its disposable income was higher. In the above example, it is obvious that all families with incomes of $6,100 or less would choose the negative income tax. Some families with incomes above $8,000 would also choose the negative income tax, because the switch from the negative to the positive income tax at precisely $8,000 would raise the tax rate on an additional dollar of income above 100 percent. At $8,000, the positive tax for a family of four (at 1977 rates and exemptions) would be $294, leaving the family with a disposable income of $7,706 instead of the $8,000 it would have had without the additional dollar of income. Paradoxically, the option of paying the higher negative income tax rate would give a family of four a higher disposable income until its income exceeded $8,888 in this example (see figure 4-4). The exact location of this "tax break-even" point need not concern the individual taxpayer because the final tax return would provide a reconciliation between the positive and negative income taxes. To operate the system

Figure 4-4. Illustration of a Negative Income Tax Plan for a Four-Person Family with a $4,000 Basic Allowance and a 50 Percent Tax Rate

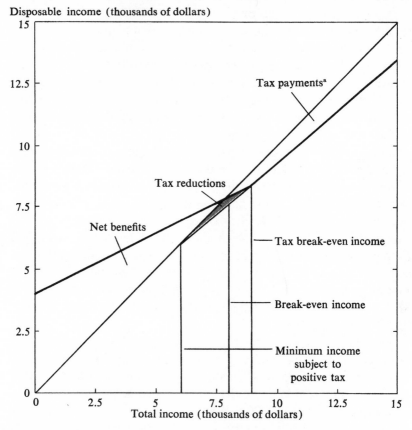

Disposable income (thousands of dollars)

a. Tax is based on rates, exemptions, low-income allowance, and credits applicable to 1977.

efficiently, consistent definitions of income and filing unit under the two taxes would be necessary.

THE FAMILY ASSISTANCE PLAN. In 1969 the Nixon administration proposed a family assistance plan to guarantee a small annual income to poor families with children. The plan—a limited negative income tax—provided for an allowance of $500 for the first two members of the family and $300 for each additional member. Benefits were reduced by fifty cents for each dollar earned after the first $720. To be eligible for the plan, nonworking members of the family, except for mothers with children under six years of age, would have been required to register for training or employment at a public employment office. Single persons and married couples without children were not eligible. The plan was seriously debated for several years, but was not approved by Congress.

The negative income tax is a novel idea for welfare and tax experts, as well as for the American public. With the proliferation of overlapping programs for the poor, it is again being given serious consideration.

Personal Deductions

Personal deductions itemized on taxable returns in 1976 amounted to an estimated $130 billion. Of this total, about $69 billion would have been deductible through the standard deduction in any event. The tax savings from the additional $61 billion of itemized deductions amounted to over $20 billion.

The relative importance of the itemized deductions at different income levels is shown in figure 4-5. Because taxpayers had the alternative of taking the low-income allowance or the standard deduction, it is not surprising to find that, at low income levels, those who itemize their deductions subtract much more than these minima provide. Deductions account for a decreasing percentage of income as incomes rise to $100,000, but increase in the highest brackets. In 1974 they averaged about 21 percent of adjusted gross income on taxable returns with itemized deductions. They were even more important for nontaxable returns, where they accounted for three-quarters of adjusted gross income.

The largest deductions at most income levels are interest and taxes, but medical deductions—which are subject to a 3 percent floor except for one-half of health insurance premiums up to $150—are heaviest in the lowest income classes. Interest is particularly important for those with incomes below $15,000 because of the high incidence of mortgage-financed homeownership.

In 1974 the standard and itemized deductions combined amounted to 58.5 percent of adjusted gross income on all tax returns below $5,000, declined to 17.2 percent of income between $30,000 and $50,000, and rose to 19.6 percent above $100,000. The high percentage in the lower income classes reflects the importance of the minimum standard deduction (i.e., the low-income allowance),

Figure 4-5. Itemized Deductions as a Percentage of Adjusted Gross Income, Taxable and Nontaxable Federal Individual Returns, 1974

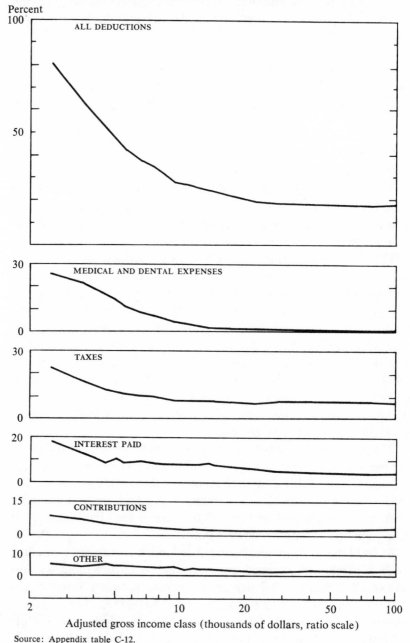

Percent

Adjusted gross income class (thousands of dollars, ratio scale)

Source: Appendix table C-12.

which greatly exceeds itemized deductions in these classes. The rise at the top is due to an increase in the ratio of contributions to income, reflecting the importance of philanthropy among the wealthy and the incentive for giving provided by the tax deduction.

There is no recorded explanation of the justification for many of the personal deductions. Most of them have been allowed since the beginning of the income tax. Given the definition of income stated earlier, deductions would be allowed only for expenditures that were essential to earn income. An exception might be made for unusual personal expenditures that create hardships when incomes are low; but to avoid subsidizing personal consumption, the personal expense deductions should be kept to a minimum. The current tax law departs from these criteria to a substantial degree.

PURPOSES OF THE PERSONAL DEDUCTIONS. There are four major groups of itemized deductions under present law. The first is for large, unusual, and necessary personal expenditures. Deductions for extraordinary medical expenses are the best examples of this group. Such expenses are often involuntary and unpredictable and may exhaust a large proportion of the taxpayer's total income in a particular year. When a serious illness strikes a member of a family, its ability to pay taxes is clearly lower than that of another family with the same income whose members are healthy. For these reasons, taxpayers are permitted to deduct medical expenses in excess of 3 percent of their income. Since 1967 one-half of premiums paid for private health insurance have been deductible separately from other medical expenses, up to a maximum of $150. Other deductions for large, involuntary, and unpredictable costs are those for uninsured losses resulting from thefts, fires, storms, or other casualties. Since 1964 these deductions have been limited to the amount of loss from each casualty that exceeds $100.

The second group of deductions in effect subsidizes particular groups of taxpayers. For instance, deductions for taxes paid on owner-occupied residences and for interest on home mortgages help the homeowner. Since the rental value of an owner-occupied house is not included in the owner's income, the deduction of expenses—including interest and taxes—connected with the home is not warranted. In addition to the direct benefit from the deductions and the exclusion from taxable income of the rental value of their homes, homeowners also benefit indirectly from itemizing deductions. Tenants with low and middle incomes rarely accumulate deductions aggregating more than the standard deduction. The result is that homeowners are the primary beneficiaries of the remaining deductions. Moreover, when a new deduction is introduced, homeowners who already itemize ordinarily receive the full benefit. Other taxpayers must sacrifice the standard deduction before receiving any value from the new deduction.

Another deduction of the subsidy type is for contributions to religious, educational, and other nonprofit organizations, which may be deducted as long as they do not exceed 50 percent of a taxpayer's adjusted gross income (20 percent for foundations and other organizations not considered "public" charities). A few question whether private philanthropy should be encouraged at the expense of the federal treasury, since in effect it permits individuals to divert tax funds to certain kinds of organizations. But most people believe the activities of these organizations are in general socially desirable.

The deduction for interest is justifiable when the interest is paid on a loan used to produce taxable income. The interest payment is in effect a negative income, which should be offset against the positive income produced by the asset purchased with the loan proceeds. Alternatively, an individual may prefer to borrow money and pay interest rather than sell an asset; in such cases, the interest deduction is also required to measure the individual's true net property income. A substantial proportion of the interest deducted on tax returns, however, is for loans on homes and consumer durables or for other purposes that do not produce income. In addition, people with high incomes often deduct interest on debt incurred to carry investment assets that produce no current income, causing a mismatching of income and expenses. (See the section on tax shelters below.)

The most recent addition to the list of itemized deductions is the deduction for political contributions, which became effective in 1972. Individuals are permitted to deduct up to $100 ($200 on joint returns) for contributions to candidates for political office and political parties. As an alternative, they may deduct one-half of the contribution up to $25 ($50 on joint returns) as a credit against their tax. In 1973 political contributions amounting to $75 million were reported on 1.8 million tax returns. In addition, as of June 30, 1976, a total of $95 million was placed in a special fund by individuals who exercised the option, also introduced in 1972, to set aside $1 ($2 on joint returns) of their annual tax liabilities for financing presidential campaigns.

The third group of deductions is for income, property, gasoline, and sales taxes paid to state and local governments. A deduction for income taxes reduces the combined impact of federal, state, and local income taxes; it is also an effective way of moderating interstate tax differences in the higher income brackets. For example, if an income were subject to the highest state rate of 19.8 percent and also to the 70 percent rate for federal tax, the combined marginal rate would be 89.8 percent. By allowing taxpayers to deduct the state tax on their federal returns, the maximum combined rate is reduced to 75.9 percent. If the state also permits a deduction for federal taxes, the maximum combined rate is 72.1 percent. (Deductibility is discussed more fully in chapter 9.)

At one time, federal excises and all the minor state and local taxes were allowed as deductions, but these were gradually eliminated. The deductions for general sales and property taxes survived because it was felt that some federal relief for these taxes was needed to encourage state and local governments to raise needed revenue without coercing them to use a particular source. The deduction for gasoline taxes was retained for the same reasons, but here the rationale is strained.

The fourth group contains the only theoretically necessary deductions, namely, those that make allowances for the expenses of earning income. These deductions are required to correct the deficiencies of the adjusted gross income concept. To avoid complicating the tax return, expenses incurred in earning nonbusiness income (that is, wages and salaries, interest, and dividends) are generally not allowed as deductions in arriving at adjusted gross income, but taxpayers are permitted to deduct some of these expenses in arriving at taxable income. Examples of these deductions are fees for investment counselors, rentals of safe deposit boxes used to store income-producing securities, custodian fees, work clothing, and union dues. Moving expenses and nonreimbursed travel expenses of employees are deductible in arriving at adjusted gross income, as are alimony payments, which are taxable to the recipient.

In lieu of a deduction for child care, the 1976 act allows employed single persons and married couples (with both husband and wife employed) a 20 percent nonrefundable tax credit on expenditures of up to $2,000 made for the care of a dependent while they are at work and up to $4,000 for two or more dependents. The credit is also available when one parent works full time and the other is a part-time worker or a full-time student, and to a divorced or separated parent with custody of the children. Congress justified this deduction on the ground that child care expenditures must be incurred by many taxpayers to earn a livelihood and are comparable to ordinary business expenses.

A major problem with using deductions to distinguish the taxpaying ability of different families and individuals is that the tax benefit depends on the tax rate. A person who would not be taxable even without the deduction receives no benefit; a 25 percent taxpayer receives a 25 percent benefit; and so on. Thus the deductions should be pruned to the minimum necessary for an effective and equitable income tax. Opponents of the deductions argue that, if they are not pruned, they should be converted to tax credits so that the tax benefit would be the same in all income classes. At the very least, a distinction should be made between deductions that help to refine income as a measure of ability to pay—such as unusual medical expenses and casualty losses—and those that provide an incentive for particular activities—such as charitable contributions.

POSSIBLE REVISIONS OF THE PERSONAL DEDUCTIONS. Revision of the personal deductions might begin with those that subsidize personal expenditures, which account for the major share of itemized deductions on taxable returns (appendix table C-12). The deductions that receive the most attention are those for charitable contributions, interest on personal loans, and state and local taxes other than income and sales taxes.

Proponents of the deduction for charitable contributions have persuaded Congress that the organizations benefiting from the deduction have such overwhelming social priority under present institutional arrangements that they warrant the use of tax incentives. Recent econometric analyses suggest that the tax deduction encourages charitable giving at all income levels, although the response in the lower income classes is uncertain. If an income tax deduction is considered necessary to encourage contributions, it might be better to allow the deduction only when the contribution is larger than some average amount. For example, the deduction might be allowed for the amount of contributions in excess of, say, 2 or 3 percent of adjusted gross income, with the total deduction limited to the present 50 percent of adjusted gross income. This revision was recommended by the outgoing Treasury in 1969, but was not accepted by Congress because of the strong opposition of tax-exempt organizations. On the other hand, various methods of increasing the deduction have been recommended in order to increase contributions to charitable organizations.

As for the 3 percent floor for the medical deduction, surveys indicate that 3 percent of income is about the median expenditure of families with incomes below $10,000. The median, however, is only an arbitrary dividing line between "usual" and "extraordinary." The lower limit could be restored to 5 percent for all taxpayers without violating its basic rationale. This would permit medical deductions by about 30 percent of all family units. The separate deduction for health insurance premiums, which was enacted to broaden coverage, is clearly not a substitute for national health insurance and will doubtless be eliminated when a comprehensive national plan is adopted.

The interest deduction presents a special difficulty because interest is paid on both business and personal debts, and it is difficult to distinguish between the two. Clearly, the deduction should be allowed for interest on a loan made to the owner of a grocery store to carry inventory, while interest on a loan to purchase a consumer durable hardly merits a deduction. The inventory loan produces taxable income, while the consumer durable goods loan generates income in the form of services that do not enter into the tax base. But it is often difficult to identify the purpose of loans because owners of unincorporated enterprises take out personal loans to finance their business activities, and vice versa.

The best way to handle this problem would be to permit deductions (with carry-over privileges) for interest paid up to the amount of property and business income reported by the taxpayers, on the ground that interest paid must be subtracted to obtain *net* income from these sources. This test would make nondeductible about three-fourths of the interest now deducted.

The 1969 act adopted a variant of this approach by allowing a taxpayer to deduct interest paid to purchase investment assets up to $25,000, plus his or her net investment income (dividends, interest, long-term capital gains, and so forth), plus one-half the amount of such interest in excess of net investment income. In 1976 the limit on deductible investment interest was reduced to $10,000 plus the tax-payer's net investment income other than capital gains. Any interest disallowed in one year may be carried over to offset investment income in subsequent years. Even after the 1976 change, the provision accounts for only a small fraction of the $5 billion revenue loss from all interest deductions in excess of property income.

Among the deductible taxes, gasoline taxes are least justified as a deduction. In effect the federal deduction places part of the burden of user charges levied for automobile use on the general taxpayer. This is unfair to those who do not itemize their deductions, to non-users of automobiles, and to people who are not taxable. Furthermore, the deduction reduces the cost of driving an automobile at a time when there is urgent need for energy conservation.

The omission of the rental value of owner-occupied houses from the tax base discriminates against renters; to redress the balance, the deductions for property taxes and interest payments on house mortgages (to the extent they exceed property income reported) might be eliminated. This would leave deductions for state and local income and sales taxes, which are justified as encouraging the use of general taxes for state and local purposes.

It may be concluded that the itemized deductions allowed are too generous and that substantial increases in revenues might be gained by trimming them to the most essential items. But this is not all. If the itemized deductions were curtailed, the standard deduction could also be reduced. To an important degree, the standard deduction violates the rationale of the itemized deductions since it tends to reduce differentiation in tax liabilities. The existence of both standard and itemized deductions suggests that there is some ambivalence toward many of the personal deductions.

Interest has recently been expressed in alternative approaches that would not involve direct repeal or modification of the questionable deductions. One possibility would be to eliminate the standard deduction and convert it to a floor for itemized deductions. Taxpayers might be permitted to deduct only the amount of their itemized deductions exceeding, say, 16 percent of their adjusted gross income. The attractive feature of this approach is that, without increasing the overall burden of the income tax, it would greatly increase the yield of the tax at present rates and thus permit substantial reductions in

Table 4-7. Increases in Revenue under Various Sets of Revisions of Personal Deductions under the Federal Individual Income Tax, 1976

Billions of dollars

Revision	Set A	Set B	Set C
Eliminate deduction for state gasoline taxes	0.8	0.8	0.8
Eliminate separate deduction for health insurance premiums	0.3	0.3	0.3
Raise floor on medical expense deduction from 3 to 5 percent	...	0.8	0.8
Introduce 2 percent floor in the charitable contribution deduction	...	2.5	2.5
Eliminate deduction for property taxes	...	...	4.5
Limit interest deduction to the amount of business and property income	...	...	5.1
Convert standard deduction and low-income allowance to a flat $2,000[a]	...	2.4	3.0
Total	1.1	6.6[b]	14.5[b]

Source: Brookings 1972 tax file, projected to 1976.
a. Assumes revisions in itemized deductions as indicated above.
b. Total is less than the sum of the individual revisions because the standard deduction would exceed the sum of the remaining deductions for many of those now itemizing deductions.

these rates. A variant of this proposal was recommended by the Treasury in 1963, but it was virtually disregarded by the congressional tax-writing committees.

Another approach would be to increase the standard deduction so that fewer people would choose to itemize personal deductions. Proposals call for increasing the rate of the standard deduction and raising the ceiling, or converting the standard deduction to a flat amount. President Ford recommended a standard deduction of $2,500 for married couples and $1,800 for single persons. (The lower limit for single persons is to avoid both a "tax penalty" on marriage and excessive generosity to single persons who do not maintain separate households.) The main objection to raising the standard deduction is that it corrects one inequity by further reducing the tax base. Nevertheless, since 1969, whenever Congress has been in a tax-cutting mood, it has raised the standard deduction and accepted the resulting revenue loss.

Estimates of the revenue gains of three combinations of revisions of the personal deductions are given in table 4-7. These gains, which range from $1 billion to $14.5 billion a year, would come mainly from the middle and higher income classes. On balance, equity would be better served by pruning the itemized deductions in these or other ways and using the revenues to reduce tax rates. But although it recognizes the inequity of the present system, Congress hesitates to remedy the situation directly for fear of alienating the large groups of taxpayers who benefit from the deductions. The only progress in recent years was made in 1964, when deductions for numerous state-local taxes and casualty losses of less than $100 were eliminated.

The Family

During most of the history of the income tax, differentiation for family responsibilities was made among taxpayers through the personal exemptions. More recently, there has been a trend toward differing tax rates to provide additional differentiation, particularly in the middle and higher tax brackets. In the United States and West Germany this has been accomplished by adopting the principle of "income splitting" between husband and wife. In France, income splitting among all family members is permitted. Other countries achieve a similar objective by providing separate rate schedules for families of different size.

The adoption of income splitting in the United States arose out of the historical accident that eight states had community property laws, which treated income as if divided equally between husband and wife. By virtue of several Supreme Court decisions, married couples residing in these eight states had been splitting their incomes and filing separate federal returns. Shortly after World War II, a number of other states enacted community property laws for the express purpose of obtaining the same advantage for their residents, and other states threatened to follow suit. In an effort to restore geographic tax equality and to prevent wholesale disruption of local property laws and procedures, Congress universalized income splitting in 1948.

The effect of income splitting is to reduce progression for married couples. The tax rates nominally begin at 14, 15, 16, and 17 percent on the first four $500 segments of taxable income and rise to 70 percent on the portion of taxable income above $100,000. A married couple with taxable income of $2,000 splits this income and applies the first two rates to each half; without income splitting, the first four rates would apply to the income. Thus, whereas the nominal rate brackets cover taxable incomes up to $100,000, the actual rates for

Figure 4-6. Federal Tax Saving for Married Couples Filing Joint Returns, Heads of Households, and Single Persons, as a Percentage of the Basic Rate Schedule[a] Tax, by Taxable Income, 1977 Rates

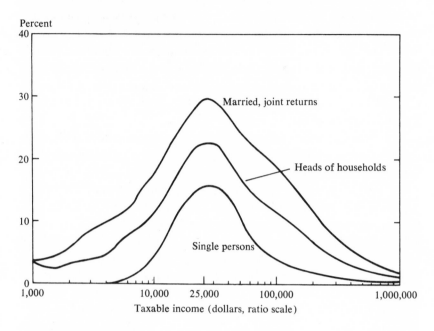

Percent

Taxable income (dollars, ratio scale)

Source: Appendix table C-10.
a. Married, separate returns.

married couples extend to $200,000 (table 4-2). The tax advantage rises from $5 for married couples with taxable income of $1,000 to $14,510 for couples with taxable income of $200,000 or more. In percentage terms, the tax advantage reaches a maximum of almost 30 percent at the $28,000 level (figure 4-6 and appendix table C-10).

The classic argument in favor of income splitting is that husbands and wives usually share their combined income equally. The largest portion of the family budget goes for consumption, and savings are ordinarily set aside for the children or for the enjoyment of all members of the family. Two conclusions follow from this view. First, married couples with the same combined income should pay the same tax irrespective of the legal division of income between them; second, the tax liabilities of married couples should be computed as if they were two single persons with their total income divided equally between them. The first conclusion is now firmly rooted in our tax law and seems to be almost universally accepted. It is the second conclusion on which opinions still differ.

The case for the sharing argument is most applicable to taxpayers in the lower income classes, where incomes are used almost entirely for the consumption of the family unit. At the top of the income scale, the major rationale of income taxation is to reduce the economic power of the family unit, and the use made of income at these levels for family purposes is irrelevant for this purpose. Obviously, these objectives cannot be reconciled if income splitting is extended to all income brackets.

The practical effect of income splitting is to produce large differences in the tax burdens of single persons and married couples, differences that depend on the *rate of graduation* and not on the level of rates. Such differences are difficult to rationalize on any theoretical grounds. It is also difficult to justify treating single persons with families more harshly than married persons in similar circumstances. As a remedy, widows and widowers are permitted to continue to split their incomes for two years after the death of the spouse, and half the advantage of joint returns is given (through a separate rate schedule) to single persons who maintain a household for children or other dependents or who maintain a separate household for their parents. This, of course, is a makeshift arrangement that does not deal with the problem satisfactorily. For example, a single taxpayer who supports an aunt in a different household receives no income-splitting benefit; if he supports an aged mother, he receives these benefits. Pressures on Congress to treat single persons more liberally—by broadening the head-of-household provision, increasing their exemptions, and other devices—resulted in the adoption of a new rate schedule for single persons under the 1969 act. In this schedule, the single persons' tax never exceeds by more than 20 percent the tax for married couples filing joint returns. In keeping with prior practice, the rate schedule for heads of households is halfway between the single-person and joint-return rate schedules. The result has been the introduction of the so-called tax penalty on marriage: two persons with roughly equal earnings pay more tax after marriage than the total tax they paid before marriage; under the pure version of income splitting, they pay the same tax before and after marriage. There is a marriage penalty even if the earnings are not equal.

One of the major reasons for acceptance of the consequences of income splitting may well be that personal exemptions do not provide enough differentiation among taxpayers in the middle and top brackets. Single persons, it is felt, should be taxed more heavily than married couples because they do not bear the costs and responsibilities of raising children. But income splitting for husband and wife clearly does not differentiate among taxpayers in this respect since the benefit is the same whether or not there are children.

One problem with the income-splitting approach is that differentiation among families by size is made through the rate structure rather than through personal exemptions. It would be possible to differentiate among taxpayer units by varying the personal exemptions with the size of income as well as the number of persons in the unit, with both a minimum and a maximum. This procedure could be used to achieve almost any desired degree of differentiation among families while avoiding most of the problems and anomalies produced by income splitting. The tax rates for single persons and married couples could be equalized either by extending the rate advantages of income splitting to single persons or by requiring married couples to use the same tax rate schedule as single people.

Another problem with income splitting is that married couples with one and two earners pay the same tax. The one-earner couple has more ability to pay, because the spouse who stays at home produces income in the form of household services which is not subject to tax. Some portion of the earnings of the two-earner couple is absorbed in providing such household services. Furthermore, the high marginal tax rate on the earnings of the second spouse may discourage some from seeking employment.

Elimination of income splitting would restore all of the problems of the pre-1948 law and would not adjust correctly for the understatement of the taxable income of the one-earner couple. Since the understatement cannot be calculated, an adjustment of the taxable income of the two-earner couple would be necessary. For example, a deduction or tax credit might be allowed on the income of the spouse with the lower earnings. The difference between the two approaches is that the tax value of the deduction would increase as incomes rose, whereas the tax credit would provide the same tax reduction per dollar of earnings in all income classes. The adoption of a deduction or a tax credit would eliminate or greatly moderate the penalty on marriage.

Table 4-8. Revenue Effects of Changes in Income Splitting and Allowances for Two-Earner Married Couples, by Adjusted Gross Income Class, 1976

Income classes in thousands of dollars

Revenue change and adjusted gross income class	Extend rate advantages of income splitting to single persons			Eliminate rate advantages of income splitting for married couples		
	No special deduction for married couples	With special deduction of 25 percent of earnings of spouse with lower earnings[a]	With special tax credit of 10 percent of earnings of spouse with lower earnings[b]	No special deduction for married couples	With special deduction of 25 percent of earnings of spouse with lower earnings[a]	With special tax credit of 10 percent of earnings of spouse with lower earnings[b]
Revenue change (billions of dollars)	−3.4	−8.1	−12.5	32.5	25.5	23.3
Percentage distribution of revenue change						
0–3	*	*	*	*	*	*
3–5	2.0	0.8	0.6	*	*	*
5–10	23.7	10.3	9.7	1.7	1.9	0.5
10–15	27.2	17.0	21.0	8.7	8.7	4.8
15–20	19.2	20.7	26.6	16.8	15.5	11.8
20–25	8.4	19.3	20.0	18.3	15.5	15.9
25–50	11.5	24.3	18.0	36.8	37.4	43.3
50–100	4.9	5.4	2.8	12.9	15.2	17.2
100–200	2.1	1.6	0.8	3.8	4.6	5.2
200–500	0.9	0.5	0.3	0.8	1.0	1.1
500–1,000	0.1	0.1	*	0.1	0.1	0.1
1,000 and over	0.1	*	*	*	*	*
All classes[c]	100.0	100.0	100.0	100.0	100.0	100.0
Percentage change in tax liabilities						
0–3	0.2	0.2	0.2	*	*	*
3–5	−14.9	−14.9	−15.8	1.0	1.0	*
5–10	−8.3	−8.9	−12.6	5.7	5.0	1.3
10–15	−4.8	−7.4	−13.7	14.7	11.4	5.8
15–20	−2.8	−7.5	−14.5	23.6	17.2	12.0
20–25	−1.6	−8.8	−13.7	32.4	21.6	20.2
25–50	−1.3	−6.7	−7.4	39.2	31.3	33.1
50–100	−1.1	−2.9	−2.3	27.0	25.0	25.8
100–200	−0.9	−1.7	−1.4	16.1	15.2	15.6
200–500	−0.9	−1.2	−1.0	7.6	7.2	7.4
500–1,000	−0.5	−0.6	−0.6	3.1	3.0	3.0
1,000 and over	−0.2	−0.2	−0.2	1.0	0.9	0.9
All classes[c]	−2.6	−6.4	−9.6	25.0	19.6	17.9

Source: Brookings 1972 tax file, projected to 1976. Figures are rounded.
* Less than 0.05 percent.
a. Assuming maximum deduction of $2,500.
b. Assuming maximum tax credit of $1,000.
c. Includes negative incomes not shown separately.

The revenue effects of the two types of revisions of the tax rates applying to single persons and married couples and the introduction of a deduction or a tax credit for two-earner couples are illustrated, by income class, in table 4-8. The revenue implications are large, but they can be offset by adjusting the tax rates.

The Aged

Personal exemptions and deductions for extraordinary medical expenses automatically allow for special circumstances of the taxpayer. Beyond this, the federal income tax has been particularly solicitous of the special circumstances of the aged. Taxpayers sixty-five or over have an additional personal exemption, pay no tax on their social security or railroad retirement pensions, and receive a 15 percent tax credit on the first $2,500 of other income (less any social security, railroad retirement, or other exempt pension income) for single persons and a couple only one of whom is over sixty-five and $3,750 for a couple both of whom are over sixty-five. The base for computing the credit is reduced by half of earned income above $7,500 for single persons and $10,000 for couples.

The exemptions for age and blindness, which amounted to over $5 billion on taxable returns in 1976, were justified on the ground that these taxpayers have less ability to pay than do other members of the community. The aged and the blind are in fact concentrated at the lower end of the income distribution. But the personal exemptions, the low-income allowance, and the graduated income tax rates were specifically designed to differentiate among the taxpaying abilities of individuals with different incomes. The aged and the blind might have a claim for an additional exemption if it could be shown that they have to spend more out of a given income than other taxpayers. There are no data on the expenditures of the blind, but the available evidence indicates that a family headed by an individual over sixty-five actually spends less than a family headed by a young person in the same income group. It has also been argued that the aged find it difficult to obtain employment and therefore have less resilience to financial reverses than do other taxpayers. However, many other groups of taxpayers are handicapped in one way or another (for example, by physical or mental disability or lack of opportunity to receive training) or are required to spend more than others for geographical or other reasons, and it would be impractical and undesirable to take account of all these individual differences under an income tax.

The omission of social security and railroad retirement benefits from the tax base dates from the 1930s, when incomes were so low that it did not matter whether these payments were subject to tax or not. As incomes grew and social security was extended to almost the entire population, it became clear that the tax exemption for these benefits is extremely generous. Contributions by employees do not account for more than 10 to 20 percent of their benefits at present and will account for much less than 50 percent even when the systems mature. By contrast, recipients of pensions from other publicly administered retirement programs and from industrial pension plans are fully taxed on the portion of their benefits that exceeds their contributions. This discrimination was deeply resented by the recipients of taxable pensions. As a result, a credit against tax of 20 percent of the first $1,200 of retirement income (other than social security and railroad retirement benefits) was enacted in 1954. The maximum income subject to the credit was raised to $1,524 in 1962 and $2,500 in 1976, and the credit was lowered to 15 percent in 1965, when tax rates in the lower brackets were reduced.

Not only is special relief of this sort questionable, but the additional exemption gives greater tax advantage to aged persons the higher their income. In principle, it would be fairer to remove the exemption for age and make all retirement income taxable (with an allowance, of course, for the portion contributed by the employee, on which tax was paid when earned). The additional revenue could be used to good advantage to raise social security benefits for all the aged. But these suggestions do not seem politically acceptable at this time.

Earned Income

Personal exemptions for the taxpayer and his or her dependents and deductions for business and certain personal expenses are the only adjustments now made under the federal income tax in deriving the taxable income from an individual's total income. One further adjustment was made in the United States in the years 1924–31 and 1934–43, and is still made in the United Kingdom and other countries. This is an allowance for income earned from work rather than from property ownership. The earned income allowance is justified by its supporters on the ground that earned income is not on a par with unearned income. In 1969 the top marginal rate on earned income was limited to 50 percent as a method of increasing the work and management incentives of professional people and corporate executives, and also to make the use of tax shelters less attractive to high earners. In 1975 a refundable earned income tax credit was adopted to reduce the burden of the social security payroll tax for those in the lowest earnings classes. Special deductions for savings set aside for retirement purposes by the self-employed and workers not covered by a pension plan have also been added to the law.

THE EARNED INCOME ALLOWANCE. In the United States the earned income allowance was granted in the form of a deduction that ranged from 10 percent to 25 percent of earned net income. In some years the deduction was allowed for normal tax purposes only; in others it was allowed for both normal tax and surtax. In all years a certain minimum amount of income ($3,000 or $5,000) was presumed to be earned whether it actually was or not, and the deduction was limited to a maximum ranging from $10,000 to $30,000. The tax value of the deduction was always small. It was never worth more than $496 for a family of two (in the period 1928–31); immediately before it was eliminated in 1944 as part of the wartime simplification program, the maximum value was $84. One state—Massachusetts—taxes investment income at a higher rate than earned income.

The equity argument in favor of an earned income allowance is that one person with a given income that is earned has less ability to pay than another who has the same amount of income that is unearned. Several reasons are cited to support this view. First, recipients of earned income do not have the benefit of an allowance for depreciation, and yet their productive capacities often decline as they grow older and are ultimately exhausted. Second, expenses of earning an income are not taken into account fully by the individual income tax deductions. It was only recently (in 1964) that the law permitted a deduction for nonreimbursed moving expenses in connection with a new job. But such outlays as commuting expenses, the additional cost of lunches and other meals away from home, office clothing, and laundry and dry cleaning make the costs of generating earned income higher than the costs of generating the same amount of income from property. Third, earning an income involves psychic costs and the sacrifice of leisure, warranting special income tax relief.

While these arguments appear to have some merit, there are good counterarguments. An earned income allowance is at best only a rough method of correcting for the alleged inequities. To the extent that there are inequities, they should be corrected directly by adjustments either in the structure of the income tax or in other government programs. For example, the depreciation argument is essentially a question involving old age insurance; if retirement benefits are inadequate, the best method of providing more adequate benefits is to increase them. If there are special costs involved in earning income, income tax deductions should be liberalized. Finally, to counter the view that recipients of earned income have greater psychic costs, it can be argued that the accumulation of capital which produces unearned income also involves costs and sacrifices.

On balance, the case for an earned income allowance does not seem overwhelming. Where it has been employed, the allowance has been given to all people with incomes below a certain level and denied to those with incomes above a certain level, whether the income was earned or not. This means that, in practice, there was only a rough differentiation between earned and unearned income. There is also no basis for calculating the earned income element of the incomes of the self-employed (for example, farmers and professional persons); in practice, this separation is based on an arbitrary formula. And a substantial earned income credit could be very expensive. For example, if the rate of tax on all earned incomes were reduced 10 percent below the ordinary rates, the annual cost would be more than $7 billion. Furthermore, an earned income credit is not simple, and it would complicate the tax return form.

MAXIMUM TAX RATE ON EARNED INCOME. The 1969 legislation took a new approach to increasing work incentives by placing a maximum marginal tax rate of 50 percent on earned income beginning in 1972 (60 percent in 1971). Such income includes wages and salaries, professional fees, and self-employment income. (Where capital is a material income-producing factor, not more than 30 percent of the net profit of a business is considered to be earned income.) In 1976 earnings subject to the maximum tax rate were defined to include deferred compensation and pension and annuity income. Taxpayers are required to subtract all preference income from earned income before applying the 50 percent rate.

This provision gives significant tax reductions to business managers, highly paid lawyers, physicians, and other professionals, sole proprietors, and other successful businessmen who operate in the corporate form and pay themselves high salaries. The action was justified on the ground that it would substantially reduce the incentive to seek out tax avoidance schemes and would permit diversion of effort from tax planning to normal business operations. Since most tax preferences apply to unearned income, it is hard to see how a tax reduction on earned income materially affects the search for tax avoidance schemes. No evidence has been produced to show that the provision has had a measurable impact on the work actually performed by those who benefit from it. The 50 percent maximum tax rate will cost an estimated $500 million in fiscal year 1977, all of which will go to people with very high incomes.

DEDUCTION FOR RETIREMENT SAVINGS. The law also permits self-employed persons to deduct savings set aside for their retirement (called the Keogh plan after Congressman Keogh, who introduced the idea) up to 15 percent of earned income or $7,500, whichever is less. A deduction of $750 is allowed, regardless of the maximum limitations, up to the amount of the individual's earned income. This provision was adopted because it was felt that self-employed persons find it difficult to accumulate tax-free savings for purposes of retirement. By contrast, wage earners and salaried employees do not pay tax on the amounts contributed to qualified pension plans in their behalf by employers. The savings deduction for the self-employed was intended as an analogous provision for them, since they cannot participate in such plans.

When originally proposed, the Keogh plan did not have an upper limit on the allowable deduction for these contributions, and it also granted capital gains treatment to withdrawals from the retirement funds in which the savings were invested. As a result, it was regarded as a device to avoid taxes rather than to correct an inequity. These defects were corrected before the legislation was enacted. Although an increasing number of taxpayers have made use of this provision, there is no longer much concern about its abuse. In 1973, 417,500 individuals reported $611 million for this deduction.

Beginning in 1975 persons not covered by a pension plan were allowed to deduct 15 percent of their income up to maximum of $1,500 for amounts invested in an individual retirement account (IRA). In 1976 the limit was raised to $1,750 for married couples with one nonworking spouse ($875 for each). The rationale for this deduction is the same as the rationale for the Keogh plan. The IRAs were devised to encourage those who are not active participants in a retirement plan to set aside their own savings for this purpose. It was felt that the same deferral of tax granted employees under pension plans qualified under the law should be allowed those who work for an employer that has not set up such a plan or who, because of the nature of their employment, cannot be covered. The additional $250 allowance for married couples was enacted in recognition of the household work done by the spouse who stays at home.

THE EARNED INCOME CREDIT. The latest concession to those with earned income was the enactment of a refundable tax credit for earned income received by people with children. The credit is 10 percent of earned income up to $4,000 and is phased down to zero at $8,000. The credit is "refundable" because a payment is made to the person for the amount of the credit that exceeds his or her income tax liability.

The purpose of the earned income credit is to moderate the burden of the social security payroll tax on low-income earners. During the discussions of the negative income tax, it was emphasized that the working poor are required to pay the social security tax even though they are not subject to the individual income tax. The credit against the income tax was devised to avoid disturbing the social security tax arrangements. This is one of the most significant steps taken by the federal government in recent years to relieve the tax burdens of the poor. (See the discussion in chapter 7.) The credit is denied to persons without children to avoid making grants to students, retired people, and other part-time workers who have small amounts of earned income, even though they are also subject to the social security tax.

The combined employee-employer social security tax rate is 11.7 percent (5.85 percent each for the employer and employee) on earnings up to $16,500 in 1977. Thus 85 percent of the total social security tax paid is refunded to those eligible to receive the full credit. The estimated cost of the credit for fiscal year 1977 is $1.4 billion.

Extending the credit at the full 11.7 percent social security tax rate to persons without children would cost approximately an additional $6 billion a year at 1976 earnings levels.

ALLOWANCE FOR WORKING SPOUSES. Wholly apart from the treatment of earned income generally is the difficult question of taxing the incomes of working spouses. A special exemption is given working spouses under the British income tax system. In the United States, except for an allowance of up to $15 against the normal tax in 1944 and 1945, a working spouse credit or deduction has never been granted.

As indicated in the discussion of income splitting, allowances for working spouses are supported partly on incentive grounds and partly on equity grounds. The incentive argument is that, if one spouse already earns income, the other spouse's earnings are taxable beginning at the first dollar. The higher the income of one spouse, the higher is the marginal rate of tax on the additional income of the other spouse. This high rate plus the additional costs of operating the household deter some spouses from seeking employment.

The equity argument is that the ability to pay taxes is not commensurate with the actual earnings of the working spouse. The services that a wife, for instance, performs at home (housework, care of children) may be performed by a domestic servant if she obtains gainful employment; moreover, clothing, laundry bills, and food are usually more expensive if she works, and the family purchases are, in general, less efficient. It is not fair to tax all the additional earnings of the wife since they are partly absorbed in meeting these extra expenses.

A deduction for working wives that would be generous enough to encourage many to enter the labor market would be fairly costly. For example, if a deduction were allowed for 25 percent of the earned income of the spouse with the lower earnings up to a maximum of $2,500, revenues would be reduced by about $6 billion a year. A tax credit of 10 percent of the earnings of the spouse with the lower earnings would cost about $9 billion annually. Most of this benefit would go to married couples with total incomes between $15,000 and $100,000 (see table 4-8).

Indexing for Inflation

With prices rising at unsatisfactorily high rates, increasing attention has been given in recent years to the relation between inflation and the tax system. Inflation affects real tax burdens in two ways. First, it affects the measurement of several types of income for tax purposes, particularly capital gains, business profits, and interest.

Table 4-9. Effect of a 10 Percent Inflation on the Tax Liabilities of a Family of Four, Selected Income Levels, 1977

Amounts in dollars; effective rates in percent

Income before inflation[a]	Tax before inflation		Tax after 10 percent inflation				Effect of not indexing[d]		
			Without indexing[b]		With indexing[c]				
	Amount	Effective rate	Amount	Effective rate	Amount	Effective rate	Percent increase in tax	Percentage-point increase in effective rate	Percent reduction in income after tax
8,000	294.0	3.7	429.0	4.9	323.4	3.7	32.7	1.2	1.2
10,000	651.0	6.5	841.0	7.6	716.1	6.5	17.4	1.1	1.2
12,000	1,031.0	8.6	1,237.6	9.4	1,134.1	8.6	9.1	0.8	0.9
15,000	1,552.0	10.3	1,829.2	11.1	1,707.2	10.3	7.1	0.7	0.8
20,000	2,530.0	12.6	2,950.0	13.4	2,783.0	12.6	6.0	0.8	0.9
25,000	3,640.0	14.6	4,232.0	15.4	4,004.0	14.6	5.7	0.8	1.0
30,000	4,904.0	16.3	5,739.2	17.4	5,394.4	16.3	6.4	1.0	1.2
50,000	11,510.0	23.0	13,496.0	24.5	12,661.0	23.0	6.6	1.5	2.0
100,000	33,740.0	33.7	38,640.0	35.1	37,114.0	33.7	4.1	1.4	2.1
200,000	86,800.0	43.4	98,242.0	44.7	95,480.0	43.4	2.9	1.3	2.2
500,000	262,700.0	52.5	292,100.0	53.1	288,970.0	52.5	1.1	0.6	2.1
1,000,000	556,700.0	55.7	615,500.0	56.0	612,370.0	55.7	0.5	0.3	0.6

a. Assumes all income is fully subject to tax.
b. Assumes tax law applying in 1977. Tax liability computed on the assumption that the family deducts the low-income allowance of $2,100 or 16 percent of income, whichever is greater, and that the maximum tax rate on earned income does not apply.
c. The exemptions, the exemption credit, the low-income allowance, and the rate brackets of the 1977 law are increased by 10 percent. Assumes maximum tax rate on earned income does not apply.
d. Percentages are computed from unrounded data.

These problems will be discussed in the capital gains section below and in chapter 5. Second, the personal exemptions, low-income allowance, tax credits, tax rate boundaries, and other structural features of the income tax are expressed in dollar terms. As prices and incomes rise, if the dollar value of such features remains unchanged, taxpayers' incomes are thrown into higher tax brackets and effective tax rates increase even if there has been no increase in real income.

The effect of inflation is illustrated in the first four columns of table 4-9, which compare the tax liabilities of a family of four at selected income levels before and after a 10 percent inflation. Effective tax rates increase at all income levels as a result of the inflation. In percentage terms, those at the bottom of the income scale fare the worst. However, the increases in effective rates and the percentage changes in income after tax (shown in the last two columns of the table) are much more uniform throughout the income classes. The maximum effect occurs at the lower end of the income scale, where progressivity is determined primarily by the personal exemptions and the low-income allowance, and between $50,000 and $200,000 of income, where rate graduation increases most rapidly.

Several countries with high rates of inflation automatically index their income taxes for inflation. The technique is to raise the value of the personal exemptions, standard deductions, and rate brackets by the rate of inflation once a year on the basis of an overall price index, usually the consumer price index. As the inflation rate has risen in the United States, indexing the income tax in this way has received increasing support. So far Congress has shown no interest in this technique; instead, it has adopted the policy of increasing the personal exemptions and low-income allowance to keep pace with inflation and occasionally reducing tax rates. From 1960 to 1975 the discretionary changes more than compensated for inflation overall, but the distribution of these cuts was not the same as the adjustments that would have been made under an indexed system. The actual tax reductions were larger than the indexed reductions for adjusted gross incomes below $25,000 and above $200,000 and smaller between these levels.

The major argument for indexing is that the increases in effective income tax rates are unintentional by-products of inflation. Total tax receipts rise faster than incomes and the public sector grows more rapidly than it would in a noninflationary situation. Moreover, the increases in the real tax burdens are not selected by Congress but depend on the rate of progression and the rate of inflation.

On the other hand, indexing would reduce the built-in stabilizing effect of the income tax during periods of inflation. The rise in effective rates of tax automatically reduces the growth of demand and thus contributes to the stability of the economy. Indexation does contribute to stabilization policy when prices rise during periods of recession, but the automatic reduction in tax revenues would not be precisely the amounts required except by accident. In any event, if revenues are increasing too rapidly, Congress always has the option of taking discretionary action—as it has done frequently in recent years.

Capital Gains and Losses

An economic definition of income would include all capital gains in taxable income as they accrue each year. This would be difficult for three reasons: first, the value of many kinds of property cannot be estimated with sufficient accuracy to provide a basis for taxation; second, most people would regard the requirement to pay tax on income that had not actually been realized as unfair; and third, taxation of accruals might force liquidation of assets to pay the tax. Thus capital gains are included in taxable income only when they are realized.

The United States has taxed the capital gains of individuals since it first taxed income. But this has not been the practice elsewhere until recently, when many countries began to tax capital gains, although at generally much lower rates of taxation than those applied to ordinary incomes.

PRESENT LAW. In the United States, realized capital gains were originally taxed as ordinary income, but since the Revenue Act of 1921 they have been subject to preferentially low rates. The provisions applying to such gains changed frequently during the 1920s and 1930s, but were stabilized beginning in 1942. In general, half of the capital gains on assets held for periods longer than six months were included in taxable income, and the amount of tax on such gains was limited to a maximum of 25 percent. The 1969 act left all the old provisions intact, but added a new maximum rate of 35 percent on long-term capital gains of $50,000 or more, and included in the base of the tax on preference income the half of the capital gains that are excluded from taxable income. Gain on the sale of an owner-occupied house is exempt if it is applied to the purchase of a new home within eighteen months. For persons over sixty-five, such gains are entirely exempt up to $35,000 of the sale price. The holding period separating short- from long-term capital gains was lengthened from six to nine months in 1977 and twelve months beginning in 1978 (but the holding period for gains on farm commodity contracts remains six months).

ALTERNATIVE SOLUTIONS. From the standpoint of equity, it is well established that capital gains should be taken into account in determining personal income tax liability. Moreover, preferential treatment of capital gains encourages the conversion of ordinary income into capital gains. Preferential legislation and business manipulation of this sort distort patterns of investment and discredit income taxation. The low capital gains rates now apply to patent royalties, coal and iron ore royalties, income from livestock, income from the sale of unharvested crops, and real estate investments. The amount of ordinary income thus converted into capital gains is unknown, but a great deal of effort goes into this activity and it must be very substantial.

In addition to the overwhelming rate advantage, the law permits capital gains to escape income tax if they are passed from one generation to another and are never realized. The gain is taxed only if the assets are later sold by the recipient. (Gains on the first $60,000 of assets transferred at death and gains accrued before January 1, 1977, on such assets are completely tax exempt, and there is also an exemption of $10,000 for household and personal effects.) The result is that increases in the value of securities and real estate held in wealthy families may never be subject to income tax. Suppose a stock is now selling for $100 a share. An investor who bought 100,000 shares at $50 a share has a capital gain of $5,000,000. If he sold the stock (in a year in which his ordinary income was equal to the sum of his exemptions and deductions), under the 1977 law he would pay a capital gains tax of about $1,721,000 and a minimum tax of about $246,000, making a total tax of $1,967,000, or over 39 percent of the total gain. If he bequeathed the stock to his children, no income tax would be paid on the $5,000,000 gain until the stock was sold. In 1969 Congress removed this tax advantage for gifts to private foundations. In such cases, the charitable deduction is reduced by one-half of the unrealized appreciation.

On the other hand, taxation on a realization basis requires some provision to moderate the effect of progression when large capital gains accumulated over many years are realized in a single year. Full taxation of gains is also criticized because it might have a substantial "locking-in" effect on investors and reduce the mobility of capital. It is also argued that preferential treatment of capital gains helps stimulate a higher rate of economic growth by increasing the attractiveness of investment generally and of risky investments in particular.

The "bunching" problem that would arise with full taxation of capital gains could easily be handled either by prorating capital gains over the length of time the asset was held or by extending the present general averaging system to the full amount of capital gains. (It now applies only to the portion of long-term gains that is included in taxable income.) Unless the present marginal rates were reduced, however, the tax might still discourage the transfer of assets. Part of the difficulty is that adherence to the realization principle permits capital gains to be transferred tax free either by gift or at death.

The solution to this problem is to treat capital gains as if they were constructively realized at gift or at death, with an averaging provision to allow for spreading the gains over a period of years. (This method was proposed by President Kennedy in 1963 and by President Johnson's Treasury Department in early 1969, but has not been approved by Congress.) Under such a system, the only advantage to taxpayers from postponing the realization of capital gains would be the accumulation of interest on the tax postponed. Unless the assets were held for many years, this advantage would be small compared to the advantage of the tax exemption accorded to gains transferred at death; in any event, the interest on the tax postponed would be subject to income tax when the assets were transferred. In these circumstances, the incentive to hold gains indefinitely for tax reasons alone would be greatly reduced.

In the quest to reconcile equity and economic objectives in the taxation of capital gains, tax experts differ about the best approach. A sizable number believe that realized capital gains and those transferred by gift or at death should be taxed in full, with a provision for averaging either over the period during which the asset was held or over an arbitrary but lengthy period. Some believe that present arrangements may be the best that can be devised, while others insist that the capital gains rates are still too high. Most experts agree that there is little justification for granting preferential treatment to income that is not a genuine capital gain.

From 1948 through 1976 the preferential rates applied to capital gains on assets that had been held for longer than six months. This "holding period" was criticized as being both too long and too short. Investor groups urged that the holding period be reduced to three months, and some even recommended that it be eliminated entirely, maintaining that the resulting additional security transactions would increase capital gains tax revenues. On the other hand, if the purpose of the holding period is to differentiate between gains that are bunched and those that are not, there is no logical reason under an annual income tax to reduce the tax rate on incomes earned in less than a year. On this rationale, Congress raised the holding period from six to nine months in 1977 and to twelve months beginning in 1978.

The revenue effects of various revisions in the capital gains tax are shown in table 4-10. Since capital gains are heavily concentrated in the higher income classes, tax liabilities at the bottom of the income scale would not be much affected by changes in the capital gains tax while those in the top classes would be substantially altered. The estimates assume that capital gains realizations would not be affected by the tax change, an assumption that may be unrealistic if present high marginal tax rates remain unaltered. However, this effect could be moderated or completely offset if the revenue gains were used to lower marginal rates in the top brackets substantially.

In principle, capital losses should be deductible in full against either capital gains or ordinary income. However, when gains and losses are recognized only upon realization, taxpayers can easily time their sales so as to take losses promptly when they occur and to postpone gains for as long as possible. This type of asymmetry can be avoided under the U.S. system of capital gains taxation only by charging interest on the deferred tax on capital gains, a device that has never been seriously considered by Congress. The stopgap used in the United States is to limit the deduction of losses. From 1942 through 1963, individuals were allowed to offset their capital losses against capital gains plus $1,000 of ordinary income in the year of realization and in the five subsequent years. In 1964 the loss offset up to $1,000 of ordinary income was extended to an indefinite period. In 1976 the loss offset limit was raised to $2,000 for 1977 and $3,000

Table 4-10. Revenue Effects of Various Capital Gains Tax Revisions, by Adjusted Gross Income Class, 1976

Income classes in thousands of dollars

Revenue change and adjusted gross income class	Constructive realization of gains from gift and at death	Reduce inclusion percentage from 50 to 25 percent	Taxation at regular rates	
			Realized gains only	Realized and constructively realized gains
Revenue change (millions of dollars)	2,200	−2,300	6,200	11,100
		Percentage distribution of revenue change		
0–3	*	*	0.1	0.1
3–5	2.5	0.4	0.6	1.5
5–10	7.4	3.1	3.0	5.4
10–15	8.1	4.2	3.7	6.0
15–20	5.6	6.4	6.2	6.1
20–25	11.0	5.3	4.8	7.7
25–50	28.3	16.9	15.8	21.0
50–100	11.2	19.3	18.3	15.1
100–200	11.0	16.4	16.7	13.9
200–500	7.0	13.3	13.5	10.4
500–1,000	3.1	5.9	6.3	4.7
1,000 and over	4.9	8.9	10.9	8.0
All classes[a]	100.0	100.0	100.0	100.0
		Percentage change in tax liabilities		
0–3	2.2	*	15.6[b]	26.0[b]
3–5	4.7	−0.7	3.0	14.4
5–10	1.5	−0.6	1.7	5.4
10–15	0.9	−0.5	1.2	3.3
15–20	0.5	−0.6	1.6	2.8
20–25	1.3	−0.7	1.6	4.6
25–50	2.1	−1.3	3.2	7.6
50–100	1.6	−2.9	7.5	10.9
100–200	3.2	−5.0	13.6	20.2
200–500	4.4	−8.8	24.0	32.8
500–1,000	6.9	−14.1	40.1	53.7
1,000 and over	9.6	−18.6	60.8	79.5
All classes[a]	1.7	−1.7	4.7	8.3

Source: George F. Break and Joseph A. Pechman, *Federal Tax Reform: The Impossible Dream?* (Brookings Institution, 1975), table 3-1, p. 49.

* Less than 0.05 percent.

a. Includes negative incomes not shown separately.

b. Percent increase in tax is unusually high because many persons with large incomes have tax shelters that reduce their adjusted gross income to less than $3,000 and pay virtually no individual income tax.

for 1978 and later years. In computing the offset, long-term losses were taken into account in full between 1952 and 1969; before 1952 and after 1969 only 50 percent of the net long-term loss could be offset against ordinary income up to the limit.

The annual limit on the amount of the offset is most harmful to people with modest investments, since they are unlikely to have large gains against which to subtract the losses they may incur. The only solution to this problem would be a pragmatic one that was reasonably liberal for the modest investor without opening the door to widespread abuse of the provision and large revenue losses.

CAPITAL GAINS AND INFLATION. Capital gains cannot be treated on a par with current income flows when measuring income during a period of rising prices. An asset does not give the owner command over additional resources until the value of the asset exceeds its purchase price at prices prevailing when the asset is sold (or during the period of accrual, if the accounting is on an accrual basis). Thus to measure the income from appreciated assets, the portion of the capital gain that results from inflation should be deducted from the nominal capital gain. The correction can be made by multiplying the purchase price of the asset by the ratio of a general price index (usually the consumer price index) on the date of sale to the value of the same index at the time of purchase before computing the gain. No correction is necessary for current income flows like wages and salaries, because they give the recipient command over resources in the prices of the period during which they are earned. (The bracket effect of inflation discussed in the previous section is a separate matter. Here the concern is with the measurement of income, which can be taxable under a fixed set of rates or rates that are indexed for inflation.)

A system corrected for inflation would have a dramatic effect on the distribution of taxable income. Many apparent capital gains would be converted to real losses, and real losses and gains that are now ignored would be recognized. For example, an individual who purchases an asset for $1,000 and sells it for $1,200 after holding it for a period during which prices have risen 50 percent would have a $200 nominal gain but a real loss of $300 at current prices. Assets that are fixed in money terms, such as bonds, mortgages, and bank deposits, generate real losses as prices increase. On the other hand, those who borrow money on fixed dollar contracts repay their debts in depreciated dollars and thus gain from the rise in prices. All such gains and losses would have to be taken into account to calculate inflation-corrected income correctly.

The percentage of capital gains included in taxable income under an inflation-corrected system would not be a flat percentage, as it is under present U.S. tax law; it would vary with the rate of inflation and the length of time the asset was held. If the inflation rate were stable, the inclusion rate would actually rise with the length of time the asset was held. For example, suppose an asset purchased for $1 appreciates in real terms at the rate of 10 percent a year in a period in which prices also rise 10 percent a year. The real gain for a single year is just over half the nominal gain of 21 percent ($1.21 - 1.10 = 0.11$). After five years, the nominal value of the asset is 2.59 (1.21^5), the purchase price expressed in current prices is 1.61 (1.1^5), and the real gain measured in current prices is 0.98, or 62 percent of the nominal gain of 1.59.

The realization criterion would also create problems if an inflation-corrected system were implemented on an equitable basis. If capital gains are taxed only when realized, the interest on the tax that is deferred during the period assets are held can be substantial. It would therefore be necessary to require taxpayers to correct nominal gains for the value of the tax deferral, as well as to permit them to adjust their gains for inflation. Such correction factors could be calculated in advance for all possible holding periods and provided in special tables to accompany the annual tax return.

Many proponents of the present treatment of capital gains favor an inflation adjustment for capital gains without making all the necessary refinements, including the adjustments for the real losses on assets fixed in money terms. Those who oppose the present treatment would argue against an inflation adjustment unless capital gains were fully included in income and the value of tax deferral were taken into account in computing tax liabilities.

State and Local Government Bond Interest

Interest received from state and local government bonds has been exempt from income tax ever since its enactment in 1913. The tax exemption has been criticized by secretaries of the treasury, tax experts, and others who believe that it is inequitable, reduces risk investment by high-bracket taxpayers, and costs the federal government an excessive amount. Interest rates on these bonds have increased as state-local debt has risen, and the relative advantage of the exemption to the top income classes has greatly increased. Proponents of the exemption argue that its elimination would make state-local borrowing costs prohibitive, which would be unwise in view of the mounting needs of these units of government. Bills to remove the exemption have reached a vote in Congress six times, but each time they have been defeated. Although Congress has not voted on the question since 1942, it is doubtful that a move to repeal the exemption would be successful today.

By discriminating between income from municipals and from other securities, and by giving investors in the high income brackets an advantage (see table 4-11), the exemption violates the generally accepted principles that an income tax should apply equally to equal incomes and should be progressive. It also reduces investment in productive enterprises by diverting risk or venture capital from the private sector. It distorts the allocation of resources within the private sector, and between the public and private sectors, when state and local governments issue tax-exempt securities to finance such "business" enterprises as public utilities and housing developments or to subsidize the growth of local industry. Even many who favor the exemption agree that the use of so-called industrial development and pollution control bonds to build tax-exempt facilities for private firms should be stopped. Since 1968 interest on such bonds has been subject to tax if the value of the amount issued for a single project exceeds $1 million. An exception to this limitation was provided for pollution control and airport construction bonds, and large numbers of these bonds have been issued in recent years.

The exemption is an inefficient type of subsidy. Empirical studies suggest that the saving in interest payments by state and local governments is a little less than half the revenue loss to the federal government. There are not only less costly ways to assist or subsidize capital outlays by state and local governments, but also more equitable methods, since governmental units benefit not on the basis of need but on the basis of the amount of debt they issue.

Proposals to remove the exemption have usually been limited to new issues. This reflects the belief that taxing outstanding securities would be a breach of faith by the federal government, causing capital losses and the inequitable application of taxes to holders of existing securities.

Table 4-11. Revenue Effects of Taxing Interest on State and Local Government Bonds, by Adjusted Gross Income Class, 1976
Income classes in thousands of dollars

Revenue change and adjusted gross income class[a]	Individuals	Corporations	Total
Revenue change (millions of dollars)	1,300	3,600	4,900
	Percentage distribution of revenue change		
0–3	*	1.6	1.2
3–5	0.5	4.2	3.2
5–10	0.5	8.6	6.4
10–15	0.8	8.6	6.6
15–20	1.3	8.8	6.8
20–25	1.4	5.4	4.3
25–50	13.3	19.7	18.0
50–100	41.7	18.7	24.8
100–200	34.7	10.5	16.9
200–500	5.3	7.1	6.6
500–1,000	0.2	2.7	2.0
1,000 and over	0.1	3.2	2.4
All classes[b]	100.0	100.0	100.0
	Percentage change in tax liabilities		
0–3	0.9	138.6[c]	139.4[c]
3–5	0.6	13.1	13.7
5–10	0.1	2.8	2.9
10–15	0.1	1.6	1.6
15–20	0.1	1.3	1.4
20–25	0.1	1.0	1.2
25–50	0.6	2.3	2.9
50–100	3.6	4.4	8.0
100–200	6.0	5.0	11.0
200–500	2.0	7.3	9.3
500–1,000	0.2	9.8	10.1
1,000 and over	0.1	10.4	10.5
All classes[b]	1.0	2.7	3.7

Source: Break and Pechman, *Federal Tax Reform*, table 3-2. Figures are rounded.
* Less than 0.05 percent.
a. Assumes corporation tax is borne by individuals in proportion to their dividend income.
b. Includes negative incomes not shown separately.
c. Percent increase in tax is unusually high because many persons with large incomes have tax shelters that reduce their adjusted gross income to less than $3,000 and pay virtually no individual income tax.

Some lawyers have argued that taxing state-local bond interest is unconstitutional, whether the proposal is to apply the tax to new issues only or to existing ones as well. The majority opinion is that there is no constitutional bar to taxing state-local bond interest if Congress wants to do so.

Interest costs of state and local governments would rise if the exemption were removed. Municipals are more difficult to market than corporates and other securities. Many issues are too small to appeal to large institutional buyers, and lack of information about the finances of small units of local government discourages some investors. Thus, if the municipals were fully taxable, they would have to bear higher interest rates than do corporate bonds of comparable quality. This would probably discourage borrowing in some localities and thereby reduce capital expenditures for public purposes. If total outlays were to rise in some areas, state and local taxes would ultimately be increased to meet higher interest charges. Since local taxes tend to be regressive, a greater burden might fall on the lower income groups. It has also been argued that the heavier financial burden on state and local governments, added to existing unmet needs for public facilities, would intensify pressure for federal aid, bring greater federal participation in local affairs, and further reduce the fiscal independence of states and localities.

Because opponents of the exemption concede that some desirable investment in social capital might be curtailed if the localities had to pay higher interest charges, they have often coupled suggestions for abolishing the exemption with proposals to provide alternative federal subsidies. These have generally taken one of two forms: (1) subsidies tied to state and local borrowing (for example, the payment of a portion of the interest on state and local debt by the federal government) as a quid pro quo for giving up the exemption or (2) subsidies tied to capital outlays rather than borrowing and thus not allocated strictly according to exemption benefits lost. In 1976 a House Ways and Means Committee bill included a provision that state and local governments could voluntarily relinquish the tax-exemption privilege for any specific bond issue and the Treasury would pay 35 percent of the interest on the issue, depending on the value of the tax exemption in the market. The provision was not acted on by the House.

With the growing difficulties of marketing municipals during the inflation of the 1970s, state and local officials who once opposed the taxable bond option are reversing their position and are increasingly supporting the enactment of the option with a federal subsidy of 30 to 50 percent. The Ford administration also supported this legislation, and the congressional committees have been giving it sympathetic consideration.

The major problem is political. If the tax exemption is replaced by a generous subsidy, many people fear there will be an unhealthy increase in federal control over state and local fiscal affairs. Even the possibility of this is often sufficient to arouse opposition to removal of the exemption. Those opposed argue that the inefficiencies or tax inequities arising from the exemption are trivial compared with the dangers of more centralization of fiscal activity and possible disruption of the credit channels used by the state and local governments. Others argue that efficiency and tax equity are important enough to justify exploring the possibility of substituting for the tax exemption an alternative formula that would not mean greater federal control.

These differing views are irreconcilable, and it seems that even the taxable bond option will not be adopted unless state and local government officials are assured that it will not involve any federal participation, let alone interference, in the purposes for which state and local borrowing is undertaken.

Income Averaging

The use of an annual accounting period, combined with progressive income taxes, results in a heavier tax burden on fluctuating incomes than on an equal amount of income distributed evenly over the years. For example, a single taxpayer who has a taxable income of $25,000 in each of two successive years pays a total tax before credit of $14,380 (1977 rates) in the two years. If $50,000 was received one year and nothing the next, the tax would be $20,190.

This type of discrimination is hard to defend on either equity or economic grounds. Taxpayers usually do not and cannot arrange their business and personal affairs to conform with the calendar. Annual income fluctuations are frequently beyond the control of the taxpayer, yet he or she is taxed as if twelve months were a suitable horizon for decisionmaking. In addition, in the absence of averaging, there is great pressure for moderating the impact of the graduated rates on fluctuating incomes by lowering the rates applicable to them.

As already indicated, reduced rates on capital gains have been justified on this basis although the rate reductions for such gains have more than compensated for the lack of averaging.

There is general agreement on the need for averaging, but the roadblock has always been the administrative problem. Keeping an accurate account for a number of years is difficult for the government as well as for the taxpayer. It was therefore considered desirable to start modestly.

A start was made under the Revenue Act of 1964, which permitted averaging income over a five-year period if the income in the current year exceeded the average for the four prior years by one-third and if this excess was more than $3,000. Taxpayers who had been at least 50 percent self-supporting for the four prior years could average. The averaging technique is first to compute a tentative tax on one-fifth of the "averageable income" and then to multiply the tentative tax by five. The 1969 act increased the amount of income that can be averaged by permitting averaging if the current year's income exceeds the average of the four prior years by 20 percent and this excess is over $3,000. The 1969 act also permitted for the first time the averaging of the portion of capital gains included in taxable income.

The restriction of averaging to those who have an *increase* in income eliminated from the averaging system the millions of persons who have a sharp reduction in income. It would be desirable to allow those who have reductions in income to average if a suitable way to avoid including retired persons in the averaging system could be devised.

In 1973 the averaging provision was used by 2,174,000 taxpayers who saved $1.4 billion, or about 9 percent of the tax that would otherwise have been due.

Minimum Tax and Allocation of Deductions

The introduction of the minimum tax was an attempt to obtain some tax contribution from wealthy people who had previously escaped income taxation on all or most of their income. The tax is now levied at a 15 percent rate on a selected list of preference incomes to the extent that income from all the items exceeds $10,000 or half the regular income tax for the year, whichever is higher. The most important preference incomes in the minimum tax base for individuals are the 50 percent of long-term capital gains excluded from taxable income, itemized deductions (other than those for medical expenses and casualty losses) in excess of 60 percent of adjusted gross income, depletion deductions in excess of the amount that would be allowed on the basis of cost, intangible drilling costs for oil and gas to the extent they exceed the amount of deductions that would be allowed if these costs were capitalized and amortized, and accelerated depreciation on real property and equipment leases. The minimum tax yielded a total of $516 million in 1973—$182 million from individuals and $334 million from corporations. The 1976 revisions raised the yield to an estimated $1.3 billion for individuals and $500 million for corporations, a total of $1.8 billion in a full year.

The present minimum tax may be criticized on three grounds. First, the application of a low flat rate of tax violates the principle of progression. Since the tax applies only to wealthy people, the preference incomes would be taxed at or near the top-bracket rates if they were included in the regular income tax base. Second, the list of preferences is not comprehensive. The most important preferences omitted from the minimum tax base are tax-exempt interest and unrealized capital gains transferred by gift or at death. Third, the exemption restricts the applicability of the minimum tax to a small number of taxpayers.

An alternative method, proposed by the Treasury Department in 1973, of accomplishing the same objective as the minimum tax would be to require that every individual be taxable on no less than half of his or her total income, including income from preference items. In computing the minimum taxable income subject to tax, allowances could be made for personal exemptions and essential deductions, such as extraordinary medical expenses and casualty losses. The advantage of this approach is that the regular progressive tax rates automatically apply to minimum income subject to tax.

Another method of cutting down the benefits of tax-exempt income would be to allocate personal deductions proportionately between the individual's taxable and nontaxable sources and to permit a deduction only for the amount allocated to the taxable sources. This proposal is based on the reasonable assumption that personal outlays—whether deductible or not—come out of the taxpayer's total income, rather than out of his taxable income alone. The House version of the 1969 act included this provision, but it was eliminated by the Senate, largely because of the opposition of representatives of tax-exempt institutions and of state and local governments, who generally are against any proposal that would reduce the tax advantages of the charitable contribution deduction and of state-local securities.

Although allocation of deductions was rejected, the enactment of the minimum tax reflects an awareness on the part of Congress of the growing public resentment of unwarranted tax privileges. It was a weak compromise, but the minimum tax was the first break in the long struggle to achieve a more comprehensive income tax base. Mere publication of the amount of the tax preferences reported on tax returns has helped dramatize the inequities of the present tax structure. In 1973, $7.3 billion of preference income was reported on almost 119,000 individual tax returns; of these, only 26,000 paid additional tax on the preference income.

Compulsory allocation of deductions would increase revenues by $1.9 billion a year (at 1976 income levels) and the minimum tax by $1.3 billion. Both provisions are highly progressive (table 4-12).

Tax Shelters

Tax shelters permit individuals to reduce drastically or even to wipe out tax liabilities on large incomes by taking advantage of preferential provisions in the tax law. A number of spectacular examples were presented to the Ways and Means Committee by the staff of the Joint Committee on Internal Revenue Taxation in 1975. In one case, a man who participated in a real estate partnership reduced his economic income of $448,000 to an adjusted gross income of only $37,000 on the basis of an investment of $225,000 made by the partnership only three days before the end of the year.

A tax shelter contains three basic elements: tax deferral through large depreciation deductions, heavy reliance on borrowing, and capital gains treatment when the investment is terminated. For example, a $1,000,000 investment with a depreciable life of ten years would generate in the first year $200,000 of declining-balance depreciation at twice the straight-line rate plus interest on any funds borrowed to pay for the investment. If 80 percent of the $1 million were borrowed at a 10 percent rate, the interest deduction would amount to $80,000, and total deductions would come to $280,000 in the first year. Such deductions would ordinarily be sufficient to offset not only any current earnings from the investment, but also income from other

Table 4-12. Revenue Effects of the Minimum Tax and Compulsory Allocation of Personal Deductions between Taxable and Nontaxable Income, by Adjusted Gross Income Class, 1976

Income classes in thousands of dollars

Revenue change and adjusted gross income class	Minimum tax	Compulsory allocation of deductions[a]
Revenue change (millions of dollars)	1,300	1,900
	Percentage distribution of revenue change	
0–3	0.3	*
3–5	0.4	*
5–10	1.2	2.5
10–15	0.7	8.1
15–20	3.2	12.3
20–25	1.0	10.5
25–50	7.6	19.9
50–100	17.5	14.7
100–200	14.8	11.9
200–500	12.1	7.7
500–1,000	6.2	3.9
1,000 and over	12.1	8.4
All classes[b]	100.0	100.0
	Percentage change in tax liabilities	
0–3	c	*
3–5	1.2	*
5–10	0.2	0.4
10–15	*	0.8
15–20	0.2	1.0
20–25	0.1	1.1
25–50	0.3	1.3
50–100	1.4	1.9
100–200	2.4	3.1
200–500	4.3	4.3
500–1,000	8.1	7.8
1,000 and over	14.2	14.8
All classes[b]	1.0	1.5

Source: Brookings 1972 tax file, projected to 1976. Figures are rounded.
* Less than 0.05 percent.
a. All itemized personal deductions in excess of $2,000 allocated between adjusted gross income and nontaxable income (state-local bond interest, excluded capital gains, and other preference items subject to the minimum tax).
b. Includes negative incomes not shown separately.
c. Percentage cannot be computed because tax liabilities other than minimum tax are negative for the entire class.

sources. Ultimately, as the depreciation and interest deductions decline, the investor will sell the asset and can frequently apply capital gains treatment to most of the gain even though the depreciation was deducted at regular income tax rates.

Gains from the sale of property held for twelve months or less or of equipment regardless of the time held are treated as ordinary income up to the amount of depreciation previously taken, thus in effect "recapturing" the tax benefit of depreciation deductions. In the case of commercial, industrial, and unsubsidized residential buildings, the recapture provision applies only to the excess of accelerated depreciation over straight-line depreciation. In the case of low-income housing projects subsidized by the government, excess depreciation is fully recaptured if the property is held less than one hundred months (twenty months for low-income housing) and the full gain, including excess depreciation, is taxable at capital gains rates after two hundred months (one hundred months for low-income housing). However, tax shelters remain a serious problem because many other activities permit the conversion of ordinary deductions into capital gains, including equipment leasing, sports franchises, motion pictures, real estate on which straight-line depreciation is taken, oil and gas drilling, and farming.

The proper way to remove the advantages of tax shelters would be to eliminate the favorable tax provisions and tax "economic" income. This would require limiting depreciation deductions to actual depreciation based on the taxpayer's own investment (that is, excluding depreciation on borrowed capital) and treating the gain on the disposition of assets as ordinary income. Alternatively, the artificial deductions arising in a tax shelter might be allowed only against the income generated by the shelter itself, thus limiting the loss offset to the earnings from the same project in future years. This provision, known as the limitation on artificial losses, was incorporated in the House Tax Reform Bill of 1976, but was rejected by the Senate. Instead, Congress allowed taxpayers to take all the deductions available under the tax law up to the full amount of capital "at risk" (which is defined as the amount of cash or other property contributed to the business plus borrowed money on the taxpayer's personal liability or secured by personal assets). The provision applies to farming (except operations involving trees other than fruit or nut trees), oil and gas, motion pictures, and equipment leasing. Real estate investors are not subject to the at-risk provision, but will be required to capitalize and amortize taxes paid during the construction period over five years beginning in 1977 (over four years beginning in 1978 for residential housing) and increasing annually to a permanent level of ten years in 1982 (1984 for residential housing). Subsidized housing projects are allowed current deductions for construction period interest and taxes through 1981, and then amortized deductions over a four-year period starting in 1982 and rising to ten years in 1988.

Summary

The individual income tax—the most important tax in the federal tax structure—is widely regarded as the fairest source of government revenues. Its yield expands or contracts more rapidly than personal income during a business cycle, imparting built-in flexibility to the revenue side of the federal budget. The tax is less burdensome on consumption and more burdensome on saving than a consumption or expenditure tax of equal yield would be. Its potential effect on work and investment incentives is unclear. There is no evidence to support the contention that the income tax significantly retards growth. The nation has grown at a satisfactory rate during most of the period since the income tax was enacted.

Many unsettled problems remain regarding some of the major features of the individual income tax. These include the treatment of the family, the aged, earned income, special deductions for personal expenditures, capital gains and losses, tax-exempt interest, eligibility for averaging, the minimum tax, and tax shelters. Even in its present form, however, the individual income tax continues to be the best tax ever devised. Further improvement through broadening the tax base and lowering the tax rates would pay handsome dividends in still greater equity, simplification, and better economic performance.

CHAPTER FIVE

The Corporation Income Tax

THE CORPORATION INCOME TAX was enacted in 1909, four years
before the introduction of the individual income tax. To avoid a constitutional issue, Congress levied the tax as an excise on the privilege
of doing business as a corporation. The law was challenged, but the
Supreme Court upheld the authority of the federal government to
impose such a tax and ruled that the privilege of doing corporate
business could be measured by the corporation's profits.

The corporation income tax produced more revenue than the
individual income tax in seventeen of the twenty-eight years before
1941, when the latter was greatly expanded as a source of wartime
revenue. From 1941 through 1967 corporation income tax revenues
were second only to those of the individual income tax, but they were
overtaken by payroll taxes in 1968. In fiscal year 1976 the corporation income tax accounted for about 14 percent of federal receipts.

A business enterprise enjoys special privileges and benefits when
it operates in the corporate form. These include perpetual life, limited
liability of shareholders, liquidity of ownership through marketability
of shares, growth through retention of earnings, and possibilities of
intercorporate affiliations. Moreover, the modern corporation—particularly the large "public" corporation in which management and

123

ownership are separated—generates income that nobody may claim for personal use. The growth of the corporate sector could not have taken place if the corporation had not been endowed with these valuable privileges. The Supreme Court's acceptance of the constitutionality of the corporation income tax was based on the view that the corporation owes its life, rights, and power to the government.

Few experts accept this rationale for a substantial tax on corporate profits. Instead, one justification seems to be that the corporation is a mechanism for accumulating capital that is managed by the corporate officers and directors, and is not really subject to the control of the owners—the stockholders. Proponents of the corporation tax believe that the earnings and economic power derived from this large stock of capital are a proper base for taxation.

Another reason for the corporation income tax is that it is needed to safeguard the individual income tax. If corporate incomes were not subject to tax, people could avoid the individual income tax by accumulating income in corporations. Short of taxing shareholders on their shares of corporate incomes whether the incomes are distributed or not (a method that has been receiving increasing attention of late), the most practical way to protect the individual income tax is to impose a separate tax on corporate incomes. The existence of two separate taxes side by side creates other problems; these will be discussed at some length in this chapter.

Despite its prominence in the federal revenue system, the corporation income tax is the subject of considerable controversy. In the first place, there is no general agreement about who really pays it. Some believe the tax is borne by the corporations and hence by their stockholders. Others believe it depresses the rate of return to capital throughout the economy and is therefore borne by owners of capital in general. Still others argue that the tax is passed on to consumers through higher prices, or may be shifted back to the workers in lower wages. Some believe that it is borne by all three groups—stockholders, consumers, and wage earners—in varying proportions. This uncertainty about the incidence of the tax makes strange bedfellows of individuals holding diametrically opposed views and often puts them in inconsistent positions. Some staunch opponents of a sales tax vigorously support the corporation income tax even though they believe it is shifted to the consumer, while many who believe that the corporation tax is "just another cost" (and is consequently shifted) demand that the tax be reduced and some form of consumption tax substituted for all or part of it.

Second, the proper relation between individual and corporation income taxes has never been settled. At various times, dividends have been allowed as a credit or deduction in computing the tax on individual income. Today, a $100 exclusion is allowed for dividends, which is intended to relieve the small shareholder from paying both individual and corporation income taxes on dividends. The present situation is makeshift and satisfies few people.

A third set of issues has to do with the impact of the corporation tax on the corporate sector and on the economy in general. It has been argued that, particularly during periods of inflation, the tax places a heavy burden on corporations and thus curtails business investment and reduces the nation's growth rate. Since interest paid is deductible in computing taxable corporation profits but dividends paid are not, the tax is said to favor debt over equity financing. Some question the desirability of a tax that discourages the corporate form of business; others believe that alternative tax sources yielding the same revenue would be much more harmful to the economy.

Characteristics of the Tax

Since the corporation income tax is a tax on business, many of the refinements required in computing the taxable income of individuals do not arise. For example, the deductions allowed under the corporation income tax, with the exception of that for charitable contributions, are confined to expenses incurred in doing business. State and local bond interest is exempt from the corporation income tax as well as from the individual income tax, and capital gains and losses receive special treatment. Corporations are also required to pay taxes in quarterly installments as profits are earned during the year.

The Tax Base

The corporation income tax is a complicated instrument because it must be applied to a wide variety of organizations doing business in the corporate form or in a form that closely resembles a corporation. The major features will be discussed in a later section of the chapter, but at this point a number of the significant provisions may be noted.

1. As in the case of individuals, corporations may elect to be taxed

on the capital gains they realize on assets held more than twelve months (nine months for 1977) at a lower rate than that applying to ordinary income. The alternative tax rate on taxable corporate capital gains is 30 percent instead of the 35 percent maximum that applies to capital gains of individuals. However, gains on the sale of assets when the sale is associated with a corporate liquidation, as well as gains on assets distributed to stockholders in kind, are not taxable to the corporation.

2. Whereas individuals may deduct half of net capital losses up to $3,000 from ordinary income ($2,000 in 1977) and have an un-limited carry-forward, corporations are allowed to offset capital losses only against capital gains. The remaining capital losses may be carried back for three years and forward for five years to be offset against capital gains.

3. Net operating losses may be carried back and offset against taxable income of the three preceding years. If the income in these years is not sufficient, the remaining losses may be carried forward for seven years (nine years for regulated transportation firms). In effect, this provides an eleven-year period for offsetting losses against gains (thirteen years for regulated transportation firms). The tax-payer is allowed to waive the carry-back for any year and just carry that year's losses forward.

4. Generous provision is made for recovery of capital. In the case of plant and equipment, the original cost may be depreciated or re-covered over the useful life of the asset. Formerly, the law in effect limited the rate of depreciation for most corporations to the straight-line method (that is, the cost was allocated evenly over the life of the asset). New methods adopted in 1954 permit a faster rate of depre-ciation in the early years. In 1969 the most rapid methods were re-stricted to machinery and equipment and residential buildings. Service lives were shortened in 1962 and 1971. An investment tax credit has also been allowed, with some interruptions, since 1962 for purchases of new equipment (buildings are not entitled to the credit). The credit was originally set at 7 percent of investment, and was raised to 10 percent in 1975 (an extra 1 percent was allowed for 1975–80 if contributed to an employee stock ownership plan and another 0.5 percent was allowed for 1976–80 if matched by employee contributions). For minerals and gas and oil, the law allows deduc-tions for the costs of exploration, discovery, development, and deple-

tion, which often exceed the cost of the mine or oil or gas fields. In 1975 Congress limited the integrated oil companies to cost recovery.

5. All current outlays for research and development may be deducted in full in the year they are made. Taxpayers may elect to capitalize such expenditures and, if regular depreciation cannot be used because the useful life cannot be determined, the expenditures may be written off over a period of five years.

The provisions for net operating losses, recovery of capital, and research and development expenses (items 3, 4, and 5 above) are also available to individuals and partnerships under the individual income tax.

6. Intercorporate dividends paid by one corporation to another are subject to tax at a relatively low rate. Corporations are allowed to deduct 85 percent of the dividends they receive from other domestic corporations. This means that intercorporate dividends are subject to an extra tax of 7.2 percent (the regular 48 percent rate multiplied by 15 percent). The tax on intercorporate dividends is waived, however, if the two corporations are members of a group of affiliated corporations eligible to file a consolidated return.

7. Corporations are subject to U.S. tax on foreign as well as domestic income. Income earned by foreign branches (and certain corporations located in tax havens) is included in the corporation's tax return in the year it is earned. If the corporation operates through a foreign subsidiary, foreign earnings are subject to tax when they are distributed to the U.S. parent corporation as dividends. However, credit against the domestic tax is allowed for foreign income and withholding taxes paid on earnings and dividends received from abroad. Special rate reductions for western hemisphere and China trade corporations are being phased out (by 1980 for the former, by 1978 for the latter).

8. Half the earnings in excess of 67 percent of the 1972–75 annual average of a domestic international sales corporation (DISC), which may be organized to handle the export business of a U.S. corporation, is not subject to tax until the earnings are returned to the parent corporation. In 1980 the four-year base will start moving forward one year at a time. Military exports receive only half the regular DISC benefits.

9. Corporations with no more than ten shareholders may elect to be treated as partnerships for tax purposes. Such shareholders are

subject to individual income tax on the entire earnings of the corporation, whether distributed or not, and may deduct any losses from
other personal income. In 1973, 308,457 corporations reporting
profits of $5.2 billion and deficits of $1.5 billion elected this treatment.

10. Religious, educational, and charitable organizations, trade
associations, labor unions, and fraternal organizations are exempt
from the corporation income tax, but the tax does apply to the "unrelated business income" of these organizations. Private foundations
are subject to a special excise tax of 4 percent on their investment
income. Cooperatives are subject to special provisions designed to
tax their earnings at least once under the individual or corporation
income tax, but the revenue collected from them is small. Investment
funds that distribute at least 90 percent of their dividends and realized
capital gains to their shareholders are not taxable on the distributed
amounts. Mutual financial institutions, including savings and loan associations, mutual savings banks, and insurance companies, are taxed,
but they are permitted to accumulate substantial tax-free reserves.

Tax Rates

Since "ability to pay" does not apply to corporations as it does to
individuals, the corporation income tax is levied at a flat rate on most
corporate incomes. Lower rates are applied to the first $50,000 as a
concession to small businesses; the remainder is taxed at one rate.
The corporation tax is 20 percent on the first $25,000 of income, 22
percent on the next $25,000, and 48 percent on the excess over
$50,000. About 90 percent of corporate taxable income is subject to
the 48 percent rate (appendix table B-9).

A minimum tax is imposed on the preference items of corporations
as well as individuals. The most important of these items for corporations are: eighteen forty-eighths of long-term capital gains (that is,
the proportion of gains not subject to the full corporation tax), accelerated depreciation on real property and equipment leases in excess
of straight-line depreciation, depletion in excess of adjusted basis depletion, and bad debt deductions of financial institutions in excess of
loss experience. Timber companies include only two-thirds of their
capital gains less $20,000 in the minimum tax base. The minimum
tax is applied at a 15 percent rate to the total amount of the preferences above an exemption of $10,000 or the regular income tax paid,
whichever is higher.

Tax Payment

The provision for paying taxes currently applied only to individuals when it was enacted during the Second World War. Corporations continued to pay their tax, as they had from the beginning, in four installments in the year following the tax year. This state of affairs continued until 1950, when payments were gradually shifted over a period of five years to two installments to be paid in the first six months of the year following the tax year (appendix table C-16).

Further acceleration of corporation tax payments was legislated in 1954. After another transition period of five years, corporations were required to pay half of their estimated tax over $100,000 in September and December of the tax year, and the remaining liability in two installments in March and June of the following year.

Further steps to place corporations on a current payment basis were taken in 1964 and 1966. After an additional transition period of four years (originally seven years under the 1964 legislation), corporations paid their estimated tax (in excess of $100,000) in four installments in the current year. Since 1967 large corporations and individuals filing declarations of estimated tax have paid tax on the same time schedule. The 1968 act extended the current payment system to all corporate tax liabilities, to be fully effective in 1977.

The Shifting and Incidence of the Tax

There is no more controversial issue in taxation than the question, *who bears the corporation income tax?* On this question, economists and businessmen alike differ among themselves. The following quotations are representative of these divergent views:

The initial or short-run incidence of the corporate income tax seems to be largely on corporations and their stockholders. . . . There seems to be little foundation for the belief that a large part of the corporate tax comes out of wages or is passed on to consumers in the same way that a selective excise [tax] tends to be shifted to buyers. (Richard Goode, *The Corporation Income Tax,* Wiley, 1951, pp. 71–72.)

. . . the corporation profits tax is almost entirely shifted; the government simply uses the corporation as a tax collector. (Kenneth E. Boulding, *The Organizational Revolution,* Harper, 1953, p. 277.)

Corporate taxes are simply costs, and the method of their assessment does not change this fact. Costs must be paid by the public in prices, and corporate taxes are thus, in effect, concealed sales taxes. (Enders M. Voorhees, chairman of Finance Committee, U.S. Steel Corporation, address before the Controllers' Institute of America, New York, September 21, 1943.)

The observation is frequently made that because in the long run the [corporate] tax tends to be included in the price of the product, it is to this extent borne by consumers. This observation miconstrues the nature of the tax. Fundamentally, it is a tax on a factor of production: corporate equity capital. (Arnold C. Harberger, "The Corporation Income Tax: An Empirical Appraisal," *Tax Revision Compendium,* House Ways and Means Committee, vol. 1, 1959, p. 241.)

. . . an increase in the [corporate] tax is shifted fully through short-run adjustments to prevent a decline in the net rate of return [on corporate investment], and . . . these adjustments are maintained subsequently. (Marian Krzyzaniak and Richard A. Musgrave, *The Shifting of the Corporation Income Tax,* Johns Hopkins Press, 1963, p. 65.)

. . . there is no inter-sector inefficiency resulting from the imposition of the corporate profits tax with the interest deductibility provision. Nor is there any misallocation between safe and risky industries. From an efficiency point of view, the whole corporate profits tax structure is just like a lump sum tax on corporations. (Joseph E. Stiglitz, "Taxation, Corporate Financial Policy, and the Cost of Capital," *Journal of Public Economics,* vol. 2, 1973, p. 33.)

Unfortunately, economics has not yet provided a scientific basis for accepting or rejecting one side or the other. This section presents the logic of each view and summarizes the evidence.

The Shifting Mechanism

One reason for the sharply divergent views is that the opponents frequently do not refer to the same type of shifting. It is important to distinguish between short- and long-run shifting and the mechanisms through which they operate. The "short run" is defined by economists as a period too short for firms to adjust their capital to changing demand and supply conditions. The "long run" is a period in which capital can be adjusted.

SHORT RUN. The classical view in economics is that the corporation income tax cannot be shifted in the short run. The argument is as follows: all business firms, whether they are competitive or monopolistic, seek to maximize net profits. This maximum occurs when output and prices are set at the point where the cost of producing an additional unit is exactly equal to the additional revenue obtained from the sale of that unit. In the short run, a tax on economic profit should make no difference in this decision. The output and price that maximized the firm's profits before the tax will continue to maximize profits after the tax is imposed. (This follows from simple arithmetic. If a series of figures is reduced by the same percentage, the figure that was highest before will still be the highest after.)

The argument against this view is that today's markets are characterized neither by perfect competition nor by monopoly; instead, they show considerable imperfection and mutual interdependence or oligopoly. In such markets, business firms may set their prices at the level that covers their full costs *plus* a margin for profits. Alternatively, the firms are described as aiming at an after-tax target rate of return on invested capital. Under the cost-plus behavior, the firm treats the tax as an element of cost and raises its price to recover the tax. Similarly, if the firm's objective is the after-tax target rate of return, imposition of a tax or an increase in the tax rate—by reducing the rate of return on invested capital—will have to be accounted for in making output and price decisions. To preserve the target rate of return, the tax must be shifted forward to consumers or backward to the workers, or be shifted partly forward and partly backward.

It is also argued that economists' models are irrelevant in most markets where one or a few large firms exercise a substantial degree of leadership. In such markets, efficient producers raise their prices to recover the tax, and the tax merely forms an "umbrella" that permits less efficient or marginal producers to survive.

When business managers are asked about their pricing policies, they often say that they shift the corporation income tax. However, there is little evidence to support this position. Economists have debated it without reaching a consensus.

Even if this behavior on the part of business firms is accepted, some doubts must be expressed about their ability to fully shift the corporation income tax in the short run. In the first place, the tax depends on the outcome of business operations during an entire year. The businessman can only guess the ratio of the tax to his gross receipts, and it is hard to conceive of his setting a price that would recover the precise amount of tax he will eventually pay. (If shifting were possible, there would be some instances of firms shifting more than 100 percent of the tax, but few economists believe that overshifting actually occurs.)

Second, the businessman knows that should he attempt to recover the corporation income tax through higher prices (or lower wages) other firms would not necessarily do the same. Some firms make no profit and thus pay no tax; among other firms, the ratio of tax to gross receipts differs. In multiproduct firms, the producer has very little basis for judging the ratio of tax to gross receipts for each product. All these possibilities increase the uncertainty of response by other firms and make the attempt to shift part or all of the corporation income tax hazardous.

LONG RUN. Unless it is shifted in the short run to consumers or wage earners, or both, the corporation income tax influences investment in the long run by reducing the rate of return on corporate equity. The tax may discourage the use of capital altogether or encourage investment in debt-intensive industries (for example, real estate) and unincorporated enterprises. The result is a smaller supply of corporate products, unless the reduction in equity investment is offset by an increase in borrowing.

The incidence of the corporation income tax depends on whether the tax is shifted in the short run. Short-run shifting means that net after-tax rates of return are maintained at the levels prevailing before the tax; the burden of the tax falls on consumers or wage earners. If the tax is not shifted in the short run, net after-tax rates of return are depressed, and the amount of corporate investment is reduced. After-tax rates of return tend to be equalized with those in the noncorporate sector, but in the process corporate capital and output will have been permanently reduced. Thus, in the absence of short-run shifting, the burden of the tax falls on the owners of capital in general.

Where use is made of debt capital, the corporation tax cannot affect investment decisions because interest on debt is a deductible expense. If the marginal investment of a firm is fully financed by debt, the corporation tax becomes a tax on residual profits at the margin and is borne entirely by the owners of the corporation, the stockholders. In view of the recent large increase in debt financing (see the section on equity and debt finance below), a substantial proportion of the corporation income tax may now rest on stockholders and not be diffused through the shifting process just described to owners of capital in general.

Figure 5-1. Percentage of Business Income Originating in the Corporate Sector, 1929–75[a]

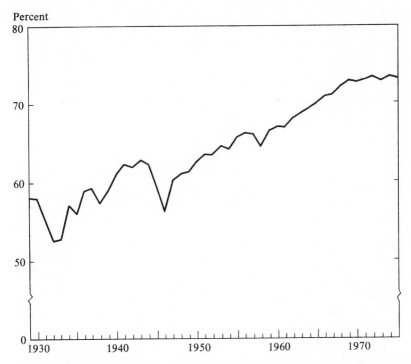

Percent

Source: Appendix table C-17.
a. Business income is national income originating in business enterprises.

The Evidence

The evidence on the incidence of the corporation income tax is inconclusive. The data do not permit a clear determination of the factors affecting price and wage decisions: different authors examining the same set of facts have come to diametrically opposite conclusions.

For the long run, unincorporated business has not grown at the expense of incorporated business. Corporations accounted for 58 percent of the national income originating in the business sector in 1929, 61 percent in 1948, and 73 percent in 1975 (figure 5-1). Much of the increase comes from the relative decline of industries, particularly farming, in which corporations are not important; but even in the rest of the economy, there is no indication of a shift away from the

Table 5-1. Rates of Return and Debt–Capital Ratio, Manufacturing Corporations, Selected Periods, 1927–71
Percent

Item	1927–29	1936–39	1953–56	1957–61	1964–67	1968–71
Return on equity[a]						
Before tax	8.8	7.8	18.4	14.1	17.8	13.6
After tax	7.8[b]	6.4[b]	9.2	7.3	11.0	8.0
Return on total capital[a,c]						
Before tax	8.7	7.3	15.7	12.2	14.9	11.6
After tax	7.8[b]	6.2[b]	8.2	6.8	9.7	7.8
Ratio of debt to total capital[d]	15.2	15.0	19.0	20.5	25.1	32.7
General corporation tax rate[e]	12.2	17.0	52.0	52.0	48.5	50.7

Source: Appendix table C-18.
a. Equity and debt capital are averages of book values for the beginning and end of the year.
b. Rates of return are slightly understated (probably by 0.3 percentage point or less) because no allowance has been made for the foreign tax credit.
c. Profits plus interest paid as a percentage of total capital.
d. End of year.
e. Statutory rate of federal corporation income tax applicable to large corporations (average of annual figures).

corporate form of organization. The advantages of doing business in the corporate form far outweigh whatever deterrent effects the corporation tax might have on corporate investment.

Beyond this, the data are conflicting. On the one hand, rates of return reported by corporations after tax were slightly higher in the 1950s and 1960s than in the late 1920s, when the corporation income tax was much lower. After-tax rates of return on equity capital in manufacturing were 7.8 percent in 1927–29, 9.2 percent in 1953–56, 11.0 percent in 1964–67, and 8.0 percent in 1968–71. On total capital (equity plus debt), the returns were 7.8 percent, 8.2 percent, 9.7 percent, and 7.8 percent, respectively (table 5-1). Before-tax rates of return were 50 to 100 percent higher in the 1950s and 1960s than in the late 1920s.

On the other hand, except for recession years, the share of property income before tax (profits, interest, and capital consumption allowances) in corporate gross product changed little over the same period (figure 5-2). Corporations have been able to increase their before-tax profits enough to avoid a reduction in the after-tax return, without increasing their share of income in the corporate sector. This suggests that corporations have increased rates of return before tax not by marking up prices or lowering wages, but by making more efficient

Figure 5-2. Property Income Share in Corporate Gross Product less Indirect Taxes, 1922–75[a]

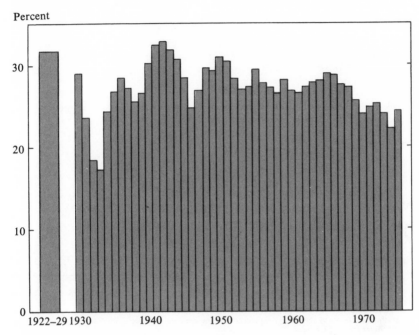

Percent

Sources: 1922–29, worksheets of the U.S. Department of Commerce; 1930–75, appendix table C-17.

a. Property income includes corporate profits before taxes with inventory valuation and capital consumption adjustments, capital consumption allowances with capital consumption adjustment, and net interest.

use of their capital. But what might have occurred without the tax is unknown, and its long-run effect remains unclear.

The burden of taxation borne by individuals is strikingly different under the different incidence assumptions. The tax is slightly regressive in the lower income classes and mildly progressive in the higher ones if as much as one-half is shifted forward to consumers in the form of higher prices and the remainder is borne by owners of capital in general. If the entire tax is borne by capital, progressivity increases in the higher income classes. The tax is even more progressive if it rests entirely on stockholders (table 5-2).

Economic Issues

The corporation income tax has been subject to a continuous barrage of criticism on economic grounds. The most critical issues have

Federal Tax Policy

Table 5-2. Effective Rates of the Corporation Income Tax, by Income Class, 1970
Income classes in thousands of dollars; tax rates in percent

Income class[a]	If half the tax is borne by owners of capital and half is shifted forward to consumers	If the tax is borne by owners of capital in general	If the tax is borne by stockholders
0–3	4.6	3.1	0.8
3–5	3.5	2.9	0.6
5–10	3.1	2.2	0.7
10–15	2.7	1.8	0.6
15–20	2.6	1.9	0.8
20–25	2.5	2.0	1.3
25–30	2.6	2.3	1.7
30–50	2.9	3.3	2.9
50–100	3.8	5.5	7.0
100–500	5.0	8.2	14.1
500–1,000	7.7	12.1	27.6
1,000 and over	8.6	13.4	32.0
All classes[b,c]	3.0	2.8	2.4

Source: Brookings 1970 MERGE data file.
a. Income is defined as money factor incomes plus transfer payments, accrued capital gains, and indirect business taxes.
b. The average burden of the corporation income tax is different under the different assumptions because the portion of it borne by the tax-exempt sector (and therefore not included in the household sector) varies.
c. Includes negative incomes.

been its effect on investment and saving, equity and debt finance, resource allocation, the built-in flexibility of the tax system, and the
balance of payments. The charges and countercharges reflect different assumptions about who bears the tax and the inherent difficulty
of separating the effect of taxation from other factors.

Investment and Saving

The corporation income tax may affect investment in either of two
ways: through investment incentives or through the availability of
funds for investment.

INVESTMENT INCENTIVES. New investments will be undertaken by
corporations if they promise to yield a satisfactory rate of return *after
tax*. The higher the corporation tax, the higher the pre-tax rate of
return must be to preserve the after-tax return. To remain equally
attractive, an investment that promised a 10 percent return in the
absence of the tax must yield a pre-tax rate of return of 19.2 percent

with a tax rate of 48 percent. If 10 percent after tax is required to induce investments, corporations will defer the construction of new facilities and the purchase of new equipment unless there are projects that yield 19.2 percent or more before tax. This is the process, discussed earlier, through which the tax exercises its effect on investment; it depends crucially on the assumption that the corporation income tax is not shifted in the short run and that the marginal investment is financed out of equity rather than debt capital.

Is it possible to detect any reduction in the rate of investment that can be attributed to the high corporation income tax? The answer is no, for two reasons. First, high tax rates were introduced during the Second World War, when wartime demands and support by government helped maintain investment at a high level. In the immediate postwar period, the rate of investment was extremely high because of the huge backlog of demand. Investment demand receded in the late 1950s, but this is attributed primarily to the slowdown in the rate of economic growth. The ratio of investment to the gross national product rose during the recovery of the early 1960s and stayed at high levels throughout the decade and the early 1970s.

Second, the proportion of corporate capital financed by debt has been increasing steadily since 1946 (see the section on equity and debt finance below). Since the corporation income tax is levied only on the residual after the payment of interest, the burden of the tax on investment has been declining.

Third, although the corporation tax rate has remained at a high level in recent years, part of its adverse effect on investment has been cushioned by substantial increases in investment allowances. Whereas straight-line depreciation was the rule before the Second World War, the tax law has allowed more liberal depreciation methods since 1954. In addition, as was noted above, a tax credit has been allowed, with some interruptions, for investment in machinery and equipment since 1962. The effect of these changes may be illustrated by the following figures: in 1954 the corporation tax amounted to 43.3 percent of corporation profits before tax; it was reduced to 34.7 percent in 1965 and to 29.9 percent in 1975 (table 5-3). This thirteen-point reduction in the effective rate occurred during a period when the general corporation income tax rate was reduced four percentage points (from 52 to 48 percent).

AVAILABILITY OF FUNDS. All other things being equal, the corpora-

Table 5-3. General Corporation Income Tax Rate and Effective Rate of the Federal Income Tax on Profits of U.S. Corporations, 1946–75

Year	Corporation income tax rate (percent)	Corporation profits before tax[a] (billions of dollars)	Federal corporation taxes[b]	
			Amount (billions of dollars)	Percent of profit before tax
1946	38	24.0	8.3	34.6
1947	38	30.4	10.6	34.9
1948	38	33.8	11.6	34.3
1949	38	27.5	9.4	34.2
1950	42	41.0	15.6	38.0
1951	50.75	42.5	18.9	44.5
1952	52	37.9	16.7	44.1
1953	52	39.5	17.6	44.6
1954	52	38.3	16.6	43.3
1955	52	49.3	20.8	42.2
1956	52	49.1	20.5	41.8
1957	52	47.6	19.9	41.8
1958	52	43.3	17.5	40.4
1959	52	52.1	21.6	41.5
1960	52	50.5	20.5	40.6
1961	52	50.6	20.7	40.9
1962	52	57.1	21.7	38.0
1963	52	61.4	23.7	38.6
1964	50	68.2	24.5	35.9
1965	48	79.5	27.6	34.7
1966	48	85.2	29.8	35.0
1967	48	82.6	28.0	33.9
1968	48[c]	91.2	30.4[c]	33.3[c]
1969	48[c]	89.8	29.8[c]	33.2[c]
1970	48[c]	76.3	26.5[c]	34.7[c]
1971	48	87.9	30.1	34.2
1972	48	105.4	33.4	31.7
1973	48	122.1	38.7	31.7
1974	48	125.9	40.0	31.8
1975	48	124.6	37.2	29.9

Source: U.S. Department of Commerce, Bureau of Economic Analysis. For method of calculation, see Emil M. Sunley, Jr., "Effective Corporate Tax Rates: Toward a More Precise Figure," *Tax Notes*, vol. 4 (March 1, 1976), pp. 15–24.

a. Profits before taxes as defined in the national income accounts plus accelerated depreciation over straight-line depreciation, taxable foreign income, dividends paid by corporations to noninsured private pension plans, and net gain from sales of property, less state and local income taxes, Federal Reserve Board earnings, and Subchapter S income.

b. Federal corporation income tax as defined in the national income accounts plus the foreign tax credit less the Federal Reserve Board payment to the U.S. Treasury less the temporary surcharge of 1968–70. Excludes excess profits taxes.

c. Excludes the temporary surcharge of 1968–70.

tion income tax may be expected to reduce the amount of corporate funds available for investment, but other factors have been operating to maintain internal corporate funds at a high level. The rise in the corporation tax has been accompanied by a much larger rise in high-bracket individual income tax rates. Recent studies indicate that these high individual rates and the preferential rate on capital gains have stimulated a higher rate of corporation retentions (that is, lower dividend pay-out rates) than in the 1920s. In addition, the generous depreciation allowances enacted in recent years have enabled corporations to set aside large amounts for investment purposes.

Since the end of the Second World War, dividends have been close to 25 percent of the cash flow of corporations (appendix table C-17). This is considerably lower than the rate in the late 1920s. As a result of the lower dividend rates and higher depreciation allowances, gross corporate saving has kept pace with the growth of the economy. From 1929 to 1975 gross national product increased 1,366 percent, while gross corporate saving increased 1,383 percent. During the large upswing in investment in the first half of the 1960s, internal sources of funds generally exceeded plant and equipment expenditures of corporations in each year; in the last half of the decade and in the 1970s, internal funds were insufficient to finance all corporate investment (appendix table C-19). This was due in part to the high level of investment demand and to a decline in the rate of corporate profits. After the burst of inflation beginning in 1973, corporation taxes were relatively high because profits were inflated by inventory gains, but the major reason for the decline in investment in 1974 and 1975 was the reduced level of demand rather than the corporation tax. Thus the evidence suggests that the supply of corporate funds has not been impaired by the corporation income tax.

Equity and Debt Finance

Corporations are allowed to deduct from taxable income interest payments on borrowed capital, but there is no corresponding deduction for dividends paid out to stockholders in return for the use of their funds as equity capital. At the present 48 percent tax rate, a corporation must earn $1.92 before tax to be able to pay $1 in dividend, but it needs to earn only $1 to pay $1 of interest. This asymmetry makes the cost of equity more "expensive" for the corporation than an equal amount of borrowed capital.

Large corporations borrow long-term capital funds at interest rates ranging from 6 to 10 percent. With stocks selling at ten to twenty times net earnings, corporate earnings *after* tax on equity capital range between 5 and 10 percent. Under these conditions, the earnings rate before tax (at the rate of 1.92:1) must range between 9.6 and 19.2 percent to prevent equity financing from reducing the rate of return. It is in this sense that equity capital costs more than borrowed capital.

Financial experts discourage large amounts of debt financing by corporations. Debt makes good business sense if there is a safe margin for paying fixed interest charges. But business firms may be tightly squeezed when business falls off, and the margin will evaporate rapidly. At such times, defaults on interest and principal payments and bankruptcies begin to occur. Even though borrowed capital may increase returns to stockholders, corporations try to finance a major share of their capital requirements through equity capital (mainly retained earnings) to avoid these risks.

The available data suggest that these reasons for caution have tended to restrain the use of borrowed capital despite its lower cost. However, the ratio of debt to total capital rose gradually after the war and increased rapidly during the investment boom and the heightened inflation expectations of the 1960s and the early 1970s. The ratio for manufacturing corporations was about 15 percent in 1927–29, 20 percent in 1957–61, 25 percent in 1964–67, and 33 percent in 1968–71 (table 5-1).

Resource Allocation

If the corporation income tax is not shifted in the short run, it becomes in effect a special tax on corporate capital. This does not necessarily mean that the tax permanently reduces rates of return on capital in the corporate sector. Capital may flow out of the taxed sector into the untaxed sectors, and rates of return will tend to equalize. In the process, the allocation of capital between corporate and noncorporate business will be altered from the pattern that would have prevailed in the absence of the tax.

How much capital, if any, has left the corporate sector as a result of the corporation income tax is not known. It is possible that the corporate form of doing business is so advantageous for nontax reasons that, for the most part, capital remains in the corporate sector despite the tax. To the extent that corporate investment is financed by debt, the corporation income tax does not affect investment incentives because interest on debt is deductible as a business expense. In addition, the preferential treatment of capital gains under the individual income tax provides an offsetting incentive to invest in the securities of corporations that retain earnings for reinvestment in the business. These earnings show up as increases in the price of common stock rather than as regular income. In any case, the corporate sector has been getting larger, both relatively and absolutely, for several decades (figure 5-1 and appendix table C-17). The discouragement of investment in the corporate form induced by the tax system, if any, must have been comparatively small.

Distortions may also take place if the tax is shifted in the short run. If prices increase in response to an increase in the tax, they rise in proportion to the use of corporate equity capital in the various industries. Consumers will buy fewer goods and services produced by industries using a great deal of corporate capital because the prices of these products have risen most, and will buy more goods and services produced by industries with less corporate capital. Within the corporate sector, profits will fall in the "capital-intensive" industries as a result of the decline in sales and will rise in the "labor-intensive" industries. In the end, not only will less capital be attracted to the corporate sector, but less will be attracted to the capital-intensive industries in that sector, and the economy will suffer a loss in efficiency as a result. The quantitative effect of this process is heavily dependent, of course, on the degree to which the noncorporate form of doing business can be substituted for the corporate form and production can be transferred from capital-intensive to labor-intensive industries. As in the nonshifting case, even a shifted corporate tax would tend to distort the composition of output, but in the aggregate this effect too is probably small.

Built-in Flexibility

Receipts from the corporation income tax are volatile over the business cycle because corporate profits rise and fall more sharply than other incomes. However, this characteristic does not necessarily qualify the tax as an effective built-in stabilizer. To qualify, a tax must automatically moderate the changes in consumer disposable income or reduce fluctuations in investment. When profits fall, dividends are

Federal Tax Policy

Table 5-4. Changes in Real Gross National Product and Disposable Personal Income in Six Postwar Recessions

Billions of 1972 dollars

Pre-recession peak[a]	*Recession trough*[a]	*Gross national product*[b]	*Federal receipts*[b]	*Federal corporation tax*[b]	*Undistributed corporate profits*[b]	*Disposable personal income*[b]
1948:4	1949:2	−7.0	−5.5	−4.0	−7.5	−3.9
1953:2	1954:2	−20.6	−16.8	−8.5	−3.0	−3.6
1957:3	1958:1	−22.2	−10.7	−7.0	−8.0	−1.7
1960:1	1960:4	−8.8	−6.0	−7.0	−7.0	4.1
1969:3	1970:4	−12.0	−20.5	−8.3	−8.9	22.4
1973:4	1975:1	−81.5	−13.5	−11.5	−16.9	−37.9

Source: *Survey of Current Business.*
a. As measured by real GNP.
b. Current dollar magnitudes deflated by the GNP deflator.

apt to be maintained, but this appears to be due largely to the dividend policy of corporations rather than to the reduction in tax paid by corporations. Similarly, corporate investments are determined largely by current and prospective sales volume and rates of return, although the reduced tax liability may have an effect through its impact on cash flow. Thus the corporation income tax is not regarded as one of the significant built-in stabilizers, despite its heavy contribution to the large swings in federal surpluses and deficits during business cycles.

The more important stabilizing feature of the corporate sector is the policy of cutting into saving rather than reducing dividends when economic activity declines. A reduction in retained corporate earnings prevents a corresponding decline in disposable personal income, thus maintaining spending on the part of consumers. Quantitatively, corporate saving is second only to the federal tax structure as a built-in stabilizer. In four of the six recessions following the Second World War, undistributed profits of corporations declined about as much as or more than federal receipts; in the last recession, undistributed profits fell $16.9 billion while total federal receipts declined $13.5 billion (table 5-4). Largely because of the decline in corporate saving and federal receipts, real disposable personal income rose in the 1960–61 and 1969–70 recessions and declined much less than the real gross national product in the other four recessions since the end of World War II.

Balance of Payments

During the 1950s and 1960s the corporation income tax figured prominently in discussions of ways to improve the U.S. balance of payments. Many countries have a general, broad-based commodity tax, which is rebated on exports, and firms in these countries can sell goods abroad at prices below those charged their domestic customers. Imports are subject to a compensating tax. American exporters, on the other hand, are not subject to a federal consumption tax; they receive no refund for taxes on exports and cannot cut their prices in foreign markets. It was contended that the United States should, for competitive reasons, reduce the corporation income tax, enact a value added tax (see chapter 6) as a substitute, and rebate the value added tax on exports.

Two major questions are involved in this issue. The first relates to the effects of the two taxes on prices; the second, to the nature of the international monetary system. Under fixed exchange rates, if the corporation income tax is not shifted, substitution of a value added tax with a rebate for exports would accomplish little. The value added tax would raise prices on all goods and services, and the rebate would return export prices to their former level. Trade in commodities produced by U.S. firms would not change because their prices in international markets would remain unchanged. On the other hand, if the corporation tax were shifted and exchange rates were fixed, the switch to a value added tax would keep domestic prices the same as before, but export prices would decline by the amount of the rebate. Prices of U.S. goods in foreign markets would be lower, and the trade balance would improve (if the demands for goods produced in the United States were price elastic; that is, if foreign customers actually increased their total expenditures on U.S. goods as prices were reduced).

To the extent that the corporation income tax is not shifted in the form of higher prices, it reduces the rate of return to investment in this country. Removal of the corporation income tax and substitution of a value added tax that would bear more or less equally on all factors of production would raise the net yield to capital. Capital would be attracted from abroad and the outflow of capital from the United States would be discouraged. Over the long run, the larger investment would increase the productivity and better the competitive position of U.S. industry, leading to an improvement in the balance of payments.

Since views on corporation tax shifting are divided, no consensus was reached on these matters. When the exchange rate of the dollar was fixed, some improvement in the balance of payments on either trade or capital account might have been expected if a value added tax had been substituted for the corporation income tax, but the improvement would probably have been small because the spread in effective corporation tax rates between the United States and most developed countries was, and remains, small (appendix table C-5).

The analysis is different in a world where countries rely on flexibility in exchange rates to adjust external imbalances; this has been the case since 1973. When exchange rates are free to find their own levels in international financial markets, changes in tax rates or in the taxes used have little lasting effect on the competitiveness of the goods manufactured by a single country or its attractiveness as a place to invest. For example, if an unshifted corporation income tax were eliminated in the United States, rates of return would increase and the country would become temporarily more attractive to foreign investors. But the inflow of funds from abroad would raise the value of the dollar and make U.S. exports of goods less competitive in world markets. Ultimately, the advantage of eliminating the corporation income tax would be wiped out. Similarly, with a shifted corporation tax, the price of U.S. exports would decline if the tax were eliminated, but the increased trade balance would also raise the value of the dollar, again make U.S. products more expensive on world markets, and soon wipe out the advantage gained by eliminating the corporation tax. In effect, floating exchange rates (without intervention to moderate fluctuations) would permit countries to decide what type of tax structure they wish to have for domestic reasons, without being constrained by fear of foreign repercussions.

Structural Features

The structural features of the corporation income tax are highly technical and therefore rarely understood by the average taxpayer. The major features are (1) allowances for capital consumption; (2) depletion and other allowances for the mineral industries; (3) multiple incorporations to secure multiple tax exemptions; (4) financial institutions; (5) tax-exempt organizations; (6) foreign and export income; and (7) recognition of gain or loss on intercorporate asset transfers and on asset distributions to stockholders. (The first, second, and sixth features also apply to individual income taxation, but they are treated here because their revenue and economic implications are much more important in the corporation income tax.) The purpose of this discussion is to show how these technical features affect particular firms and industries, the economy as a whole, and the equity and yield of the corporation income tax.

Capital Consumption Allowances

The law has always permitted "a reasonable allowance for the exhaustion, wear and tear" of capital as a deduction for depreciation. Such a deduction is necessary to avoid taxing capital rather than income. In addition, liberalized capital consumption allowances are proposed as devices to stimulate investment.

DEPRECIATION. The annual deduction for depreciation is determined by spreading the cost of the depreciable asset over its "service life." Before 1954 the law and regulations were relatively strict, requiring fairly exact estimates of the period of use. Asset costs were amortized primarily by the "straight-line" method, which assumes a uniform amount of depreciation each year. The declining-balance method at 1.5 times the straight-line rate, while not specifically authorized by statute, was also permitted but seldom used. In 1954 the law was amended to permit the use of the declining-balance method for new property with an annual depreciation rate twice the straight-line rate or the sum-of-years-digits method.

The differences between the three methods are illustrated for a $1,000 asset with a service life of ten years in table 5-5. The straight-line method provides a uniform annual depreciation deduction of $100 a year. The declining-balance method permits the taxpayer to use a *rate* of depreciation and to apply this rate to the undepreciated amount each year. In the first year, the double declining-balance method provides a 20 percent allowance, or $200, leaving $800 undepreciated. In the second year, the 20 percent is applied to $800, giving an allowance of $160, and so on. (The taxpayer is permitted to switch to straight-line depreciation at any time; as is shown in the example, this is profitable beginning in the seventh year.) Under the sum-of-years-digits method, the fraction allowed as depreciation each

Table 5-5. Three Methods of Depreciation for a Ten-Year, $1,000 Asset
Dollars

	Depreciation		
Year	Straight-line	Double declining-balance	Sum-of-years-digits
1	100	200	182
2	100	160	164
3	100	128	145
4	100	102	127
5	100	82	109
6	100	66	91
7	100	65.5	73
8	100	65.5	55
9	100	65.5	36
10	100	65.5	18
Total	1,000	1,000	1,000
Present value at 8 percent			
Depreciation allowances	671	733	748
Tax value of depreciation allowances[a]	322	352	359

a. At a tax rate of 48 percent.

year is computed by dividing the number of years still remaining by the sum of years in the useful life. With a ten-year asset, the sum of the years is 55 (10 + 9 + 8 ... + 2 + 1), so that the depreciation allowance is ten fifty-fifths in the first year, nine fifty-fifths in the second year, and so on until it reaches one fifty-fifth in the tenth year.

As table 5-5 shows, the two accelerated depreciation methods concentrate a larger percentage of the deductions in the early years. Under straight-line depreciation, half the original cost of a ten-year asset is written off in the first five years, compared with 67 percent under the double declining-balance method and 73 percent under the sum-of-years-digits method. A useful way of comparing the value of the three methods is shown in the last line of the table. At a corporation income tax rate of 48 percent, the present value at the time of investment of the tax savings from the depreciation deductions (assuming an 8 percent interest rate) is $322 for straight-line depreciation, $352 for double declining-balance depreciation, and $359 for sum-of-years-digits depreciation. In relation to the original cost, the tax saving amounts to 3 percent under the declining-balance method and 3.7 percent under the sum-of-years-digits method.

SERVICE LIVES. A small pamphlet containing narrative material on useful lives for purposes of depreciation calculations was first published by the Bureau of Internal Revenue in 1920. Numerical useful lives for about 5,000 separate items were published in *Bulletin F* in 1942. *Bulletin F* remained substantially unchanged until 1962, when the Internal Revenue Service issued a new set of depreciation rules, Revenue Procedure 62-21, in a pamphlet titled *Depreciation Guidelines and Rules*. The new procedure assigned guideline lives to much broader classes of assets, numbering less than one hundred. These guidelines reduced the write-off period in manufacturing industries about 15 percent below those used earlier.

A second innovation made in the 1962 revenue procedure was a set of rules governing the determination of depreciation allowances, which was called the "reserve ratio test." This test required taxpayers to gear depreciation allowances to actual experience in replacing facilities. (The reserve ratio was the ratio of depreciation actually taken to the cost of the asset or group of assets in a depreciation account.) Taxpayers who replaced assets more frequently than was implied by the guideline lives found that their reserve ratios were lower than the ratio computed by the Internal Revenue Service. In such cases, they were allowed to shorten the service lives of their assets. On the other hand, taxpayers who used assets for periods longer than those implied by the guideline lives were required to lengthen service lives. The test was to go into effect three years after the adoption of the guideline lives, but the effective date was further delayed in 1965.

Many businessmen and accountants believed that the reserve ratio test was inequitable and unworkable; they urged that the guideline lives be permitted as a matter of right without requiring use of the test. On the other hand, the test protected both the equity and the yield of the corporation income tax. Nevertheless, the unpopularity of the reverse ratio test led to its discontinuation in 1971 (and it was never actually put into effect because of generous transition rules provided in 1962 and 1965). Instead, on the recommendation of the Treasury Department, Congress authorized the use of an "asset depreciation range" system that permits taxpayers to use service lives for machinery and equipment that are within 20 percent (above or below) of the 1962 guideline averages. Most firms use the lower option to write off their investments at a faster rate. The cost of this system is higher than the published guideline lives by an estimated $1.8 billion in fiscal year 1977.

In addition to the asset depreciation range system, which may be used for investment generally, the tax law permits five-year straight-line depreciation for investments in specific assets that are regarded as having high social priority. The 1969 law authorized the use of this fast write-off for pollution control activities, coal mine safety equipment, railroad rolling stock, and rehabilitation expenditures for low-income housing. This provision, which was scheduled to expire in five years, was extended to the end of 1977 for low-income housing rehabilitation (up to $20,000 per dwelling unit) and was made permanent for pollution-control equipment. Firms electing the fast write-off option are required to forgo the use of the investment credit, except that one-half the credit is allowed for pollution-control equipment beginning in 1977.

INVESTMENT CREDIT. The investment tax credit has been in effect since January 1, 1962 (except for two short periods). Under this provision, business firms are permitted to deduct as a credit against their tax 10 percent of the amount of new investment with service lives of seven years or more (5 percent for ships used in U.S. waters that are financed from previously earned net income set aside in a tax-free construction fund). One-third of the full credit is allowed for assets with service lives of three to four years and two-thirds for those with service lives of five to six years. Qualified investments include all new tangible personal property and up to $100,000 of used property, and exclude all buildings except research and certain storage or special purpose facilities. The credit is allowed to offset the first $25,000 of tax liability and 50 percent of the tax above $25,000 (100 percent for utilities in 1975 and 1976 and for railroads and airlines in 1977 and 1978, phasing down by 10 percent a year until it returns to the regular 50 percent in 1981 for utilities and in 1983 for railroads and airlines). Unused credits may be carried back for three years and forward for seven. The 10 percent credit is scheduled to be reduced to 7 percent at the end of 1980.

The 1962 law required deduction of the credit from the cost of the asset before computing depreciation for tax purposes. However, this requirement complicated accounting for the credit and reduced its incentive effects, and it was eliminated in the 1964 act. Taxpayers now have the benefit of the full credit plus the liberalized depreciation allowances adopted in 1954, 1962, 1965, and 1971. In fiscal 1977 the revenue cost of the credit is expected to be $9.1 billion.

The effect of an investment credit is similar to that of an increase in the depreciation allowances above 100 percent of the cost of the asset. For corporations subject to the 48 percent rate, the same results could be achieved by allowing the taxpayer to deduct an additional 20.8 percent in the first year. But a credit has two virtues. First, it is simpler to understand and does not interefere with depreciation accounting. Second, it provides the same credit for all taxpayers regardless of their marginal rate. (It will be recalled that individuals are subject to rates up to 70 percent; corporations are subject to only a 20 percent rate on profits below $25,000 and 22 percent on profits of $25,000 to $50,000.)

Even though the credit seems small, it provides a sizable incentive for new investment (assuming that the corporation income tax is not shifted to higher prices). In effect, the credit reduces the cost of the asset and hence increases the rate of return. For example, for an investment yielding 10 percent after straight-line depreciation and after the 48 percent corporation income tax, the credit increases the rate of return to 12.2 percent for an asset with a ten-year life, 11.7 percent for a fifteen-year life, and 11.4 percent for a twenty-year life. To increase the rates of return by equivalent amounts would require reductions in the 48 percent corporate tax rate of 13.2, 10.4, and 8.9 percentage points, respectively.

COMBINED EFFECT OF INCREASED CAPITAL CONSUMPTION ALLOWANCES. It has already been noted that the liberalization of capital consumption allowances beginning in 1954 reduced the effective rate of the corporation income tax, even though the tax rate remained constant through 1963 (table 5-3). Another measure of the benefits of the various provisions is given in figure 5-3, which shows their effects on after-tax rates of return for assets with ten-, fifteen-, and twenty-year service lives if the assets yield 10 percent on a straight-line depreciation basis.

The combined effect is dramatic in all three cases. The rate of return is increased by double declining balance depreciation, asset depreciation range, and a 10 percent investment credit to 14.7 percent for a ten-year asset, 13.2 percent for a fifteen-year asset, and 12.7 percent for a twenty-year asset. The investment credit accounts for about half of the increase in rates of return. To reproduce the

150   *Federal Tax Policy*

Figure 5-3. Effect of Various Investment Allowances on the Rate of Return of Assets Yielding 10 Percent[a]

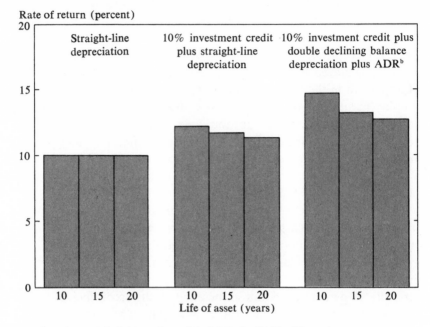

Rate of return (percent)

| Straight-line depreciation | 10% investment credit plus straight-line depreciation | 10% investment credit plus double declining balance depreciation plus ADR[b] |

Life of asset (years)

a. Assuming a constant stream of annual receipts during the life of the asset.
b. Asset depreciation range system.

rates of return through rate reductions alone, it would be necessary to reduce the corporation tax rate by 28.4, 20.0, and 17.5 percentage points, respectively.

When the investment credit was first introduced, there was substantial resistance on equity grounds to liberalizing allowances for investment. But the attitude toward liberalization changed in the early 1960s, when the government began using its fiscal powers aggressively to promote a rapid rate of economic growth. The widespread use of accelerated depreciation in other countries also made it more acceptable in the United States. Today, there is still continued disagreement about the merits of the reserve ratio test. Many believe that, with the adoption of the asset depreciation range, depreciation allowances are now too generous.

The investment credit also encountered resistance before it was finally enacted—even from businessmen who were to benefit from the new provision. While many still oppose the credit on equity grounds, few deny its effectiveness as a method of stimulating investment.

The credit was originally enacted as a permanent feature of the tax system, but the rate of the credit could be raised, lowered, or eliminated entirely as a stabilization measure. The investment credit was suspended from October 10, 1966, to March 9, 1967, and from April 19, 1969, to August 15, 1971, to counteract inflationary pressures, but it was increased to 10 percent in 1975 to help stimulate economic recovery.

Allowances for the Mineral Industries

In computing their taxable income, firms engaged in extracting oil and gas and other minerals from the ground are entitled to a "depletion" allowance for exhaustion of the mineral deposit, just as other firms are entitled to a depreciation allowance for wear and tear on the capital they use.

Although there is little distinction in theory between depletion and depreciation, there are substantial differences in practice. First, it is difficult to estimate what proportion of a mineral deposit has been used up. Second, the value of a mineral deposit may be substantially larger than the amount invested in discovering and developing it. Some argue that depletion allowances should be based on the higher "discovery value" of the deposit, rather than on the amount invested. Others argue that there is no reason to treat minerals differently from other investments and that only the original investment in bringing the mine or oil field into production should be amortized.

Present allowances for the mineral industries are more generous than depreciation allowances. Allowances in excess of depletion based on costs were first permitted in 1918 in the form of *discovery depletion* to stimulate exploration for war purposes and to reduce the taxes of small-scale prospectors who often made discoveries after years of fruitless searching. (The 1918 act was not actually passed until after the war was over.) Discovery value proved difficult to estimate, and in 1926 Congress permitted the use of *percentage depletion* for oil and gas properties. Under percentage depletion, taxpayers deduct a fixed percentage of receipts from sales as a depletion allowance, regardless of the amount invested. The percentage depletion deduction for gas and oil, which was 27.5 percent from 1926 to 1969 and 22 percent from 1969 to 1975, has been eliminated entirely for the major oil companies and is being gradually reduced for unintegrated small producers to 15 percent on the first 1,000 barrels of oil or 6 million cubic feet of gas a day by 1984. Beginning in 1932, percentage depletion was extended to other products taken from the ground, at percentages ranging from 22 for sulfur, uranium, and other rare metals to 5 for gravel, sand, peat, clay used in the manufacture of tile, and pumice. In all industries, firms must use *cost depletion* (depletion based on the actual cost of the property) if it is higher than percentage depletion. Percentage depletion cannot reduce the net income from the property (computed before taking the depletion allowance) by more than 50 percent.

In addition to depletion, an immediate write-off is permitted for certain capital costs incurred in intangible drilling expenses and exploration and development without limit for oil and gas and other minerals. This treatment of expenses does not reduce percentage depletion, so a double deduction is allowed for the same capital investment. Studies made over the years by the Treasury Department indicate that the annual depletion deductions greatly exceed the deduction computed on the basis of the original investment (after allowance for depletion). The tax benefits of these special provisions will be $2.6 billion in fiscal year 1977—$1.6 billion from percentage depletion and $1.0 billion from the expensing of intangible drilling costs and exploration and development costs.

This special treatment is justified by its proponents on several grounds: there are unusual risks in oil and gas exploration and development; national defense requires continuous exploration and development; the allowances are needed to finance new discoveries; and the present provisions serve as a strong impetus for taxpayers who discover new sources of oil and gas to operate these properties rather than to sell them for the preferential capital gains rates.

On the other hand, the risks in these industries could be satisfactorily handled by the general deductibility of losses; the industries are no more strategic from a national defense standpoint than many other industries; and the large revenue cost of the benefits requires the imposition of higher tax rates than would otherwise be necessary to raise a given amount of revenue, thus penalizing other taxpayers. Moreover, the provisions lead to overinvestment in the favored industries and hence seriously distort the allocation of resources.

The allowances for oil and gas and other minerals have been the subject of acrimonious debate for many years. In 1950 President Truman recommended the reduction of percentage depletion to a maximum of 15 percent. Congress took no action and in later years extended percentage depletion to other minerals and also raised percentage depletion rates. Bills were introduced frequently to curtail the allowances, but only minor changes were made until 1969, when the depletion allowance for oil and gas was reduced to 22 percent, and "excess" depletion was made subject to the minimum tax beginning in 1970. In 1975 percentage depletion was eliminated for the major oil and gas producers. In 1976 intangible drilling expenses for oil and gas in excess of the deductions that would be made if they were capitalized were included in the base of the minimum tax.

Multiple Surtax Exemptions

The surtax exemption, which was intended to help small corporations, provided a strong monetary incentive for larger business firms to form multiple corporations. Since incorporation is relatively inexpensive, many firms took the opportunity to spin off a large number of subsidiaries. In some instances, several hundred corporations were involved, and the tax savings were large.

There are valid business reasons for incorporating different units of a business enterprise, but this hardly justified treating each unit for tax purposes as if it were an independent small business. Moreover, the income tax rules often led to uneconomic corporate arrangements and discriminated against firms and industries in which multiple corporations are impractical. Chain stores, personal finance companies, motion pictures, and other businesses involving separate outlets were particularly easy to break up into separate corporations. As a consequence, the reduced rate for the first $25,000 of profits ($50,000 after 1974) conveyed unintended benefits to many medium-sized and large businesses.

After several attempts, Congress finally eliminated the advantage of multiple surtax exemptions for affiliated groups in 1969. Such groups of corporations are now limited to one surtax exemption and are not taxed on intergroup dividends. These amendments have effectively curbed abuses in this area.

The 1964 act eliminated the 2 percent penalty tax previously paid by a group of affiliated corporations for the privilege of filing a consolidated return. Consolidated reporting of income results in a more meaningful and fair representation of taxable income than does unconsolidated reporting. Consolidation also has the advantage of providing offsets for losses of one corporation against the gains of other members of the group and of eliminating the tax on intercompany dividends (15 percent of which are included in taxable income). Now that the rules against multiple corporations have been tightened to prevent abuses of the surtax exemption, the dividend tax could be eliminated entirely.

Financial Institutions

Financial institutions have always presented a difficult problem for income taxation because many of them are organized on a mutual basis. At one time, mutuals were completely exempt from tax on the theory that they belonged to their members and were not corporations in any ordinary sense. But with the growth in number and size of mutuals, it became increasingly evident that the mutual status was not sufficient reason for exempting them from taxation. Attempts have been made to tax financial institutions—whether they organize as mutuals or not—like other corporations, but many observers feel that they are still not paying their fair share of the tax burden. Since the problems depend on the type of business conducted, it is necessary to discuss separately the thrift institutions (mutual savings banks and savings and loan associations), life insurance companies, fire and casualty insurance companies, and commercial banks.

THRIFT INSTITUTIONS. Mutual savings banks and savings and loan associations were made subject to the corporation income tax by the Revenue Act of 1951, which required them to pay the regular corporation income tax rate on retained earnings exceeding allocations to reserves. Payments of interest to depositors were allowed as a deductible expense, as in the case of ordinary commercial banks. However, the law permitted thrift institutions to build a reserve for bad debts of up to 12 percent of their deposits, while the regulations permitted commercial banks to set aside a reserve of three times their annual loss experience over a twenty-year period (less than 3 percent on the average). With steady growth in deposits, the amounts covered by the 12 percent ceiling increased steadily, and the result was that savings banks and building and loan associations paid very little tax.

The ineffectiveness of the 1951 law was partly remedied by a 1962 amendment that, in effect, allowed thrift institutions to add to their reserves for bad debts an amount equal to 60 percent of their taxable income (or an amount equal to actual loss experience). While this fell far short of full taxation, the tax paid by savings and loan associations and mutual savings banks increased from $6.4 million in 1960 to $184 million in 1968. The 1969 act eliminated the 3 percent of assets rule and gradually lowered the deduction for additions to reserves from a maximum of 60 percent to 40 percent of taxable income over the period 1970–79. By 1971 the tax paid by savings and loan associations had increased to $289 million.

LIFE INSURANCE COMPANIES. The problem in life insurance company taxation also concerns the method of computing appropriate reserves. The intention of the law is to exempt that part of their income judged necessary to meet contractual obligations to policyholders. Methods of achieving this objective have been considered periodically by Congress over the past fifty-five years.

Initially, life insurance companies were taxed as ordinary corporations, but this method was abandoned because of the administrative difficulties of establishing deductions for additions to reserves. Beginning in 1921, a deduction of a specified percentage of legal reserves (4 percent from 1921 to 1931 and 3.75 percent from 1932 to 1941) was permitted. Because of this high allowance, insurance companies paid practically no tax during the 1930s, and the law was again amended in 1942. This time they were allowed a tax credit for the amount presumed to be needed to meet policy commitments. The credit was a flat percentage of net investment income, determined by the secretary of the treasury on the basis of a formula that yielded high reserve figures for the industry when interest rates declined during the war. Again, the life insurance companies paid virtually no tax.

A new formula for taxing the industry was enacted as stopgap legislation in 1951. Life insurance companies were subjected to a tax of 6.5 percent on their net investment income (3.75 percent on the first $200,000) in lieu of the regular corporation income tax. This rate was equivalent to the 52 percent tax, on the assumption that the industry required 87.5 percent of its investment income for policy reserves.

The present method of taxing life insurance companies was enacted in 1959, effective for 1958 incomes. The theory is that life insurance companies should be taxed not only on their net investment income but also on the "underwriting" profits resulting from the fact that the life expectancy tables on which premiums are based usually understate actual life expectancies. To reach such profits, the 1959 law required companies to report premium as well as investment income and allowed deductions for benefit payments, insurance losses, and other ordinary business expenses. Additions to reserves were also allowed, but were to be computed on the basis of each company's needs and experience.

The 1959 law had a number of technical provisions that did not become fully applicable until 1961. Tax payments of life insurance companies rose from $294 million in 1957, the year before the 1959 law became effective, to $529 million in 1960. Most of this increase was due to the new method of taxation, which has remained unchanged since 1961. Tax payments by the industry rose to $2.1 billion in 1973, reflecting the tremendous growth of life insurance in this country.

FIRE AND CASUALTY INSURANCE COMPANIES. Stock companies selling fire and casualty insurance have long been taxed on both their investment and underwriting profits (as life insurance companies have been taxed since 1958). Between 1942 and 1962, however, mutual fire and casualty insurance companies paid tax under special formulas that excluded underwriting profits. In 1963 underwriting profits were included in the formula for these companies, but they were allowed to set up a deferred income account which, in effect, permanently defers one-eighth of their underwriting gains from taxation and also defers taxation of another large portion of their underwriting gains for five years.

COMMERCIAL BANKS. Commercial banks are regarded as ordinary business corporations for tax purposes and are subject to tax on their profits, after allowing for payment of interest on their deposits. One peculiarity of their taxation in the past was the treatment of capital gains and losses. Long-term capital gains of commercial banks were taxed at a maximum rate of 25 percent, as were the gains of ordinary business corporations. Capital losses of commercial banks, however, were deductible in full not only against capital gains but also against ordinary income. This treatment was justified on the grounds that dealings in securities are part of normal business operations in commercial banking and losses should therefore be treated as ordinary losses. By this reasoning, capital gains from the sale of bonds should have been regarded as ordinary income and subjected to the ordinary corporation income tax rate. The 1969 legislation finally corrected this asymmetrical treatment, and such gains are now treated as ordinary income.

Commercial banks were also allowed to maintain a reserve for bad debts that was about three times their actual loss experience. Before 1969 the allowable reserve was set by regulation at 2.4 percent of outstanding loans. The 1969 law reduced this percentage to 1.8 in 1970–75, 1.2 in 1976–81, and 0.6 in 1982–87. Beginning in 1988, the actual loss experience for the current and the preceding five years will be the only criterion.

Another feature of the corporation tax that is helpful to commercial banks is that expenses are fully deductible from taxable income, even though part of the expenses are incurred to earn tax-exempt income. Commercial banks invest heavily in tax-exempt municipal securities and are now allowed to deduct all the interest they pay rather than allocating it between taxable and tax-exempt income.

Tax-Exempt Organizations

The federal tax law exempts a variety of nonprofit organizations, including religious, charitable, educational, and fraternal organizations. Favorable tax treatment for these organizations dates from a time when the federal government assumed little responsibility for relief and welfare activities and the value of the tax exemption was relatively small. Today, the federal government has substantial responsibility for public assistance, and the revenue loss from the exemptions has become significant.

The tax status of these organizations might never have been altered had they remained small and not entered into business and public affairs. But numerous complaints were made against tax-exempt organizations for unfair competition and for involvement in public activities that seem political in nature to those who disapprove of them. As a result, the permissible activities of private foundations have been spelled out in some detail in the Internal Revenue Code, and the business income of all exempt organizations has been made taxable under the corporation income tax, even though they are still "exempt" under the Internal Revenue Code. The special taxes apply to unrelated business income, rental income from "lease-back" arrangements, investment income of private foundations, and the income of cooperatives.

UNRELATED BUSINESS INCOME. The major change in the tax status of exempt organizations was made in 1950, when Congress decided to tax their "unrelated business income." This is defined as income from a business that is not substantially related to carrying out charitable, educational, or other exempt purposes. Unrelated business income is subject to the regular corporation income tax rates; the Tax Reform Act of 1969 eliminated the original exemption of $1,000 and extended coverage to all exempt organizations except government agencies (other than publicly supported colleges and universities).

LEASE-BACK ARRANGEMENTS. Exempt organizations often purchased property from private business firms with borrowed funds and then leased the property back to the same firms. In some cases, the original owners were given lower rentals or were paid a higher price for the property than going market rates. Even when the transaction was at arm's length, the exempt organization was trading on its tax exemption to accumulate property. To solve these problems, the 1950 legislation defined unrelated business income to include rental income from leased property owned by tax-exempt organizations to the extent that the ownership was financed by borrowed funds. The 1969 legislation extended the definition still further to include rental income for property held less than five years. These changes permit tax-exempt organizations to use their funds for investment in real estate, but make it difficult for them to use their exempt status as a means of acquiring property.

PRIVATE FOUNDATIONS. Private foundations are defined as tax-exempt organizations other than (a) religious, charitable, and educational institutions and (b) organizations that derive more than one-third of their income from contributions and less than one-third from investment income. These foundations were made subject to a new tax on investment income and to a variety of restrictions under the 1969 legislation; the tax is 4 percent of net investment income. Foundations are also required to distribute all their income each year or 5 percent of the value of their assets, whichever is greater; financial or "self-dealing" transactions between a foundation and persons with a direct or indirect interest in the foundation ("disqualified persons") or government officials are prohibited; and the amount of stock a foundation and disqualified persons may hold in any business enterprise is limited. These provisions are supported by a variety of sanctions for noncompliance.

COOPERATIVES. Farm, irrigation, and telephone cooperatives and like organizations are exempt from income tax. Other nonfinancial cooperatives are taxable. However, all cooperatives are allowed to deduct from their income amounts paid as "patronage dividends" to their patrons on the ground that they represent readjustments in prices initially charged patrons.

Originally, patronage dividends were deductible even if distributed in noncash form ("written notices of allocation"). The deductibility of noncash patronage dividends enabled cooperatives to expand from earnings not taxed at the cooperative level. Furthermore, patrons often were not taxed on such dividends until they were redeemed because the written allocations had no fair market value.

The law was revised beginning with the income year 1963. Earnings of taxable cooperatives distributed as written notices of allocation cannot now be deducted by the cooperatives unless at least 20 percent of the face amount of the allocation is in cash. Deductibility of noncash allocations is further limited to those that the patron, at his option, can redeem in cash for the face amount within ninety days of the payment thereof or that the patron has consented to include at face value in his or her income in accordance with the federal income tax laws. Thus taxable cooperatives may, in effect, retain 80 percent of their earnings by the use of noncash patronage dividends. At the same time, patrons are currently taxed on noncash dividends to the extent that the dividends are related to transactions entered into for business purposes. Dividends on purchases for personal consumption do not have to be included in a patron's income.

Corporate Acquisitions, Reorganization, and Liquidations

The law permits the reorganization of corporations through acquisitions, mergers, divisions, and other arrangements without recognizing gains and losses as a result of the transaction. The purpose is to permit corporations to arrange their affairs in a flexible manner without incurring tax liability in the process. But the provisions are highly complicated and arbitrary, with the result that the unwary or ill-advised taxpayer may be subject to large amounts of tax for purely procedural rather than substantive reasons, while others escape paying taxes that ought to be paid. Under existing law, for example, corporations are often permitted to transfer appreciated assets to shareholders without recognizing the gains that have accrued.

The objective of tax reform should be to enact simpler and consistent rules for the treatment of corporate transactions and to ensure that profits are subject to corporation income tax in full and at an appropriate time for recognition. Neither shareholders nor corporations should escape tax on corporate profits permanently.

Foreign and Export Income

The income earned by foreign subsidiaries of U.S. corporations is subject to tax when it is "repatriated" through the payment of dividends to the parent corporation. To avoid double taxation, the parent is allowed a credit against the U.S. tax for any tax paid on these dividends to a foreign government up to the U.S. tax liability on that income. Income of foreign branches is included in the taxable income of the parent in the year earned, but credit is allowed for any foreign tax paid on this income.

The deferment of tax on income of foreign subsidiaries was at one time considered a desirable feature of the tax system because it encouraged foreign investment by U.S. firms. Attitudes toward this policy changed in the 1950s and early 1960s as a result of two developments. First, the United States encountered a serious balance-of-payments problem, which was aggravated by private capital outflows. Second, some U.S. corporations were using the deferral privilege as a method of tax avoidance. This was done by establishing "tax haven" subsidiaries in countries with little or no tax on foreign income and using these subsidiaries as base companies for accumulating earnings from foreign operations.

To solve both problems, President Kennedy in 1961 recommended elimination of the deferral of taxes on earnings of U.S.-owned foreign subsidiaries, except for those in underdeveloped countries. The deferral provision had originally been designed to achieve *foreign neutrality* in the taxation of U.S. companies doing business abroad (that is, to permit their foreign income to be taxed at the rates applicable abroad). In view of the changed balance-of-payments circumstances, the government argued that it was time to give priority to *domestic neutrality* (that is, to eliminate the tax as a factor in the choice between domestic and foreign investment).

The business community launched a successful campaign to convince Congress that complete elimination of deferral was too extreme. Congress agreed but was annoyed by the factual evidence that some foreign subsidiaries were able to avoid paying taxes in any country through the use of tax havens. In the end, the Revenue Act of 1962 included new ways of dealing specifically with tax havens for business operations in developed countries, but left the basic deferral provisions unchanged. The technique was to single out certain tax avoidance transactions of tax haven corporations for inclusion in the taxable income of the parent corporation in the year in which income was earned even if the income was not repatriated. Although the restrictions were tightened even more in 1975, the revenue loss from the deferral provision will amount to $365 million at fiscal year 1977 income levels.

To encourage U.S. exports, the law was amended in 1971 to permit domestic manufacturers to create for their export businesses domestic international sales corporations, which can defer tax on half their earnings. In 1975 the DISC privilege was removed for exports of energy products and natural resources subject to depletion. In 1976 deferral was permitted for only half the earnings in excess of 67 percent of the 1972–75 annual average (the four-year base will move forward one year at a time beginning in 1980). The original estimate of the cost of the DISC provision was modest ($170 million a year), but the practice of funneling export earnings through DISCs mushroomed and the revenue loss is expected to amount to $950 million in fiscal year 1977 even after the restrictions enacted in 1976.

Corporations that take part in international boycotts based on race, nationality, or religion are denied the benefit of the foreign tax credit, deferral of earnings of foreign subsidiaries, and the DISC provision for profits earned in the boycotting countries.

Several other, less important provisions provide favorable treatment for foreign income. Dividends from corporations in less developed countries are measured net of foreign tax, yet the recipients are entitled to a full tax credit for any foreign income tax. Profits earned in U.S. possessions, such as Puerto Rico, are not subject to U.S. tax. Persons other than U.S. employees who live abroad for at least three years are permitted to exclude up to $15,000 of their earnings abroad in computing their U.S. income tax ($20,000 for employees of U.S. charitable organizations). The revenue cost of these provisions is not insignificant (table 5-6).

Table 5-6. Revenue Effects of Special Provisions Applying to Foreign Income of U.S. Citizens and Corporations, Fiscal Year 1977
Millions of dollars

Provision	Individuals	Corporations	Total
Deferral of tax on domestic international sales corporations	...	950	950
Exemption for certain income earned abroad by U.S. citizens	115	...	115
Deferral of income of controlled corporations	...	365	365
Exclusion of income earned in U.S. possessions	5	345	350
Total	120	1,650	1,780

Sources: Joint Committee on Internal Revenue Taxation, Congressional Budget Office, and Department of the Treasury.

The foreign tax credit is essential to prevent double taxation of foreign income. However, the other special provisions greatly complicate the tax law and are of dubious value from an economic standpoint. Congress has been considering proposals to eliminate all or most of them in recent years, but they are staunchly defended by those who benefit from them as essential either to promote foreign investment or, in the case of DISCs, to protect employment at home. The economic effects tend to be exaggerated because they ignore changes both in the value of the dollar under floating exchange rates that would offset the tax incentive to do business abroad and in macroeconomic policies that operate to maintain the growth of overall demand and total employment at satisfactory rates.

Inflation Accounting

Business net income is calculated by subtracting from the gross receipts of a firm the expenses of generating these receipts. If all expenses were incurred at the time sales are made, the difference between the two would provide a correct measure of net income. But there are two complications: first, business outlays are frequently made long before sales are realized; and second, the outlays and expenses are expressed in different prices. The first of these problems is handled by estimating sales and expenses on an accrual basis. If the accounting methods match expenses and sales correctly, the difference between the two will accurately represent the net income of the firm—provided the general price level is stable. If prices change, accrual accounting alone will not suffice; a further correction is required to express sales and expenses in the same prices. (The tax rates and exemption, if any, that should apply to the price-corrected net income are another matter. Under a flat-rate tax without exemptions, there is no problem. If the tax is progressive, the real tax burden will rise as money income rises. Chapter 4 discusses whether, and how, a correction for this effect should be made.)

The elements in a set of business accounting statements that are affected by inflation are depreciation allowances, costs of goods sold, and financial assets and liabilities. Separate adjustments are required for each of these elements to arrive at a measure of real income expressed in prices of the current period.

Depreciation

As indicated earlier in this chapter, the purpose of the depreciation allowance is to write off the portion of the cost of a depreciable asset that is used up in producing the income of the enterprise. Even if the wear and tear on plant and equipment could be measured, the funds accumulated in a depreciation reserve based on historical costs would not be adequate to replace worn-out equipment during periods of rising prices.

Two types of adjustment are suggested by economists to correct depreciation for inflation. The first would permit firms to calculate depreciation on the basis of the replacement cost of each of its depreciable assets (or groups of like assets). The second would correct the deduction based on historical costs for the rise in the average of all prices. This could be done by multiplying the amount of historical cost depreciation by the ratio of the general price level in the current period to the level in the period when the asset was purchased. (Accelerated depreciation methods based on historical costs, which are used in many countries, are often justified on inflation grounds, but they can approximate direct adjustments for inflation only accidentally.)

The basic difference between the two types of inflation adjustments concerns the treatment of accrued gains and losses resulting from changes in the relative prices of different depreciable assets. Depreciation at replacement cost permits the tax-free recovery of the cost of such assets at the time they wear out. Consequently, gains and losses on depreciable assets reflecting both changes in the general price level and changes in relative prices are ignored until the firm is liquidated or sold. Under the adjusted historical-cost approach, depreciation is corrected by the change in the average of all prices, with the result that gains and losses on depreciable assets exceeding those that reflect increases in the general price level are included in income as they accrue.

Inventories

The tax law permits firms to use either the first-in-first-out (FIFO) or last-in-first-out (LIFO) methods of inventory valuation. Under FIFO, the deduction for the cost of materials is calculated on the basis of the earliest price paid for similar items in the closing inventory. Under LIFO, the valuation is based on the price last paid for similar items in the closing inventory. In a period of rising prices, the cost of materials is higher—and net income is lower—under LIFO than under FIFO and hence LIFO results in the lower tax.

As in the case of depreciation, gains and losses on items of inventory are taken into account at different times under FIFO and LIFO. Under FIFO, the change in the price of materials between date of purchase and date of use is treated as a realized gain or loss which is included in income for tax purposes. LIFO defers the date of realization of gains and losses on inventories so long as the number of units in stock does not decline.

LIFO is in effect the analogue to replacement cost depreciation— inventory gains and losses are not included in income unless inventories are depleted or the firm is liquidated. FIFO treats the full gains and losses on inventories, including the gains and losses resulting from changes in the general price level and in relative prices, as realized on the date of use. An intermediate possibility, analogous to the use of inflated historical-cost depreciation, would be to modify FIFO by raising the historical cost of materials used by the percentage increase in the general price level between the date of purchase and date of use. This would protect the firm against taxation of inventory gains caused by general inflation, but would include in net income any gains or losses caused by changes in the prices of its inventories relative to all other prices.

Net Financial Assets and Liabilities

A business that lends $1,000 at a 10 percent interest rate realizes no real return on its investment if prices go up 10 percent a year. At the end of the first year, for example, it receives interest of $100 but the value of the loan has declined $100. The enterprise that borrows is in the exact opposite position. It is better off because the real value of the loan it must repay has declined by $100. Under the present tax laws, the lending firm is taxed on $100 of interest even though it has earned no income in real terms, while the borrowing firm is permitted to deduct the $100 of interest paid even though the loan cost nothing in real terms.

In an inflation-corrected accounting system, real gains and losses on net financial assets and liabilities are included in business profits. Enterprises with net financial liabilities gain from inflation; their profits are increased by the reduction in the real value of their liabilities. Enterprises with net financial assets find that the value of these assets erodes during an inflation and their incomes are reduced by the fall in the value of their assets. In each case, the correction is calculated by multiplying the average market value of the financial assets or liabilities during the accounting period by the percentage rise in the price level in that period. The same effect can be achieved by subtracting from interest income or interest deductions the product of the percentage change in prices and the nominal value of the assets to which the interest is related. These two adjustments are precisely equivalent.

Neither of these adjustments deals with the real gains or losses of issuers and holders of bonds when interest rates rise or fall. During a period of inflation, interest rates rise and the market value of long-term bonds declines. This decline in value is a real loss to the bondholders, which they can realize by exchanging holdings for similar bonds. The issuers of bonds enjoy a corresponding real gain as the value of their debt obligations declines (a gain that many corporations realize by redeeming their bonds at the lower prices). When interest rates decline, the gains and losses are reversed—bondholders gain and bond-issuers lose. But there is substantial disagreement about whether such gains and losses should be taken into account in calculating the real income of business enterprises.

Choice of Adjustments

It is evident that, even if it is decided to convert the tax base to a measure of real income, no single set of adjustments can be regarded as "correct." The choice depends on which income concept is considered appropriate for taxing business profits.

One concept that is widely regarded by economists as the best measure of income but is not embodied in current tax law is the "accretion," or "economic power," concept. Applied to an individual, this is the sum of consumption plus the change in the value of his or her assets during the taxable period including all accrued gains and losses (see chapter 4). Applied to a business firm, it is equivalent to the change in the market value of the firm during the taxable period before distributions to shareholders.

To correct for inflation on the basis of the economic power concept, nominal gains resulting from an increase in the general price level are eliminated from income, but all gains and losses resulting from changes in relative prices should be recognized in the period in which they accrue. Depreciation would be based on historical costs and adjusted for the increase in the general price level. Inventories would be valued on a FIFO basis and then adjusted for the increase in the general price level between the date of purchase and the date of use. Finally, real gains and losses on net financial assets and changes in the value of bonds would be recognized in the calculations of income.

An alternative concept of income, which is regarded as more appropriate for business accounting purposes even by some economists who endorse the use of the economic power concept for individuals, is the "capital maintenance" concept. According to this concept, the purpose of the business entity is to produce or distribute a product or service. Changes in the value of the assets of the firm should not be taxed until the firm liquidates some of its assets or goes out of business entirely. There is thus a distinction between operating profits, which are measured on an accrual basis, and capital gains and losses, which are measured only when they are actually realized.

The capital maintenance concept would defer until liquidation recognition of gains and losses on depreciable assets and inventories resulting from changes in relative prices as well as changes in the general price level. Depreciation would be calculated on a replacement cost basis, and a strict form of LIFO, in which historical costs are disregarded even if inventories are liquidated, would be used in accounting for inventories. Real profits on net financial liabilities would be included in income, while changes in the real value of bonds would be ignored.

A major consideration in appraising real income tax accounting, under either the economic power or the capital maintenance concept of income, is that many provisions already provide generous treatment for business and property income, some of which are justified in part as an offset to the distortions caused by using historical prices during inflation. For example, accelerated depreciation and the asset depreciation range system are not equivalent to replacement cost depreciation or to adjusted historical cost depreciation and would be harder to justify if prices were certain to remain stable. Preferential income tax treatment for capital gains would clearly be inappropriate if nominal gains from inflation were eliminated from the tax base. For these reasons, many believe that adjustment of the taxable income concept for inflation should be considered only as part of a thorough revision of the tax law which reexamined all preferences and taxed income from all sources at the same rates.

Table 5-7 compares reported corporate profits of U.S. nonfinancial corporations for the years 1946 through 1974 with estimates of real profits under the two concepts of real income. The adjustments for depreciation and inventories reduce profits substantially, while the financial adjustments raise them. The net adjustments go in both directions, but the overall trend of profits is similar. In some years, the differences are substantial. Real profits are lower than reported profits in nineteen years of the twenty-nine-year period under the economic power concept and in twenty years under the capital maintenance concept.

The aggregates for the entire period since the end of the Second World War differ by less than 4 percent: for the years 1946–74, total profits were $1,461 billion as reported, $1,490 billion under the economic power concept of real income, and $1,408 billion under the capital maintenance concept. However, the inflation correction would have a significant effect on the relative distribution of taxes among various industries and firms. In general, those that rely heavily

Table 5-7. Reported Corporate Profits before Taxes and Real Profits under Two Concepts of Real Income, U.S. Nonfinancial Corporations, 1946–74

Billions of dollars

Year	Reported profits[a]	Real profits[b]	
		Economic power concept	Capital maintenance concept
1946	22.0	20.9	15.1
1947	29.1	26.4	22.0
1948	31.8	27.0	27.2
1949	24.9	19.6	23.2
1950	38.5	32.6	31.0
1951	39.1	37.2	34.5
1952	33.8	27.1	31.2
1953	34.9	31.9	30.6
1954	32.1	26.5	29.8
1955	42.0	41.4	39.7
1956	41.8	46.9	38.6
1957	39.8	35.8	37.3
1958	33.7	30.2	31.9
1959	43.2	46.7	41.3
1960	40.1	35.3	39.2
1961	40.3	37.3	39.0
1962	44.7	43.6	46.6
1963	49.1	50.7	50.7
1964	55.8	54.2	57.5
1965	65.8	69.8	67.3
1966	71.2	84.8	74.0
1967	66.2	73.1	70.1
1968	72.4	74.3	74.6
1969	68.0	92.7	71.1
1970	55.7	37.1	57.8
1971	63.2	39.6	61.4
1972	76.3	73.3	73.9
1973	95.8	124.1	92.7
1974	110.1	149.5	98.4

Source: John B. Shoven and Jeremy I. Bulow, "Inflation Accounting and Nonfinancial Corporate Profits: Financial Assets and Liabilities," *Brookings Papers on Economic Activity, 1:1976*, pp. 40, 41, 44.
a. As estimated in the official national income accounts before the January 1976 revision.
b. Expressed in current dollars. For definitions of the income concepts, see the text.

on equity capital and use long-lived depreciable assets would benefit, while those that rely heavily on borrowed capital and use short-lived depreciable assets would be worse off.

Integration of the Corporation and Individual Income Taxes

Taxation of corporate earnings continues to be controversial. Some people regard taxation of total profits under the corporation tax and of distributed profits under the individual income tax as inequitable. Others believe that taxation of the corporation as a separate entity is justified. Whether something needs to be done depends on an evaluation of the economic issues discussed earlier and on the effect of the proposed changes on the distribution of tax burdens. Few people realize that the problem is tricky and that there is no easy solution.

The Additional Burden on Dividends

On the assumption that all, or a significant portion, of the corporation tax rests on the stockholder, the effect of the tax is to impose the heaviest burden on dividends received by persons in the lowest income classes. This can be seen by examining the illustrative calculations in table 5-8, which show the total and additional tax burden (ignoring the effect of the present $100 exclusion) on stockholders who receive $52 of dividends under present tax rates. Given the present rate of 48 percent, the corporation income before tax from which the $52 of dividends were paid must have amounted to $100. If this $100 had been subject to individual income tax rates only, the tax on these dividends would go from zero at the bottom of the income scale to a maximum of 70 percent at the top. With the corporation tax, the combined individual and corporation income tax increases from $48 for those subject to a zero rate to $84.40 for those subject to a 70 percent rate (table 5-8, column 6).

However, the *additional* burden resulting from the corporation tax falls as income rises. For example, the taxpayer subject to a zero individual rate would have paid no tax on the $52 of dividends; the additional burden of the corporation income tax in this case is the full $48 tax. By contrast, a taxpayer subject to the 70 percent rate pays an individual income tax of $36.40 on the dividend, and the

Table 5-8. Additional Burden on Dividends of the Corporation Income Tax on $100 of Corporation Income[a]

Dollars

Marginal individual income tax rate (percent) (1)	Corporate income before tax (2)	Corporation tax at 48 percent (3)	Dividends received by stockholders (4)	Stockholder's individual income tax (5)	Total tax burden[b] (6)	Additional burden of the corporation tax (7)
0	100	48	52	0	48.00	48.00
10	100	48	52	5.20	53.20	43.20
20	100	48	52	10.40	58.40	38.40
30	100	48	52	15.60	63.60	33.60
40	100	48	52	20.80	68.80	28.80
50	100	48	52	26.00	74.00	24.00
60	100	48	52	31.20	79.20	19.20
70	100	48	52	36.40	84.40	14.40

Column 3 = 0.48 × column 2.
Column 4 = column 2 − column 3.
Column 5 = column 4 × column 1.
Column 6 = column 3 + column 5.
Column 7 = column 6 − column 1 × column 2.
a. Assumes that corporation income after tax is devoted entirely to the payment of dividends.
b. Does not take into account the effect of the exclusion of the first $100 of dividends from the individual income tax base.

total tax burden on the original $100 of corporate earnings is $84.40. But since the taxpayer would have to pay $70 under the individual income tax in any case, the additional burden is only $14.40 (table 5-8, column 7).

One test of an equitable method of moderating or eliminating the additional tax burden on dividends is whether the method removes a uniform portion of the additional burden shown in table 5-8. If the percentage removed is the same for all dividend recipients in every individual income tax bracket, the method deals evenly at all levels. Deviations from a constant percentage indicate the dividend recipients who are favored or penalized by the method.

A second test is whether the method increases or reduces the progressivity of the tax system as a whole. Since corporate ownership is heavily concentrated in the highest income classes (see table 5-2), moderation or reduction of the additional tax burden on dividends alone would reduce progressivity, unless the change were accompanied by fundamental revisions in the individual income tax base to prevent windfalls for the minority of taxpayers who have large stockholdings.

Methods of Integration

Five methods of integrating the corporation and individual income tax have been used at various times in different countries: (1) a dividend-received credit for individuals; (2) a deduction for dividends paid by the corporation in computing the corporation income tax; (3) a "split-rate" corporation income tax, which applies a higher tax rate to undistributed than to distributed corporate earnings; (4) a method that considers all or a portion of the corporation income tax to be withholding on dividends at the source; and (5) an exclusion of all or a portion of the dividends received from the individual income tax base. These methods would only "partially" integrate the corporation and individual income taxes, because the relief would be given only to distributed earnings. A sixth method would be to treat all corporations like partnerships and tax their income to the stockholders whether distributed or not. This is the only method that would "fully" integrate the corporation and individual income taxes; in other words, it would eliminate the corporation income tax on both distributed and undistributed corporate earnings and would rely entirely on the individual income tax for the taxation of corporate profits. Of the various methods, 2, 3, and 4 and the partnership plan would remove the same proportion of the additional burden of the corporation tax at all individual income levels. All the methods except the sixth would make the federal tax system less progressive without offsetting changes. It is assumed that there is no shifting of the corporation income tax.

THE DIVIDEND-RECEIVED CREDIT. Under this method, dividend recipients are allowed to deduct a percentage of their dividends as a credit against their individual income tax. Between 1954 and 1963, U.S. taxpayers were allowed a credit of 4 percent for dividends in excess of a $50 exclusion ($100 for joint returns).

Although the credit grants the same relief on a dollar of dividends at all income levels, it removes an increasing proportion of the additional burden of the corporation tax as incomes rise. For those subject to a zero rate, the credit is worthless. For a taxpayer subject to a 10 percent rate, the 4 percent credit would remove 4.8 percent of the additional burden, and for a taxpayer subject to the maximum 70 percent rate, the credit would remove 14.4 percent (table 5-9). This regressive pattern of relief led to its repeal.

Table 5-9. Portion of the Additional Burden of the Corporation Income Tax Removed by the 4 Percent Dividend-Received Credit

Marginal individual income tax rate (percent) (1)	Additional burden resulting from corporation tax (dollars) (2)	Dividend-received credit (dollars) (3)	Percentage of additional burden removed by the dividend credit (4)
0	48.00	0	0
10	43.20	2.08	4.8
20	38.40	2.08	5.4
30	33.60	2.08	6.2
40	28.80	2.08	7.2
50	24.00	2.08	8.7
60	19.20	2.08	10.8
70	14.40	2.08	14.4

Column 2 = column 7 of table 5-8.
Column 3 = 4 percent of $52.
Column 4 = column 3 ÷ column 2.

THE DIVIDEND-PAID DEDUCTION. This is the simplest method of dealing with the problem; it was used in the United States in 1936 and 1937. Corporations deduct from their taxable income all or a portion of the dividends they pay out, and the corporation tax applies to the remainder. Table 5-10 shows the relief that would be granted under this method if the corporation were allowed a deduction of 11.79 percent of dividends paid. As shown in column 6, the relief would be exactly 6.5 percent of the additional tax imposed by the corporation income tax at all income levels.

Aside from granting the same proportionate relief at all income levels, the dividend-paid credit has the merit of treating dividends more like interest. (If a full deduction were allowed, the treatment would be identical.) This would increase the attractiveness of equity financing by corporations.

The dividend-paid deduction raised a storm of protest when it was used briefly in the United States during the 1930s. Corporations complained that by encouraging payouts of earnings it reduced their ability to save and invest at a time when the market for corporate equities was almost dried up. The method is also criticized on the ground that it discourages internal financing by corporations and might reduce total saving and investment. On the other hand, some believe it unwise to permit corporations to avoid the capital markets

The Corporation Income Tax

Table 5-10. Portion of the Additional Burden of the Corporation Income Tax Removed by the Dividend-Paid Deduction
Assuming a deduction by the corporation of 11.79 percent of dividends paid

Marginal individual income tax rate (percent) (1)	Additional burden resulting from corporation tax (dollars) (2)	Tax benefit of dividend-paid deduction (dollars)			Percentage of additional burden removed by the dividend-paid deduction (6)
		Reduced corporation tax (paid to stockholders as additional dividends) (3)	Tax on additional dividends (4)	Net benefit (5)	
0	48.00	3.12	0	3.12	6.5
10	43.20	3.12	0.31	2.81	6.5
20	38.40	3.12	0.62	2.50	6.5
30	33.60	3.12	0.94	2.18	6.5
40	28.80	3.12	1.25	1.87	6.5
50	24.00	3.12	1.56	1.56	6.5
60	19.20	3.12	1.87	1.25	6.5
70	14.40	3.12	2.18	0.94	6.5

Column 2 = column 7 of table 5-8.
Column 3 = amount of additional dividends corporations could pay out with an 11.79 percent dividend-paid deduction. This percentage was used to remove exactly 6.5 percent of the additional burden of the corporation income tax (as shown in column 6).
Column 4 = column 1 × column 3.
Column 5 = column 3 − column 4.
Column 6 = column 5 ÷ column 2.

for financing their investment programs. Forcing them "to stand the test of the marketplace" might exercise a desirable restraint on bigness and also give investment-owners more control over the disposition of their funds. In 1975 the Treasury Department recommended a deduction for 50 percent of dividends paid as part of a proposal to partially integrate the individual and corporation income taxes.

An alternative method of equalizing the treatment of dividends and interest would be to eliminate the deduction for interest in computing the taxable income of corporations. Since the base of the tax would be raised, the tax rate could be reduced substantially. (At 1977 income and borrowing levels, the rate could be reduced by 20 percentage points.) Such a plan has merit if a separate tax on corporate capital —whether financed by debt or equity capital—is justified. However, it has not been seriously considered in the United States because it would drastically alter the distribution of the corporation tax burden among firms and industries. In general, manufacturing corporations, which rely mainly on equity capital, would benefit; utilities and transportation and financial companies, which rely heavily on borrowed capital, would pay much higher taxes.

THE "SPLIT-RATE" CORPORATION INCOME TAX. A number of countries tax undistributed earnings at a higher rate than distributed earnings. This split-rate plan is similar in effect to a deduction for dividends paid. For example, a 50-25 percent split rate would be equivalent to a 50 percent tax on total corporate earnings with a deduction of 50 percent for dividends paid. The percentages actually used by various countries differ greatly, reflecting the absence of accepted criteria for establishing the split rates.

THE IMPUTATION METHOD. Under this method, all or a portion of the individual income tax is regarded as having been paid at the source (through the corporation tax). For example, if 6 percent of the dividend were regarded as having been withheld, a shareholder receiving a $52 dividend would "gross up" the dividend by adding $3.12 ($0.06 \times 52$) to taxable income and then take the $3.12 as a credit against tax. In this illustration, the portion of the additional burden of the corporation income tax removed is also exactly 6.5 percent at all income levels (table 5-11).

The imputation method achieves the same result as the dividend-paid deduction for corporations but is less likely to discourage corporate saving. This advantage frequently makes the imputation method more attractive, even though it is more difficult to understand and would also complicate the individual income tax return.

The imputation method was a basic part of the British tax structure from 1803 until 1965, when a separate corporation income tax was enacted for the first time. The same method, with a "gross-up" factor of 50 percent of dividends received, was recommended by the U.S. Treasury Department in 1975 to accompany its proposal for a 50 percent dividend-paid deduction at the corporate level. In combination, the two methods were intended to eliminate the entire burden of the corporation income tax on distributed corporate earnings. However, since the corporation tax on retained earnings would remain, the proposal would represent only a partial integration of the corporation and individual income taxes.

THE DIVIDEND EXCLUSION. This method, adopted in the United States in 1954, permits the individual income taxpayer to exclude all

Table 5-11. Portion of the Additional Burden of the Corporation Income Tax Removed by the Imputation Method

Assuming 6 percent of dividends received regarded as withheld

| Marginal individual income tax rate (percent) (1) | Additional burden resulting from corporation tax (dollars) (2) | Withholding credit (dollars) | | | Percentage of additional burden removed by the dividend credit (6) |
		Amount withheld at source (3)	Tax on amount withheld (4)	Net credit (5)	
0	48.00	3.12	0	3.12	6.5
10	43.20	3.12	0.31	2.81	6.5
20	38.40	3.12	0.62	2.50	6.5
30	33.60	3.12	0.94	2.18	6.5
40	28.80	3.12	1.25	1.87	6.5
50	24.00	3.12	1.56	1.56	6.5
60	19.20	3.12	1.87	1.25	6.5
70	14.40	3.12	2.18	0.94	6.5

Column 2 = column 7 of table 5-8.
Column 3 = 6 percent of $52.
Column 4 = column 1 × column 3.
Column 5 = column 3 − column 4.
Column 6 = column 5 ÷ column 2.

or a portion of his or her dividends from taxable income. In 1964 the maximum exclusion was raised from $50 to $100 ($200 on joint returns). Like the dividend-received credit, the exclusion grants an increasing amount of relief on a dollar of dividends as incomes rise. Accordingly, it cannot remove the same proportion of the additional tax burden at all levels of income.

THE PARTNERSHIP METHOD, OR "FULL" INTEGRATION. The most far-reaching solution is to regard the income of corporations as belonging to their stockholders in the year in which it is earned, regardless of whether the earnings are distributed. The corporation income tax as such would be abolished, but a tax would be retained at the corporate level as a withholding device for the individual income tax. Stockholders would pay individual income tax on their prorated share of the earnings of corporations in which they held stock and would receive credit for the amount of tax withheld at the source, just as in the case of wages and salaries.

This method would automatically apply the correct individual income tax rates to all corporate earnings and thus equalize the tax rates on corporate and noncorporate earnings. It would also be more

Table 5-12. Revenue Effects of Full and Partial Integration of the Corporation and Individual Income Taxes, by Adjusted Gross Income Class, 1976[a]
Income classes in thousands of dollars

Revenue change and adjusted gross income class	Full integration— allocate corporate earnings to individual shareholders	Partial integration— full individual income tax credit. for corporation tax paid on dividends[b]
Revenue change (billions of dollars)[c]	−6.9	−15.3
	Percentage distribution of revenue change	
0–3	10.1	2.5
3–5	14.2	6.3
5–10	29.2	12.3
10–15	22.4	10.7
15–20	19.8	11.2
20–25	12.3	6.6
25–50	14.7	19.8
50–100	(7.5)[d]	14.8
100–200	(8.9)[d]	7.0
200–500	(7.3)[d]	4.0
500–1,000	(2.1)[d]	1.5
1,000 and over	(0.9)[d]	1.9
All classes[e]	100.0	100.0
	Percentage change in tax liabilities	
0–3	−488.6[f]	−890.5[f]
3–5	−90.6[f]	−86.7[f]
5–10	−18.0	−17.4
10–15	−7.6	−8.1
15–20	−5.7	−7.2
20–25	−4.5	−5.5
25–50	−3.3	−10.0
50–100	3.4	−14.9
100–200	8.0	−14.0
200–500	14.2	−17.3
500–1,000	14.7	−23.2
1,000 and over	5.5	−25.4
All classes[e]	−5.1	−11.5

Source: Brookings 1972 tax file, projected to 1976. Figures are rounded.
a. Assumes corporation tax is borne by individuals in proportion to their dividend income and there is no change in the 1976 individual income tax rates.
b. Assumes effective rate of the corporation tax is 48 percent.
c. Assumes no refunds to tax-exempt organizations.
d. Indicates tax increase.
e. Includes negative incomes not shown separately.
f. Percent reduction in tax is unusually large because persons with incomes below $5,000 pay very little tax.

progressive and less costly than partial integration for dividends alone, because retained as well as distributed corporate earnings would be subject to the individual income tax (table 5-12).

A major drawback of the plan is that, unless the withholding rate was set at a very high level, some stockholders would not have funds to pay tax on earnings they did not receive. This would force them to liquidate security holdings or apply pressure on corporations to distribute a much larger portion of their retained earnings. In the former case, stock ownership among people with modest means would be discouraged; in the latter, corporate saving would be reduced.

Treatment approximating this method is available under present law for closely held corporations with no more than ten shareholders. These corporations operate much like partnerships and can arrange to distribute enough earnings to the partners to avoid forced liquidations. The decision to be treated like a partnership for tax purposes is made only if it is advantageous to the shareholders. Experts disagree about whether it would be practical to extend the partnership method to large, publicly held corporations with complex capital structures, frequent changes in ownership, and thousands or millions of stockholders.

In 1966 the Canadian Royal Commission on Taxation devised a new procedure that would approximate the effect of the partnership method and avoid its liquidity problems. Under this procedure, corporations would be permitted to allocate all or a portion of their undistributed earnings to their shareholders. The corporation income tax would be converted to a withholding tax for the individual income tax, and the corporate rate would be set at the top-bracket individual income tax rate. Shareholders would include the allocated dividends as well as cash dividends in their taxable income and would deduct the amount of tax withheld as a credit against their income tax. The only difference between this procedure and the original partnership method is that the allocation of earnings by corporations to shareholders would not be mandatory. But since shareholders would be denied immediate credit for the withheld tax, the pressure on corporate management to allocate all undistributed earnings would probably be irresistible. The commission's proposal has merit (if a separate corporation tax is considered inappropriate), but it was not adopted by the Canadian government and has not been seriously considered elsewhere.

Full integration of the corporation and individual income taxes raises a number of difficult issues. First, if present individual tax rates are retained, the corporate withholding rate would have to be set at a high enough level to prevent widespread taxpayer liquidity problems. Even a 48 or 50 percent rate may not be adequate for many stockholders who are subject to the top-bracket individual income tax rate of 70 percent. A withholding rate higher than the present 48 percent corporate tax rate would force a reduction in corporation retentions and might reduce saving for the economy as a whole.

Second, it would be difficult to decide how to treat foreign shareholders and tax-exempt organizations under an integration plan. The corporation income tax now applies to the earnings of the entire corporation, including those that would be allocated to foreign shareholders and tax-exempt organizations under an integration plan. If foreign shareholders and tax-exempt organizations were not eligible for refunds, the cost of the plan would be greatly reduced.

Third, it would be inappropriate to assume that corporate earnings were subject to a 48 percent rate in crediting the individuals with the amount of tax withheld on their corporate earnings. For one thing, all corporations are taxed at reduced rates on the first $50,000 of earnings. For another, numerous preferential provisions reduce the effective rate of the corporation tax. In principle, the effective tax rates at the corporate level would have to be computed separately by each corporation, and individuals with multiple shareholdings would credit the corporation tax at different effective rates for each of their holdings. This procedure might be regarded as too complicated and some intermediate—and less equitable—technique might be substituted.

Fourth, full integration might have a significant effect on the progressivity of the tax system. If the present individual income tax rates were retained, the maximum tax on corporate retained earnings would be raised from 48 to 70 percent and progressivity would be increased. Such an increase would be strongly resisted by those who would be affected by the increased tax burdens and those who are concerned with the possible effect of such a tax increase on national saving. If the top-bracket individual income tax rate were reduced to, say, 50 percent in response to these objections, it would be necessary to raise the tax rates in the lower brackets to avoid a revenue loss, and progressivity would be reduced (see table 5-13).

Table 5-13. Effective Rates under Present Law and under a Fully Integrated Individual and Corporation Income Tax, by Comprehensive Income Class,[a] 1976

Income classes in thousands of dollars; tax rates in percent

Comprehensive income class[a]	Present law	Effective rates — Integrated tax with		Change in effective rates under integrated tax with	
		Present rates (14–70 percent)	Rates of 18–50 percent[b]	Present rates (14–70 percent)	Rates of 18–50 percent[b]
0–5	2.6	2.1	2.7	−0.5	*
5–10	8.2	7.6	9.0	−0.6	0.8
10–15	10.7	9.9	11.8	−0.8	1.1
15–20	12.6	12.0	14.0	−0.7	1.3
20–25	14.6	13.8	15.8	−0.8	1.2
25–50	18.9	17.6	18.8	−1.3	−0.2
50–100	29.5	27.8	26.3	−1.7	−3.2
100–200	34.9	35.6	30.9	0.8	−4.0
200–500	38.9	42.2	33.8	3.3	−5.1
500–1,000	41.9	46.8	35.3	4.9	−6.6
1,000 and over	41.9	47.3	34.4	5.4	−7.4
Total[c]	15.9	15.3	15.9	−0.6	*

Source: Brookings 1972 tax file, projected to 1976.
* Less than 0.05 percent.
a. Includes adjusted gross income, the share of corporate earnings and the corporate tax allocated to individuals, half of total capital gains transferred at death or by gift, percentage depletion over cost depletion, and interest on state and local government bonds.
b. Present brackets for married couples filing joint returns with rates per bracket increasing 1 percentage point up to $4,000 of taxable income, 2 percentage points from $4,000 to $28,000, 3 percentage points from $28,000 to $36,000, 2 percentage points from $36,000 to $44,000, and 1 percentage point from $44,000 to $100,000. Assumes all taxpayers use the same schedule.
c. Includes negative incomes not shown separately.

Summary

The corporation income tax ranks third in the federal tax system despite continued criticism. It produces a large amount of revenue that would be hard to replace with any other tax and protects the equity and yield of the individual income tax. Without it, a substantial part of the individual income tax would be permanently lost from the tax base through retention of earnings by corporations.

The arguments that are made against the corporation income tax are largely economic. The tax may reduce the saving capacity of corporations and their incentives to invest; encourage debt financing by discriminating against equity financing, thus exposing many corporations to unnecessary risks; protect marginal producers by keeping up the prices of more efficient producers; and distort the allocation of resources both between the corporate and noncorporate sectors and between capital and labor-intensive industries. There is no evidence in the available data, however, that high corporation tax rates have impaired the growth of the corporate sector or of the economy as a whole.

Numerous changes have been made in the structure of the corporation income tax since the end of the Second World War. Foremost among these are the liberalization of depreciation and the adoption of the investment credit to encourage investment. Revisions have also been made to prevent tax avoidance by tax-exempt organizations, financial institutions, and cooperatives. The tax advantage of multiple incorporation has been eliminated, and a minimum tax now applies to income items that receive special treatment. Nevertheless, some difficult problems remain. The reserve-ratio test for depreciation allowances was never given a fair chance and the asset depreciation range system is regarded by many as excessively generous. The treatment of oil and gas and other mineral industries is still a major issue. The loss of revenue from the DISC provision is difficult to justify on economic grounds, and the tax treatment of foreign incomes is still in dispute. Gains on assets distributed in kind or sold in connection with a corporate liquidation frequently escape taxation at the corporate level.

In periods of inflation, the reported profits of most corporations are not representative of their real incomes. Depreciation is understated, inventory profits may be overstated, and accrued gains and losses on financial assets are not taken into account. Correcting for all the distortions would radically alter the distribution of the corporation income tax among different firms and industries.

Another difficult issue is the additional tax burden on dividends resulting from the taxation of corporate earnings at both the corporation and the individual levels. Even if it were agreed that something needs to be done about double taxation, there is no easy solution. Among the various alternatives, the only theoretically correct method is the partnership method, which would fully integrate the two taxes, but many regard this solution as impractical. The partial integration methods (the deduction of dividends from the corporation tax base and the imputation method) would be more costly than full integration and would tend to discourage corporate saving.

CHAPTER SIX

Consumption Taxes

CONSUMPTION TAXES are not very popular in the United States. It is true that general sales taxes are used by state and local governments (see chapter 9), but even when they are taken into account, consumption taxes are less important here than anywhere else in the world. In fiscal year 1976 excise taxes accounted for less than 6 percent of federal budget receipts.

Types of Consumption Taxes

There is a bewildering variety of consumption taxes. An *expenditure* tax is levied on the total consumption expenditures of the individual; a *sales* tax is levied on the sales of goods and services; and a *value added* tax is levied on the difference between a firm's sales and its purchases. Expenditure taxes may be proportional or progressive; sales and value added taxes are imposed at a uniform rate on all commodities or at differing rates on various groups of commodities. Expenditure taxes are collected from the consumer; sales and value added taxes, from the seller. Sales taxes are in use throughout the world; the value added tax, a relative newcomer, is now widely used in Western Europe and many other countries; the expenditure tax has been used—without much success—only in India and Sri Lanka.

The sales tax can be a single-stage or a multistage tax. Canada levies its sales tax at the manufacturers' level, Great Britain at the wholesale level, and U.S. state and local governments at the retail level. The *turnover* tax is so called because the tax is levied every time a commodity "turns over" from one firm to another. The value added tax is also a multistage tax, but it is figured on the *net* value added by each firm.

A common form of consumption tax is the *excise* tax on the sale of a particular commodity or group of commodities. Excise taxes are levied almost everywhere on alcoholic beverages and tobacco products, but they apply to many other products as well. They are also employed as "user charges" to collect part or all of the cost of government services enjoyed by specific groups of taxpayers. Gasoline taxes and taxes on motor vehicles, for instance, are used to pay for highway construction and maintenance. Appendix table A-6 summarizes the major excises imposed by the federal government since 1913.

Customs duties, which are levied on imports, are used in this country primarily to protect domestic industries against foreign competition. The policy of the U.S. government is to reduce trade barriers in the interest of promoting world trade, but the size and pace of the reductions depend on international negotiations, which are complicated and time-consuming. The negotiations are concerned with the role of customs duties in the nation's foreign economic policy rather than with their role as taxes to produce revenue. Customs duties are therefore not discussed in this book.

The major issue regarding consumption taxes in this country is equity. Because the poor consume more of their income than do the rich, the burden of a flat rate sales tax falls as incomes rise. The sales tax also bears more heavily on families that have larger expenditures relative to their incomes, such as families with a large number of children or those just starting a household. Some excise taxes may be progressive (if levied on luxury goods), but since they are usually levied on mass consumption items, they tend to be regressive on balance.

Sales and excise taxes are also criticized on economic grounds. Consumption taxes are never levied at a uniform rate on all goods and services, and thus they interfere with the freedom of choice of consumers and misallocate the nation's resources (except, as will be discussed below, when they are employed as pollution and user charges or to discourage consumption of items, such as narcotics, that lead to increased social costs). They rank low as automatic stabilizers because they respond no more than in proportion to changes in income. Moreover, purchasers may be charged more than the amount of the tax through *pyramiding* when successive markups are applied to the same goods as they move through the channels of production and distribution. On the other hand, sales and excise taxes are often supported for their relative stability of yield, a characteristic that is important for financing state-local government activities, but not federal.

Because of the equity and economic shortcomings of sales and excise taxes, other forms of consumption taxation have been proposed as substitutes. Some economists are partial to a graduated expenditure tax, but this is generally regarded as difficult to administer. Value added taxation, on the other hand, has spread rapidly in recent years, particularly among countries that have relied heavily on turnover and selective excise taxes and have come to recognize their economic deficiencies.

In this country, the allocation between the federal and state-local governments of consumption taxes as a source of revenue has been stabilized and is not a major issue. Federal consumption taxes are restricted to selective excises, while the state and local governments levy general sales taxes as well as excises. In 1965 all but a few major federal excise taxes were eliminated. Substitution of a value added tax for part or all of the corporation income tax has been suggested, but Congress has not shown interest in such a trade. Forty-five states and many local governments levy retail sales taxes, and the trend is toward greater use of this tax at the state and local levels.

Issues in Excise Taxation

The imposition of heavy taxes on particular commodities substantially alters the results of the market mechanism. Such interference should be avoided, but there are circumstances in which excise taxes are useful and even necessary.

Economic Effects of Excise Taxes

The immediate effect of an excise tax is to raise the price of the taxed commodity. The consumer will respond by buying less of the taxed commodity, purchasing other commodities, or saving more.

Table 6-1. Federal Excise Tax Revenue by Major Sources, Fiscal Year 1976

Major source	Amount (millions of dollars)	Percentage of total
Alcohol	5,362	31.7
Tobacco	2,430	14.4
Highway		
Gasoline	4,154[a]	24.6
Trucks, buses, and trailers	375	2.2
Tires, inner tubes, and tread rubber	566	3.3
Other[b]	647	3.8
Telephone and teletype services	1,900	11.2
Airport and airway	976	5.8
Other[c]	491	2.9
Total	16,901	100.0

Source: *The Budget of the United States Government, Fiscal Year 1977*, pp. 324–26. Figures are rounded.
a. Includes trust fund revenue plus federal funds of $31 million.
b. Includes diesel fuel, lubricating oils, truck parts and accessories, and use tax on certain vehicles, less refunds.
c. Includes (1) taxes on firearms, shells, and cartidges, fishing equipment, wagering, sugar, gaming devices, investment income of foundations, foreign insurance policies, and "other," less refunds; and (2) undistributed tax collections.

The burden of the tax is thus borne in part by consumers and in part by producers (and distributors) of the taxed commodity. If demand is relatively inelastic (that is, if consumers do not reduce their consumption of the particular item as much as its price increases), most of the burden is borne by the consumers. On the other hand, if supply is relatively inelastic (if the producer does not or cannot reduce production as price declines), the burden is borne mainly by the producer.

In general, the objective of excise taxation is to place the burden of the tax on consumers, and most excise revenues are derived from taxes imposed on articles for which the demand is relatively inelastic. For example, taxes on alcohol, tobacco, and gasoline accounted for over two-thirds of federal excise revenues in 1976 (table 6-1). Furthermore, supply is generally so highly elastic in the taxed industries that, even where demand is relatively elastic, very little of the burden of consumer taxes is borne by the producers.

BURDEN OF EXCISES. The effects of excise taxes on the allocation of economic resources depend on the sensitivity of consumption to a rise in price. If consumption is not reduced much by the increased price, consumers respond by cutting their consumption of other commodities as well as the taxed commodity. The effect is much like that of an income tax, which reduces disposable income, leading the consumer to reduce consumption of a wide range of commodities. There is little incentive for labor and capital to move out of the taxed industry, and the allocation of resources elsewhere in the economy is not altered significantly.

When consumption is fairly sensitive to price, however, production and employment in the industry producing the taxed commodity decline. Demand for other products increases at the expense of the taxed industry, and over time the labor and capital will move to other industries (if full employment is maintained). In this case, the tax substantially alters the pattern of production and consumption in the private economy. It also may create hardship for the employees and owners of capital in the industries affected.

Thus an excise tax imposes a burden on the economy because consumers are not as well off as they would have been if the same revenue had been raised by another tax that did not change patterns of consumption. The loss resulting from this distortion is called the *excess consumer burden* of the excise tax. The amount of the excess burden is the difference between the value placed by consumers on the consumption they give up and the yield of the tax. Excess burden is, in other words, the loss in economic efficiency caused by the imposition of the tax.

This analysis holds only in a world in which the allocation of resources before the imposition of the commodity tax is optimal. In the real world there are substantial departures from the conditions necessary for this optimum for reasons other than taxes, and there is no a priori basis for making the judgment that a new excise tax necessarily involves a loss in consumer welfare. Consumers may value the newly taxed commodity less highly than other commodities they consume in its place after the tax is imposed, particularly if the new tax makes them shift their consumption to commodities that are already heavily taxed.

Nevertheless, the case for selective excise taxes is weak. Conceivably, there are excise taxes that would not reduce consumer welfare, but there is no basis for making such a selection. Excise taxes should be avoided unless there is a compelling reason for altering the allocation of resources and for discriminating among individuals and families on the basis of their consumption preferences.

EXCISE TAXES IN WARTIME. One situation in which the government has a definite interest in changing the pattern of resource use is in wartime or in a similar national emergency. Many materials are needed for production in war industries. In extreme cases, as in the two world wars, the government is forced to replace the market mechanism with direct rationing and to halt production of items that conflict with the war effort. In a more limited emergency, such as the Korean War, it may not be necessary to take such drastic steps. In this situation, excise taxes may be helpful both as a rationing device and as a selective way of reducing consumer demand. By increasing the prices of the taxed commodities, the government can reduce demand and divert it to other, more plentiful commodities or to saving.

Excises are among the first taxes to be increased in a national emergency. Criticism of this practice usually arises because the taxes chosen are hard to justify on economic and equity grounds. And the rationale of discouraging consumption on a selective basis is quickly forgotten once excises are imposed and the revenue objective becomes paramount. Even in wartime, excise taxes should be used sparingly; first, because there are better ways to raise general revenues and, second, because wartime taxes are apt to linger on—and do considerable damage—for many years. For example, the excises levied by the federal government on many electric, gas, and oil appliances in 1941 were not repealed until 1965.

POLLUTION AND USER CHARGES. Selective excise taxes may be used to good advantage to obtain payments from individuals and businesses that impose special costs on society or that benefit from particular public services. Demand for private activities that result in uncompensated damages to other or for public services that are provided at less than cost is artificially stimulated, and too many resources may be used in carrying them out. An excise tax, or some other means of compensating for the damage or charging for the service, is needed to maintain economic efficiency.

Despite the sound theoretical justification for such excise, or benefit, taxes, they are not employed nearly enough for this purpose at any level of government in the United States. Specific excise taxes are allocated to the federal Highway Trust Fund, which was established in 1956 to finance the interstate highway system, and to the Airport and Airway Trust Fund, established in 1970 to finance airport and airway development. Recent presidents have recommended the adoption of a much wider range of special taxes or user charges, including taxes on sulfur emissions and payments for the use of federal air and inland waterway transportation facilities, recreation facilities, and many other federally financed benefits.

The pollution of water and air by private individuals and businesses imposes heavy costs on society, which should not be borne by the general taxpayer. Charges to pay for these costs would give producers incentives to use production processes and equipment that reduce pollution and would discourage consumption of products that generate the most pollution. Economic efficiency and equity would be improved and the burden of other taxes would be eased. But successive administrations have had little success in persuading Congress to accept this approach. Pollution taxes and user charges are strongly resisted by the groups that would be required to pay, and past experience suggests that this resistance is politically potent and difficult to overcome.

SUMPTUARY TAXES. Excises on commodities or services that are considered socially or morally undesirable are known as *sumptuary* taxes. The best examples are the excises on liquor and tobacco. The rationale for sumptuary taxes is that the consumption of some products creates additional costs for society that are not borne by the producers and are not reflected in the prices they charge. For example, consumption of liquor can generate costs in the form of lost working time, accidents, broken homes, and increased delinquency; and consumption of cigarettes has been shown to be associated with higher frequencies of a wide range of illnesses. An excise tax raises prices on such commodities to a level that more nearly reflects total social costs as well as private costs.

In some cases, the costs imposed by certain items or activities are so great that society prohibits them. This is true, for example, of narcotics and gambling. The federal government prohibits the sale of narcotics except under very strict rules, while most states either outlaw or regulate gambling. Taxes are imposed on these items largely to aid in regulation and law enforcement.

In a democratic society, complete prohibition of the use of any commodity or service requires virtually unanimous agreement that it is harmful or immoral. Where this unanimity does not exist, the majority expresses its view by levying a heavy tax that will discourage consumption without eliminating it entirely. Those who place a high value on such items are allowed to purchase them but at a higher price. This is why gambling is illegal in some states and is subject to

Table 6-2. Effective Rates of Federal Excise Taxes and of a Hypothetical General Sales Tax, 1970

Income classes in thousands of dollars; tax rates in percent

Family income classa	Federal excise taxes	5 percent retail sales tax	
		Including food	Excluding food
0–3	2.5	3.8	2.7
3–5	2.0	3.3	2.7
5–10	2.1	3.4	2.7
10–15	2.0	3.3	2.7
15–20	1.8	3.2	2.7
20–25	1.7	3.0	2.5
25–30	1.6	2.8	2.4
30–50	1.4	2.4	2.1
50–100	1.0	1.9	1.7
100 and over	0.4	1.2	1.1
All classes	1.7	2.9	2.5

Source: Brookings 1970 MERGE data file.
a. Family income is a comprehensive definition of income, which includes estimated accrued capital gains.

regulation and to special taxes in others. Similarly, since opinion on the harmful effects of alcoholic beverages and cigarettes is not unanimous, purchases of these items are permitted but are heavily taxed by the federal and state governments and even by some local governments. The main effects of these taxes as levied in the United States are to tax smokers and drinkers heavily without curtailing their consumption very much and to introduce an element of regressivity into the system.

Equity Considerations

Excise taxes rank low in terms of equity on a number of grounds. First, consumers probably bear the major burden of the excise taxes that have been levied in the United States. How this burden is distributed depends on what proportion of income is allocated to consumption of the taxed items at the various income levels. For example, excise taxes on beer and cigarettes are highly regressive, while those on furs and some consumer durables are progressive. On balance, the present federal excise tax structure is regressive throughout the income scale (table 6-2).

Second, excise taxes are unfair for different people with the same incomes. Families whose preferences for the taxed commodities are high are taxed much more heavily than those who prefer to spend their incomes in other ways. This violation of horizontal equity is not justified unless there are overriding social reasons for discouraging the use of particular goods or services. But where special costs or benefits associated with the production or distribution of a particular commodity are not borne or paid for by the individuals and firms creating the costs or receiving the benefits, the imposition of a selective excise tax improves equity and the allocation of resources.

Third, while most of the pre-1965 excise taxes were levied on goods and services used by consumers, some applied to items that were used primarily or exclusively by business (such as business and store machines, lubricating oils, long-distance telephone services, and trucks). Taxes levied on such items enter into business costs and are generally reflected in higher prices for consumer goods. Since people with low incomes spend a larger proportion of their income than those in the higher income classes, taxes that enter into business costs are regressive. Furthermore, they often create unfair competitive situations by discriminating against firms that use the taxed commodity or service and distorting the choice of production methods. The classic example of a bad excise tax was the one on freight, since it discriminated against firms with distant markets. It was eliminated in 1958.

The Excise Tax Reduction Act of 1965 eliminated most federal excises, except for a few regulatory taxes and highway taxes that recover the costs of services or facilities directly benefiting individuals and business firms. The act reduced the tax on passenger cars in stages from 10 percent to 1 percent on January 1, 1969. It also stipulated that the 10 percent telephone tax be reduced in stages until it was completely eliminated by January 1, 1969. However, the scheduled reductions were postponed in 1966, 1968, 1969, and 1970. The repeal of the automobile tax became effective December 11, 1971, and the telephone tax is scheduled to expire on December 31, 1981.

A General Consumption Tax?

The major drawback of selective excise taxes is that they are not neutral; that is, they discriminate among different items of consumption. A broadly based tax is much more appropriate for taxing consumption. The three broad-based taxes mentioned most often are the general sales tax, the value added tax, and the expenditure tax.

The General Sales Tax

Sales taxation has been used extensively throughout the world, and there is almost no limit to the variations in the structure of these taxes. On the whole, experience suggests that a single-stage tax is preferable to a multistage or turnover tax and that the scope of the tax should be as broad as possible. Among single-stage taxes, the retail sales tax is preferable on economic and equity grounds, but it is somewhat more costly to administer than either a manufacturers' or a wholesalers' tax.

SINGLE-STAGE VERSUS MULTISTAGE TAXES. The advantage of a multistage tax is that any particular revenue goal can be realized at the lowest possible rate. This makes the turnover tax politically attractive, but it is highly objectionable on other grounds. A turnover tax levied at a uniform rate results in widely varying total rates of tax on different goods, depending on the complexity of the production and distribution channels. This means that the total tax burden differs among commodities, much as it does under a selective excise tax system. Moreover, the multistage tax gives firms a strong incentive to merge with their suppliers and contributes to greater concentration in industry and trade.

Even the uniform rate turns out to be a will-o'-the-wisp whenever the turnover tax is tried. The discriminatory effects of the uniform rate soon become very serious, and the government finds it difficult to resist pressures to moderate the tax load where it is demonstrably out of line. Once introduced, modifications of the uniform rate proliferate, and the tax becomes a maze of complications and irrational distinctions. Thus a tax that was originally intended to be relatively simple turns out to be an administrative monstrosity and highly inequitable.

WHOLESALERS' AND MANUFACTURERS' SALES TAXES. Administrative complications are reduced if the tax is levied at the wholesale or manufacturing level. The number of firms is smaller, their average size larger, and their records more adequate. These advantages are offset, however, by the difficulty of identifying taxable transactions and of determining the price on which the tax is based.

The most troublesome feature of the wholesalers' tax is the determination of wholesale values when manufacturers sell directly to retailers. To avoid discrimination among industries with differing degrees of integration, these manufacturers' prices are usually raised to include a normal wholesale markup. The adjustment goes the other way in the case of the manufacturers' tax: the price a manufacturer charges a retailer must be lowered to eliminate the value of the wholesale services.

Both taxes are subject to the criticism that the rate tends to pyramid as goods move to the retail level. A 10 percent manufacturers' tax may become a 20 percent tax at the retail level after the wholesaler and the retailer have applied their customary markups. There is less pyramiding under a wholesalers' tax, but the problem is by no means avoided. In time, competition tends to wipe out the effect of pyramiding, but the adjustment process may be slow.

On balance, there is little to choose between the wholesalers' and the manufacturers' tax. The wholesalers' tax is more practical when the wholesale and retail stages are fairly distinct; on the other hand, complications arise if there is much integration between manufacturers and retailers. The manufacturers' tax is more practical when there is either a high degree of integration in most consumer lines or none at all; the mixed situation raises the most difficulties.

RETAIL SALES TAX. A retail sales tax is meant to apply uniformly to most goods and services purchased by individual consumers and is basically much less complicated than a wholesalers' or manufacturers' tax. But retail sales taxes are rarely completely general, although they are usually imposed on a broad base. It is difficult to reach many consumer services, although it is possible to include such services as admissions, repairs, laundry, and dry cleaning. The retail sales tax does not apply to housing—the largest service in most consumer budgets—but housing is subject to the property tax. Many state sales taxes in the United States exempt food and other commodities that are regarded as necessities.

Although the retail sales tax often falls short of complete generality, it is in many ways better than the taxes levied at earlier stages of the production or distribution process. Its most important advantage is that there is little or no pyramiding. For goods purchased by consumers, wholesale and retail markups are not inflated by the tax since it applies only to the final price. An attempt is sometimes made to exempt from the retail sales tax investment goods purchased by business firms, but taxes on business purchases often run as high as one-fifth of sales tax receipts, making such exemptions expensive. These taxes enter into business costs and are probably pyramided, but the extent of pyramiding must be only a small fraction of that which occurs under a manufacturers' or wholesalers' sales tax.

The broader base of the retail sales tax means that lower rates can be used than with other single-stage taxes to yield a given amount of revenue. And this difference in rates is not small, since prices may be 50 or 100 percent higher at the retail level. Thus a retail tax of 5 percent may yield the same revenue as a manufacturers' tax of 7.5 or 10 percent.

On administrative grounds, the retail sales tax has both advantages and disadvantages. It is more difficult to deal with the large number of small retailers than with the less numerous and more sophisticated manufacturers or wholesalers. On the other hand, the problems of defining a transaction and of determining the base of the tax are more easily handled at the retail level, although even there the problems are not insignificant. State governments have had retail sales taxes for many years, and most of them have learned that they are not easy to administer and enforce.

The introduction of a retail sales tax by the federal government would involve duplication of existing state and local taxes. The state and local governments would interpret this as unwarranted interference with their freedom of action concerning the rates and coverage of their own taxes. At a minimum, some effort would have to be made to coordinate the definition of the tax bases and perhaps also to administer collection of the taxes on a cooperative or joint basis.

The strongest objection to a retail tax, which also applies to wholesale and manufacturing taxes, is its regressivity. Estimates indicate that in 1970 a 5 percent sales tax on all tangible commodities, including food, would have amounted to 3.8 percent of income for families below the $3,000 level and 1.2 percent for those above $100,000 (table 6-2). These figures, based on income and consumption in a one-year period, overstate the regressivity of the sales tax, since persons temporarily in the lower income classes do not reduce their consumption by the entire amount of the reduction in their incomes, and those temporarily in higher classes do not raise their consumption by the entire increase in their incomes. Some economists have suggested that the burden of the sales tax should be measured against income over a longer period. On this basis, a retail sales tax would be less regressive and might even be proportional, but it is unlikely that it would turn out to be progressive to any significant degree, regardless of the time period examined.

Many units of government have exempted food and certain other items of consumption from the sales tax to alleviate its burden on the poor. Although these exemptions moderate the regressivity of the tax, they do not eliminate it. As an alternative, experts have long suggested refunding the estimated tax paid by people with low incomes. This suggestion was ignored until 1963, when Indiana introduced a retail sales tax and adopted a small tax credit against the income tax as a relief measure for the sales tax paid by low-income recipients. Since then, Indiana has repealed its sales tax credit, but Colorado, Hawaii, Idaho, Massachusetts, Nebraska, Vermont, and the District of Columbia have adopted it. New Mexico provides a credit for all state and local taxes for persons with incomes of less than $8,000.

The Value Added Tax

The value added tax, first proposed in 1918 by a German industrial executive, was discussed sporadically for more than three decades before it was actually put to use. A modified version was adopted in 1953 by the state of Michigan and repealed in 1967; in 1954 the central government of France imposed such a tax, and most European countries and many other countries have since followed suit. Some have advocated the inclusion of a value added tax in the U.S. federal tax system to provide a revenue source that could be raised or lowered in the interest of stabilization.

FORMS OF VALUE ADDED TAXATION. Conceptually, the value added tax is a general tax on the national income. For any given firm, value added is the difference between receipts from sales and amounts paid for materials, supplies, and services purchased from other firms. The total of the value added by all firms in the economy is equal to total wages, salaries, interest, rents, and profits and is therefore the same as the national income.

In practice, there are two types of value added taxes that differ only in the way outlays for investment purposes are treated. The first type permits business firms to subtract purchases of capital goods in computing the tax base. Total value added is thus equal to total retail sales of final consumer goods. With the second type, purchases of capital goods are not deducted; instead, firms are permitted to deduct an allowance for depreciation over the useful life of the asset.

Thus only the second type is equivalent to a tax on the national income; the first, which is proposed most often, is a general consumption tax.

There are two methods of computing the allowance to be made for purchases from other firms. Under the "tax credit" method, the tax rate is applied to the total sales of the firm, and the tax paid on goods purchased is then deducted. Where this method is used, the tax on all goods shipped must be shown separately on each invoice. Under the second, the "calculation" method, purchases are subtracted from sales, and the tax rate is then applied to the net figure.

The two methods may be illustrated as follows. Suppose a retailer who pays $52.50 for an item (including a 5 percent tax of $2.50) applies a markup of 100 percent. Under the tax credit method, he charges his customer $105 ($100 plus $5 tax) and takes a credit of $2.50 in computing the amount to be paid to the government, leaving a net tax of $2.50. If the calculation method is used, the retailer deducts from the $100 the $50 paid to his supplier and then applies a tax rate of 5 percent to the remainder to obtain the same $2.50 net tax. The customer pays the same total price of $105, which consists of the $100 price net of tax, the $2.50 tax paid by the supplier, and the $2.50 tax paid by the retailer.

Although both approaches have the same result, some administrators believe that noncompliance is easier to control under the tax credit method. In addition, the tax credit method automatically provides an accounting of the tax to be remitted on exports (the standard practice to avoid putting domestic firms at a competitive disadvantage in foreign markets) and solves some of the problems raised by the inclusion or exclusion of various items, such as charitable contributions, that are troublesome under the calculation method. In general, however, the taxation of goods and services produced in the tax-exempt and government sectors present difficult problems under a value added tax.

ECONOMIC EFFECTS OF THE VALUE ADDED TAX. The value added tax reduces or eliminates the pyramiding that would occur under the turnover tax or the manufacturers' and wholesalers' sales taxes. Since a firm receives credit for the tax paid by its suppliers, it is unlikely to apply a markup to its purchases in computing the price to be charged.

The base of the consumption-type value added tax is the same as that of a retail sales tax and is confined to goods for consumption. On the other hand, the income-type value added tax is equivalent to a proportional income tax. Whether the patterns of distribution of the burden of the income-type and consumption-type value added taxes are the same is in dispute, reflecting a difference of opinion about the impact of a proportional income tax and a general tax on consumption. The income-type value added tax is paid on capital goods at the time the purchase is made, and the tax is presumably recovered as it is depreciated. Under the consumption-type value added tax, purchases of capital goods are free of tax. Thus, at any given time, the income-type value added tax imposes an extra tax on net investment. Some argue that prepayment of the tax under the income-type tax reduces the return on capital; others believe that it is reflected in higher prices for final consumption goods and has no effect on the rate of return. The difference is not likely to be significant, however.

THE VALUE ADDED TAX VERSUS THE RETAIL SALES TAX. The consumption-type value added tax and the retail sales tax are similar on both economic and equity grounds. Both are taxes on general consumption. The retail sales tax involves fewer administrative problems because the determination of tax liability is less complicated and the number of taxpayers is smaller. But in practice retail sales taxes always exclude many items of consumption, while a value added tax could probably be levied on a more general basis.

Sales or Value Added Taxes versus Income Taxes

Until recently, the major argument for adoption of a sales or value added tax by the federal government was the arbitrariness of the excise tax system. Except for sumptuary and benefit taxes, the excises that were in effect between 1944 and 1965 could hardly be defended on rational grounds. If revenues from consumption taxes were needed permanently, it would have been better to replace the miscellaneous excises with a general low-rate tax on consumer goods.

This argument was eliminated by the enactment of the Excise Tax Reduction Act of 1965. It can be said that, for all practical purposes, the federal government has reduced consumption taxation to a minimum. The appeal of a low-rate consumption tax must now rest on the substantive ground that it would be better national policy to replace part of the income tax with a tax on consumption.

Heavier reliance on a sales or value added tax by the federal government is opposed for several reasons.

First, the shift from income taxes to a consumption tax would impair the built-in flexibility of the tax system. The automatic reductions in income tax revenues during the postwar recessions were of major importance in moderating the declines in disposable income and contributed to the brevity and mildness of the recessions. Maintenance of built-in flexibility is good insurance against the possibility of a serious business contraction.

Second, a sales or value added tax would bring the federal government into an area that is now the most important source of state revenue and is also becoming important at the local level. Federal use of this tax source would almost surely restrict its use by the state and local governments, and their fiscal capacities would be impaired.

Third, because of the opposition of state and local governments, a consumption tax enacted by the federal government might be a tax at the manufacturers' or at the wholesalers' level. Such taxes tend to pyramid through conventional markups and thus to burden the consumer by more than the amount of revenue collected. Moreover, experience in other countries has shown that it is hard to define the tax base so as to avoid serious inequities.

Fourth, the load of federal, state, and local taxes on low-income recipients is already heavy. Increases in state-local revenues in the years immediately ahead will come largely from taxes that burden low-income groups. Additional consumption taxes at the federal level would make the combined structure less progressive. Such a policy would be particularly inappropriate in light of attempts by the federal government to lessen poverty in the United States.

On the other hand, several arguments are advanced in support of greater use of consumption taxes by the federal government.

First, even though income tax rates were lowered in 1964 and 1969, they are still too high, particularly for individuals with high incomes. These high rates may reduce incentives and the willingness and capacity to save.

Second, built-in flexibility does not require that all elements of the federal tax system be highly sensitive to changes in income. A large automatic growth in tax receipts has the effect of promoting higher federal expenditures. If these revenues were not so easily obtained, federal expenditures might be much lower.

Third, the federal government need not impair the fiscal capacities of the state and local governments to build up its own consumption tax revenue. If a value added tax were adopted, the federal government would not encroach on state-local revenue. Since practically all business enterprises already file income tax returns, the administrative and compliance problems of a value added tax should not be insurmountable.

Fourth, adoption of a general consumption tax in lieu of part of the corporation income tax would improve the U.S. balance-of-payments position. This substitution would improve either the trade surplus, if the corporation income tax were shifted to the consumer in the form of higher prices, or the capital account, if the tax were borne by the owners of capital, but this argument has less validity under floating exchange rates (see chapter 5).

While there are a number of important peripheral considerations, the major issue in the income tax versus consumption tax controversy concerns the degree of progression. Proponents of a general consumption tax rarely recommend a graduated expenditure tax (see the next section) as an alternative to income taxation. Their concern is to reduce progression, and they propose a flat rate sales or value added tax as a way of accomplishing this objective. On the other hand, those who oppose a general consumption tax either defend the present degree of progression or believe it is inadequate. Most of them would support a graduated expenditure tax if a new consumption tax were necessary, but oppose the adoption of a sales or value added tax.

The Expenditure Tax

The expenditure tax has long been discussed in the economic literature but was not seriously considered until the Treasury Department recommended it during the Second World War. It was also advocated by a minority of the British Royal Commission on the Taxation of Profits and Income in 1955. Although neither recommendation was adopted, the tax has since come to be regarded as a respectable possibility.

Unlike the consumption taxes already discussed, the expenditure tax is levied on the consumer rather than on the seller of goods and services. In practice, there is little difference in the methods of administering the expenditure tax and the individual income tax. The individual taxpayer submits a form at the end of the year estimating the amount of his or her expenditures. Deductions for selected expenditures may be allowed, as well as personal exemptions. The rates may be proportional or graduated, although it is usually suggested that the expenditure tax be graduated. To achieve a given degree of progression through the income classes, expenditure tax rates would have to be higher than income tax rates to make up for the exemption for savings.

It is advocated that the expenditure tax either replace or supplement the income tax. This is supported strongly by those who believe that the income tax has an adverse effect on the incentive to save and invest (see chapter 4) and that private saving must be incréased to increase the level of output and income. It is also supported as a method of taxing persons who receive capital gains and other income that are either not taxed or taxed at preferential rates. Although preferential income is not reached by the expenditure tax as such, the tax does apply to consumption financed out of this income.

Some have argued that an income tax is inequitable because it taxes income when it is saved and then again when the savings earn additional income. It is now generally agreed that this double taxation argument is sterile. Both the expenditure tax and the income tax may be progressive and redistributional in effect. If income is considered the better measure of ability to pay, the expenditure tax is inferior. If expenditures are considered the better measure, the income tax is inferior. Expenditure tax advocates usually support effective wealth or estate and gift taxes to prevent excessive concentrations of wealth that might result from the tax exemption for savings.

On the assumption of equal yields, an expenditure tax would distribute the burden of taxation very differently from an income tax. Tax burdens would be heavier under an expenditure tax for households with high consumption ratios relative to income, such as young and large families and elderly persons, and lower for those with relatively low consumption ratios, such as families whose children have finished school and single persons in general. Tax rates on outlays for "big-ticket" items such as automobiles, furniture, and homes would be extremely high, and would probably be regarded as excessive by many people. Consequently such expenditures would have to be averaged over the assets' lives, and this would add complications. Some economists believe that the expenditure tax is superior to an income tax because current expenditures reflect normal or permanent income better than current income does. But it is far from obvious that current taxation should be related to income earned in the distant past or future.

Because expenditures tend to be relatively more stable than incomes, an expenditure tax would have less built-in flexibility than an income tax of equal yield over a business cycle. On the other hand, discretionary changes in tax rates for countercyclical purposes would be more effective under the expenditure tax, since expenditure tax changes would directly affect the net cost of current purchases (relative to future purchases) and would therefore have a much greater effect on consumption than income tax changes of equal amount.

Taxpayers cannot estimate their expenditures directly, since almost no one keeps adequate expenditure records. They must be estimated by subtracting investment outlays made during the year from total receipts. This calculation requires the taxpayer to furnish information on the proceeds of all dispositions of assets, the costs of newly acquired assets, and changes in cash holdings and bank and savings accounts, as well as on the ordinary income receipts now reported on income tax returns. Administration and compliance would be more difficult under the expenditure tax than under the income tax in some respects and easier in others. Changes in cash holdings, personal debts, and purchases and dispositions of personal assets (such as jewelry and paintings) would be hard to trace. On the other hand, the expenditure tax would avoid the problems created by the use of the realization principle for calculating capital gains and losses; and since capital outlays would be treated as an expense when the outlays were made, the complications of accrual accounting adjustments for depreciation and depletion would be eliminated. In distinguishing between business and personal expenditures, both taxes are subject to somewhat similar problems, and both are subject to tax base erosion through the proliferation of personal deductions. On balance, the administrative and compliance problems are difficult but probably not insuperable for advanced countries that have effective income tax administrations. But most countries would find it difficult to enforce such a tax with the present state of administrative know-how.

Summary

The federal government has relied exclusively on selected excises for consumption tax revenues. These taxes were increased during every major war and were subsequently de-emphasized as the need for revenue declined. The cycle lasted somewhat longer during and after World War II, but the last vestige of the wartime excises was eliminated by the 1965 Excise Tax Reduction Act. When this law becomes fully effective (scheduled for January 1, 1982), the only excise taxes remaining in the federal revenue system will be the sumptuary taxes on alcohol and tobacco, the benefit taxes for highways, airways, and some recreational activities, and certain regulatory taxes.

Sumptuary taxes help offset the additional cost to society of the consumption of certain commodities; taxes imposed on those who benefit from particular government services are needed to prevent excessive use of such services; and special charges would help discourage private activities that lead to pollution. Otherwise, excise taxes are bad taxes: they discriminate arbitrarily against the consumption of the taxed commodities and distort the allocation of resources in the economy.

If consumption taxes are needed to boost revenue, economic and equity considerations suggest that a general consumption tax would be more appropriate than a series of selective excise taxes. A general tax does not discriminate against particular forms of consumption and therefore produces less distortion in the economy.

Among general consumption taxes, manufacturers' and wholesalers' sales taxes are probably the easiest to administer, but they are pyramided through the markup of prices as goods go through production and distribution channels. Retail sales taxes and the value added tax involve much less pyramiding, if any. All these taxes are regressive or, at best, proportional. Progression can be achieved by adopting a credit for sales taxes paid against the individual income tax or by taxing consumption through a graduated expenditure tax. The expenditure tax has a number of attractive features, but it is regarded as too difficult to administer.

Consumption taxes are more burdensome than income taxes on the low income classes, and they have less built-in flexibility. Adoption of a general consumption tax by the federal government would also interfere with a revenue source that has become a mainstay of state and some local tax systems. However, consumption taxes are vigorously supported by those who believe that the federal tax system is too progressive and that income taxation has impaired economic incentives. More recently, there has been some support for the adoption of a graduated expenditure tax to replace part or all of the individual and corporation income taxes to help increase the national saving rate and to promote a higher rate of economic growth.

CHAPTER SEVEN

Payroll Taxes

TAXES ON PAYROLLS, first introduced into the federal revenue system by the Social Security Act of 1935, have grown markedly since the end of the Second World War. They rank second in importance, accounting for 31 percent of federal budget receipts in fiscal year 1976 (figure 7-1). Payroll taxes will continue to rise as scheduled rate increases go into effect. Unlike income, excise, estate, and gift taxes, payroll taxes are "earmarked"—through trust funds—to finance the nation's social security programs.

The Development of Payroll Taxes

Most countries levy special taxes on payrolls (or income) to finance social insurance. When the United States passed its Social Security Act, twenty-eight countries had well-developed national retirement systems. The depression of the 1930s demonstrated that the state and local governments and private industry did not have the capacity to develop and finance a stable and adequate retirement program for the general population.

The 1935 act established two social insurance programs: a federal system of old-age benefits (now old age, survivors, disability, and health insurance—OASDHI—commonly called "social security") and a federal-state system of unemployment compensation. The first

**Figure 7-1. Payroll Taxes as a Percentage of Gross National Product, Federal
Budget Receipts, and Individual Income Tax Receipts, Fiscal Years 1954–76**

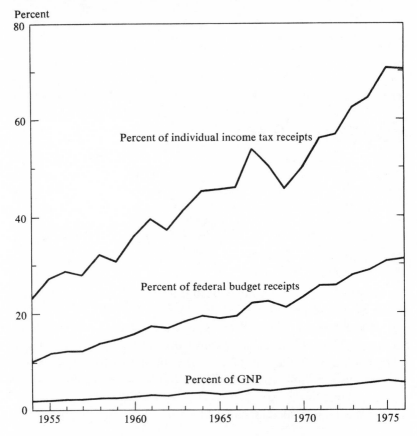

Source: *The Budget of the United States Government,* various years.

is financed by payroll taxes collected from employees and employers
in equal amounts; the second is financed mainly by payroll taxes on
employers (a few states tax both employers and employees). The
major characteristics of these programs are summarized in table 7-1.

The original programs have undergone considerable change in
coverage, benefits, and tax rates. Old-age benefits were supplemented
by survivors' benefits in 1939, disability benefits in 1957, and hospital
and medical benefits for persons sixty-five and over in 1966. The tax
rate, initially 1 percent each on employers and employees for wages
and salaries up to $3,000 annually, is now (1977) 5.85 percent on

each and is scheduled to rise to 6.45 percent by 1986. Since 1972 the top limit on earnings subject to tax has been automatically adjusted upward by the rise in average wages; in 1977 the maximum taxable earnings limit is $16,500. Self-employed persons with net earnings in excess of $400 a year were added to the social security system in 1951, with a tax rate 1.5 times the rate applied to employees. However, the tax rate for the self-employed has been frozen at 7.9 percent since 1974.

The federal unemployment compensation tax rate started at 1 percent of payrolls of employers of eight or more persons; in 1977 the rate is 3.4 percent for employers of one or more persons on wages and salaries up to $4,200 (rising to $6,000 in 1978). Lower rates (with a minimum stipulated by the federal government) are permitted in most states, depending on the stability of the employer's past record of employment.

Railroad workers are covered, though at higher rates, for both retirement and unemployment under their own systems. As under social security, employer and employee each pay half of the railroad retirement insurance tax; as under the federal-state system, the employer pays all of the railroad unemployment insurance tax.

The employees' share of payroll taxes is withheld at the source by employers, but these taxes differ from the pattern established by the individual income tax in other respects. In the first place, they are levied at a flat rate on gross wages and salaries up to a certain maximum amount each year, with no exemptions or deductions. Second, the employee—even though liable for half the OASDHI tax—does not file a return. The reporting of earnings, which provide the basis for calculating benefits, is handled entirely by the employer. Taxes are paid quarterly by the self-employed on an estimated basis.

In 1976 the federal old age, survivors, disability, and health programs covered more than 90 percent of all persons in paid jobs; 90 percent of the population sixty-five and over drew benefits. The hospital insurance program covered about 22 million people sixty-five and over. Unemployment insurance covered about 66 million people, or over 85 percent of the total number of wage and salary earners.

When the social security program was enacted in 1935, considerable emphasis was placed on its resemblance to private insurance: "contributions" were paid by the worker and the employer into a trust fund, interest was credited on trust fund balances, and benefits were

Table 7-1. Major Characteristics of the Social Insurance Programs as of July 1, 1976

Program	Contribution rates (percent except as marked)		Maximum earnings subject to tax (dollars)	Eligibility requirements for benefits	Benefits
	Employee	Employer			
Old age, survivors, and disability insurance	4.95	4.95	15,300 a year (16,500 in 1977)	OASI: 1½ to 10 years of coverage; age 62 and over for men and women workers and wives; age 60 for widows	Individual: maximum $577.60 a month[a] Individual: minimum $107.90 a month[b] Family: maximum $1,010.70 a month[a] Family: minimum $161.90 a month[b]
				Disability: insured status for OASI and recent employment; 5-month waiting period following total disability	Same as OASI
Hospital	0.9[c]	0.9[c]	15,300 a year (16,500 in 1977)	Age 65 and over; entitled to disability benefits under OASDI or railroad retirement for at least 24 consecutive months; or chronic renal disease	60 days (with $104 deductible) plus 30 days at $26 a day; also post-hospital services;[d] and a lifetime reserve of 60 days with a $52 daily coinsurance
Supplementary medical (voluntary)	$7.20 premium a month[e]	...	...	Age 65 and over; entitled to disability benefits under OASDI or railroad retirement for at least 24 consecutive months; or chronic renal disease	$60 deductible and 20% coinsurance[f]

Unemployment compensation	...	3.2[g]	4,200 a year (6,000 in 1978)	3–6 months of covered employment, depending on state law	Typically 50% of weekly wage: from 26 to 36 weeks, with additional weeks of extended and emergency benefits payable in states with high unemployment rates
Railroad retirement	5.85[h]	15.35[h]	1,275 a month	10 years of coverage, age 65 and over[i]	Maximum: $726 (for worker retiring at age 65 in July 1976),[j] with spouse $1,068[k]
Railroad unemployment compensation	...	5.5[l]	400 a month	Compensation of at least $1,000 in base year[m]	Typically 60% of daily pay for last employment in base year (subject to maximum of $25 a day), up to 130 days; extended benefits payable to long-term employees and to others during periods of high unemployment

Source: Social Security Administration.

a. Generally not payable for many years to come. Maximum payable to a male worker who retired at sixty-five in January 1976 was $364.00; to a family, $648.40.

b. Permanently reduced benefits payable for retirement between sixty-two and sixty-five, or between sixty and sixty-five and sixty-two for widows. Minimum benefits are before the reduction for early retirement.

c. To increase to 1.10 percent in 1978–80, to 1.35 percent in 1981–85, and to 1.5 percent after 1985.

d. Post-hospital services include care in a skilled nursing facility (cost of first 20 days and excess over $10.50 a day for next 100) under a registered professional nurse or care in a private home (for 100 visits) if only intermittent nursing is needed.

e. In December of each year the secretary of health, education, and welfare determines the premiums necessary to collect one-half the projected expense of the program, not to exceed the percentage increase in OASDI benefits for the current year.

f. Includes most physicians' and related services.

g. Scheduled to rise to 3.4 percent in 1977. In most states, rates are reduced on the basis of experience rating.

h. Increases in steps in accordance with OASDHI increases. Includes hospital insurance.

i. Benefits payable at age sixty with 30 years of service or reduced benefits at sixty-two to sixty-four with less than 30 years of service. Survivors and disability insurance also available.

j. $769 if supplemental annuity is payable.

k. $1,071 if supplemental annuity is payable.

l. Statutory rates vary from 0.5 to 8.0 percent depending on balance in trust fund.

m. Base year is calendar year preceding the beginning of the benefit year, which runs from July 1 to the following June 30.

formally based on the worker's previous earnings. This emphasis promoted public acceptance of the system as a permanent government institution.

The insurance analogy no longer applies to the system as it has developed. Present beneficiaries as a group receive far larger benefits than those to which the taxes they have paid, plus a reasonable rate of return, would entitle them, and this situation will continue indefinitely as long as Congress keeps benefits in line with higher current wage levels. Although the trust fund balances have tended to increase over the long run, they are not large enough to finance even one year's worth of benefits (appendix table C-20), so the payroll taxes paid by workers are not stored up or invested but are paid out currently as benefits. When the benefits promised to current workers become due, they will be paid from the tax revenues of that future date. Thus social security is really a compact between the working and nonworking generations that is continually renewed and strengthened by every amendment to the basic program.

In this concept of social security, payroll taxes are not insurance premiums but rather a financing mechanism for a large, essential government program. Those who hold this view believe that payroll taxes should be evaluated like any other major tax of the federal government; increases in benefits and expansion of the social security program should not be financed automatically by higher payroll taxes as they have been in the past, but by the best tax source or sources available to the federal government. On the other hand, since the retirement and disability benefits are related to past wages, many believe that the system has sufficient insurance elements to justify taxing payrolls to finance it.

Features of Payroll Taxes

As the second largest source of federal revenue, payroll taxes have a significant effect on the distribution of tax burdens and may also have a substantial impact on the economy. From the standpoint of tax analysis their important features are their regressivity; their built-in flexibility; their effect on prices, employment, and wages; and their effect on personal and public saving.

Regressivity

A payroll tax of 11.7 percent on earnings up to $16,500 (the maximum limit in 1977) is progressive for income up to about $12,000, roughly proportional for income between $12,000 and $22,000, and regressive thereafter (figure 7-2). This pattern ʊf tax incidence reflects the changing importance of covered earnings as incomes rise. In the lower part of the income scale, the ratio of covered earnings to total income increases; the ratio begins to fall at

Figure 7-2. Effective Tax Rates of the Payroll Tax and of Alternative Methods of Raising the Same Revenue, 1977[a]

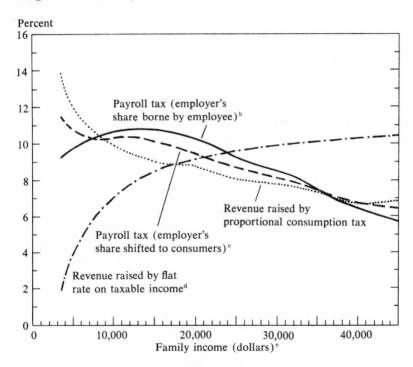

Percent

Payroll tax (employer's share borne by employee)[b]

Revenue raised by proportional consumption tax

Payroll tax (employer's share shifted to consumers)[c]

Revenue raised by flat rate on taxable income[d]

Family income (dollars)[e]

Source: Brookings 1970 MERGE data file projected to 1977.

a. Tax is 11.7 percent for wage earners and 7.9 percent for the self-employed. Maximum earnings subject to tax are $16,500.

b. Both the employer and the employee portions of the tax are assumed to be borne by the employee; the self-employment tax by the self-employed.

c. The employer tax is distributed in proportion to consumption by income class; the employee tax and self-employment tax by the employee and the self-employed, respectively.

d. The tax is applied to taxable income as defined in the income tax law for 1977.

e. Family income is a comprehensive definition of income, which includes estimated accrued capital gains.

Table 7-2. Maximum Combined Employer-Employee Taxes and Maximum Taxes on Self-Employed under the OASDI and Hospital Insurance Programs, 1970–77
Dollars

Year	Maximum employer-employee tax			Maximum tax on self-employed		
	OASDI	Hospital insurance	Total	OASDI	Hospital insurance	Total
1970	655.20	93.60	748.80	491.40	46.80	538.20
1971	717.60	93.60	811.20	538.20	46.80	585.00
1972	828.00	108.00	936.00	621.00	54.00	675.00
1973	1,047.60	216.00	1,263.60	756.00	108.00	864.00
1974	1,306.80	237.60	1,544.40	924.00	118.80	1,042.80
1975	1,395.90	253.80	1,649.70	987.00	126.90	1,113.90
1976	1,514.70	275.40	1,790.10	1,071.00	137.70	1,208.70
1977	1,633.50	297.00	1,930.50	1,155.00	148.50	1,303.50

Source: Social security statutes enacted in 1969 and later years.

higher levels because the payroll tax applies to only the first $16,500 and because property income, which is not subject to these taxes, becomes increasingly important as incomes rise above this point.

On the basis of 1970 data, the 1977 social security payroll tax is more progressive than a proportional tax on consumption up to the maximum taxable earnings level and less progressive thereafter. The income tax is much more progressive than the payroll tax throughout the income scale. These conclusions are the same if the employer and employee portions of the OASDHI taxes are assumed to be borne entirely by the wage earners or if it is assumed that only the employee tax is borne by wage earners and the employer tax is shifted to consumers.

Payroll taxes have a significant impact on the tax payments of the lowest income groups. In 1977 the employee and employer taxes for social security, disability, and hospital care will reach 11.7 percent of wages up to $16,500, or a maximum of $1,930.50 (table 7-2). This exceeds the 1976 income tax liabilities of single persons with incomes of about $13,000, married persons with incomes of $15,000, and married persons with two children and incomes of $17,000. In 1977 the federal payroll tax for OASDHI purposes will be the highest tax paid by about two-thirds of the nation's income recipients (assuming backward shifting of the employer tax), $2.5 billion will be paid by persons in families officially classified as living below poverty levels.

To moderate the burden of the social security tax on low incomes, Congress introduced in 1975 a refundable income tax credit of 10 percent of earnings (phasing down to zero at $8,000) for persons with children. (The credit is "refundable" because cash payments are made to those who are not subject to tax.) About 85 percent of the payroll tax liability is eliminated for those eligible for the full amount of the credit.

Built-in Flexibility

Payroll taxes are much less sensitive than the federal individual income tax to fluctuations in national income and employment. Since the social security tax is levied at a flat rate up to a limit that increases with the consumer price index, its yield (if the tax rate is constant) fluctuates no more than in proportion to personal income, unlike the individual income tax, which fluctuates more than proportionately to income over a business cycle. Automatic increases in the payroll tax rates enacted for many years ahead have occasionally come at the wrong time. Such increases went into effect when the country was in the midst of the 1953–54 recession, and only a few months before the onset of recessions in 1957 and 1960. The automatic escalation of the maximum taxable earnings ceiling raised payroll taxes twice during the 1974–75 business contraction. However, benefits have usually been raised along with or shortly after tax increases, offsetting their deflationary impact. Since 1973 benefits have been raised automatically each year on the basis of increases in average covered earnings.

Pressure for increasing payroll taxes at inappropriate times in the business cycle has also been experienced in state unemployment compensation programs. When the trust funds are threatened by a lack of reserves, the states are forced to raise tax rates regardless of the level of economic activity. Almost all states have adopted the "experience rating" system, which reduces tax rates for firms with stable employment. As a result, state unemployment taxes may fluctuate *inversely* with national income and employment levels.

By contrast, the expenditure side of the social insurance trust accounts has been extremely effective in promoting economic stability.

Unemployment insurance benefits increase automatically as demand slackens and unemployment increases; they decline automatically as employment picks up. This automatic effect is supplemented (by advances from the federal government's general fund, if necessary) during periods of high national or state unemployment by the payment of thirteen additional weeks of benefits to workers who have exhausted their benefits under the regular state programs. In addition, older workers fall back on old-age insurance when they cannot find employment during slack periods.

On balance, despite the regressivity of the taxes and the inappropriate timing of tax rate increases, the social insurance system has contributed notably to the nation's economic stability during the postwar period.

Effect on Prices, Employment, and Wages

It is popularly assumed that the employees' share of the payroll tax is borne by wage earners and that the employer's share is shifted forward to the consumer in the form of higher prices. But economists believe there is no difference in the incidence of the payroll taxes legally levied on employers and employees.

The OASDHI tax is a proportional tax on wages and salaries up to a given ceiling. Although a few categories of workers are excluded, the tax may be regarded as virtually universal for workers in the private sector; public employees have their own contributory retirement systems and may also be covered by social security at the option of state and local governments. Since the social security tax is paid in almost every occupation and industry, employees have no incentive to move elsewhere to avoid it. Thus, like the personal income tax, the payroll tax is not shifted.

In the short run, producers treat the payroll tax like any other production cost and try to recover it through higher prices. At the higher prices they do not sell as much as they did at pre-tax prices, and output and employment tend to decline. This effect can be offset if the government maintains real demand at the old level (through a combination of monetary and fiscal policies), but relative prices and output will be altered in any event. If money demand does not expand sufficiently, output and employment will fall.

In the long run, the impact of the payroll tax depends on the reaction of wage earners to reduced wages. Business firms aim at using just the right combination of labor and capital to produce at lowest cost. A payroll tax does not make labor any more productive, so employers have no reason to pay higher total compensation after the tax is imposed unless some wage earners react to their reduced earnings by withdrawing from the labor force (that is, unless the supply of labor is less than completely inelastic with respect to wages). If some wage earners do withdraw, employers will have to offer higher wages to attract additional employees or to keep those that remain; wages will rise as a result of the tax (though not necessarily by the exact amount of the tax), and less labor will be employed.

But it is generally agreed that the aggregate supply of labor is inelastic with respect to wages: lower wages will not induce wage earners to withdraw from the labor force. In these circumstances, the same number of workers will be seeking the same number of jobs, wages will be lower by the amount of the tax, and the workers will bear the full burden. Although wages may not actually fall, they will increase less rapidly than they would have without the payroll tax, thereby shifting the burden of the tax to the wage earner in the long run.

It is also possible that workers will bear the tax even if the supply of labor is not completely inelastic with respect to wages. Employees may be willing to accept a lower wage after the tax is imposed if they regard the benefits financed by the tax as an adequate quid pro quo. If this were the prevailing attitude, the tax would be similar to a user charge, the supply of labor would not be altered, earnings would fall by the amount of the tax, and the full burden would be borne by the wage earners.

One qualification must be applied to the conclusion that the burden of payroll taxes falls on the wage earner. The economic model on which the analysis is based assumes rational behavior in labor markets and takes no account of the possible effect on wages of collective bargaining agreements between large firms and labor unions. Labor unions will resist any cut in the wages of their members and may succeed in inducing management to raise gross wages by an amount sufficient to offset the effect of the payroll tax. In such circumstances, part or all of the employer and employee portions of the tax may be transferred to the consumer. Critics of this view argue that, if such market power existed, labor and management could have exercised it to raise wages and prices before the tax was imposed. Nevertheless, one cannot dismiss the possibility that the adoption of a new payroll tax or an increase in the old one may be the occasion when labor and management choose to exercise this power.

Personal and Public Saving

National social insurance provides protection against loss of income resulting from retirement, death, unemployment, permanent disability, and illness. Before these government programs were enacted, people's savings were their only protection against these hazards. Social insurance may encourage individuals to set aside a smaller amount of personal saving on the ground that a major reason for saving has been removed. On the other hand, the availability of social insurance gives people an incentive to retire earlier, and this encourages them to save more.

So far these tendencies have probably offset one another and total personal saving has not been greatly affected on balance. In fact, personal saving rose from 5.0 to 7.8 percent of disposable income between 1929 and 1975, but many other factors influenced this ratio. The effect on retirement, however, has been virtually exhausted (since most people are retired by the age of sixty-five), so the incentive to save less because of the existence of social security may predominate in the future.

The effect of the social security programs on government saving is less clear. As of June 30, 1976, the trust fund accumulations were over $67 billion, half of which was there in 1956 (appendix table C-20). Had these balances not been accumulated, other taxes might have been raised to yield approximately the same revenue, expenditures might have been reduced, or additional debt might have been issued to the public. Since the administrative budget, which was used by the federal government throughout this period, excluded trust fund saving, federal saving was probably larger (or dissaving smaller) because of the trust funds. This may well have been a factor in slowing economic growth during the late 1950s.

The unified budget, which is now used for federal budget purposes, takes trust fund balances into account. Presumably this implies that other taxes might have been higher had the payroll taxes been lower. But it is still uncertain whether the philosophy behind the unified budget has been completely accepted.

The trust fund balances rose rapidly between mid-1966 and mid-

1970, when prices and wages were rising sharply. The existence of large surpluses in the trust funds probably made it easier to achieve a higher level of taxes, which was needed to help contain the inflation. In view of the great difficulties faced by the Johnson and Nixon administrations in enacting and extending the Vietnam War surtax on individual and corporation income taxes, other taxes probably could not have been raised sufficiently to provide the receipts that were obtained from the trust funds during this period.

The recession-induced decline in the old age, survivors, and disability fund balances in 1975 and 1976 created a great deal of concern in both the Ford administration and Congress. Proposals for increasing social security taxes to restore the trust fund balances were seriously considered even though the economy was still in the early stages of recovery, but action was deferred primarily on grounds of countercyclical policy. With continued emphasis on the unified budget by federal policymakers, the short-term condition of the trust funds may have less impact on fiscal policies than in the past.

Financing Social Security

In view of the multiple objectives of the social security program, it is not surprising to find disagreement over financing methods. Some advocate recourse to general revenues to finance future increases in benefits; others favor continued use of payroll taxes; still others prefer a combination of the two.

The Contributory System

Financing social security through regressive contributory taxes is well established in most countries. Although the benefits are not based on the actuarial value of taxes paid, they are related to the earnings record of the individual worker. Receipts are earmarked to make workers feel they are receiving benefits as a right rather than as a gift from the government. The earmarked taxes emphasize the statutory nature of the benefit and may discourage reduction in benefits when the budget is tight. And it is believed easier to obtain increases in benefits if they are financed by the contributions of future beneficiaries rather than from general tax revenues.

Those who oppose financing social security through the contributory system point out that benefits are not closely tied to the tax payments. There are both minima and maxima to the level of benefits. Congress has been lenient in extending eligibility to people with minimum periods of covered employment. Under the circumstances, the benefit payments can hardly be said to approximate contributions even loosely. The regressivity of the taxes adds to dissatisfaction with the contributory system.

In practice, the financing of OASDHI in the United States is a compromise between these conflicting points of view. Although the taxes are regressive, the social security system does give to the lowest-paid workers the largest benefits relative to their contributions. The existence of balances in the reserve fund gives assurance to the millions of covered workers that their rights to benefits are protected. The present OASDHI system could be administered without the reserve fund device, but every impartial commission that has ever examined this question has concluded that the reserve fund should be continued. However, the appropriate size of the reserve remains at issue.

A significant departure from the precedent of relying entirely on payroll taxes to finance social security benefits occurred in 1965, when Congress added medical and hospital insurance to the OASDI system. Hospital care for the insured aged was funded by payroll tax contributions from employers and employees; the general fund pays for those not insured. Medical insurance was made available to aged persons who voluntarily paid a fee of $3 a month; an equal amount was transferred to a new trust fund by appropriation from the general fund. The premium rate for medical insurance was subject to change after 1967, depending on actual experience, but the general fund continues to match the individual's payment, which rose to $7.20 a month July 1, 1976.

Another departure from payroll tax financing was made in 1966, when all those reaching the age of seventy-two before 1968 were granted a special benefit, regardless of whether they were covered by social security. The benefit, which as of July 1976 amounted to $74.10 a month ($111.08 when husband and wife both qualify), is reduced by an amount equal to the benefits of any other federal, state, or local retirement program for which the individual is qualified. This extension of coverage, which affects fewer and fewer individuals as time passes, is financed out of the federal funds.

In 1972 the federal supplemental security income (SSI) program was enacted to provide a uniform minimum income guarantee for the aged, blind, and disabled. Some states are continuing to supplement SSI payments for beneficiaries who were receiving higher benefits under the earlier system of public assistance, but the basic SSI payments are made entirely by the federal government out of general revenues. In 1976 SSI supplemented the monthly income (earned and unearned) of those eligible up to a maximum of $167.80 for single persons and $251.80 for married couples, plus $20 from another source. It has been proposed that social security benefits be converted to a flat percentage of earnings and SSI be relied on to bring the lowest benefits up to an adequate level.

Proposals for Reform

Suggestions for changing the method of financing social security fall into four categories.

REDUCE REGRESSIVITY. One way to reduce regressivity would be to raise the amount of earnings subject to tax and eventually to remove the limit entirely. The taxes would then become proportional taxes on payrolls and would still be regressive for total income but much less so than under present law. Increases in the earnings base have helped to finance higher benefits in recent years and will doubtless continue to be used in the future.

A major share of the burden of the payroll tax at the lower end of the income scale would be eliminated if the 10 percent refundable income tax credit enacted in 1975 were increased to the 11.7 percent social security tax rate and if people without children were made eligible for the credit. The cost of such an expanded credit would be about $6 billion a year at 1977 earnings levels.

CONVERT TO A PROGRESSIVE EARNINGS TAX. Introducing into the payroll tax personal exemptions and a low-income allowance to approximate the poverty levels, as in the income tax, and eliminating the maximum taxable earnings ceiling would make the payroll tax a progressive tax on earnings even if there were only a single tax rate. The exemption and low-income allowance would eliminate taxes paid by earners who were below the poverty levels, and with no taxable earnings limit an increasing proportion of earnings would be taxed as earnings rose. At 1976 price levels, a per capita exemption of $900 and a $2,000 low-income allowance would closely approximate the poverty levels. With such an exemption and low-income allowance, it would be necessary to raise the employer and employee tax rates by 1.7 percentage points each (from the combined total of 11.7 percent to 15.1 percent) to yield the revenues produced by the 1976 social security tax.

INTEGRATE THE PAYROLL AND INCOME TAXES. Another way to moderate regressivity would be to incorporate the employee contribution into the individual income tax, either directly or through the credit device. With coverage now available to more than 90 percent of workers (in the case of OASDHI), the income tax population for any given generation of workers is not very different from the payroll tax population. The differences that do exist between the two taxes—the exemptions, personal deductions, and broader income concept—argue in favor of using the income tax rather than the payroll tax. The psychological advantage of having a special earmarked tax to finance the social security programs can be duplicated either by the credit device or by allocating some percentage of the income tax receipts, or a given number of percentage points of the income tax rates, to the reserve funds.

The decision to integrate the employee tax with the individual income tax would not necessarily require a change in the employer tax, although the two would undoubtedly be considered together. One method might be to replace the employer tax by adding the necessary number of percentage points to the individual and corporation income taxes. For example, the OASDHI tax paid by employers on 1977 payrolls is equivalent to a 5-percentage-point increase in all individual and corporation income tax rates.

USE THE GENERAL FUND. As indicated, precedent exists for using general fund receipts to finance social insurance. With the combined employer-employee OASDHI tax scheduled to be 12.1 percent in 1978–80 and higher in later years, use of the general fund might be considered in lieu of rate increases when additional funds are required to finance benefits. Since the general fund relies primarily on progressive taxes, this would automatically improve the equity of the overall tax system.

One way to introduce general revenue financing would be to adopt the recommendation of the 1975 Quadrennial Advisory Council on Social Security that the payroll tax receipts of the hospital insurance fund be gradually shifted to OASDI and that general revenue receipts be used to replace the payroll tax receipts in the hospital fund. The council pointed out that the benefits under the hospital program for the aged are not related to wages and that consequently there is no justification for using a payroll tax to finance these benefits.

EFFECT ON BENEFITS. None of the methods of moderating or eliminating the regressivity of the social security payroll tax would necessarily require a change in the method of calculating benefits. Benefits are now related to earnings; since the basic objective of the system is to moderate the decline in earnings at retirement, the relation between benefits and past earnings can be preserved whatever the structure of the tax used to finance the benefits. Under the present system, benefits are calculated by declining percentages up to the taxable earnings ceiling. A ceiling on benefits is appropriate because the national retirement system should be used to guarantee benefits based on earnings up to some reasonable level, beyond which private pension arrangements and personal saving could be expected to take over. The decision to eliminate the earnings ceiling entirely or to replace the payroll tax by the income tax or general revenues would require an explicit decision on the point at which earnings replacement would terminate. Those who wish to protect the insurance image of the system would oppose any move to divorce the maximum benefit from the maximum earnings or income subject to tax. Those who do not regard the system as insurance see no practical difficulty in establishing reasonable maximum benefit levels without tying them to the tax limit.

Financing Unemployment Insurance

Two major financial features of the unemployment insurance system have been subject to criticism in recent years: the variation of tax rates among firms in accordance with their employment experience and the inadequacy of trust funds in states suffering heavy and prolonged unemployment.

Although experience rating has survived for four decades, it is still the subject of considerable debate. The principle was adopted to induce employers to stabilize their employment and also to avoid the criticism that firms with stable employment would be subsidizing those with irregular employment records. Some believe that the minima and maxima applying to the payroll tax for unemployment insurance should be removed so that the full cost of its own unemployment would be borne by each firm. The major argument against experience rating has been that individual firms have little control over unemployment, particularly of the cyclical variety. It has also been suggested that, since the contribution rates of firms vary, only the lowest tax paid by any firm can be shifted to consumers or wage earners. This may well account for the resistance of employers to increases in coverage and benefits. Despite these objections, there is considerable reluctance to abandon experience rating, partly because it gives individual employers an incentive to prevent abuse of the system and partly because there is strong objection to the redistribution of tax burdens among firms. On the other hand, there seems to be little support for basing the tax entirely on the actual experience of each firm.

The concentration of unemployment in particular industries and regions has had an uneven effect on the state trust funds. The federal government has extended coverage for workers who had exhausted their benefit rights in every recession in response to the needs of many states for assistance. In 1958 funds were advanced to states that elected to participate. In 1961 extended coverage was financed through a temporary increase in the federal unemployment compensation tax.

In 1970 Congress enacted permanent legislation to finance the automatic extension of benefits when unemployment becomes serious. Benefits of up to thirteen additional weeks are paid when the national unemployment rate reaches 4.5 percent and stays there for three months or in a state when unemployment in that state increases by 20 percent over the average of the preceding two years and is at least 4 percent.

In addition, the federal government now finances retraining or readjustment allowances under the Manpower Development and Training Act of 1962, the Trade Expansion Act of 1962, and the Economic Development Act of 1965. The multiplicity of programs points to the need for a thorough review and realignment of methods used to ease the financial strain on unemployed workers seeking employment or undergoing training.

In 1976 benefits were extended temporarily to a maximum of sixty-five weeks for covered workers and twenty-six weeks for workers who were not covered. (This extension is now scheduled to expire December 31, 1977.) Benefits under the unemployment insurance program have not kept pace with the rise in wages; their liberalization will require either an increase in the earnings base, increases in the tax rate, or contributions from the general fund.

Summary

Payroll taxes paved the way for the enactment of a comprehensive system of social security and unemployment compensation that protects workers against income losses from retirement, unemployment, and disability. Legislation passed in 1965 also provided protection for retired workers against the high costs of hospitalization and medical care. Although these programs were originally described as "social insurance," they have developed into a large (and essential) tax-transfer system. The payroll taxes that are now used to finance them should therefore be evaluated like any other major federal tax. These taxes lack the built-in flexibility of the individual income tax and are regressive. In the long run, payroll taxes are probably paid by the worker; it makes no difference whether the law imposes the tax on the employee or on the employer.

Although the trust fund device was introduced simultaneously with the payroll taxes, the two are separable issues. Money for the trust funds could be raised from other earmarked tax sources or from the general fund. On the other hand, payroll taxes could be continued as the basic method of obtaining employee and employer contributions without a trust fund. The past accumulation of reserves was probably deflationary, but there is no reason for federal fiscal policies to disregard the effect of the trust funds on stability and growth. The use of a unified budget for federal accounting has probably been helpful.

In view of the present importance of the payroll taxes and the increases in tax rates already scheduled, the effects of these taxes on the distribution of income can no longer be ignored. Improvement of the earned income tax credit, introduction of personal exemptions and a low-income allowance into the payroll tax and removal of the maximum taxable earnings ceiling, integration of the payroll and income taxes, or use of the general fund for financing increased social security benefits would improve the equity of these taxes.

CHAPTER EIGHT

Estate and Gift Taxes

TAXES ON PROPERTY left by an individual to his heirs are among the oldest forms of taxation. In societies in which property is privately owned, the state protects the property rights of the individual and supervises the transfer from one generation to the next. Consequently, the state has always regarded property transfers as appropriate objects of taxation.

Transfer taxation can take several forms, depending on when the transfers are made and how the tax base is figured. The federal government imposes an *estate* tax on the privilege of transferring property at death, while most states impose *inheritance* taxes on the privilege of receiving property from the dead. In general, both taxes are graduated, the former on the basis of the size of the entire estate and the latter on the basis of the size of individual shares in the estate. Usually the inheritance tax is also graduated on the basis of the relationship of the heir to the decedent, the rate being lowest for the closest relative.

Taxes at death could be avoided simply by transferring property by gift *inter vivos* (between living persons). Accordingly, the federal estate tax is associated with a *gift* tax, which is imposed on the donor. (However, only sixteen of the forty-nine states with death taxes levy a gift tax.) In the United States, the estate and gift taxes were origi-

220

nally separate taxes, but they were unified by the Tax Reform Act of 1976, effective January 1, 1977.

The Role of Estate and Gift Taxes

Opinions about death taxes vary greatly in a society relying heavily on private incentives for economic growth. Some believe that these taxes hurt economic incentives, reduce saving, and undermine the economic system. On the other hand, there is general agreement that death taxes have less adverse effects on incentives than do income taxes of equal yield. Income taxes reduce the return from effort and risk-taking as income is earned, whereas death taxes are paid only after a lifetime of work and accumulation and are likely to be given much less weight in decisions to work, save, and invest.

Death taxes have been supported by people in all income classes. One of their strongest supporters was Andrew Carnegie, who had doubts about the institution of inheritance and felt that wealthy persons are morally obligated to use their fortunes for social purposes. In his *Gospel of Wealth,* Carnegie wrote that "the parent who leaves his son enormous wealth generally deadens the talents and energies of the son, and tempts him to lead a less useful and less worthy life than he otherwise would." He applauded the growing acceptance of estate taxes and said: "Of all forms of taxation this seems the wisest." According to Carnegie, it is the duty of a wealthy man to live unostentatiously, "to provide moderately for the legitimate wants of those dependent upon him, and, after doing so, to consider all surplus revenues which come to him simply as trust funds . . . to administer in the manner . . . best calculated to produce the most beneficial results for the community."

Bequests and gifts, like income from work or investments, are a source of ability to pay. In theory, therefore, they should be taxable as income when received. However, bequests and gifts are taxed separately from income, partly because death taxes antedate the income taxes and partly because it would be unfair to tax these transfers at the full graduated income tax rates in the year of receipt. Of course, the impact of income tax rate graduation could be moderated by averaging, but this approach to transfer taxation has never been seriously considered in this country (although the income tax levied in 1894, which was held unconstitutional, included in the definition of income "money and the value of all personal property acquired by gift or inheritance"). In 1966 the Royal Commission on Taxation (the Carter Commission) in Canada recommended that the Canadian estate and gift taxes be repealed and that gifts and inheritance be included in the recipient's taxable income. Although this forced many people to think seriously about this alternative method of taxing transfers, the Canadian government did not follow the commission's recommendation.

Despite the appeal of estate and gift taxes on social, moral, and economic grounds, taxes on property transfers have never provided significant revenues in this country. The federal government used an inheritance tax briefly for emergency purposes from 1862 to 1870, and an estate tax from 1898 to 1902; the present tax was enacted in 1916. The gift tax was first levied for two years in 1924 and 1925 and then was enacted permanently in 1932. During and after World War II, income and excise tax rates were increased substantially; but the estate and gift tax rates and exemptions remained unchanged from 1942 through 1976, and structural changes made in the postwar period greatly reduced their importance in the federal revenue system. Estate and gift taxes accounted for 4.4 percent of cash receipts in fiscal year 1941, 2 percent in 1948, 1.2 percent in 1953, and 1.7 percent in 1976 (appendix table C-4). The 1976 legislation, which almost tripled the effective exemption between 1977 and 1981, will cut the yield of the estate and gift taxes to about 1 percent of budget receipts in 1981.

One can only guess why heavier reliance has not been placed on the estate and gift taxes. A possible explanation is that equalization of the distribution of wealth by taxation is not yet accepted in the United States. In some countries, economic classes tend to be fairly stable, with little crossing-over by succeeding generations. In the American economy, membership in economic classes is fluid. The average family in the United States still aspires to improved economic and social status, and the estate and gift taxes are erroneously regarded as especially burdensome to the family that is beginning to prosper through hard work and saving.

Moreover, property transfer taxes are not considered equitable by many people. A surprising number resent even the relatively low taxes now imposed on small estates. This may be because the base of the property transfer taxes in certain respects includes more than what the public considers "wealth" properly subject to tax. The family home, the family car, Series E bonds, savings bank deposits, and similar property are not regarded as appropriate objects of taxation. The public generally is not aware that the major part of the estate tax base consists of stocks, bonds, and real estate, and that the exemption removes the property in most estates from the estate tax base.

Characteristics of the Taxes

The calculation of the estate and gift taxes follows the pattern established by the income taxes. The total amount of property transferred is reported, deductions are subtracted, and the graduated rates are applied to the remainder, but there are many complications. Before 1977 the estate and gift taxes were separate taxes; effective January 1, 1977, the two taxes were unified.

The Estate Tax

The gross estate consists of all property owned by a decedent at the time of death, including stocks, bonds, real estate, mortgages, and any other property that technically belonged to the decedent. (The property is valued either on the date of death or on an alternate valuation date, generally six months later, at the option of the estate's executor.) The gross estate also includes gifts made during life plus any gift taxes paid within three years of death, insurance owned by the decedent, and the value of any trusts created by the decedent while alive that could have been revoked or even modified by the decedent. Deductions are allowed for funeral expenses and expenses of settling the estate, debts, legal fees, charitable bequests, for property passing to a surviving spouse (the marital deduction), and for property passing to an orphan of the decedent. The marital deduction is limited to $250,000 or one-half of the estate, whichever is larger. The deduction for bequests to orphans is limited to $5,000 for each year of the orphan's age under twenty-one.

Estate and gift tax rates begin at 18 percent on the first $10,000 of the taxable estate and rise to 70 percent on the amount of the taxable estate in excess of $5,000,000 (appendix table A-9). Credits are provided for any gift tax paid and for state death taxes up to 80 percent of the 1926 federal tax. In addition, a credit is deducted from the tax liability computed from the official rate schedule in lieu of an exemption. The credit for both estate and gift tax purposes— called the *unified credit*—is $30,000 in 1977, $34,000 in 1978, $38,000 in 1979, $42,500 in 1980, and $47,000 in 1981 and later years. These credits are equivalent to exemptions of $120,667; $134,000, $147,333, $161,563, and $175,625, respectively.

For example, assume that a married man who made no taxable gifts during his life dies in 1981 owning $1,000,000 in securities and bequeaths half his wealth to his wife and half to his children. Assume also that the expenses of settling the estate amount to $25,000 and his debts at the time of his death amount to $75,000. If this decedent had been single or had not left anything to his spouse, the net estate would be $900,000. But the marital deduction reduces the net estate to $450,000.

The tax rates would produce a tax before credits of $138,800 on a taxable estate of $450,000. From this, two credits are deductible: the lifetime credit in lieu of an exemption and the credit for state death taxes. The former is $47,000 and the latter, in this case, is $8,400. Thus the net tax payable to the federal government would be $83,400 ($138,800 minus $47,000 and $8,400). If the decedent had made taxable gifts after December 31, 1976, the gifts would be included in his gross estate and a credit would be allowed for any gift tax paid.

The Gift Tax

The gift tax is calculated in much the same way, except that the exemptions are more complicated and the tax is computed on the basis of total gifts made after 1932. The tax due in any particular year is the additional tax resulting from the gifts made in that year. The unified credit (in lieu of an exemption) is used first against the tax on gifts; the remainder is used against the tax on the estate of the same person.

A marital deduction is provided for the first $100,000 of gifts made to a spouse and 50 percent for amounts above $200,000 (no deduction is allowed for amounts between $100,000 and $200,000). For married persons, a gift to third persons can be treated as if half were given by the husband and half by the wife. Although the gift tax rates appear to be the same as the estate tax rates, the gift tax is actually lower because the property given to the government in payment of tax is excluded from the gift tax base, but not from the estate tax base. In higher brackets, this makes the effective gift tax rates considerably lower than the estate tax rates. However, gifts made within three years of the decedent's death and the gift tax paid on such gifts are included in the gross estate.

Suppose a married man with an estate of $1,000,000 decides to distribute it to his two children systematically over a period of ten years beginning in 1981. The law gives him and his wife an annual exclusion for each child of $3,000. The annual exclusions amount to $6,000 a year for each child, or $120,000 over the ten-year period. The total amount remaining for additional gifts and gift taxes is $880,000. The amount of gift tax is $131,940 for both spouses, leaving $748,060 for gifts. By contrast, if the same amounts (including the gift tax paid) were subject to the estate tax, each spouse would pay an estate tax of $108,800, or a total of $217,600. Disposition of the estate through gifts would save $85,660, or almost 40 percent.

The Tax Base

Estate and gift taxes are levied on only a small proportion of privately owned property in the United States. Before 1977 less than one-fourth of the total wealth owned by those who died in any one year—and only about 6 percent of their estates by number—were subject to estate or gift taxes (appendix table B-10). The relatively small size of the tax base is explained in part by the generous exemptions, which excluded a large proportion of the wealth transfer, and also by other provisions that permitted the tax-free transfers of substantial amounts of property. The proportions of wealth and decedents will be reduced even more as a result of the 1976 legislation, which substantially increases the effective exemptions through the use of a tax credit.

The total number of estate tax returns filed in 1973 for citizen and resident alien decedents was 174,899 (appendix table C-21); of these, 120,761 were taxable. The value of the gross estates reported on taxable returns was $33.3 billion. Exemptions and deductions reduced this amount by more than 50 percent, leaving an estate tax base of $15.8 billion. The estate tax before deductions amounted to

$4.7 billion, or 30 percent of the taxable base (appendix table B-11). The tax after credits was $4.2 billion, or 26 percent of the taxable base.

Two-thirds of the taxable returns reported total estates of less than $200,000, but these accounted for only 10 percent of the tax before the state tax credit. Returns on estates of $1,000,000 or more, on the other hand, accounted for almost 50 percent of the total tax and only 3 percent of the number of taxable returns. The tax before state tax credit ranged from 4 percent of gross estates in gross estate classes below $200,000 to 27 percent for estates of $10,000,000 and over.

Gifts reported for the year 1966 amounted to $4.0 billion, of which $2.4 billion were reported on 29,547 taxable returns. Taxable gifts totaled $1,455 million, and gift tax paid amounted to $413 million, or 17 percent of the total gifts on taxable returns and 28 percent of the taxable gifts (appendix table C-22).

Structural Problems

Since property transfers can take many forms, estate and gift taxation is inherently complicated. Many of the structural features of the estate and gift taxes have unequal impact, depending on how and when dispositions of property are made. Such disparities are hard to justify, because many people—for personal or business reasons or because of early death—cannot avail themselves of the opportunity to minimize the taxes on their estates. Because property can be transferred in many different ways, it is difficult to devise one solution that will be equitable in all cases. The major problems are (1) the treatment of transfers of husband and wife, (2) imperfect unification of the estate and gift taxes, (3) the use of trusts to escape taxation for one or more generations, (4) outright transfers to escape taxation for one or more generations, (5) charitable contributions, and (6) small businesses and farms.

Transfers by Husbands and Wives

Transfers by married couples present a difficult problem because it is hard to decide whether they should be taxed as if their property is part of one estate or two. Since the estate and gift taxes are excises on transfers of property, the concept of legal ownership plays an important part in determining the amount of tax to be paid. The distinction between community and noncommunity property is crucial in this respect.

COMMUNITY AND NONCOMMUNITY PROPERTY. Under the community property system, which prevails in eight states, all property acquired during marriage by a husband and wife (except property acquired by gift or inheritance) belongs equally to each spouse. The community property states vary on whether the income from property owned before marriage or acquired during marriage by gift or inheritance belongs to both spouses equally or to the original owner or recipient alone. In noncommunity property states, each spouse retains ownership of all property acquired or accumulated out of his or her separate earnings or inheritance even after marriage.

Before 1942 federal estate and gift taxes recognized the community property system: only half the community property was taxable under the estate tax at the death of a spouse, and gifts to third parties were treated as if half were made by each spouse. In noncommunity property states the entire amount of property accumulated by a spouse was taxable to him or her.

To equalize estate and gift taxes for residents of community and noncommunity property states, the Revenue Act of 1942 made transfers of community property taxable to the spouse who had earned it. In effect, the 1942 law treated community property as if it were noncommunity property.

The Revenue Act of 1948 attempted to achieve equalization by moving in the opposite direction. In the spirit of income splitting for income tax purposes, transfers of community property were made taxable under the pre-1942 rules, while for transfers of noncommunity property a deduction was allowed for the amount of the property transferred to the surviving spouse, up to half the separate property in an estate. In the case of a gift of noncommunity property by one spouse to another, only half of the gift was made taxable. Gifts to third persons were to be treated, if so elected, as though half were made by each spouse. These rules are still in effect.

The marital deduction greatly increased the amount of property that married persons might transfer free of tax. Interspousal transfers up to half the value of estates and half of all gifts made by married persons were eliminated from the bases of the estate and gift taxes. Beginning in 1977 the marital deduction was raised to a minimum of $250,000 and the effective exemption rises by annual steps until it reaches $175,625 in 1981. As a result, the transfer tax exemption for married persons will be $425,625 in 1981, provided the decedent transferred at least $250,000 to the surviving spouse. Gift splitting also in effect doubled the annual exclusion from $3,000 to $6,000.

Transfers between spouses are subject to tax at the death of the recipient or when the recipient makes gifts, but the total tax on the couple is nevertheless significantly reduced by the marital deduction because of the effect of splitting on the applicable rates. Under progressive rates, the total tax on two estates of equal size is less than that on one large and one small estate. For example, a net estate of $10 million will be subject to a tax of $6 million in 1981. If half the estate is left to a surviving spouse, the tax is reduced to $2.5 million. Even if the $5 million received by the spouse is later taxed in full, the subsequent tax will be $2.5 million, and the total tax on the original $10 million will be $5 million, involving both a deferral of the tax and a tax decrease of $1 million, or 17 percent below the liability under the 1942 law (table 8-1).

These tax differences might be tolerable—despite the large reduction in estate and gift tax revenues—if the 1948 amendments had accomplished their objective of equalizing the tax in community and noncommunity property situations. In fact, they did so in some but not in others. Suppose a married man who accumulated a $1,000,000 estate through his own efforts bequeaths all the property to his wife and he dies first. Under the 1948 amendments, only half the estate will be taxable whether he lives in a community property state or in a noncommunity property state. (With noncommunity property, he is allowed a marital deduction of 50 percent; with community property, his wife automatically owns half the property, and he is taxable on only his half.) However, if the wife predeceases him and leaves her property to the children, she is taxable on half of the property accumulated by the husband in a community property state, and when he dies he is taxable on the second half. In the noncommunity property state, the husband is taxable on the entire estate when he dies, and because the rates are graduated, he pays more than the couple in the community property state (although he has received the often important benefits of deferral). On the other hand, a couple in a community property state will pay an even higher tax if the wife dies first and leaves her share of the community property to the husband.

Table 8-1. Estate Taxes Paid by a Married Couple, by Net Estate Level, 1981[a]

Net estate before exemption (dollars)	Tax on husband (assuming he leaves no bequest to wife) (dollars) (1)	Tax on husband (assuming he leaves half of estate to wife)		Tax on husband and wife (assuming bequest from husband is taxed in full at wife's death)	
		Amount (dollars) (2)	Percent of column 1 (3)	Amount (dollars) (4)	Percent of column 1 (5)
175,000	0	0	...	0	...
200,000	23,800	0	0.0	0	0.0
500,000	108,800	23,800	21.9	47,600	43.8
750,000	201,300	66,300	32.9	132,600	65.9
1,000,000	298,800	108,800	36.4	217,600	72.8
2,000,000	733,800	298,800	40.7	597,600	81.4
5,000,000	2,503,800	978,800	39.1	1,957,600	78.2
10,000,000	6,003,800	2,503,800	41.7	5,007,600	83.4
20,000,000	13,003,800	6,003,800	46.2	12,007,600	92.3

a. Assumes the husband owns all the property and dies first. Effective rates are before the credit for state death taxes.

INTERSPOUSAL EXEMPTIONS. If it is assumed that Congress will not restore the 1942 law, the problem of unequal treatment can be solved by extending the marital deduction to include all transfers between husband and wife. This would make transfers of noncommunity property between husband and wife tax free. A man who gave as much as half his estate to his wife *inter vivos* would be taxable on only his half whether he died first or last, as in community property states.

Complete exemption of transfers between husband and wife suggests that the husband and wife are a single unit and that their combined estates might be cumulated for estate tax purposes. The initial installment on the combined tax would be collected on the death of one spouse, and the remainder (figured on the basis of the cumulated estates) would be collected on the death of the second spouse. The attractive feature of this proposal is that it would equalize the taxes paid by married couples in all states regardless of the order in which they disposed of the estate, without ultimately weakening the estate tax base.

However, estate cumulation may produce inequitable results where the wealth of the husband or wife was separately inherited or accumulated. For example, a woman married to a wealthy man for a relatively short period might be taxed at the maximum estate tax rates even though the amount of property she owned was small. This objection could be met by cumulating only as much of the property transferred by the wife (during life or at death) as was originally acquired from the husband. Tracing difficulties could be avoided by cumulating transfers of the wife only up to the dollar amount of property received from the husband. Such a compromise, however, would fail to take into account any increase in the value of the property after the interspousal transfer. Estate cumulation would also require the solution of some intricate problems involving the treatment of gifts made before marriage and the taxation of transfers by widowed or divorced persons who had married again.

A second approach would be to provide a 100 percent exemption for all interspousal transfers without cumulating the estates of the husband and wife. The advantage of this approach is that owners of noncommunity property could arrange their affairs in the same way as owners of community property. The disadvantage is that it would substantially reduce the yield of the estate tax at least in the short run. While it is conceivable that the revenue loss could be offset by rate adjustments, it is hardly likely that the adjustment, if any, would be precise, and the benefits would go mainly to the very wealthy.

Still a third approach would be to give married couples the privilege of making an irrevocable choice between (a) exemption of interspousal transfers and cumulation of transfers to third parties and (b) waiver of the marital deduction and elimination of the automatic splitting of community property, combined with noncumulation of transfers to third parties. The major difficulty with this approach is that many complexities would arise out of the instability of the family unit. Divorce, as well as remarriage after the death of one spouse, might provide avenues of escape from the cumulation of transfers that would otherwise be required. Moreover, it is probably unwise as a matter of policy to permit taxpayers to make such a decision irrevocably, since later changes in circumstances might create inequities and considerable dissatisfaction.

The 1976 legislation provided a 100 percent marital deduction for transfers of $100,000 during life and $250,000 for transfers at death and kept the 50 percent deduction for interspousal transfers above these amounts (except for the second $100,000 transfer during life, for which no deduction is allowed). Thus Congress opted for the second approach for interspousal transfers of these magnitudes but left the inequalities in the treatment of married couples unresolved for larger transfers.

Imperfect Unification of Estates and Gifts

Even though the estate and gift taxes have been unified, wealthy people are well advised to transfer a substantial part of their property by gift during their lifetime rather than by bequest for two reasons. First, the annual exclusion of $3,000 per donee under the gift tax permits tax-free transfers in addition to the unified estate and gift tax exemption. Second, the amount paid as gift tax does not enter into the gift tax base, whereas the estate tax is computed on the basis of Furthermore, by transferring part of the estate to a spouse, a testator splits the estate into two parts, moderating the full impact of transfer tax graduation.

To minimize tax liability, a person would have to take these factors into account as well as the tax that would be due at the death of the spouse. Although there are many uncertainties, it is clear that a carefully drawn plan of wealth distribution during the life of a wealthy person can pay handsome dividends in lower tax burdens.

USE OF GIFTS. Information on the distribution of wealth during life and at death has been collected by the Treasury Department on the basis of the estate and matched gift tax returns of the wealthiest decedents for whom estate tax returns were filed in 1945, 1951, 1957, and 1959. Information on gifts made before 1932 was available from the 1945 and 1951 estate tax returns. Thus it was possible to build up an aggregate figure for the property distributed by each decedent during life and at death for the two earlier years, and a total, excluding gifts made before 1932, for the two later years.

The figures (table 8-2) show clearly that wealthy people prefer to retain the bulk of their property until death and fail to use gifts to maximum tax-saving advantage. There are a number of reasons for the small proportion of gifts. First, most people are reluctant to contemplate death. Uncertainty regarding time of death encourages delay in making estate plans even by those with considerable wealth. Second, many wish to retain control over their businesses. Disposal of stock or real estate frequently means loss of control over substan-

Table 8-2. Frequency of Gifts and Percentage of Wealth Transferred by Gift during Life among Millionaire Decedents, 1945, 1951, 1957, and 1959

Total wealth transferred during life and at death (millions of dollars)	Percent of decedents who made gifts during life				Percent of wealth transferred by gift			
	1945	1951	1957	1959	1945	1951	1957	1959
1.00–1.25	77	74	52	56	14	12	5	5
1.25–1.50	76	65	57	58	17	7	6	8
1.50–1.75	83	74	55	67	21	12	7	8
1.75–2.00	89	70	67	71	28	10	6	8
2.00–3.00	84	88	65	68	20	14	6	8
3.00–5.00	88	84	69	84	20	14	7	11
5.00–10.00	100	95	75	84	20	18	10	11
10.00 and over	91	100	92	100	38	25	15	17
Total	83	77	60	66	24	16	9	10

Source: Special tabulations by the Treasury Department. Includes only returns with total transfers before tax during life and at death of $1,000,000 or more. Data for 1945 and 1951 include gifts before 1932; those for 1957 and 1959 exclude such gifts.

tial enterprises. Third, donors may wish to delay transfers of property until their children have had an opportunity to make their own careers. Fourth, many people—even those who are wealthy—do not know the law and often do not take the advice of their tax lawyers on such personal matters.

Whatever the reason, the actual use of gifts has resulted in much less erosion of the tax base than might have taken place, and the recent unification of the estate and gift taxes will somewhat reduce the incentive to make gifts. The major criticism of the law is that it discriminates against those who, for business or personal reasons, do not dispose of a substantial portion of their wealth during their lives. And among those who do make gifts, the law discriminates in favor of wealthier donors by rewarding them with larger tax savings than less wealthy donors obtain on gifts of the same value. This feature stems from the exclusion of the gift tax from the base of the tax.

COMPLETE UNIFICATION OF ESTATE AND GIFT TAXES. The remedy for the inequalities resulting from the separate taxation of gifts and estates is to complete the unification of the two taxes begun in 1976. A truly unified system would have a single marital deduction for lifetime transfers and bequests. In addition, any gift tax paid would be included in the base of the final transfer tax.

Unification to this extent is opposed by those who believe that gifts should be encouraged. It is argued, in fact, that gifts tend to reduce the concentration of wealth by dispersing property among a relatively large number of donees.

Generation-Skipping through Trusts

The most difficult problems in estate and gift taxation arise from the existence of the *trust,* a legal institution used to administer funds on behalf of individuals or organizations. Suppose A wants his wife to have the income from his estate as long as she lives. He may place his property in a trust, the income of which would go to her for life; the trust might be dissolved at her death and the property distributed to the children. The trust is administered by a *trustee*—usually a relative or associate, the family lawyer, or a bank—who is the legal owner. He is required by law to manage the trust property strictly in accordance with the terms of the trust instrument.

Legal terms are used as shorthand in trust language for the various beneficiaries of a trust. In the above example, A's wife, who is entitled to receive the income from the trust, is the *life beneficiary.* Any number of life beneficiaries may be designated, and they need not be confined to members of the same generation. The creator of the trust may designate his wife and children as joint or successive life beneficiaries and prescribe the proportions in which the income is to be distributed among them. When the trust is terminated, the trust property is legally transferred to the *remaindermen,* who then own the property outright. More often than not, children are the remaindermen of family trusts; but grandchildren or other relatives as well as unrelated persons may also be remaindermen. In some cases, the trust is created with the wife and children as life beneficiaries and the remainder is distributed, after the last one dies, to one or more charities. In all but a few states, all interests in a trust must vest not later than twenty-one years after the death of the last survivor among a reasonably small number of persons who were alive when the trust was created (*lives in being*). This rule has the effect of restricting most noncharitable trusts to a duration of less than a century.

The trust has a profound influence on the taxation of property transfers. Before 1977, if the trust was properly planned, the trust property was not subject to estate tax when one life beneficiary was succeeded by another or when the property was received by the remaindermen. An estate or gift tax was paid when the trust was cre-

Table 8-3. Frequency of Noncharitable Transfers in Trust and Percentage of Wealth Transferred in Trust by Millionaire Decedents, 1945, 1951, 1957, and 1959[a]

Total wealth transferred during life and at death (millions of dollars)	*Percent of decedents with noncharitable transfers in trust*				*Percent of noncharitable transfers made in trust*			
	1945	*1951*	*1957*	*1959*	*1945*	*1951*	*1957*	*1959*
1.00–1.25	75	72	57	56	44	39	28	26
1.25–1.50	75	78	53	61	48	44	25	29
1.50–1.75	80	77	53	62	38	44	24	30
1.75–2.00	71	80	63	69	37	49	37	31
2.00–3.00	89	69	61	64	55	39	34	34
3.00–5.00	84	87	63	70	42	51	32	35
5.00–10.00	87	74	77	67	44	44	43	30
10.00 and over	91	100	73	92	58	59	33	30
Total	80	76	59	63	47	46	32	31

Source: Special tabulations by the Treasury Department.

a. Includes only returns with total transfers before tax during life and at death of $1 million or more. Data for 1945 and 1951 include gifts made before 1932; those for 1957 and 1959 exclude such gifts.

ated, but tax was not paid again until the remaindermen transferred the property. Given these characteristics, the trust was frequently used by wealthy people to avoid estate and gift taxes for at least one generation and sometimes more. In extreme cases, trusts were set up to last for the lives of the children and grandchildren, with the remainder going to the great-grandchildren, thereby skipping two estate and gift tax generations.

USE OF TRUSTS. The trust device has been used frequently by the wealthy to transfer property to later generations. The data from the Treasury studies of 1945, 1951, 1957, and 1959 returns indicate the following patterns:

1. In the 1940s and 1950s more than three of every five millionaires transferred at least some of their property in trust. Transfers in trust accounted for at least one-third of noncharitable transfers by millionaires in this period (table 8-3). The data also indicate that trusts were used primarily by wealthy people. Those with smaller estates gave much more of their property outright.

2. There was little difference in the eventual disposition of property transferred outright and property transferred in trust. Outright transfers were received in the first instance largely by the wife and children; these properties were in turn transferred to grandchildren and great-grandchildren. In the case of trust transfers, wives, children,

and grandchildren frequently received only a life interest, so the grandchildren and great-grandchildren received the property undiminished by estate or gift taxes. As table 8-4 indicates, about half the trust property of wealthy decedents escaped estate and gift taxes until the death of the grandchildren or great-grandchildren. Only a very small proportion of the property transferred outright escaped tax for a similar period.

THE 1976 LEGISLATION. There are legitimate reasons for trusts, and it would be unwise to abolish them altogether. On the other hand, some economists have pointed out that it is also unwise to encourage excessive use of the trust device, thus reducing the supply of capital available for risky investments, since trust property is managed more conservatively than property owned outright. And as trust transfers and outright transfers go to the same people, it seems unfair to impose lower taxes on trust transfers. Equity suggests that the two types of transfers should be treated equally.

Several methods were devised to remove or reduce the tax advantage of trust transfers. The 1976 legislation, which is effective for transfers in trust beginning May 1, 1976 (except transfers pursuant to a will in existence on April 30, 1976, of a decedent dying before January 1, 1982), used the direct method. Under this legislation, life estates are treated as if the property generating their income is owned by the income beneficiaries, a procedure followed in Great Britain. The capital from which the life estate is supported is included in the life beneficiary's gross estate. The tax is computed by adding the trust property to the other taxable transfers of the life beneficiary. In effect, the trust property is taxed at the marginal transfer tax rate of the life beneficiary. The tax is paid from the assets of the trust.

The mechanism for taxing life estates in the 1976 legislation is a new tax which is imposed on "generation-skipping" transfers of trust property. A generation-skipping trust is one in which income or remainder interests are given to two or more generations that are younger than the generation of the grantor of the trust. The tax applies when the trust assets are distributed to a generation-skipping heir (for example, a great-grandchild of the transferor) or when an intervening interest in the trust terminates (for example, when the life interest in a trust is transferred from a child to a grandchild); but an exclusion of $250,000 is provided for transfers to all the children

Table 8-4. Timing of Next Estate Taxes on Outright and Trust Transfers of Millionaire Decedents, 1945, 1951, 1957, and 1959

Person at whose death the next estate tax falls due	Outright transfers		Trust transfers[a]	
	Amount (millions of dollars)	Percentage of total	Amount (millions of dollars)	Percentage of total
			1945	
Spouse	77	24	...	...
Children	154	48	...	...
Grandchildren	9	3	...	...
Great-grandchildren	b	b	...	...
Other	80	25	...	...
Total	320	100	...	...
			1951	
Spouse	164	41	2	1
Children	137	34	95	28
Grandchildren	11	3	124	37
Great-grandchildren	b	b	20	6
Other	89	22	96	28
Total	400	100	337	100
			1957	
Spouse	405	39	2	*
Children	362	35	90	18
Grandchildren	56	5	209	43
Great-grandchildren	b	b	24	5
Other	212	21	162	33
Total	1,034	100	487	100
			1959	
Spouse	468	42	4	1
Children	366	33	91	18
Grandchildren	68	6	208	42
Great-grandchildren	b	b	37	7
Other	214	19	160	32
Total	1,117	100	500	100

Source: Special tabulations by the Treasury Department. Figures are rounded.
* Less than 0.5 percent.
a. Data not available for 1945.
b. Outright transfers to great-grandchildren were not tabulated separately, but the amount is negligible and is included in transfers to "other."

of each child of the grantor. For trust transfers outside the family, individuals not more than twelve and a half years younger than the grantor are treated as members of his generation; those who are twelve and a half to thirty-seven and a half years younger than the grantor are regarded as members of his children's generation; and so on. In the case of a discretionary trust, the tax is postponed until the death of the last member of an intervening generation.

The 1976 legislation is a major effort to plug the former generation-skipping loophole under the estate and gift taxes. The provisions are complex and there will undoubtedly be many difficult problems of compliance and administration. Nevertheless, the legislation is a significant step toward equalizing tax burdens on transfers in trust and those on outright transfers.

Generation-Skipping through Outright Transfers

Transfers in trust and outright transfers are to some degree substitutes for one another. If they are subject to taxes of unequal size, many persons will avoid the more heavily taxed kind of transfer and will make the one that is taxed more lightly. It is just such an inequality in tax burdens that caused many wealthy people to tie up property in trust for one or two generations rather than have it taxed each time it passed from one generation to the next. Now that a tax is imposed on generation-skipping transfers in trust, some people who would otherwise create such trusts may instead make generation-skipping outright transfers that are not subject to an additional tax under the 1976 legislation. Instead of establishing a trust and naming the children as life tenants and grandchildren as remaindermen, a donor could transfer property outright to them in amounts equal to the present value of the interests in trust they would otherwise receive. The gift of property to a grandchild is the generation-skipping component of the outright transfers. The great similarity between the outright transfer and single transfer in trust has led some to argue that a tax imposed on generation-skipping trusts ought to be accompanied by an equivalent tax on generation-skipping outright tranfers, in order to preserve fairness in the tax system and to prevent tax avoidance.

It is easier to reach generation-skipping outright transfers than generation-skipping transfers in trust, because property given outright can ordinarily be valued exactly at the time it is transferred, whereas interests in trust are often difficult to value at the time the trusts are created. Many state inheritance taxes already incorporate some form of relationship discrimination in their rate schedules, and the same principle could be used in designing a generation-skipping tax on outright transfers under the federal estate tax. Arbitrary rules based on the age and relationship of the transferor and the recipient could take care of transfers to persons outside the transferor's direct line of descent. The tax rate could be set in any one of a number of ways. It might be set at some fraction above the transferor's average tax rate on all other transfers. Or the transfer might be taxed according to a separate rate schedule, whose rates were graduated according to the total of all generation-skipping transfers that the transferor had ever made. Whatever method was adopted, the additional tax clearly would add features of the inheritance tax form of death taxation to the federal estate tax.

Charitable Contributions

Unlike the deductions allowed under income taxes, charitable bequests and gifts are deductible without limit from the estate or gift tax bases. (Contributions are deductible up to 50 percent of income in the individual income tax and up to 5 percent in the corporation income tax.) Although a minority of people allocate substantial portions of their estates to charity, the charitable deduction does stimulate giving at death. Slightly over half the estate tax returns of millionaire decedents in 1957 and 1959 reported no contributions above the annual exclusion during life or at death, and about 15 percent of their total transfers were given to charitable organizations. Nevertheless, the total amounts deducted are significant; they rose from $254 million on all 1945 estate and gift tax returns to $2.0 billion on 1973 estate tax returns.

The large growth of private foundations, some of which have been suspected of abusing the tax exemption privilege, has led to concern about the charitable deduction. Owners of closely held corporations may avoid the impact of the estate tax by dividing the stock into voting stock, which is retained in the family, and nonvoting stock, which is transferred to a foundation. In this way, the family continues to control the assets without being subject to the full estate and gift tax rates when control passes from one generation to the next. In many cases, the economic power of the family grows rapidly as the enterprise continues to expand; the estate tax does not encroach on the property because the property belongs to the foundation and has been permanently removed from the estate tax base. This type of transfer amounts to giving up the income from the property rather than the property itself, yet the transfer is treated as if control of the property has also been relinquished by the donor.

Private foundations were not even required to file financial statements until 1950, when the tax law was amended to require public information returns on their assets, earnings, and expenditures. These reports did not completely eliminate shady dealings on the part of a few donors and foundation officials. Investigations by congressional committees revealed abuses ranging from excessive salaries for foundation officials to the use of loans from foundation funds for personal investment purposes.

Although the large majority of foundations operate in the public interest, by 1969 there was substantial agreement that their affairs should be subject to stricter public controls. As a result, the Tax Reform Act of 1969 included prohibitions against loans to contributors, officers, and directors; rules to prevent the use of foundation funds to influence legislation and to prevent accumulation of income; and requirements to broaden the foundation's management so as to avoid indefinite control by one family. The legislation also included a 4 percent tax on the investment income of private foundations. These measures appear to have curbed abuses by foundations of their tax exemption privilege.

Small Business and Farm Property

A perennial problem in estate taxation is its effect on small business and farms. Small businessmen and farmers have always felt that the estate tax is especially burdensome. Often their estates consist of little more than the business. Heavy taxation or a rule requiring payment of taxes immediately after the death of the owner-manager would necessitate liquidation of the enterprise and loss of the business by the family.

As the previous discussion indicated, a little advance estate planning would be sufficient to prevent or mitigate most of these problems. Nevertheless, payment difficulties may arise even in carefully planned situations. The law, which was made much more liberal in 1976, contains two provisions to help in these cases.

First, tax payments on estates of which a small business or a farm is a large proportion may be made in installments over a period of fifteen years. There is a special 4 percent interest rate for the first million dollars of closely held property. Only interest is paid the first five years; thereafter the tax is payable in equal installments over the next ten years. This option, which is exercised by the executor, is available if the value of the business exceeds 65 percent of the gross estate. Installment payments are limited to the portion of the estate tax accounted for by the business. A special lien is provided for payment of the deferred taxes, and when this lien procedure is followed, the executor is discharged from personal liability.

Second, redemptions of stock in closely held corporations to pay the estate tax are taxed as capital gains rather than dividend income. To qualify for this treatment, the value of the decedent's stock in the closely held corporation must exceed 50 percent of the gross estate. The allowable redemption period is four years for all estates and fifteen years when an election has been made for the deferred payment of taxes. Such stock redemptions are, of course, indistinguishable from ordinary distributions of profits by private corporations, which are subject to tax.

In addition to the payment problems, spokesmen for farm interests alleged that farmland was often assessed for estate tax purposes at a value far in excess of its value in agricultural production. As a result, heirs to the property, who frequently wanted to keep it in family hands and continue to farm it, were forced to sell to pay the tax. Under the 1976 legislation, farmland and other closely held business property may be assessed at its "current use" value rather than at its market value.

It is hard to estimate how far the difficulties described are attributable to an estate tax squeeze. Prices of farmland have been rising rapidly, and the increase must be due in some cases to mounting demand for the land for nonagricultural uses, particularly when it is located on the fringes of metropolitan areas. If decedents' assets are included in their estates at fair market value, it must be expected that the estate taxes will often force the heirs to sell to people who will put the property to more profitable use. The generous liberalization of payment provisions enacted in 1976 should be sufficient to avoid the liquidation of farms to pay the estate tax. A similar valuation provision, which was once in effect in the United Kingdom but was recently repealed, reportedly caused much mischief by encouraging wealthy people to shift their investments into agricultural property to reduce their death duties.

Other Methods of Taxing Wealth

Some have argued that, instead of relying on estate and gift taxes, it would be better to start afresh. The alternatives most often recommended are based on the inheritance or accessions tax principle. Another type of wealth tax, which has recently been enacted in a number of European countries, is an annual tax on net wealth. This tax is regarded primarily as a supplement to, rather than a substitute for, the estate and gift taxes.

Inheritance or Accessions Taxes

Although widely used by the states, the inheritance tax is rarely considered for use at the federal level. Its most serious deficiency in its unmodified form is that each receipt of a gift or inheritance is taxed separately. Thus two individuals would pay the same tax on equal inheritances received from the same decedent. However, if one received the inheritance in a lump sum and the other received it from several decedents, they would pay different taxes.

This deficiency would be remedied by the modern modification of the inheritance tax principle—the *accessions tax*. This is a progressive, cumulative tax on the total lifetime acquisitions of an individual through inheritances and gifts. The tax in any one year would be computed by subtracting the tax paid on earlier acquisitions from the tax on total acquisitions received. There would be small annual exclusions and a lifetime exemption. Although tax rates could be varied on the basis of the relationship of donor and donee, there is little support for such differentiation under an accessions tax.

The accessions tax has appeal for those who advocate a more equal distribution of wealth than the present estate tax provides. It would also be more equitable than the estate tax since it would be graduated according to the total wealth received by any one person. It is probably true that the accessions tax would encourage individuals to distribute their property among a larger number of heirs, but the result would not necessarily be a different distribution of wealth, since property is ordinarily kept in the immediate family. Moreover, in practice, only the wealthiest could afford to divert property from wife and children to more distant relatives to take advantage of the tax savings offered by an accessions tax. To the extent that the accessions tax did encourage a more equal distribution of estates, it might do so by shifting some of the burden of the wealthiest estates to the smaller estates.

The accessions tax offers some practical advantages. For one thing, it would equalize the taxes on transfers during life and at death. Some of the proponents of the accessions tax also claim that it would facilitate the inclusion of property settled in trust in the tax base. For example, receipt of trust property by remaindermen would automatically be subject to the accessions tax, but not to the estate tax. On the other hand, the estate tax collected when the trust is created would not automatically be recovered by the accessions tax. To include such transfers in the accessions tax base, the benefits received by the life beneficiaries would have to be valued—a problem that has not been solved satisfactorily even after years of experience with the estate tax.

A practical argument against the accessions tax is that it would probably not raise as much revenue as the estate and gift taxes. To obtain a given yield, accessions tax rates would have to be higher and exemptions lower than under the present transfer taxes. In view of the recent reduction in estate tax rates and increase in exemptions, the revisions necessary to preserve the revenue yield might be difficult to obtain.

The Wealth Tax

Annual taxation of wealth is perhaps the most recent development in tax policy among the advanced industrial countries. The tax is now levied in eight European countries (Austria, Denmark, Finland, Ireland, the Netherlands, Norway, Sweden, and West Germany) and is being seriously considered in the United Kingdom. In all these countries, estate or inheritance taxes are levied in addition to an annual net wealth tax.

The base of the wealth tax is the value of assets less the liabilities of the individual or household. Exemptions are high in order to exclude all but the top wealthholders. Tax rates are graduated, but the top rates are very low compared with income tax rates. The maximum rate in the European countries is 2.5 percent, the top rate in Sweden.

A major objective of an annual tax on wealth is to reduce the concentration of wealth directly. A wealth tax would also be an effective method of taxing people who have not paid tax on large, unrealized capital gains. Even with a low rate, the wealth tax may be a significant fraction of the income from property. For example, a 2 percent wealth tax rate is a 25 percent tax on the income from an asset yielding 8 percent; a 10 percent rate might be confiscatory of the income of most assets. For this reason, a moderate wealth tax rate is often proposed as a substitute for high individual income tax rates, which may impair incentives to work and to save.

Since the wealth tax is paid on the value of an asset regardless of its rate of return, people in ventures yielding low rates of return have an incentive to shift into risky enterprises that could yield high rates of return if successful. On the other hand, since a wealth tax would fall more heavily on accumulated savings than an equal-yield income tax on earnings from all sources, substituting a wealth tax for an income tax might reduce the incentive to save.

The possibility of adopting an annual net wealth tax at the federal level in the United States has never been seriously considered. Local governments, which rely heavily on property taxes, might regard federal entry into this field as an unwarranted invasion of a revenue source that has been reserved exclusively for them. Questions about the constitutionality of a national wealth tax may also arise, since the Constitution requires apportionment of all direct taxes other than income taxes on the basis of population. Nevertheless, the experience of the European countries will be worth watching to see whether a wealth tax can be used effectively in a modern tax system.

Summary

In theory, estate and gift taxes are among the better taxes devised by man; in practice, their yield is disappointing, and they have little effect on the distribution of wealth. Tax rates are high, but there are ways to escape them. The major avenues are the marital deduction, distribution of estates by gifts during lifetime, and use of the tax-free charitable foundation to maintain control without paying tax on the bulk of the estate. Generation-skipping through trusts was at one time a major avenue of tax avoidance, but the 1976 legislation included such transfers in the base of the estate tax. The remaining problems can be solved, but the solutions are technical, and some would regard them as unnecessarily harsh. The revenue potential of estate tax reform is, in any case, relatively modest.

Although tax theorists almost unanimously agree that estate and gift taxation should play a larger role in the revenue system, they have not been successful in convincing Congress. The public does not appear to accept the desirability of a vigorous estate and gift taxation system. The major obstacles to the increased use of these taxes are public apathy and the difficulty of understanding their major features and how they apply in individual circumstances. The merits of property transfer taxes will have to be more widely understood and accepted before they can become effective revenue sources.

CHAPTER NINE

State and Local Taxes

THE STATE-LOCAL SEGMENT of the national revenue system is its most dynamic element. State and local expenditures have grown rapidly in recent years and will continue to grow in the foreseeable future. These governments spent (from their own sources) about $185 billion in fiscal year 1976, almost 50 percent of federal expenditures and 70 percent of federal nondefense expenditures. Whereas the federal government income tax rates are at their lowest levels in more than thirty years, state and local tax rates continue to increase.

The growth in expenditures and taxes during the 1950s and 1960s reflected the persistent demand for more state and local services to meet the large backlog of unmet needs at the end of the Second World War and the requirements of the rapidly growing population. The mobility of the people accentuated the problems of population growth. Entire new communities had to be developed, with schools, roads, sewers, police and fire protection, and other public services. The rate of growth of state-local expenditures declined in the 1970s in part because population growth subsided, but there has been a continued fiscal squeeze as a result of inflation and high rates of unemployment.

The major characteristics of the state-local tax system are its regressivity and sluggish response to income growth. The states rely heavily on consumption taxes and local governments on property taxes—revenue sources that are particularly burdensome for the poor. Fear of driving out commerce and industry and discouraging the entry of new business restrains the use of most taxes; this is true particularly of the income tax, which is the most equitable and most responsive to growth. At constant tax rates, state and local tax receipts rise barely in proportion to the gross national product, while expenditures grow at a much faster rate than GNP.

In these circumstances, the federal government has filled a major part of the gap. Federal grants-in-aid to state and local governments rose from $6.8 billion in 1959 to $20.3 billion in 1969 and are estimated to reach $59 billion in 1976. Most of them help finance needed expenditures for education, health, welfare, and roads. In addition, revenue sharing was enacted in 1972 to link the states more directly to the superior tax resources of the federal government.

The pressure for larger revenues has generated a great deal of fiscal activity throughout the country. Tax systems are being examined by official and unofficial commissions, legislative committees, and experts in an effort to increase revenues, achieve greater equity, improve administration, and reduce the cost of compliance by taxpayers. Many states have adopted new taxes, increased rates on old taxes, introduced withholding for income tax payments, and reformed their tax administrative machinery. Under pressure from the states, local governments have improved property tax administration. Some large cities have adopted municipal income and sales taxes. But much remains to be done to satisfy state and local financial needs.

The State-Local Tax Structure

In the ten years ending June 30, 1974, annual state and local expenditures for general purposes (all activities other than public utilities, liquor stores, and insurance trust funds) rose from $69.3 billion to $198.6 billion, an increase of $129.3 billion. In the same period, state and local revenues rose from $68.4 billion to $207.7 billion, an increase of $139.3 billion. Only 23 percent of the revenue increase came from federal grants; 77 percent came from state and local sources. Although the rise in receipts slightly exceeded the rise in expenditures for the entire period, expenditures were larger than receipts in every year except 1966, 1973, and 1974, and state-local debt rose from $92.2 billion to $206.6 billion (appendix tables C-23, C-24, and C-25).

The state and local governments relied on all their major sources to produce their share of the additional revenue: 25 percent came from property taxes, 28 percent from consumption taxes, 19 percent from income taxes, and the remaining 28 percent from user charges and other miscellaneous taxes (figure 9-1).

While state and local tax sources are often considered together, the two levels of government have very different tax systems. The state governments rely heavily on consumption and income taxes; local governments are dependent largely on the property tax.

State Taxes

State tax structures have changed dramatically since the turn of the century. In 1902 almost half of state revenue came from property taxes and the rest from selective excise taxes. Today, the general sales tax is the largest single source of state revenue, with automotive and income taxes next. Most states have relinquished the general property tax to their local governments; only Arizona and Washington raise 6 percent or more of their revenues from this tax.

SALES AND EXCISE TAXES. State legislatures have been irresistibly attracted to the productivity and stability of revenues from consumption taxes. Selective excise taxes on gasoline, cigarettes, and liquor are now in extensive use throughout the country. In recent years, these taxes have been supplemented increasingly by the retail sales tax.

The retail sales tax emerged as a major source of state revenue in the 1930s. It is now in use in forty-five states and the District of Columbia, at rates ranging from 2 to 7 percent. To moderate its regressivity, twenty-one states exempt food, and thirty-six exempt medicine. A recent development is a credit against state personal income tax for sales tax paid. For example, Massachusetts provides a credit of $4 for the taxpayer and spouse and $8 for dependents if taxable income does not exceed $5,000. (For a family of four, the $16 credit is equivalent to the 3 percent tax on $533 of purchases.) Colorado, the District of Columbia, Hawaii, Idaho, Nebraska, and Vermont have similar provisions. Cash refunds are made to individ-

Figure 9-1. Sources of Growth of State and Local Revenue, 1964–74

Billions of dollars

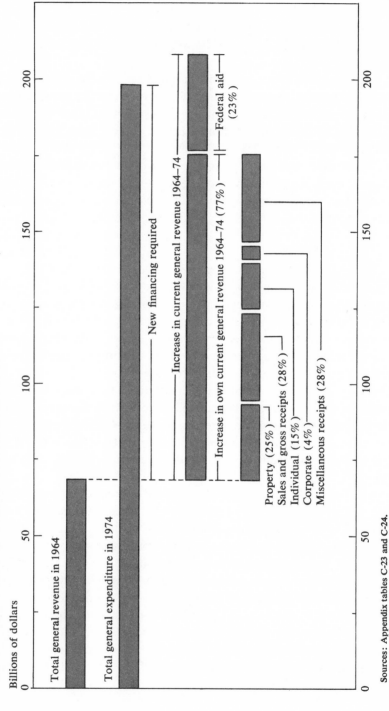

Sources: Appendix tables C-23 and C-24.

uals and families who do not pay enough income tax to recover the entire credit. In New Mexico, a credit is provided for all state-local taxes for those with incomes of $8,000 and under.

INCOME TAXES. State individual and corporation income taxes in their modern form began in Wisconsin in 1911. (Hawaii had adopted both taxes in 1901, but this experience apparently had no influence on the states.) General individual income taxes are now in force in forty-one states and the District of Columbia, and the corporation income tax in forty-five states and the District of Columbia. New Hampshire and Tennessee tax only dividends and interest (though interest on savings deposits is excluded in New Hampshire), and Connecticut taxes only capital gains. State tax rates are much lower than the federal rates, and personal exemptions are generally higher. Tax brackets used for the individual income tax are narrower, and graduation is steeper but terminates at a much lower level, usually between $5,000 and $25,000. The maximum individual income tax rates are levied in Delaware, where the rate is 19.8 percent. Minnesota has the highest corporation income tax, with a rate of 12 percent.

The nominal tax rates overstate the *net* impact of the state income taxes because these tax payments are deductible from taxable income in computing federal taxes. In addition, many states permit the deduction of federal taxes in computing taxable income for state tax purposes. In most cases the net effect of deductibility is to make the burden imposed by state individual income taxes considerably heavier on the lower and middle income classes than on the higher income classes. Of the forty-one state income taxes, eighteen place a higher net burden on those in the lowest federal tax bracket (taxable incomes of $0 to $500) than on those in the highest bracket (taxable incomes over $100,000), and twenty-eight of the states place the highest net burden on a bracket below $16,000. After allowing for deductions, the maximum net burden is found in New York, where those with taxable incomes between $25,000 and $28,000 pay a net additional rate of 9.8 percent. The corporation income tax burden is highest in Minnesota, where the net additional rate is 6.2 percent (appendix table C-27).

State income taxes are generally patterned after the federal taxes, and in recent years there has been a movement toward uniformity with federal definitions. All but eight of the personal income tax states have an optional standard deduction. All states modify the adjusted gross income concept by subtracting interest on federal securities, and most states add state income taxes and interest on out-of-state state-local bonds. Withholding for individual income tax purposes was introduced by Oregon in 1948, and all the states except North Dakota now withhold from wages and salaries. Most of these states complement withholding by requiring declarations of estimated tax for income on which tax is not withheld.

DEATH AND GIFT TAXES. Death taxes were levied by states long before the federal government enacted an estate tax in 1916. Pennsylvania taxed inheritances as early as 1825, and Wisconsin set the modern pattern by adopting a progressive inheritance tax in 1903. Only Nevada does not tax bequests. The gift tax is levied in sixteen states. For the United States as a whole, death and gift taxes amount to less than 3 percent of total state tax collections.

LOTTERIES. The states have recently begun to use lotteries in their quest for new sources of revenue. Lotteries were used early in American history, but fell into disuse when it was found that they generated crime and corruption. Recent experience, which began with the New Hampshire Sweepstakes in 1964, has been more acceptable from the social point of view. As of mid-1976, thirteen states, representing about 40 percent of the total population, had adopted a lottery. But net amounts after the payment of prizes and administrative costs have been disappointing. In fiscal year 1975 net revenues from lotteries amounted to about $400 million, or less than 0.5 percent of state revenues from their own sources. Aside from the danger of encouraging criminal activity, lotteries are criticized on the ground that they appeal too often to people who cannot afford to participate and are therefore regressive.

Local Taxes

The tax sources of municipal and county governments are limited. They have always relied heavily on the property tax, and despite persistent efforts to diversify their sources of funds, the majority of local governments assign nonproperty taxes a relatively unimportant place in their finances.

PROPERTY TAX. The property tax provides 56 percent of the general revenues from all local sources (nearly 80 percent of the tax revenue). Dependence on this tax reflects the reluctance of many state governments to give localities authority to levy other taxes. It also reflects fears that high local income or sales taxes might induce emigration to or purchases in neighboring communities. Taxation of real property may have significant effects on the price and use of land but not on its location.

Although critics have long predicted the demise of the property tax, it has performed creditably in the postwar period. State and local property tax collections rose from about $6 billion in fiscal 1948 to $47.8 billion in 1974, an annual rate of growth of 8.3 percent during a period when the gross national product (in current dollars) grew at a rate of 6.8 percent. In 1971 the median effective state rate for single-family homes with FHA-insured mortgages was 2.0 percent, and only five states had average rates in excess of 3 percent. Among 146 cities with a population of 100,000 or more, 11 had an effective rate for houses of 4 percent or more and 9 of the 11 were located in the northeastern part of the country.

To moderate the burden of the property tax on the poor, twenty-four states and the District of Columbia have provided credits for property tax payments against the personal income tax. In most of these states, the credit is also given to renters on the basis of an assumed relation between property taxes and rental payments. Like the sales tax credit, the property tax credit is paid directly to the taxpayer if he or she is not subject to income tax or if the income tax does not cover the entire credit.

NONPROPERTY TAXES. Some large cities in a limited number of states have successfully diversified their revenue sources. Sales taxes are the most productive nonproperty taxes, with taxes on earnings or income next. Local general sales taxes are now used in twenty-six states by over 4,700 local governments. Local income taxes are levied in eleven states but are widespread only in Indiana, Kentucky, Maryland, Michigan, Ohio, and Pennsylvania.

NONTAX REVENUES. Nontax revenues are most important at the local level. In 1974 they accounted for 26 percent of local general revenues from own sources and for 17 percent of comparable state revenues. Such nontax revenue sources include charges for water, electric power, and gas, special assessments, license and other fees, and user charges for transportation, medical care, and housing. Payments for most government services that yield measurable benefits are substantially below marginal cost, primarily because it is feared that user charges will hurt low-income families.

State and Local Fiscal Performance, Capacity, and Effort

The fiscal performance and tax capacity of the fifty states during fiscal 1974 are summarized in figure 9-2. *Performance* is measured by per capita revenue collected from state and local sources; *capacity* is measured by personal income per capita; and *revenue effort* is the ratio of performance to capacity, or the ratio of revenue collected to personal income.

When the states are arrayed by size of per capita personal income, the per capita revenue obtained from state-local sources increases from low- to high-income states. In 1974 the ten poorest states raised only $618 per capita, whereas the ten richest states raised $949 per capita. This pattern of performance cannot be attributed to a lack of effort on the part of the poorest states. In fact, the average revenue

Figure 9-2. State and Local Revenue and Revenue Effort, by Quintiles of State Personal Income per Capita, Fiscal Year 1974[a]

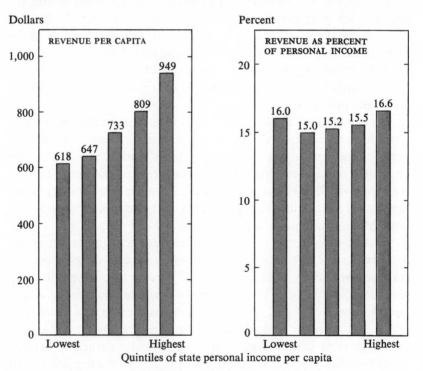

Quintiles of state personal income per capita

Source: U.S. Bureau of the Census, *Governmental Finances in 1973–74.*
a. State and local revenue excludes federal grants.

effort in the poorest one-fifth of the states is greater than the average effort made in the next three-fifths. Even if the poorest states increased their revenue effort from their 16.0 percent in 1973–74 to the 16.6 percent of the highest one-fifth, they would raise only $641 per capita —still far below the amount raised by other states. These figures indicate that the poorest states will not be able to provide adequate levels of public services just by increasing their revenue effort.

Major Issues

The state and local tax systems are still in transition. The fiscal squeeze from inflation and unemployment requires higher taxes, which create equity and economic problems. Most of these problems are not new, but they have become acute as tax burdens have increased.

Income Taxes versus Sales Taxes

The relative merits of an individual income tax and a sales tax for state use continue to provoke emotional responses in many areas of the country. The debate is primarily over equity, but other considerations enter into it.

The major argument in favor of the income tax is its progressivity. Proponents of the income tax believe that state as well as federal taxes should be based on ability to pay. Moreover, the deductibility of state income taxes in calculating the federal income tax greatly moderates the impact of the top state rates on high-income taxpayers (see the discussion of deductibility below). The income tax is also much more responsive to economic growth than the sales tax.

Proponents of the sales tax believe it is undesirable to pile a state income tax on top of the high federal tax. Even with deductibility, they fear that high-income taxpayers will emigrate to avoid the state income tax. They feel that tax progressivity is not essential at all levels of government, provided the entire federal-state-local tax system is progressive on balance.

Both the income and the sales taxes can be productive revenue sources for state governments if they are levied on a broad base. Most states levying both sales and income taxes derive more revenue from the sales tax. While it is possible to devise an income tax with a yield equal to that of almost any sales tax, sales taxes of 3 to 5 percent are

Table 9-1. Combined Federal and State Income and Sales Tax Liabilities, Married Couple with Two Dependents, Oregon and Washington, 1975

Dollars

| Adjusted gross income | Federal income tax[a] plus | | Difference (income tax less sales tax) |
	Oregon income tax[b]	Washington sales tax[b,c]	
3,000	−300	−182	−118
4,000	−400	−263	−137
5,000	−262	−35	−227
8,000	521	655	−134
10,000	1,000	1,003	−3
15,000	2,253	1,927	326
20,000	3,588	2,985	603
25,000	5,037	4,168	869
35,000	8,340	7,052	1,288
50,000	14,302	12,528	1,774

a. After the refundable earned income credit, indicated by minus signs.
b. After taking into account deductibility of the state income or sales tax in computing the federal income tax. All other deductions were assumed to be equal to the Oregon standard deduction of 13 percent of income.
c. Sales tax for 1975 as estimated by the Internal Revenue Service for purposes of federal deductibility. See Commerce Clearing House, *1976 U.S. Master Tax Guide* (1975), p. 43.

generally more productive than income taxes with rates graduated up to 10 percent. These are the ranges currently used in most states. The balance, of course, swings toward the income tax as incomes increase.

Whether an income tax would drive wealthy residents to sales tax states is difficult to determine. For example, in 1975 Oregon had an income tax and neighboring Washington had a sales tax. Table 9-1 compares the combined federal-state income and sales tax burdens of families with different incomes, after taking into account the effect of the deductibility of state taxes in computing the federal income tax. A married person with two children who was subject to the Oregon income tax would have paid $134 less tax on an income of $8,000 than a person who was subject to the Washington sales tax, but $1,774 more tax on an income of $50,000. Reactions to such differences depend heavily on individual attitudes toward equity, the need for state revenues, and the benefits of improved public services. In any case, the opposition to state income taxes is often vocal and influential and may prevent the use of income taxation regardless of its effect on location decisions. For instance, New Jersey finally enacted an income tax in 1976, but only after a long struggle.

There is little to choose between income and sales taxes on administrative and compliance grounds. Costs of administration are somewhat lower for the income tax than for the sales tax. Compliance is more difficult for the taxpayer in the case of the income tax, while the sales tax imposes a burden on retailers. Sales tax revenues are more stable than income taxes, but both taxes are responsive to changes in income and employment. Some support the sales tax because its revenues come partly from tourists and other visitors who use the facilities of the state temporarily. On the other hand, income taxes can be, and usually are, imposed on employees who live outside the state and work within the state. These differences may be significant in a few places where interstate travel and commuting are important.

In recent years, the need for revenue has tended to soften attitudes on both sides of the controversy. At one time most states had either an income tax or a sales tax, but the number of states with both has been increasing. On January 1, 1977, thirty-seven states had both, eight had only a sales tax, four had only an income tax, and one (New Hampshire) had neither (appendix table C-26). Credits for sales taxes against state individual income taxes, adopted in six states, make it possible to eliminate the burden of the sales tax on the lowest incomes. There are few remaining objections on equity grounds to the use by states of either type of tax, or both, if such credits are allowed.

Deductibility

The discussion in chapter 4 of the deductibility of state taxes in calculating the federal income tax base implied that simultaneous use of the same tax source by two (or even three) levels of government is acceptable provided the combined rates are not excessive. Deduction from the federal tax base of income, sales, and property taxes paid to state and local governments is considered desirable to encourage state and local use of these taxes and to narrow interstate and intercommunity net tax differences.

Most states with income taxes have borrowed the deductibility features of the federal law. While practices vary, state and local sales and excise taxes are deductible in arriving at taxable income in most states. In addition, sixteen of the forty-one states with an individual

Table 9-2. Marginal Burden of State Income Taxes under Federal Tax Deductibility[a]
and under Federal and State Tax Deductibility,[b] at Illustrative Marginal Rates
Percent

Marginal federal tax rate	Type of deductibility	Marginal state tax rate				
		2	3	5	7	10
14	Federal only	1.72	2.58	4.30	6.02	8.60
	Federal and state	1.48	2.23	3.72	5.23	7.50
20	Federal only	1.60	2.40	4.00	5.60	8.00
	Federal and state	1.29	1.93	3.23	4.54	6.53
30	Federal only	1.40	2.10	3.50	4.90	7.00
	Federal and state	0.99	1.48	2.49	3.50	5.05
40	Federal only	1.20	1.80	3.00	4.20	6.00
	Federal and state	0.73	1.09	1.84	2.59	3.75
50	Federal only	1.00	1.50	2.50	3.50	5.00
	Federal and state	0.51	0.76	1.28	1.81	2.63
60	Federal only	0.80	1.20	2.00	2.80	4.00
	Federal and state	0.32	0.49	0.82	1.17	1.70
70	Federal only	0.60	0.90	1.50	2.10	3.00
	Federal and state	0.18	0.28	0.47	0.66	0.97

a. State income taxes paid are deducted in computing federal income taxes.
b. Same as note a; in addition, federal income taxes paid are deducted in computing state income taxes.

income tax permit deduction of the federal individual income tax (four on a limited basis), and seven permit deduction of the state individual income tax itself; eight of the forty-five states with a corporation income tax permit deduction of the federal corporation income tax, and ten allow deduction of the state corporation income tax.

Deductibility of any tax from the base of another (or from its own base) has two effects: first, the extra burden on the taxpayer of the deducted tax is reduced by the marginal rate of the tax against which it is deductible; and second, the net yield of the tax with the deductible feature is reduced, requiring higher nominal rates to obtain any given amount of revenue. The net marginal burdens of state taxes with federal and federal plus state deductibility are illustrated in table 9-2. For example:

1. A proportional 2 percent state income tax is converted to a regressive tax by the deductibility feature of the federal income tax. Such a tax would impose a net burden of 1.72 percentage points on a taxpayer subject to the lowest federal rate of 14 percent, 1 point

on a taxpayer subject to a 50 percent federal rate, and only 0.6 point on a taxpayer subject to the top federal rate of 70 percent. If the state allowed its income tax to be deducted from its own income tax base, the regressivity would be even greater.

2. Federal deductibility of state income taxes already greatly reduces the burden of the top state income tax rates; as the following shows, state deductibility accomplishes little more for the taxpayer at a substantial cost to the state:

Tax collected as a percentage of income
(70 percent federal rate, 10 percent state rate)

Level of government	Federal deduct- ibility only	Federal and state deductibility	Difference
Federal	63.00	67.74	4.74
State	10.00	3.23	−6.77
Total	73.00	70.97	−2.03

With federal deductibility of the state tax, a top state rate of 10 percent imposes a net additional burden of only 3 percentage points on a taxpayer subject to a federal rate of 70 percent. With state deductibility of the federal tax, the net additional burden of the same 10 percent state tax is only 0.97 of a point. The 2.03-point net reduction in the taxpayer's total burden costs the state 6.77 points, or more than three times the taxpayer's saving.

3. Federal deductibility reduces the progressivity of the state tax and may actually convert it to a regressive tax. Adding state deductibility of the federal tax aggravates matters. For example, if the state rates are paired with the federal rates along the diagonal in table 9-2, the net impact of the state tax on an additional $1 of income is as follows:

Marginal federal rate	Marginal state rate	Net impact of the state tax (percent)		
		Federal deduct- ibility only	Federal and state deductibility	Difference
14	2	1.72	1.48	−0.24
20	3	2.40	1.93	−0.47
30	5	3.50	2.49	−1.01
40	7	4.20	2.59	−1.61
50	10	5.00	2.63	−2.37
60	10	4.00	1.70	−2.30
70	10	3.00	0.97	−2.03

If the federal income tax allows deductibility of the state tax, the state tax adds 1.72 percentage points to the federal tax in the lowest federal bracket, rising to 5 points in the 50 percent bracket. If, further, the state permits the federal income tax to be deducted against its own tax, the additional tax reaches a maximum of only 2.63 points.

Although the income tax rates in the top brackets raise only a fraction of their nominal values in many states, very high rates at the high income levels act as a psychological barrier to further use of the income tax for needed revenues. Since deductibility of the state tax in computing the federal tax already protects taxpayers against excessive rates, removal of the deductibility of the federal tax against the state tax would provide some additional revenue for the states and improve and simplify state income taxes.

The Property Tax

In spite of widespread and occasionally vehement criticism, the property tax continues to be the major revenue source for local governments. Its survival is mainly due to the impressive growth of revenue already noted. Recent economic analysis suggests that the tax is borne largely by owners of capital, which would make it a distinctly progressive element of the tax system.

Although the property tax was at one time intended to be a tax on all wealth, it is no longer general in coverage. While practices vary from community to community, the tax falls chiefly on real estate, business equipment, and inventories. The tax rate is determined as a residual. Local governments assess the value of property subject to the tax, estimate the revenue needed from this source, and calculate the tax rate required to obtain the predetermined result. The property tax is more adaptable to local government needs than are income or sales taxes, whose rates vary only with legislative action, and the ease with which rates can be raised has probably contributed to its durability.

ADMINISTRATION. Administration of the property tax has been subject to universal criticism. Because the value of the tax base for any particular property is not determined by a market transaction, property assessments are often arbitrary and can result in an erratic distribution of the tax burden. Substantial underassessment is the rule rather than the exception, even in the twenty states that require full valuation. In 1956, 1961, 1966, and 1971, for example, property was

Table 9-3. Distribution of States by Percentage Ratios of Assessed Value to Sales Price of Real Property, 1956, 1961, 1966, and 1971

Assessed value as percent of sales price[a]	Number of states			
	1956	*1961*	*1966*	*1971*
0–9.9	2	3	1	5
10.0–19.9	16	15	17	11
20.0–29.9	16	13	10	9
30.0–39.9	4	6	7	10
40.0–49.9	7	10	5	7
50.0–59.9	2	2	6	4
60.0–69.9	1	1	2	1
70.0 and over	0	0	2	3
Total	48	50	50	50
Average assessment (percent)	30	29.5	32.5	32.7

Sources: *Census of Governments*, 1956, 1961, 1966, and 1971.
a. Total assessed value of all properties sold that were included in the Census samples expressed as a percentage of their sales prices.

assessed at an average of about 30 percent of its market value in all states and at less than 50 percent in at least four-fifths of the states (table 9-3). Moreover, there is great variability in assessments of properties of equal value, creating irritating inequities among taxpayers and among different communities within the same state. The variability of local assessments requires state agencies to "equalize" the assessments before they are used for allocating state grants to local governments. In some places, property tax limitations are based on assessed valuations; in such cases, underassessment may impair the ability of the local government to finance its needs.

Uniform assessment can be attained at any assessment ratio, but assessors seem able to achieve more uniformity at the higher assessment ratios (table 9-4). Between 1956 and 1966 average assessment ratios increased somewhat while the variability of assessments declined significantly. Little change occurred either in average assessment ratios or in variability of assessments between 1966 and 1971, the last year for which such data are available.

The poor quality of assessments is due primarily to the difficulty of valuing property that is sold infrequently. In addition, local assessors are often not capable of making assessments or the local taxing jurisdiction lacks the staff and resources to take advantage of market evidence on property values. But good administration is possible despite the inherent difficulties. The Advisory Commission on Inter-

Table 9-4. Property Tax Assessment Ratios and Coefficients of Intra-Area Dispersion, Nonfarm Houses in Selected Local Areas, 1956, 1961, 1966, and 1971
Percent

Assessment ratio and dispersion coefficient	1956	1961	1966	1971
Median assessment ratio[a]	*Median coefficient of intra-area dispersion*[b]			
Under 20	37	33	26	27
20–30	32	27	21	21
30–40	25	23	19	21
40 and over	22	19	16	17
All areas	30	26	19	20
Coefficient of intra-area dispersion[b]	*Percentage distribution of local areas*			
Under 15	8	14	28	25
15–20	12	16	25	24
20–30	30	32	27	30
30–40	21	19	10	12
40 and over	29	19	10	9
All areas	100	100	100	100

Sources: Same as table 9-3.
a. Median ratio of assessments to sale prices for the Census samples of nonfarm houses in each local area.
b. The average deviation of assessment ratios from the median expressed as a percentage of the median ratio in the area.

governmental Relations (ACIR)—a permanent commission created by act of Congress to make recommendations on intergovernmental relations—has recommended centralization of property assessment in one state agency to take advantage of the states' superior technical resources; appointment rather than election of assessors to remove the assessment process from political influence; full information on property assessments and easy procedures for appeal so that taxpayers can help enforce good administration; publication of the value of property that is exempt from local property taxes by state action; and elimination of unnecessary and inequitable property tax limitations.

Many state governments have taken the initiative to improve local property tax administration along the lines proposed by the ACIR. The reforms involve more state participation in the administration of the tax, greater reliance on professional personnel, and reorganization of local assessment districts into larger and more efficient units. Most states collect comparative statistics on assessment ratios, which reveal the diversity in assessment practices and permit state officials to locate the major areas of administrative weakness. Many states are also taking an active part in supervising local assessment practices, training assessment personnel, and providing technical assistance where needed.

INCIDENCE AND ALLOCATION EFFECTS. Practically every economist since Ricardo has agreed that a property tax on unimproved land is borne by the landowners. Since the supply of land is fixed, the value of sites will fall by the capitalized value of the tax when it is first imposed or increased. More recently, it has been pointed out that a property tax on land may be shifted if, as a result of the reduced value of the land, investors accumulate a larger amount of reproducible capital. In these circumstances, the productivity of land would increase and interest rates would decline, and the tax would be shifted in the form of a lower rate of return on capital in general.

The incidence of a uniform property tax on reproducible capital has been disputed by economists for many years. If the supply of saving is not responsive to the rate of return, the tax will not affect the supply of capital and will be borne entirely by the owners of capital. (See chapter 5 for this analysis as it applies to the corporation income tax.) If the supply of saving responds at least to some extent to the rate of return, the tax will discourage new investment and reduce the supply of new buildings. The prices of services produced by buildings will rise and the tax will be borne partly by the consumers of these services and partly by the owners of capital.

The property tax on improvements could also be shifted forward in the form of higher prices under two conditions. First, property owners may have sufficient market power to set prices and may exercise this power when the property tax is imposed or increased, although this possibility is remote because the real estate industry is highly competitive throughout the country. Second, where rents are subject to control, property tax increases are usually considered justification for rent increases.

On the assumption that the property tax on improvements is borne entirely by capital, the distribution of the burden of this tax is regressive up to about the $15,000 income level and progressive thereafter. On the other hand, if the property tax on improvements is shifted forward to users, the property tax is regressive throughout most of the income scale (table 9-5). In both calculations it is assumed that the property tax on land is borne by landlords.

Table 9-5. Alternative Estimates of the Incidence of the Property Tax,
by Income Class, 1970

Income classes in thousands of dollars; tax rates in percent

Income class[a]	Effective rates of tax, assuming property tax on improvements is borne in proportion to	
	Housing expenditures and consumption[b]	Income from capital[b]
0–3	9.0	3.8
3–5	6.2	3.6
5–10	4.5	2.9
10–15	3.8	2.4
15–20	3.5	2.5
20–25	3.1	2.4
25–30	3.1	2.9
30–50	3.2	4.1
50–100	3.7	6.8
100–500	3.6	8.7
500–1,000	1.6	10.3
1,000 and over	0.8	10.9
All classes[c]	3.7	3.4[d]

Source: Brookings 1970 MERGE data file.

a. Income is defined as money factor income plus transfer payments, accrued capital gains, and indirect business taxes.

b. It is assumed that the property tax on land is borne by landlords.

c. Includes negative incomes.

d. The average burden of the property tax is lower because, under these assumptions, part of the tax is borne by the tax-exempt sector and is not included in the household sector.

It is also assumed that the property tax is a uniform tax levied on all property at the average rate for the country as a whole, although, in fact, taxes vary substantially among local areas and industries. Returns to owners of land and reproducible capital will fall on the average, but the interarea differences will also have significant effects. If labor and reproducible capital are not perfectly mobile, workers, property owners, and consumers will have higher real incomes in low-tax areas than those in high-tax areas.

The property tax also affects land use. In a city surrounded by farmland, the property tax will have no effect on land development if the farmland is taxed at the same rate as urban land. On the other hand, taxes on urban real estate often exceed taxes on farmland; land development for urban use will be retarded where this occurs. Similarly, heavy taxation of improvements discourages rebuilding in urban areas.

Residential property is one of the major sources of property tax revenue. The high taxes on housing might be expected to discourage the demand for housing. For many, however, the income tax advantages of homeownership offset its deterrent effects.

CIRCUIT BREAKERS. Credits against state income taxes for property tax payments by the elderly and the poor, a recent development, are sweeping the country. By the beginning of 1976, twenty-four states and the District of Columbia had enacted such a program. The credits are called "circuit breakers," the analogy being that they protect the family against a property tax overload in the same way that a circuit breaker protects an electrical line against an overload of current.

The circuit breaker is triggered when the income of a property taxpayer falls below certain levels. Some states provide a credit against the state income tax (or a refund if the income tax is not large enough to absorb the entire credit or if the individual is not subject to income tax) for the entire amount of property tax paid that exceeds the statutory percentage. In others, the credit is given on a sliding scale, with the highest percentage of relief at the lower end of the income scale. Some states assume that the property tax accounts for an arbitrary percentage of rental payments. In some states, only elderly homeowners are eligible; in others, relief is provided for elderly renters as well as homeowners; in a few states, all homeowners and renters, regardless of age, are eligible. For fiscal year 1974 the benefits under these programs amounted to $450 million, or about 1 percent of the revenue generated by the property tax.

Proponents of the circuit breaker idea believe that it is an effective device in cushioning the impact of heavy property taxes on poor families, especially the elderly, many of whom go on living in the family home even after their children have left and their incomes have declined. The benefits are financed by the state government and thus do not erode the fiscal resources of the local government.

On the other hand, although the circuit breaker is justified primarily on the ground that the property tax is regressive, economists have increasingly come to believe that the property tax is borne largely by owners of capital and is therefore progressive. If the property tax is actually borne by owners of capital, renters are not entitled to relief. Furthermore, the relief is given to those who have unusually large amounts of property in relation to their income or who spend an unusually large percentage of their current annual income on housing because their income is temporarily depressed. Where there are current difficulties in paying, provision can be made for delayed payment of property taxes, without paying benefits to those who are not entitled to them.

The relief provided by circuit breakers is far less efficient in helping the poor than a general income maintenance system. If relief for housing is desirable, a system of housing allowances to those with low incomes and low net worth would be more appropriate. Without such programs, circuit breakers will continue to be attractive because they provide apparently needy people with relief from an unpopular tax at relatively modest cost.

ALTERNATIVES. Other forms of real estate taxation have been proposed as alternatives to the general property tax. One is the use of annual rather than capital values as a base, often advocated by those who wish to "tax the profits out of the slums," where high-rent, low-capital-value housing prevails. Such a system would favor properties in low-return uses and, like the present tax, would discourage improvements to increase annual income from properties.

A second alternative is site-value taxation: taxing the value of the sites themselves while exempting the value of improvements. Site-value taxation has merit on equity grounds; since the value of land is increased by population growth and general improvements are financed by the community at large, the community has the right to tax this "unearned increment." Site-value taxation would also discourage the hoarding of land for speculative purposes and encourage more efficient use of land in and around the nation's cities. On the other hand, the supply of sites is not fixed, as the supporters of site-value taxation assume; in these circumstances, the tax on sites will be shifted in part to improvements. This is especially applicable to the fringes of city areas which are bordered by annexable land not subject to taxation. Moreover, shifting from the present system to a site-value tax would pose problems for present property holders who had paid the full current value, or close to it, for their land and who therefore have not received large unearned increments.

A third proposal, with similar equity and economic advantages, is to tax land-value increments. This would avoid the transitional problems of the site-value tax, but would yield much less revenue than the property tax if it were levied at moderate rates only at the time of transfers of ownership.

A different approach to property taxation is that of a user charge. It is argued that the distribution of taxes based on property values has little relation to the distribution of services to property provided by local governments. A series of user charges would be more clearly linked to the benefits received. For some services, like fire protection, the appropriate benefit charge would be easy to determine because the area of service is well defined; others, like transportation, would be more difficult to allocate. This proposal, however, would not deal with the bulk of the current tax revenues that finance services to persons rather than to property.

Other methods of financing local governments could be devised, but the alternatives to the property tax would not yield comparable revenues at reasonable rates. This will probably preserve the property tax as a major source of local government revenue, making the need for improved administration especially urgent.

With the growing sophistication of assessment techniques, it should be possible to further reduce the major administrative inequities. Participation in the administrative process by state governments, with their superior financial and technical resources, should accelerate the adoption of the latest techniques to the fiscal advantage of local governments.

Tax Coordination

Tax overlapping among different levels of government was at one time considered a major drawback of the national tax system, but attempts to divide revenue sources have had little success. The state and local governments failed to pick up the electrical energy tax, which was repealed by Congress in 1951, although they had urged the federal government to relinquish this tax for their use. The same was true of reductions in the federal admissions tax during the 1950s. In 1958–59 the Joint Federal-State Action Committee (consisting of state governors appointed by the chairman of the Governors' Conference and representatives of the federal government appointed by the President) could not reach agreement on a proposal to eliminate some federal grants in return for relinquishment of the local telephone tax by the federal government. Such attempts fail because it is difficult to devise a plan that all states regard as equitable and because the state and local governments are likely to view the specific federal taxes relinquished with the same reservations that motivated Congress to give them up as revenue sources in the first place.

One fairly successful transfer of a tax source did occur when federal excise taxes were reduced in 1965. At the request of the ACIR and the states, Congress delayed the effective date of the repeal of the federal stamp tax on realty title transfers to give states time to enact a replacement tax that would assure continuity of the sales information used in computing assessment sales ratio data for property tax equalization and state school aid programs. In this case, states were motivated more by the need for the tax-record information than by a desire for revenue.

Tax overlapping was moderated slightly by the 1965 federal excise tax reductions, but these cuts were made for other reasons. Experience to date suggests, therefore, that the major cases of duplication—in income, estate and gift, and selective excise taxes—will persist.

But the situation is not as serious as it appears. In recent years new methods of administrative cooperation between federal and state governments have been developed. State income taxes resemble the federal taxes in major respects; many, in fact, start with the federal definition of adjusted gross income for individuals and taxable income for corporations. Several states have simplified their tax returns. Most experts accept some tax overlapping as inevitable, and even desirable if the taxes used in common are good taxes. The present approach is to relieve major taxpayer compliance problems, remove inequities resulting from tax overlapping, and extend the area of intergovernmental administrative cooperation as much as possible.

ESTATE AND GIFT TAX COORDINATION. The administrative and compliance problems raised by overlapping estate and gift taxation are way out of proportion to their revenue yield. Most of the states use inheritance taxes, but they have a wide variety of exclusions, deductions, and exemptions. The federal credit for state death taxes (enacted in 1924 and enlarged in 1926) placed a floor under state taxes but did not produce uniformity. The states left their own taxes unchanged and later added special levies to pick up the difference between these taxes and the maximum allowable credit. Today, thirty-two states have inheritance taxes, thirty with pickup taxes; nine have estate taxes, seven with pickup taxes; two have estate and inheritance taxes, both with pickup taxes; and six have only pickup taxes. Only Nevada levies no state death tax.

The states have long felt that estate and gift taxes should be left to them, but would not have the credit arrangement repealed. They recognize that, without the protection of the federal credit, interstate competition for wealthy taxpayers would quickly dry up state death tax revenues. The credit ensures that any state can tax up to the amount of the credit without running the risk of losing its taxpayers to other states, but in its present form the credit provides no incentive for states to adopt uniform definitions of the tax base.

In 1961 the ACIR recommended the substitution of a two-bracket graduated credit for the present estate tax credit, which was originally computed as a flat percentage of the 1926 tax. The ACIR proposal would make available to the states a larger share of the tax on smaller estates on two conditions: first, that they increase their death taxes by at least the amount of the increase in the credit; second, that they enact estate taxes. The first condition was considered necessary because existing state death taxes generally exceed the federal credit; without a revenue maintenance provision, the higher credit might result in a net reduction rather than in an increase in state revenues. The second condition was intended to encourage the states to follow the pattern of the federal law, although it did not require uniformity in other respects.

The states had also asked for a federal credit for their gift taxes. The ACIR rejected a gift tax credit because it would force gift taxes on all the states, even though the revenue involved is negligible and the states do not need gift taxes to safeguard their death taxes (the federal gift tax already serves this purpose). In any event, the increased federal estate tax credit could be made generous enough to compensate the states for not having gift taxes.

Legislative action on the ACIR's recommendations for a higher estate tax credit has been deferred, and prospects for such consideration appear dim. The recommendations stimulated little interest in Congress or in the executive branch, partly because the degree of coordination they might achieve did not seem to justify the federal revenue loss. The federal government might be more receptive to the loss of revenue if the recommendations were modified to require greater uniformity.

STATE TAXATION AND INTERSTATE COMMERCE. For years the states have been reaching out to exact taxes from activities that cross state lines. On the whole, their claims have been sustained by the Supreme Court. In 1959, when the Court upheld a corporation income tax on a firm whose activities consisted solely of the solicitation of sales within a state, interstate business interests promptly appealed to the federal government for relief. Congress responded by enacting stopgap legislation under its power to regulate interstate commerce. This halted further expansion of state income tax jurisdiction pending the outcome of a congressional study to determine what legislation, if any, was needed. A few months later the Supreme Court held that an out-of-state business could be required to collect and pay over to a state a use tax on sales made to customers within the taxing state even if it maintained no facilities in the state and its sales were made entirely through independent contractors. As a result of this development, Congress expanded its study to include all matters pertaining to the taxation of interstate commerce by the states or any political or taxing subdivision.

After three years of study, the special Subcommittee on State Taxation of Interstate Commerce of the House Judiciary Committee recommended legislation affecting corporation income, sales, use, gross receipts, and capital stock taxes. These recommendations were the basis for bills passed by the House in 1968 and 1969 but not approved by the Senate in either year. The major issues are (1) the division of the income of multistate firms among the states, and (2) requirements for the collection of use taxes by firms shipping into a state.

1. The forty-five states with a corporation income tax have various formulas to compute the allocation for state tax purposes of profits of multistate firms. While twenty-six states have adopted uniform laws for allocation purposes (patterned after the proposal of the National Conference of Commissioners on Uniform State Laws), the others give varying weights to property, payroll, and sales. This diversity produces anomalous results: some interstate corporations are taxed lightly; others claim they pay state taxes on an aggregate tax base that exceeds their net income. Reporting for state income tax allocation is time-consuming and costly, especially for small and medium-sized

businesses with small accounting and legal staffs. Agreement is widespread that states should adopt uniform rules, but there is disagreement on what factors should be considered and who should administer the rules.

Under some legislative proposals, businesses subject to taxation would have the option of computing their state income tax liability under the existing state formula or under an optional, federally prescribed tax apportionment formula (presumably either the three-factor payroll, property, and sales formula or the two-factor payroll and property formula). No business would have to pay a state tax greater than that calculated under the optional prescribed formula.

The theory of the two-factor approach is that income should be apportioned according to the factors used in producing it and sales should be taken into account only to the extent that they involve the use of company facilities or labor in a particular state.

The three-factor approach is advocated on the grounds that no income is realized without sales. Sales reflect the relative importance of each state as a market for the output of any particular company and should therefore be given recognition in the division-of-income rules. Supporters of this approach hold that the elimination of the sales factor would create a competitive environment that discriminated against local firms.

Support for federal legislation reflects the interest of many small firms whose accounting and legal staffs are not prepared to cope with the current diversity in state apportionment formulas. Opposition to federal legislation mirrors the reluctance of the states to make the Treasury responsible for administrative interpretations that have traditionally been within the purview of state tax officials and the reluctance of the business community to forgo negotiations with state tax officials over income items and tax liability.

The corporation income tax accounts for much less than 5 percent of state-local revenue in all but a few states, so that the overall revenue consequences for the states of either approach are small. The two- and three-factor formulas would change tax revenues by as much as 1 percent in only two states, and in a majority by less than 0.5 percent. Nonetheless, shifts in tax burden from out-of-state to home-state firms in states with relatively high corporation income tax rates could be significant. This gives rise to concern about a state's competitive position for location of industry.

Congressional interest in state apportionment formulas may be renewed as a result of recent actions by New York and Massachusetts assigning double weight to the sales element in their three-factor formulas in an effort to attract payrolls and property. Other states are likely to consider weighting their apportionment factors as a counter-incentive, which would make the disparity in state tax treatment of multistate firms even greater.

2. All forty-five states with sales taxes levy use taxes on out-of-state purchases to complement their sales taxes. The use tax is imposed on the buyer for the privilege of using the commodity in the state and is designed to ensure that tangible personal property used in the state is subject to tax, wherever it may have been purchased. As a rule, states cannot enforce such taxes by collecting them from the purchasers except for registered automobile owners and business purchasers who are registered vendors.

To eliminate tax avoidance in connection with out-of-state purchases, states began to require out-of-state sellers to collect the use tax for them. In 1941 the Supreme Court permitted Iowa to require a mail order house with retail stores in Iowa to collect a use tax on mail order sales sent to its out-of-state customers; and in 1960 it upheld Florida's right to require use tax collections by a Georgia corporation that had representatives in Florida but no office or place of business there.

Although the volume of interstate sales in relation to local sales is small, sales across state lines create some of the most troublesome problems in sales taxation. Interstate sellers object to the requirement that they collect use taxes. The tax base is not uniform from state to state, and interstate sellers sometimes find compliance with use tax collection requirements as burdensome as compliance with state corporation income tax laws. As states rely more and more on these taxes and as rates rise, state tax officials feel an increasing obligation to protect local firms from competition by enforcing the use tax on out-of-state sellers.

The special subcommittee recommended an optional approach to vendor collection of the use tax that would maintain the status quo or permit the states to join in a cooperative federal-state sales tax administration under a uniform sales and use tax law to collect use taxes on interstate shipments. The only way to avoid the coercion of federal legislation is for the states to cooperate in mutually enforcing and collecting each other's taxes. The bill proposed by the House subcommittee would have authorized such cooperation through interstate sales tax agreements.

Resolution of the issues in state taxation of multistate business involves a balancing of the values of state tax sovereignty against the advantages of, and constitutional requirement for, the free flow of commerce across state lines. With the increasing interdependence of all regions of the country, a higher degree of uniformity and certainty in state taxation of interstate activities is both desirable and inevitable, but the process of accommodation to economic realities by the states and the federal government is painful.

Although no legislation has been enacted by Congress, the threat of federal legislation has triggered state action. Most of the states have amended their laws or regulations to eliminate practices that were criticized—for example, failing to allow the taxpayer the cost of sending a tax auditor to an out-of-state headquarters, and forbidding a trade-in allowance on out-of-state purchases but allowing it on local sales. Nineteen states have formed a tax compact that provides for a multistate tax commission composed of representatives of the member states. The commission seeks to promote the acceptance of uniform laws, regulations, and procedures, to conduct audits of a taxpayer on behalf of a number of states, and to settle disputes that involve a single taxpayer and two or more states by an arbitration procedure. Congress has as yet taken no action on bills consenting to the compact.

STATE TAXATION OF NONRESIDENTS. It is a settled rule of law that the states, like the federal government, have the right to tax all the income of their residents, wherever earned, and the right to tax all income originating in the state. Most states have eliminated multiple taxation of the same income by allowing credits for income taxes that must be paid by their residents to other states, provided the other states grant reciprocal credits. In addition to the resident credit, a number of states grant credits to nonresidents for income taxes they pay to their home states, provided those states reciprocate. In 1975 the United States Supreme Court outlawed the brazen attempt by New Hampshire, a state with no income tax, to take advantage of the resident credit available in its neighboring income tax states by imposing a tax on the income earned in New Hampshire by nonresidents.

The likelihood of an individual's owing tax to two states on the same income is now slight, although situations of multiple taxation do arise when two states, because their definitions of residence vary, claim the same person as a resident.

The problem is more acute when residents of a state without a personal income tax work in a state with such a tax. In these cases, the employees pay income tax to the state in which they are employed but receive no credit in their home states, where their principal tax payments are sales or property taxes. This problem would be solved, of course, if all states taxed personal incomes, as has been recommended by the ACIR. This group has also recommended the elimination of the nonresident credit and the adoption of a uniform definition of residence. The latter might be required as a condition either for continuing the deductibility feature of the federal income tax or for the enactment of a federal credit in lieu of, or as a supplement to, deductibility (see the discussion of federal assistance below).

COOPERATIVE TAX ADMINISTRATION. Formal federal-state cooperative tax administration dates back to the Revenue Act of 1926. The earliest form of cooperation involved examination of federal income tax returns by state tax officials; in 1950 a plan for coordinated federal-state use of income tax audits was developed. While the states benefited from these arrangements, the federal government received little in return.

In 1957 a new series of agreements on the coordination of tax administration was launched to extend cooperation to other taxes and activities. These agreements, which had been negotiated with forty-eight states by 1975, provide for examination of federal tax returns by state officials and of state returns by federal officials, including the exchange of automatic data processing tapes and information disclosed by federal and state audits. In addition, special enabling legislation permitted the Internal Revenue Service to perform statistical services for state agencies on a reimbursable basis and to enroll state enforcement officers in its training programs. In 1952 a Treasury Department regulation permitted federal agencies to withhold income taxes for state governments. In 1974 Congress passed a bill authorizing federal agencies to withhold income taxes for major cities.

These evidences of federal-state cooperation suggest that federal, state, and local tax officials are willing to coordinate their activities in the interest of greater efficiency. In the revenue sharing legislation enacted in 1972, Congress authorized the federal government to enter into agreements with the states for federal collection of state income taxes if at least two states with 5 percent of the federal individual income tax returns elected to have their income taxes "piggybacked" on the federal system. States showed no interest in this because of the high degree of federal conformity required, the widespread feeling that the federal income tax base may not be the perfect income tax instrument, and the lack of any interest at the federal level in assuming the responsibility for administering state income taxes. In 1976 Congress reduced the number of states needed to start the piggyback system to one, eliminated the requirement for 5 percent of federal returns, and made it explicit that no costs of collection would be charged to any state. Now that the legislation has been improved, most of the administrative and compliance benefits of unitary administration (including the same or similar tax returns for all units of government for any one tax, joint audits, and joint collection of taxes other than income taxes) could be achieved by agreement between the federal and state governments rather than through federal coercion.

State-Local Fiscal Relations

Most public services enjoyed directly by a resident of the United States—education, health, sanitation, and sewerage facilities, welfare aid, and police and fire protection—are provided by local governments. Yet local governments derive all their powers, including fiscal powers, from their parent state governments. Fortunately, the states are increasingly recognizing that local governments cannot be left to their own devices to finance an adequate level of public services.

INCREASING LOCAL TAX CAPACITY. There are limits to the freedom that can be given local governments in the field of taxation. Unless they were restrained by the state governments, they might soon find themselves with a maze of complicated, burdensome, and inefficient taxes that would impair economic growth. However, several techniques permit local governments to take advantage of the revenue productivity and growth potential of the major nonproperty taxes—sales and personal income taxes—within limits set by the state governments for purposes of control.

Tax supplements. Under this arrangement, the local rate is added to the state rate and the state collects the two taxes and then remits the local shares. The tax supplement has the advantages of simplicity, elimination of duplicate administrative costs, and ease of compliance for the taxpayer. It also retains the local governments' freedom to select revenue sources. Local tax supplements on sales taxes are now used in twenty-two states.

Maryland *requires* its local governments to add their own income tax to the state tax, with a minimum of 20 percent of the state tax and a maximum of 50 percent. Practically all local governments were close to the maximum within three years of the enactment of the legislation. The principal result has been that local property tax increases have been modest compared to increases in other states.

Tax sharing. Most state governments earmark one or more taxes for partial or total distribution to the local governments. The state government decides the tax to be shared, the rate to be imposed, and the formula for allocating receipts. Taxes are frequently returned to the communities where they were collected, but other methods of distribution are also used. Tax sharing imposes statewide uniformity in tax rates and automatically eliminates intercommunity competition. Like the tax supplement, it does away with duplicate tax administration and relieves local governments of unnecessary administrative costs. The device is widely used for automotive taxes, but it may be applied to the entire gamut of state taxes, including income, sales, and cigarette taxes and other excises and fees.

Tax credits. This is a little-used device to force local governments to use a particular tax. The state levies a statewide tax but gives a credit to the taxpayer for a specified portion (sometimes as much as 100 percent) of the tax paid to a local government. Credits for taxes paid to the state are given by the federal government under its estate and unemployment insurance taxes. In California and Utah tax credits are used to divide the sales tax revenues between counties and cities. The states require the counties to credit sales taxes levied by the cities within their jurisdictions. Florida credits municipal cigarette taxes and Virginia credits municipal taxes on bank shares against the corresponding state taxes. The tax credit is similar to the shared tax, except that local governments may exceed the credit if the state permits. On the other hand, the tax credit perpetuates duplicate tax administration although local governments often benefit from the spillover of experience under the state tax.

There is no a priori basis for judging which of these three devices is most appropriate in given circumstances, although each has advantages for particular objectives. In states where a specific tax is already widely used by the local governments, the tax supplement may be the best alternative. Tax sharing will be more acceptable where local taxes tend to be uniform or where the tax to be shared is not widely used at the local level. The tax credit provides the least coordination at the state-local level, but it may be the only alternative in states where the diverse interests of the local governments are difficult to reconcile.

STATE GRANTS-IN-AID. Grants are similar in many ways to shared taxes. However, instead of distributing funds according to the local tax base, grants provide financial aid to local governments according to some predetermined formula. The source of the revenue may be specified in the legislation, but the grants are often appropriated from general funds. Distribution formulas give weight to such factors as population, number of schoolchildren, income, property tax base, miles of paved streets, and so on. The grants are usually for specified purposes (such as schools, roads, and health services), but in some cases they are given unconditionally for general local use.

State assistance to local governments is not a new phenomenon. It amounted to 6 percent of local general revenue in 1902 and rose to 23 percent in 1934, 30 percent in 1950, and almost 34 percent between 1970 and 1974. In the past thirty-five years, state transfers to local governments have amounted to more than one-third of all state expenditures (figure 9-3).

Most state grant systems have grown without systematic planning. They are often complicated and inequitable, and may even defeat the purposes for which they were designed. Distribution formulas remain unchanged for decades despite huge population shifts. Many of the nation's largest cities are denied their appropriate shares of state grants by suburban-dominated state legislatures. The states have become more sensitive to the needs of their counties and cities, however, and this sensitivity is increasing as urban problems multiply. Although there are entrenched interests to overcome, state grant systems are gradually being revamped to meet current requirements.

Federal Aid

State and local governments have received some federal financial assistance since early in the nineteenth century. The early grants, financed by the sale of federal lands, were used for road construction

Figure 9-3. Federal Aid to State and Local Governments and State Aid to Local Governments, Selected Years, 1902–48; Annually, 1950–74

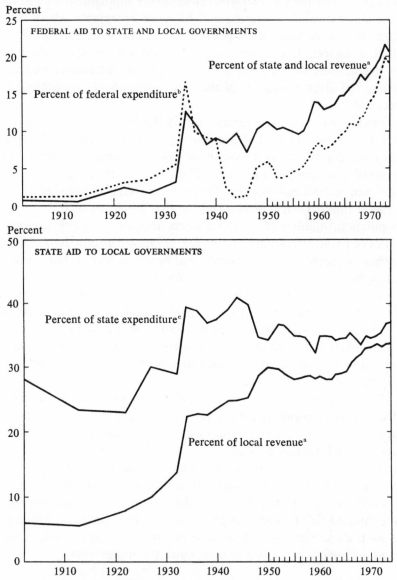

Sources: Bureau of the Census, *Census of Governments* and *Governmental Finances,* various issues.

a. Includes intergovernmental revenue and excludes utility, liquor store, and insurance trust revenue.

b. Includes intergovernmental expenditure and excludes insurance trust expenditure.

c. Includes intergovernmental expenditure and excludes liquor store and insurance trust expenditure.

and later to establish and operate the land grant colleges. The amounts were relatively modest until the 1930s, when the desperate financial condition of the states and localities led to the development of a great variety of grants to help finance their programs in education, health, welfare, transportation, housing, and other fields. Federal grants have risen from less than 1 percent of state-local general revenue in 1902 to 10 percent in 1948, and 21 percent in 1974 (figure 9-3).

CONDITIONAL GRANTS-IN-AID. Federal aid is now provided mainly through grants for specific government services. Such grants stimulate increased state and local action in particular areas that serve the national interest. They may also be justified on the ground that the benefits of many public services "spill over" from the community in which they are performed to other communities. For example, an individual may be educated in one state and migrate to another when entering the labor force. In such circumstances, investment in education will be too low if it is financed entirely by state funds, because each state is willing to pay only for benefits likely to accrue to its citizens. Federal assistance is needed to raise the level of expenditures closer to the optimum from the national standpoint.

Conditional grants permit the federal government to tailor its assistance to those activities that have the largest spillover effects. It can set minimum standards and require matching funds to assure state or local government support and participation. It can also allocate funds to states and communities where the need for a particular program is greatest or where fiscal capacity is least.

Conditional grants help finance state-local services without transferring their operation to the federal government. However, the proliferation of grants in the 1950s and 1960s made them increasingly subject to criticism. Critics charged that many specific grants involved excessive federal direction and interference with state-local prerogatives, diverted large sums from other urgently needed state-local programs, and were apt to be perpetuated long after their original objectives were met. On the other hand, the ability to control the use of funds and to require state-local financial participation appealed to Congress and private groups that trusted the federal government more than the state and local governments.

In 1971 President Nixon recommended consolidation of some 130 specific grants into six so-called special revenue sharing programs.

The complete overhaul was rejected by Congress, but elements of the special revenue sharing structure were adopted for grants to finance community development, manpower training, and urban mass transportation. President Ford added to the Nixon grant reform agenda in 1976, proposing the consolidation of grants in health, education, social services, and child nutrition into four major "block grants." The proposed consolidations are intended to give the states and local governments more flexibility in the use of federal funds, but it is still too early to judge whether they will promote the objectives of the federal grant program more effectively than the earlier arrangements.

GENERAL PURPOSE GRANTS. The federal government first appropriated funds to be given the states for any state-local purpose in 1836, when federal surplus revenues were large enough—partly as a result of receipts from the sale of public lands—to retire the entire national debt and to accumulate a Treasury balance besides. Beginning January 1, 1837, the funds were distributed quarterly on the basis of the number of congressmen and senators from each state, which was very nearly the same as a per capita distribution. The federal surplus disappeared before the end of 1837, a recession year, and the grants were terminated after three installments. From 1837 to 1971, all federal grants were conditional.

General purpose grants are justified on two grounds. First, all states do not have equal capacity to pay for public services. Even though the poorest states make a relatively larger revenue effort (see figure 9-2), they are unable to match the revenue-raising ability of the richer states and cannot provide the range or quality of services offered elsewhere. While on balance conditional grants (excluding transportation grants) have an equalizing effect (figure 9-4), the assistance they provide is inadequate for the total needs of the poorer states. Within states, conditional grants have widened fiscal disparities slightly among metropolitan areas rather than narrowing them.

Second, federal use of the best tax sources leaves a wide gap between state-local need and state-local fiscal capacity. Moreover, no state can push its tax rates much higher than those in neighboring states for fear of placing its citizens and business enterprises at a disadvantage. On this line of reasoning, all states need some federal assistance even for purely state-local activities, with the poorer states needing more help because of their low fiscal capacity.

As federal revenue increased during the 1960s, considerable sup-

Figure 9-4. State and Local General Revenue from Own Sources and from Federal Grants Other than for Transportation, by Quintiles of State Personal Income per Capita, Fiscal Year 1974

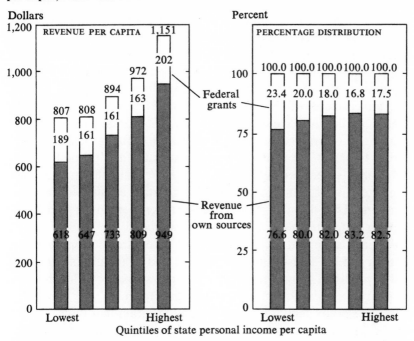

Sources: Bureau of the Census, *Governmental Finances in 1973–74,* and Department of the Treasury.

port developed for some way to use part of the increasing federal receipts for general purpose grants. Several proposals were considered in Congress, including one that was the central element of the New Federalism program of the Nixon administration. In the end, a general revenue sharing program was enacted in 1972 for the five years ending December 31, 1976, to provide financial assistance to the states and local governments with few strings attached. In 1976, the legislation was extended to September 30, 1980. The major features of the program are:

1. For the first five years a total of $30.2 billion was set aside in a special federal trust fund, with annual amounts ranging from $5.3 billion in the first year to $6.7 billion in the fifth. For the next three and three-quarter years, the annual rate is $6.85 for a total of $25.6 billion. The appropriations are automatic and are not subject to the annual budget process.

2. One-third of the revenue sharing funds are paid to the states and the other two-thirds to over 38,000 general purpose local governments. The state shares are calculated on the basis of two formulas— one devised by the House and the other by the Senate—and each state receives the higher of the two amounts. The House formula gives weight to population, per capita income, urban population, tax effort, and personal income tax revenues. The Senate formula is based on population, per capita income, and tax effort. Allocations among local governments within each state are made on the basis of a formula containing the same elements as the Senate's interstate formula.

3. Few constraints are imposed on the use of funds. States are permitted to spend the revenue sharing funds for any purpose. Local governments were permitted to spend their revenue sharing funds on a selected list of items, but the 1976 legislation eliminated these restrictions. Thus the state and local governments are given great flexibility in budgeting their total financial resources.

4. Each state and local government is required to report to the secretary of the treasury on the planned and actual use of the funds and to publish a copy of the reports in a newspaper covering the geographic area of the government making the report.

5. The funds cannot be used for any program that discriminates on the basis of race, color, national origin, or sex. Where such discrimination is found, the secretary of the treasury is directed to withhold all revenue sharing funds to which the unit of government would be entitled.

In actual practice, the revenue sharing program has helped equalize the fiscal resources of the states, though not by much (table 9-6). Metropolitan central cities receive more shared revenues than other areas on a per capita basis, but the advantage is not significant if the shared revenues are compared with the total expenditures of the various units of government. As a percentage of nonschool revenues, the assistance to the large urban counties is smaller than to the other counties. Thus far, the revenue sharing program has not altered the pattern of spending by the states and local governments, and has had a limited effect on the decisionmaking processes of states and local governments and on their institutional structure.

Reaction to the revenue sharing program depends on attitudes toward the relations between the federal and the state and local

Table 9-6. Relation of Revenue Sharing Grants to State and Local Revenues from Own Sources and to State Personal Income, by States Ranked by 1974 Personal Income per Capita

States ranked by 1974 per capita income quintile	Revenue sharing grants in 1975 as a percentage of	
	State-local revenues from own sources, 1973–74	Personal income, 1974
Top	3.20	0.50
Second	3.48	0.48
Third	3.79	0.52
Fourth	4.41	0.57
Lowest	5.57	0.78

Sources: U.S. Bureau of the Census, *Governmental Finances in 1973–74*, pp. 31–33; U.S. Department of the Treasury, Bureau of Government Financial Operations, *Federal Aid to States, Fiscal Year 1975*, p. 17; *Survey of Current Business*, vol. 55 (August 1975), pp. 10–11.

governments. The program is opposed by those who wish to control the use of federal funds in great detail, who have little faith in the willingness or ability of state and local governments to use the funds wisely, and who believe that general purpose grants will weaken the role of conditional grants. It is supported by those who wish to strengthen the role of the state and local governments and to limit federal control over state-local spending, and who believe that conditional grants are overworked in the federal system. Some oppose the expansion of federal assistance on the ground that separation of the expenditure and financing functions will lead to excessive and wasteful expenditures.

The categorical and revenue sharing grants have very different functions. Categorical grants ensure that the states do not neglect areas where the "spillover" effects are clearly in the national interest. Revenue sharing, on the other hand, links the states and localities to the superior revenue resources of the federal government and helps poorer states and localities provide services of the same scope and quality as those of the wealthier ones without putting far heavier tax burdens on their citizens.

In addition to the idea of a continuing revenue sharing program, special financial assistance for state and local governments is needed during recession periods. The programs and activities supported by these units of government cannot be turned on and off in response to changes in tax receipts. Moreover, periods of slow growth or recession have a major impact on the ability of the states and local governments to finance their expenditure commitments. In periods of stagflation particularly, local government revenues cannot keep up with the rising costs caused by inflation. Only the federal government can moderate cyclical changes in state-local receipts. On the basis of these considerations, legislation was enacted in 1976 that will automatically provide payments to the states and local governments when national unemployment exceeds 6 percent of the labor force. The legislation calls for quarterly payments of $125 million at 6 percent unemployment plus $62.5 million for each half point above 6 percent, up to a total of $1.25 billion for the five quarters ending September 30, 1977. One-third of the funds goes to the states and two-thirds to the local governments on the basis of the excess of unemployment in each state or local government over 4.5 percent and their general revenue sharing allocation. This legislation will improve countercyclical fiscal policy and prevent curtailment of urgently needed state-local programs during periods of recession, particularly if the amount of assistance is substantially increased and the unemployment trigger is lowered to 5 percent.

OTHER METHODS OF FEDERAL ASSISTANCE. Alternatives for accomplishing the objectives of federal grants involve the reduction of federal revenues. These include (1) reducing federal taxes or relinquishing specific types of federal taxes; (2) sharing federal tax collections with the states; and (3) granting credits against federal taxes for state and local taxes. These are the same methods that state governments use to provide assistance to local governments. Such measures would help state and local governments in varying degrees, but they would not achieve the broad objectives sought through the grant device, especially fiscal equalization.

If the objective is to increase state-local fiscal resources, the response of the state and local governments is bound to be spotty because it depends on action by many different executive and legislative bodies. State and local revenues would rise mainly through the indirect effect of the increased national income resulting from federal tax reduction, but this would amount to only a fraction of the released federal revenues. To the extent that state and local tax rates increased, the richer states and localities would benefit most.

As has been indicated, tax sharing is a common arrangement at the state-local level, but not at the federal-state level. Now that the federal government must rely almost exclusively on income and estate and gift taxes, the tax sharing alternative would greatly reduce federal revenues unless the states were willing to relinquish these taxes and the federal government raised its tax rates to finance the shared revenues.

Tax credits would not automatically increase state-local revenues: state and local governments now imposing the taxes that could be credited would have to raise their rates. Since this could be done without raising the total taxes paid by their citizens, they might be encouraged to do so, but there would be strong opposition from groups that would prefer the tax reduction provided by the credit. If the credit applied to income taxes, the nine states without individual income taxes would benefit only after they imposed such a tax. This might be regarded as federal coercion, however, and in some states would face formidable constitutional barriers. The earlier discussion of the estate tax credit indicated that the tax credit could be an effective coordinating device, but it would not redistribute resources to the neediest states. At best, the credit would divert federal revenues to the states where they originated.

The Plight of the Cities

In recent years, city finances have emerged as a major fiscal problem. The resources of many of the nation's largest cities, particularly those in the northeast and north central regions of the country, are inadequate to pay for their rapidly growing expenditures. In general, the problems are most acute in the old core cities, which have been losing population to the suburbs, have a high proportion of low-income families, and cannot improve their finances through annexation of or amalgamation with more affluent surrounding communities.

The distress of the old, declining core cities results from several factors.

1. The tax base has been moving from the central city to the suburbs for many years, and the expenses of operating public services for residents and commuters have been rising sharply. The poor, who cannot pay taxes, are concentrated in the cities, while the middle- and high-income recipients are in the surrounding suburbs. Some of

the large cities and counties and the urban states have been carrying a major share of the welfare burden, even though poverty is acknowledged to be a national problem.

2. The state legislatures are often controlled by representatives of the suburbs and small towns who believe that it is in their interest to prevent the cities from levying taxes on suburbanites to pay for the costs they impose on the city. The result is that many cities are shortchanged in state grant programs and others are prohibited from levying taxes on the earnings of commuters. This impoverishes the cities even more and leads to further deterioration of their fiscal capacity.

3. The coexistence of inflation and high unemployment—a relatively new phenomenon in modern economic life—imposes intolerable burdens on the cities. Inflation increases the costs of government services; high unemployment reduces tax receipts. In these circumstances, cities must either resort to borrowing or curtail essential services. Occasionally, as in the case of New York City in 1975, the borrowing exceeds the capacity of the governmental unit to service the debt and to finance growing expenditure requirements. New York City forced holders of some of its maturing bond issues to accept longer maturities and lower interest rates, and it needed massive state and federal assistance to avoid bankruptcy.

4. Many cities have overextended themselves. Salaries of local government employees have risen sharply in the last ten years, and many public employee unions have extracted unusually generous pension benefits from city governments. Budgetary controls are also lax in many cities. New York and other cities borrowed in the short-term market to cover current expenses, a practice that backfired as soon as receipts began to slack off during the 1974–75 recession.

Since the cities are creatures of the states, the states have the responsibility of supervising the city budget and debt procedures to enforce sound fiscal practices. In most states, city budgets or borrowing plans are subject to approval by the state government, but often the procedure has not been taken seriously by either side. As a result of the fiscal crisis in New York City, the state governments are exercising stricter controls over city fiscal procedures.

In addition to their supervisory role, the state governments also have the responsibility of providing adequate revenue resources for the cities, but most large cities are hamstrung in their efforts to tax suburbanites, who rarely pay their fair share of the costs they impose on the cities. In the absence of metropolitan government, the state governments could solve the problem by making special or block grants to the cities out of state funds and, in cases such as that of New York, by increasing financial assistance for such local functions as welfare, hospitals, and higher education. Another possibility is to require the suburbs to share their taxes with the cities. One such arrangement is operating in the Minneapolis–St. Paul area, where the central cities share in the growth of property tax receipts of the surrounding suburbs under a program approved by the state government. In metropolitan areas covering two or more states, the central city could be given the authority to levy a special income tax (either independently or piggybacked on the state tax) that would apply to the full earnings of its residents and to the earnings of the commuters in the city. In normal practice, commuters who are residents of other states may credit such taxes against the income tax of their state of residence, so that this arrangement should not create any serious cases of double taxation.

Since poverty is a national problem, the federal government has been urged to assume the full financial burden of the welfare system. Release of state and local fiscal resources now used to pay welfare benefits would ease the burden of a few of the cities and counties directly and would provide elbow room throughout the country for additional state support of city activities. The program of counter-cyclical revenue sharing discussed earlier would help prevent the inevitable erosion of city tax receipts during periods of high unemployment. State as well as city borrowing sources could be expanded if the federal government agreed to subsidize taxable bonds issued by the states and local governments (see chapter 4).

The cities of this country are centers of industry and commerce, education, arts and letters, theater and sports, and other economic, cultural, and recreational activities. These benefits accrue to the residents of the entire areas in which the cities are located and, to a lesser extent, to the people throughout the country. Part of the costs of the cities should therefore be shared by residents of other parts of the country. This is the reason both the states and the federal government must be concerned with city finances.

Summary

Despite the sluggish response of their taxes to economic growth, state and local governments have made a good record since the end of the Second World War. But they will continue to be hard pressed in the foreseeable future as their financial needs grow.

Most of the additional revenue needed must be raised by the state and local governments themselves. At the state level, the trend is toward the use of both income and sales taxes. In some states, there are long-standing traditions against one or the other of these two major taxes, but historical precedents have broken down under the pressure for more revenue. The adoption in six states of a credit against the income tax for sales taxes paid suggests that the objection to sales taxes on equity grounds can be dealt with effectively. The deductibility of state income taxes under the federal income tax makes income taxation at the state level more acceptable. However, states that permit the deduction of federal income taxes from their own income tax bases should recognize that they lose much more revenue than their taxpayers save and reduce the equity of their incomes taxes.

At the local level, immediate strengthening of property tax administration is needed. According to the modern theory of incidence, this tax is borne by owners of capital and is therefore progressive. The tax will continue to be the main revenue source of local governments; state governments should take a strong hand in promoting improvements in the professional quality of assessment personnel and assessment procedures. The circuit-breaker technique for moderating the property tax burdens of the poor and the elderly is based on the older notion that the property tax is regressive. In actual operation, the circuit breakers use up scarce revenues and are poor substitutes for an effective and equitable program to help the poor.

The states should supervise local budgetary and debt practices closely to prevent fiscal mismanagement, and should expand their use of the tax sharing device. They might also consider the feasibility of permitting local governments to supplement the overworked property tax with revenues from income or sales taxes. Allowing local governments to levy such taxes has some dangers, but unnecessary complications and inefficiencies can be avoided if local income and sales taxes are levied as supplements to the corresponding state taxes.

Even if they make a substantial effort of their own, state and local governments are unable to meet their needs without considerable federal assistance. Part of this assistance comes from conditional grants, which help finance activities in which the federal government has a strong interest. The recently enacted federal revenue sharing program, which gives aid to the states and local governments with few strings attached, provides assistance for other state-local programs. Both categorical and general purpose grants are essential ingredients of a federal fiscal system. The enactment by the federal government of special countercyclical grants to the states and local governments will help cushion the decline in their receipts during recessions.

Historical Summary of the Major Federal Taxes

THE FEDERAL TAX SYSTEM as we know it today is of relatively recent origin. From 1789 to 1909 the federal government relied almost exclusively on excise taxes and customs. An income tax was used for emergency purposes during the Civil War, and rudimentary death taxes were levied in the years 1797–1802, 1862–70, and 1898–1902. The corporation and individual income taxes—now the backbone of the federal revenue system—were enacted in 1909 and 1913 respectively. The modern estate tax was first levied in 1916 and the gift tax in 1924. Payroll taxation was introduced by the Social Security Act of 1935.

The Individual Income Tax

The Civil War tax on individual incomes was in effect from 1862 through 1871. The tax contained a flat $600 exemption with no allowance for children, was graduated up to 10 percent (in 1865 and 1866), and was collected at the source on wages, salaries, interest, and dividends. Total revenues under this tax amounted to $376 million. At its peak in 1866, it accounted for almost 25 percent of internal revenue collections. The tax was allowed to lapse in 1872, when the urgent need for revenue disappeared.

For almost twenty years after the expiration of the Civil War tax, there was only isolated support for the reenactment of an income tax. As the country grew and prospered, great industries and fortunes were estab-

288

lished, and inequalities in the distribution of income became more disturbing. The income tax was reenacted in 1894, when the country was in a mood for reform against the evils of monopolies and trusts, but it was declared unconstitutional by the Supreme Court in 1895.

The high court held that the portion of the personal income tax that fell on income from land was a "direct" tax, which the Constitution stipulated must be apportioned among the states according to population. The decision was assailed by many groups, and agitation for a change in the Constitution continued until the Sixteenth Amendment was ratified in 1913. This amendment stated that "Congress shall have power to lay and collect taxes on incomes, from whatever source derived, without apportionment among the several States, and without regard to any census or enumeration."

The 1913 tax, which was enacted shortly after the Sixteenth Amendment was ratified, applied to wages, salaries, interest, dividends, rents, entreprenurial incomes, and capital gains. It allowed deductions for personal interest and tax payments, as well as for business expenses. It exempted federal, state, and local government bond interest and the salaries of state and local government employees; it also exempted dividends from the normal tax but not from surtax. Taxes were collected at the source on wages and salaries, interest, rents, and annuities, with an exemption of $3,000 for single persons and $4,000 for married couples. A normal tax of 1 percent was applied to income above the exempted amounts, with a surtax of 1 to 6 percent.

The most significant changes made since the original 1913 act are the following: a credit for dependents and a deduction for charitable contributions were introduced in 1917; collection at the source was eliminated in 1916 and was reenacted for wages and salaries only in 1943; preferential rates on long-term capital gains were adopted in 1921; in 1939 the exemption of the salaries of state and local government employees was eliminated; the sale of tax-exempt federal bonds was discontinued in 1941; the standard deduction and the per capita personal exemption were adopted in 1944; income splitting for married couples was enacted in 1948; an averaging system and a minimum standard deduction were introduced in 1964; in 1969 the minimum standard deduction was replaced by a low-income allowance, and a minimum tax on selected preference incomes and a top marginal rate on earned income of 50 percent were adopted; and in 1975 a refundable earned income credit was introduced to alleviate the burden of the payroll tax on low-income recipients, and a per capita tax credit was adopted in lieu of increasing the per capita personal exemption.

Rates and exemptions have changed frequently (tables A-1, A-2, and

A-3). Maximum marginal rates reached 77 percent during World War I, 94 percent during World War II, and 92 percent during the Korean War. They declined to 24 percent in the 1920s and rose to 79 percent in the 1930s; in the late 1950s and early 1960s, the maximum rate was 91 percent. At present, the maximum rate is 70 percent. A special Vietnam War surcharge was in effect at 7.5 percent of tax in 1968, 10 percent in 1969, and 2.5 percent in 1970. Exemptions showed a downward trend during the first three decades of income taxation in this country, reaching a low of $500 per taxpayer during World War II, and then rose to $600 for each personal exemption in 1948, $625 in 1970, $675 in 1971, and $750 in 1972. In addition, a tax credit of $30 per capita was allowed in 1975 and increased in 1976 to $35 per capita or 2 percent of adjusted gross income up to a maximum of $180, whichever is larger. Beginning in 1975 families with children have been permitted to deduct as a credit against their tax (with refunds for those who are not taxable or whose tax does not equal the credit) 10 percent of their earned income up to $4,000, phasing down to zero at $8,000.

The Corporation Income Tax

The general corporation income tax rate began at 1 percent in 1909, reached 12 percent during World War I, 13.5 percent in the 1920s, 40 percent during World War II, and 52 percent during the Korean War. The Revenue Act of 1964 reduced the rate to 50 percent for 1964 and 48 percent for later years (table A-4).The Vietnam War surcharge also applied to corporations at 10 percent of tax in 1968 and 1969 and 2.5 percent in 1970.

Between 1909 and 1935 the tax was levied at a proportional rate on taxable income. A small exemption was allowed in computing taxable income for sporadic periods: $5,000 in the years 1909–13; $2,000 in 1918–27; and $3,000 in 1928–31. Graduation was introduced for the first time in 1936, with rates ranging from 8 percent on the first $2,000 of taxable income to 15 percent on income over $40,000.

Beginning in 1938 graduation was limited to corporations with incomes of $25,000 or less. Above this point, a flat rate applied to all the taxable income of the corporation, on the theory that rate graduation in the corporation income tax cannot be defended on equity grounds as in the case of individuals. The limited graduation was intended as a concession to small business. This rationale produced a peculiar rate schedule, which persisted until the end of 1949. For example, between 1942 and 1945 the rates began at 25 percent on the first $5,000 of taxable income and rose to

53 percent for taxable incomes between $25,000 and $50,000 (table A-5); beginning at $50,000, the rate was a flat 40 percent on total taxable income. The 53 percent rate—called the "notch" rate—was just enough to raise the corporation rate to 40 percent at $50,000 and thus avoided a discontinuity in effective rates at that point.

While it produced the desired result, the notch rate was regarded as a penalty on small business. After considerable agitation, the 1950 act removed the notch rate and restored a simple two-bracket system of graduation. This was accomplished by enacting a normal tax applying to all corporation profits and a surtax applying to profits in excess of $25,000. For the years 1952–63 the combined rates were 30 percent on the first $25,000 and 52 percent on the amount in excess of $25,000. In 1964 they were reduced to 22 percent and 50 percent respectively, and from 1965 through 1967 were 22 percent and 48 percent. Including the Vietnam War surcharge, the rates were 24.2 percent and 52.8 percent for 1968 and 1969, and 22.55 percent and 49.2 percent for 1970. They returned to 22 percent and 48 percent in 1971. In 1975 graduation was extended to $50,000, with rates of 20 percent on the first $25,000 and 22 percent on the next $25,000; the top rate, which remained at 48 percent, applies to the amount of taxable income above $50,000.

Dividends distributed by corporations were excluded from the individual *normal* tax before 1936 and were subject to the *surtax* (which was the progressive element of the individual income tax). In 1936 this exclusion was removed, and a tax on undistributed profits was imposed at the corporate level. This tax was intended to force corporations to distribute most of their earnings as dividends. The tax was vigorously attacked as a deterrent to corporate growth and was repealed after being in operation for only two years.

Between 1939 and 1954 the individual and corporation income taxes were levied without any attempt to integrate the two taxes as they applied to dividends. In 1954 individuals were allowed to exclude the first $50 of dividends from their taxable income ($100 for joint returns) and to subtract as a credit from the tax 4 percent of the dividends received in excess of the exclusion. After a decade of debate, Congress reduced the credit to 2 percent in 1964 and eliminated it entirely beginning in 1965; at the same time, the exclusion was increased to $100 ($200 for joint returns).

The corporation income tax was supplemented by an excess profits tax during World Wars I and II and the Korean War. The method adopted was to tax at a very heavy rate (as high as 95 percent in World War II) the excess of a corporation's profits over a prewar base period or over a "normal" rate of return (specified in the statute) on invested capital. For example, the base period for the World War II excess profits tax was 1936–39. The excess profits tax creates difficult economic, equity, and administrative problems; taxation of even a portion of a corporation's net profits at rates close to 100 percent tends to be unfair. To relieve the most glaring inequities, the law provided alternative methods of computing excess profits and also permitted adjustments for hardship cases. But such provisions made a complicated law even more difficult to administer. Experience to date indicates that excess profits taxation is appropriate only for wartime use.

Excise Taxes

Immediately after the ratification of the Constitution, the new government introduced a fairly elaborate system of excise taxes, including taxes on carriages, liquor, snuff, sugar, and auction sales. Even at that time, these taxes were considered unfair and burdensome on the poor. The Whisky Rebellion of 1794 was a revolt by farmers against the federal tax, which ran up to 30 cents a gallon. Except for the tax on salt, the early excises were abolished by the Jefferson administration in 1802, revived during the War of 1812, and then terminated again in 1817, not to reappear until the Civil War.

The Civil War excise tax system foreshadowed what was to happen during every major war thereafter. Liquor and tobacco taxes, which remained as permanent parts of the federal revenue system after the war, were supplemented by taxes on manufactured goods, gross receipts of transportation companies, advertising, licenses, legal documents, and financial transactions. During World War I, the list was again expanded, this time to include special occupational taxes and taxes on theater admissions, telephone calls, and retail sales of jewelry, toilet preparations, and luggage. After the war, tobacco and stamp taxes remained as the major excise taxes. The liquor taxes remained in effect throughout the prohibition era.

A break with peacetime precedent was made during the early 1930s, when Congress enacted a series of manufacturers' excise taxes on such items as automobiles, trucks, buses, appliances, and other consumer durables; also taxed were long distance telephone calls. These taxes were to be continued at varying rates and with varying degrees of comprehensiveness until 1965. The depression taxes were enacted after an attempt to introduce a general manufacturers' sales tax was defeated in Congress. During World War II, the rates of most of the then existing excise taxes were increased; and new excise taxes on retail sales of furs, jewelry, luggage, and toilet preparations, on local telephone service, and on passenger and freight transportation were introduced.

A bill to reduce the excise taxes was passed by the House just as the Korean War began. These changes were quickly eliminated from the Revenue Act of 1950, which was enacted three months after the beginning of hostilities. In the following year, the excise taxes on liquor, tobacco, gasoline, automobiles, consumer durables, and other products were increased, and new taxes on wagering and diesel fuel were adopted.

A major innovation in excise taxation was introduced in 1956, when a number of excise taxes were earmarked for the specially created Highway Trust Fund to finance the construction of the 41,000-mile federal highway system. The earmarked taxes included the old taxes (with increased rates) on gasoline, diesel, and special motor fuels, trucks, and tires, and new taxes on tread rubber and the use of heavy trucks and buses on the highways. The Airport and Airway Trust Fund was set up along similar lines in 1970 to finance construction of airports and improvements in the airway system. The taxes earmarked for this fund included those on passenger tickets, airfreight, gasoline used by general aviation aircraft, tires and tubes used on aircraft, a special $3 tax on international air trips, and an annual aircraft user tax.

The Korean War excise tax structure was dismantled beginning in 1954; the process took more than a decade. The original Korean War tax increases had been enacted for a period of three years, but most of them were extended each year as revenue requirements forced continued postponements of their repeal. The first significant break came in 1954, when all excise tax rates in excess of 10 percent were reduced to 10 percent, with the exception of the 20 percent cabaret tax. The freight tax was repealed in 1958; the cabaret tax was reduced to 10 percent in 1960; and in 1962 the railroad and bus passenger tax was eliminated, and the air transportation tax was reduced from 10 percent to 5 percent. An interest equalization tax on the acquisition of stock or debt obligation of a foreign issue was enacted in 1964 (retroactive to July 1963) for balance-of-payments reasons and was allowed to expire on June 30, 1974.

The present excise tax system was enacted in 1965, when Congress scaled down the Korean War excises to all but a few major taxes levied for sumptuary and regulatory reasons and as user charges (table A-6). Excises are now confined to five general categories: (1) alcohol and tobacco taxes; (2) highway and airway user taxes; (3) a tax on truck parts and accessories of 8 percent of manufacturers' prices; (4) regulatory taxes on matches, butter, cotton futures, and betting; and (5) some miscellaneous taxes. The telephone tax, levied at a 10 percent rate during the Korean

War, is being phased out gradually and is scheduled to expire at the end of 1981.

Payroll Taxes

The Social Security Act of 1935 imposed payroll taxes to finance the old age insurance system and unemployment compensation benefits. Later the tax was used to finance survivor, disability, and health insurance. Railroad employees are covered under a separate system of taxation, which is similar to, but not identical with, the general social insurance system.

The OASDHI Taxes

The 1935 act established the principle that the retirement system would be financed by equal taxes on employers and employees. Under the original act, the tax was 1 percent each for employer and employee on covered wages up to $3,000 per employee. The act also provided a schedule of rate increases for subsequent years, reaching a maximum of 3 percent for 1949 and later years. However, the original increases were deferred when the social security trust fund accumulated substantial reserves. Later, as benefits were raised and coverage of disability and health were added, both the tax and the ceiling on earnings were increased repeatedly. Beginning in 1973 the maximum taxable earnings level has been adjusted upward annually on the basis of increases in the consumer price index. In 1977 the payroll tax will apply to the first $16,500 of earnings; and the tax rate will be 5.85 percent each on the employer and the employee (table A-7).

The original act exempted agricultural and domestic labor, members of the professions, public employees, a few other classes of employees, and the self-employed. The coverage has been gradually expanded to include all employed people except federal civilian employees (who are covered by their own retirement system), self-employed persons who have self-employment income of less than $400 a year, domestic and farm workers earning less than specified amounts from a single employer, and state-local employees on an optional basis. Coverage of the self-employed began in 1951 at a rate one and one-half times the corresponding rate for employees (rounded to the nearest 0.1 percent beginning in 1962). However, beginning in 1971, the tax rate applicable to the earnings of the self-employed was fixed at lower levels—7.5 percent in 1971–72, 8.0 percent in 1973, and 7.9 percent beginning in 1974.

The Unemployment Insurance Tax

The unemployment insurance tax was originally imposed in 1936 on employers of eight or more persons at a rate of 1 percent of payrolls, with automatic increases to 2 percent in 1937 and 3 percent in 1938 and later years. The coverage was expanded to employers of four or more in 1956, and the rate was increased to 3.1 percent in 1961. The rate was raised temporarily to 3.5 percent in 1962 and 3.35 in 1963, was restored to 3.1 percent in 1964–69, raised to 3.2 percent in 1970–76 and to 3.4 percent beginning in 1977. Legislation in 1970 expanded coverage to employers of one or more, effective in 1972. The tax was originally applicable to all wages, was limited to $3,000 of wages in 1939–71, $4,200 in 1972–77, and $6,000 beginning in 1978 (see table A-8).

The federal government allows a credit against its tax for amounts contributed to state unemployment insurance programs, up to 2.7 percent of covered wages. The remainder of the federal tax is used to pay the administrative costs of the state programs.

State unemployment taxes are levied at the standard rate of 2.7 percent to use up the federal credit. In three states the tax is levied on employers and employees; in the others it is levied only on employers. In almost all states, employers are taxed according to an experience rating that may result in a larger or smaller tax than the standard 2.7 percent. This device permits states to lower the tax rates on firms with stable employment and to increase it on those with unstable employment. However, the full 2.7 percent credit is allowed against the federal tax where the tax rate has been reduced by a good experience rating. As a result of these provisions, tax rates differ greatly from one state to another as well as within a single state.

Railroad Taxes

Payroll tax rates have always been higher in the railroad industry than in other industries. The retirement tax for railroad employees dates back to 1937, when the rate was 2.75 percent each on employers and employees, and the maximum monthly wage subject to the tax was $300. Since 1937 the rates and wages subject to tax have been changed frequently, rising to 10.6 percent of wages up to $900 a month in the first nine months of 1973. Beginning on October 1, 1973, the equal contribution scheme was abolished and tax rates of 5.85 percent for employees and 15.35 for employers were adopted. As in the case of social security, the maximum taxable earnings level has been automatically raised in accordance with increases in the consumer price index since 1973. The maximum taxable level will reach $1,375 a month in 1977 (table A-7).

The railroad unemployment insurance program is supported by a tax on wages of up to $400 per month per employee paid by the employers. Before 1948 the tax rate was 3 percent. It was reduced to 0.5–3 percent in 1948–59, the variation depending on the financial condition of the trust fund, and was raised to 1.5–3.75 percent on June 1, 1959, 1.5–4.0 percent from 1962 to 1975, and 0.5–8.0 percent beginning in 1976 (table A-8).

Estate and Gift Taxes

The 1916 estate tax was levied at rates ranging from 1 percent to 10 percent, with an exemption of $50,000. During World War I the rates ranged from 2 percent to 25 percent. In 1926 the top rate was reduced to 20 percent, and the exemption was increased to $100,000.

One of the major developments during the 1920s was the enactment of a credit for state death taxes against the federal tax. Some of the states requested that the federal government abandon the death tax field entirely, but the credit was enacted instead. It was first limited to 25 percent of the federal tax in 1924 and was then raised to 80 percent in 1926. The same credit (based on the 1926 rates) exists today, even though the federal tax has been increased (table A-9).

Substantial changes in rates and exemptions were made during the 1930s. The exemption was reduced to $50,000 in 1932 and to $40,000 in 1935, and then was raised to $60,000 in 1942, when a special $40,000 exclusion for life insurance (enacted in 1918) was repealed. In 1976 the exemption was converted to a tax credit, to be used for both estate and gift tax purposes, of $30,000 in 1977, $34,000 in 1978, $38,000 in 1979, $42,500 in 1980, and $47,000 in 1981 and later years. These credits are equivalent to exemptions of $120,667, $134,000, $147,333, $161,563, and $175,625, respectively.

The top rate was increased in several steps from 45 percent in 1932 to 77 percent in 1940. It was reduced to 70 percent in 1977, when the estate and gift taxes were unified (table A-10).

The gift tax was first levied for two years in 1924 and 1925 but was repealed on the ground that it was too complicated for the revenue it yielded. It was reenacted in 1932, when the estate tax rates were greatly increased, to limit avoidance of the estate and income taxes. The gift tax was unified with the estate tax beginning January 1, 1977.

Gift tax rates were originally set at 75 percent of estate tax rates and were raised to the full estate tax rates beginning in 1977. A lifetime gift tax exemption of $50,000 was adopted in 1932, when the present gift tax was enacted. This exemption was reduced to $40,000 in 1935 and to $30,000 in 1942; beginning in 1977 the unified credit was made applicable to gifts and estates and the separate lifetime gift tax exemption was repealed. In addition to the lifetime exemption, taxpayers were allowed an annual exclusion of $5,000 for each donee under the 1932 act. This exclusion was reduced to $4,000 in 1938 and to $3,000 in 1942, which is still in effect (table A-11).

Splitting estates and gifts between husbands and wives was allowed beginning in 1948. A marital deduction is allowed for bequests of noncommunity property to surviving spouses, up to one-half of the estate. Similarly, one-half of gifts of noncommunity property by one spouse to the other are not subject to gift tax. Gifts of noncommunity property to third persons are treated as though half were made by each spouse. In the case of community property, property acquired during marriage by a husband or wife (except property acquired by gift or inheritance) belongs equally to each spouse and is therefore automatically split for estate and gift tax purposes. Beginning in 1977 the marital deduction under the estate tax was liberalized to $250,000 or one-half the estate, whichever is higher; for gifts, the marital deduction was set at 100 percent of the first $100,000 and 50 percent for amounts above $200,000 (no deduction is allowed for amounts between $100,000 and $200,000).

In addition to the conversion of the exemption to a credit and the unification of the estate and gift taxes, the Tax Reform Act of 1976 imposed a tax on "generation-skipping" transfers of trust property. This tax is intended to plug the generation-skipping loophole for transfers in trust under the former estate and gift taxes.

Federal Tax Policy

Table A-1. History of Federal Individual Income Tax Exemptions and First and Top Bracket Rates

Dollars unless otherwise specified

| | Personal exemptions[a] | | | Tax rates[b] | | | |
| | | | | First bracket | | Top bracket | |
Income year	Single persons	Married couples	Depen- dents	Rate (percent)	Income up to	Rate (percent)	Income over
1913–15	3,000	4,000	...	1	20,000	7	500,000
1916	3,000	4,000	...	2	20,000	15	2,000,000
1917	1,000	2,000	200	2	2,000	67	2,000,000
1918	1,000	2,000	200	6	4,000	77	1,000,000
1919–20	1,000	2,000	200	4	4,000	73	1,000,000
1921	1,000	2,500[c]	400	4	4,000	73	1,000,000
1922	1,000	2,500[c]	400	4	4,000	56	200,000
1923	1,000	2,500[c]	400	3	4,000	56	200,000
1924	1,000	2,500	400	1.5[d]	4,000	46	500,000
1925–28	1,500	3,500	400	$1\frac{1}{8}$[d]	4,000	25	100,000
1929	1,500	3,500	400	$\frac{3}{8}$[d]	4,000	24	100,000
1930–31	1,500	3,500	400	$1\frac{1}{8}$[d]	4,000	25	100,000
1932–33	1,000	2,500	400	4	4,000	63	1,000,000
1934–35	1,000	2,500	400	4[e]	4,000	63	1,000,000
1936–39	1,000	2,500	400	4[e]	4,000	79	5,000,000
1940	800	2,000	400	4.4[e]	4,000	81.1	5,000,000
1941	750	1,500	400	10[e]	2,000	81	5,000,000
1942–43[f]	500	1,200	350	19[e]	2,000	88	200,000
1944–45[g]	500	1,000	500	23	2,000	94[h]	200,000
1946–47	500	1,000	500	19	2,000	86.45[h]	200,000
1948–49	600	1,200	600	16.6	2,000	82.13[h]	200,000
1950	600	1,200	600	17.4	2,000	91[h]	200,000
1951	600	1,200	600	20.4	2,000	91[h]	200,000
1952–53	600	1,200	600	22.2	2,000	92[h]	200,000
1954–63	600	1,200	600	20	2,000	91[h]	200,000
1964	600	1,200	600	16	500	77	200,000
1965–67	600	1,200	600	14	500	70	100,000
1968	600	1,200	600	14	500	75.25[i]	100,000
1969	600	1,200	600	14	500	77[i]	100,000
1970	625	1,250	525	14	500	71.75[i,j]	100,000
1971	675	1,350	675	14	500	70[j,k]	100,000
1972	750	1,500	750	14	500	70[j,k]	100,000
1973 and after	750[l]	1,500[l]	750[l]	14	500	70[j,k]	100,000

Appendix A 299

Sources: Adapted from *The Federal Tax System: Facts and Problems, 1964*, Materials Assembled by the Committee Staff for the Joint Economic Committee, 88:2 (GPO, 1964); and relevant public laws.

a. Since 1948 taxpayers and their spouses who are blind or over sixty-five have been allowed additional exemptions.

b. Beginning in 1922 lower rates applied to long-term capital gains. See text, pp. 106–11.

c. If net income exceeded $5,000, a married person's exemption was $2,000.

d. After earned income credit equal to 25 percent of tax on earned income.

e. Before earned income credit allowed as a deduction equal to 10 percent of earned net income.

f. Exclusive of Victory tax.

g. Exemptions shown were for surtax only. Normal tax exemption was $500 per tax return plus earned income of wife up to $500 on joint returns.

h. Subject to the following maximum effective rate limitations:

Year	Maximum effective rate	Year	Maximum effective rate
1944–45	90.0 percent	1951	87.2 percent
1946–47	85.5	1952–53	88.0
1948–49	77.0	1954–63	87.0
1950	87.0		

i. Includes surcharge of 7.5 percent in 1968, 10 percent in 1969, and 2.5 percent in 1970.

j. Does not include 10 percent tax on tax preference items beginning in 1970.

k. Earned income was subject to maximum marginal rates of 60 percent in 1971 and 50 percent beginning in 1972. Beginning in 1975 earned income credit of 10 percent of earned income up to $4,000 (phased down to zero at $8,000) allowed.

l. In addition to the personal exemptions, a per capita tax credit of $30 was allowed for 1975, and $35 per capita or 2 percent of the first $9,000 of taxable income, whichever is higher, for 1976 and 1977.

Table A-2. Federal Individual Income Tax Rate Schedules, 1944–63ᵃ

Percent

Taxable income (dollars)	1944 act Calendar years 1944–45	1945 act Calendar years 1946–47	1948 act Calendar years 1948–49	1950 act Calendar year 1950	1951 act Calendar year 1951	1951 act Calendar years 1952–53	1951 act Calendar years 1954–63
0–2,000	23	19.00	16.60	17.40	20.4	22.2	20
2,000–4,000	25	20.90	19.36	20.02	22.4	24.6	22
4,000–6,000	29	24.70	22.88	23.66	27.0	29.0	26
6,000–8,000	33	28.50	26.40	27.30	30.0	34.0	30
8,000–10,000	37	32.30	29.92	30.94	35.0	38.0	34
10,000–12,000	41	36.10	33.44	34.58	39.0	42.0	38
12,000–14,000	46	40.85	37.84	39.13	43.0	48.0	43
14,000–16,000	50	44.65	41.36	42.77	48.0	53.0	47
16,000–18,000	53	47.50	44.00	45.50	51.0	56.0	50
18,000–20,000	56	50.35	46.64	48.23	54.0	59.0	53
20,000–22,000	59	53.20	49.28	50.96	57.0	62.0	56
22,000–26,000	62	56.05	51.92	53.69	60.0	66.0	59
26,000–32,000	65	58.90	54.56	56.42	63.0	67.0	62
32,000–38,000	68	61.75	57.20	59.15	66.0	68.0	65
38,000–44,000	72	65.55	60.72	62.79	69.0	72.0	69
44,000–50,000	75	68.40	63.36	65.52	73.0	75.0	72
50,000–60,000	78	71.25	66.00	68.25	75.0	77.0	75
60,000–70,000	81	74.10	68.64	70.98	78.0	80.0	78
70,000–80,000	84	76.95	71.28	73.71	82.0	83.0	81
80,000–90,000	87	79.80	73.92	76.44	84.0	85.0	84
90,000–100,000	90	82.65	76.56	79.17	87.0	88.0	87
100,000–136,719.10⎱	92	84.55	⎧78.32	80.99 ⎫	89.0	90.0	89
136,719.10–150,000⎰			⎩80.3225	82.503⎭			
150,000–200,000	93	85.50	81.2250	83.43	90.0	91.0	90
200,000 and overᵇ	94	86.45	82.1275	84.357	91.0	92.0	91

Sources: Same as table A-1.

a. Since 1948 married couples have been allowed to split their income for tax purposes. A separate rate schedule was adopted in 1952 for heads of households to give them approximately half the advantage of income splitting.

b. Subject to the following maximum effective rate limitations:

Year	Maximum effective rate	Year	Maximum effective rate
1944–45	90.0 percent	1951	87.2 percent
1946–47	85.5	1952–53	88.0
1948–49	77.0	1954–63	87.0
1950	87.0		

Table A-3. Federal Individual Income Tax Rate Schedules, 1964[a] and Later Years

Percent

	1964 act		1968 act		1969 act	
	Calendar	Calendar	Calendar	Calendar	Calendar	Calendar year 1971
Taxable income (dollars)	year 1964	years 1965–67	year 1968[b]	year 1969[b]	year 1970[b, c]	and later years[c, d, e]
0–500	16.0	14	14	14	14	14
500–1,000	16.5	15	15	15	15	15
1,000–1,500	17.5	16	17.2	17.6	16.4	16
1,500–2,000	18.0	17	18.275	18.7	17.425	17
2,000–4,000	20.0	19	20.425	20.9	19.475	19
4,000–6,000	23.5	22	23.650	24.2	22.55	22
6,000–8,000	27.0	25	26.875	27.5	25.625	25
8,000–10,000	30.5	28	30.1	30.8	28.7	28
10,000–12,000	34.0	32	34.4	35.2	32.8	32
12,000–14,000	37.5	36	38.7	39.6	36.9	36
14,000–16,000	41.0	39	41.925	42.9	39.975	39
16,000–18,000	44.5	42	45.15	46.2	43.05	42
18,000–20,000	47.5	45	48.375	49.5	46.125	45
20,000–22,000	50.5	48	51.6	52.8	49.2	48
22,000–26,000	53.5	50	53.75	55.0	51.25	50
26,000–32,000	56.0	53	56.975	58.3	54.325	53
32,000–38,000	58.5	55	59.125	60.5	56.375	55
38,000–44,000	61.0	58	62.35	63.8	59.45	58
44,000–50,000	63.5	60	64.5	66.0	61.5	60
50,000–60,000	66.0	62	66.65	68.2	63.55	62
60,000–70,000	68.5	64	68.8	70.4	65.6	64
70,000–80,000	71.0	66	70.95	72.6	67.65	66
80,000–90,000	73.5	68	73.1	74.8	69.7	68
90,000–100,000	75.0	69	74.175	75.9	70.725	69
100,000–200,000	76.5	70	75.25	77.0	71.75	70
200,000 and over	77.0	70	75.25	77.0	71.75	70

Sources: Same as table A-1.

a. Since 1948 married couples have been allowed to split their income for tax purposes. A separate rate schedule was adopted in 1952 for heads of households to give them approximately half the advantage of income splitting. Under the 1969 act a separate schedule for single persons who are not heads of households was provided to limit the tax paid by single persons to no more than 20 percent more than the tax paid by married couples with the same taxable income.

b. Includes surcharge of 7.5 percent in 1968, 10 percent in 1969, and 2.5 percent in 1970, beginning with the $1,000–$1,500 bracket. A partial surcharge exemption, based on a graduated scale, applied to this and the next higher bracket. The marginal rates in these brackets therefore varied slightly from those shown here.

c. A 10 percent minimum tax on certain tax preference items was imposed by the 1969 act for 1970 and later years.

d. Earned income subject to maximum marginal rates of 60 percent in 1971 and 50 percent beginning in 1972.

e. Does not allow for 10 percent rebate of 1974 taxes (maximum of $200) or a refundable earned income credit of 10 percent of earned income up to $4,000 (phased down to zero at $8,000) beginning in 1975.

Table A-4. History of Federal Corporation Income Tax Exemptions and Rates

Year	Exemptions, brackets, or type of tax	Rate (percent)
1909–13	$5,000 exemption	1
1913–15	None after March 1, 1913	1
1916	None	2
1917	None	6
1918	$2,000 exemption	12
1919–21	$2,000 exemption	10
1922–24	$2,000 exemption	12.5
1925	$2,000 exemption	13
1926–27	$2,000 exemption	13.5
1928	$3,000 exemption	12
1929	$3,000 exemption	11
1930–31	$3,000 exemption	12
1932–35	None	13.75
1936–37	Range of graduated normal tax	
	First $2,000	8
	Over $40,000	15
	Range of graduated surtax on undistributed profits	7–27
1938–39	First $25,000	12.5–16
	Over $25,000	19[a]
1940	First $25,000	14.85–18.7
	$25,000 to $31,964.30	38.3
	$31,964.30 to $38,565.89	36.9
	Over $38,565.89	24
1941	First $25,000	21–25
	$25,000 to $38,461.54	44
	Over $38,461.54	31
1942–45	First $25,000	25–29
	$25,000 to $50,000	53
	Over $50,000	40
1946–49	First $25,000	21–25
	$25,000 to $50,000	53
	Over $50,000	38
1950	First $25,000	23
	Over $25,000	42
1951	First $25,000	28.75
	Over $25,000	50.75
1952–63	First $25,000	30
	Over $25,000	52
1964	First $25,000	22
	Over $25,000	50

Table A-4 (*continued*)

Year	Exemptions, brackets, or type of tax	Rate (*percent*)
1965–67	First $25,000	22
	Over $25,000	48
1968–69[b]	First $25,000	24.2
	Over $25,000	52.8
1970[b]	First $25,000	22.55
	Over $25,000	49.2
1971–74	First $25,000	22
	Over $25,000	48
1975–77	First $25,000	20
	Next $25,000	22
	Over $50,000	48

Sources: Same as table A-1.
a. Less adjustments: 14.025 percent of dividends received and 2.5 percent of dividends paid.
b. Includes surcharge of 10 percent in 1968 and 1969 and 2.5 percent in 1970.

Table A-5. Marginal Rates of the Federal Corporation Income Tax, 1942–77
Percent

Year	Under $5,000	$5,000–20,000	$20,000–25,000	$25,000–50,000	Over $50,000
1942–45	25	27	29	53	40
1946–49	21	23	25	53	38
1950		23		42	
1951		28.75		50.75	
1952–63		30		52	
1964		22		50	
1965–67		22		48	
1968–69[a]		24.2		52.8	
1970[a]		22.55		49.2	
1971–74		22		48	
1975–77		20		22	48

Sources: Same as table A-1.
a. Includes surcharge of 10 percent in 1968 and 1969 and 2.5 percent in 1970.

Table A-6. Federal Excise Tax Rates on Selected Items as of December 31, Selected Years, 1913-76.

Dollars unless otherwise specified

Tax	1913	1919	1928	1932	1944	1952	1954	1963	1970	1972	1976
Liquor taxes											
Distilled spirits (per proof or wine gallon)	1.10	2.20	1.10	1.10	9	10.50	10.50	10.50	10.50	10.50	10.50
Still wines (per wine gallon)											
Not over 14 percent alcohol	...	0.16	0.04	0.04	0.15	0.17	0.17	0.17	0.17	0.17	0.17
14 to 21 percent alcohol	...	0.40	0.10	0.10	0.60	0.67	0.67	0.67	0.67	0.67	0.67
21 to 24 percent alcohol	...	1	0.25	0.25	2	2.25	2.25	2.25	2.25	2.25	2.25
Beer (per barrel)	1	6	6	6	8	9	9	9	9	9	9
Tobacco taxes											
Cigars, large (per thousand)	3	4-15	2-13.50	2-13.50	2.50-20	2.50-20	2.50-20	2.50-20	2.50-20	2.50-20	2.50-20
Cigarettes (per thousand, 3 pounds or less)	1.25	3	3	3	3.50	4	4	4	4	4	4
Tobacco and snuff (per pound)	0.08	0.18	0.18	0.18	0.18	0.10	0.10	0.10	...	...	...
Documentary, etc., stamp taxes											
Conveyances (per $500, or fraction thereof, if value is over $100)		0.50		0.50	0.55	0.55	0.55	0.55	...	...	...
Bond and stock issues (per $100, respectively)		0.05	0.05	0.10	0.11	0.11	0.11	0.11, 0.10	...	...	...
Playing cards (per package of not more than 54)	0.02	0.08	0.10	0.10	0.13	0.13	0.13	0.13	...	...	...
Manufacturers' excise taxes											
Lubricating oils (per gallon)	...	...	...	0.04	0.06	0.06	0.06	0.06	0.06	0.06	0.06
Matches, white, phosphorous (per hundred)	0.02	0.02		0.02	0.02	0.02	0.02	0.02	0.02	0.02	0.02
Matches, in general (per thousand)			0.02	0.02	0.02	0.02	0.02	0.02	...	...	...
Gasoline (per gallon)	...	...	...	0.01	0.015	0.02	0.02	0.04	0.04	0.04	0.04
Electrical energy (percent of sale price)				3	$3\frac{1}{3}$	...	...	...	...	...	...
Tires (percent of sale price, 1919; per pound, 1932 and after)	...	5	...	0.0225	0.05	0.05	0.05	0.10	0.10	0.10	0.10

Article (basis of tax)										
Inner tubes (percent of sale price, 1919; per pound, 1932 and after)	5	…	0.04	0.09	0.09	0.09	0.10	0.10	0.10	0.10
Tread rubber (per pound)	…	…	…	…	…	…	0.05	0.05	0.05	0.05
Trucks (percent of sale price)	3	…	2	5	8	8	10	10	7	10
Automobiles (percent of sale price)	5	…	3	7	10	10	10	7	8	8
Truck accessories (percent of sale price)	5	…	2	5	8	8	8	8	8	8
Automobile accessories (percent of sale price)	5	…	2	5	8	8	8	…	…	…
Radios and accessories (percent of sale price)	…	…	5	10	10	10	10	…	…	…
Refrigerators, household (percent of sale price)	…	…	5	10	10	5	5	5	5	…
Firearms, shells, cartridges, bows, arrows[a] (percent of sale price)	10	…	10	11	11	11	11	11	11	11
Pistols and revolvers (percent of sale price)	10	10	10	11	11	10	10	10	10	10
Sporting goods other than fishing equipment (percent of sale price)	10	…	10	10	15	10	10	…	…	…
Fishing equipment (percent of sale price)	10	…	10	10	15	10	10	10	10	10
Musical instruments and phonographs (percent of sale price)	5	…	…	10	10	10	10	10	…	…
Records (percent of sale price)	5	…	5	10	10	10	10	…	…	…
Electric, gas, and oil appliances (percent of sale price)	…	…	…	10	10	5	5	…	…	…
Business and store machines (percent of sale price)	…	…	…	10	10	10	10	…	…	…
Cameras and photographic apparatus (percent of sale price)	10	…	10	25	20	10	10	…	…	…
Photographic film (percent of sale price)	5	…	…	15	20	10	10	…	…	…
Mixed flour (per barrel containing 99–196 pounds)	0.04	0.04	0.04	…	…	…	…	…	…	…
Automatic slot vending machines (percent of sale price)	5	…	…	…	…	…	…	…	…	…
Vending weighing machines (percent of sale price)	10	…	…	…	…	…	…	…	…	…
Candy (percent of sale price)	5	…	2	…	…	…	…	…	…	…

Table A-6 (*continued*)

Tax	1913	1919	1928	1932	1944	1952	1954	1963	1970	1972	1976
Retailers' excise taxes											
Jewelry (percent of sale price)	...	5	...	10^b	20	20	10	10	...	...	...
Furs (percent of sale price)	...	10^b	...	10^b	20	20	10	10	...	...	...
Toilet preparations (per 25¢ or fraction, 1919; percent of sale price thereafter)	...	0.01	...	10^b	20	20	10	10	...	...	...
Luggage (percent of sale price)	...	10	...	...	20	20	10	10	...	...	...
Gasoline used in noncommercial aviation (per gallon)	...	...	...	...	...	...	...	...	0.03	0.03	0.03
Fuels other than gasoline used in noncommercial aviation (per gallon)	...	...	...	...	...	...	...	...	0.07	0.07	0.07
Diesel (beginning 1951) and special motor fuels for highway vehicles (per gallon)	...	...	0.01^b	0.015^b	0.02^b	0.02^b	0.02	0.04	0.04	0.04	0.04
Miscellaneous excise taxes											
Foreign insurance policies (percent of premium)											
Life insurance	...	3	3	3	1	1	1	1	1	1	1
Other insurance	...	3	3	3	4	4	4	4	4	4	4
General telephone service (percent of amount paid)	...	...	...	...	15	15	10	10	10	10	6
Toll telephone service (percent of amount paid; before 1944, per message)	...	0.05–0.10	...	0.10–0.20	25	25	10	10	10	10	6
Cable and radio messages, domestic (percent of amount paid; before 1944, per message)	...	0.10	...	0.10	25	25	10	10	...	...	...
Telegraph messages, domestic (percent of amount paid; 1919, per message)	...	0.10	...	5	25	15	10	10	...	...	...
Leased wires or teletypewriter and wire mileage service (percent of amount paid)	...	10	...	5	25	25	10	10	10^c	10^c	6^c

Item											
Wire and equipment service (percent of amount paid)	…	…	…	…	…	…	…	8	8	8	8
Transportation of oil by pipeline (percent of amount paid)	8	…	…	…	4	4.5	4.5	4.5	…	…	…
Bowling alleys, pool tables (per unit, per year)	10	…	…	…	20	20	20	20	…	…	…
Transportation of persons other than by air (percent of amount paid)	8	…	…	…	15	15	15	10	10	…	…
Transportation of persons, air (percent of amount paid)	…	…	…	…	15	15	10	10	8	8	8
International flight (per person)	…	…	…	…	…	…	…	…	3	3	3
Transportation of property (percent of amount paid)	3	…	…	…	3	3	3	3	…	…	…
Airfreight (percent of amount paid)	…	…	…	…	…	…	…	…	5	5	5
Aircraft registration (annually, per civil aircraft)	…	…	…	…	…	…	…	…	25	25	25
Aircraft poundage fees, takeoff weight above 2,500 pounds											
Propeller-driven aircraft (per pound)	…	…	…	…	…	…	…	…	0.02	0.02	0.02
Turbine-powered aircraft (per pound)	…	…	…	…	…	…	…	…	0.035	0.035	0.035
Use tax on highway vehicles weighing over 26,000 pounds (per 1,000 lbs. per year)	…	…	…	…	…	…	3	3	3	3	3
Lease of safe deposit boxes (percent of amount collected)	…	…	10	10	20	20	10	10	…	…	…
Admissions (for every 10¢ or fraction, 1919–43 and 1954–63; 5¢ or major fraction, 1944–53)[d]	0.01	0.01	0.01	0.01	0.01	0.01	0.01	…	…	…	…
Leases of boxes or seats (percent of amount for which similar accommodations are sold)	10	10	10	10	20	20	10	10	…	…	…
Cabarets, roof gardens, etc. (for every 10¢ or fraction of 20 percent of total charge, 1919–40; percent of amount paid, 1941–63)	0.015	0.015	0.015	0.015	20	20	20	20	…	…	…

Table A-6 (*continued*)

Tax	1913	1919	1928	1932	1944	1952	1954	1963	1970	1972	1976
Miscellaneous excise taxes (continued)											
Wagers (percent of amount of wager)	...	...	...	...	...	10	10	10	10	10	2
Occupation of accepting wagers (per year)	...	...	...	...	...	50	50	50	50	50	500
Dues and initiation fees (percent of amount paid)	...	10	10	10	20	20	20	20	...	...	...
Domestic oleomargarine (per pound)											
Uncolored	0.0025	0.0025	0.0025	0.0025	0.0025	...	...	...	...	...	...
Colored	0.10	0.10	0.10	0.10	0.10	...	...	...	...	...	...
Butter (per pound)											
Processed	0.0025	0.0025	0.0025	0.0025	0.0025	0.0025	0.0025	0.0025	0.0025	0.0025	0.0025
Adulterated	0.10	0.10	0.10	0.10	0.10	0.10	0.10	0.10	0.10	0.10	0.10
Filled cheese (per pound)											
Domestic	0.01	0.01	0.01	0.01	0.01	0.01	0.01	0.01	0.01	0.01	...
Imported	0.08	0.08	0.08	0.08	0.08	0.08	0.08	0.08	0.08	0.08	...
Use of boats (per foot, according to size, 1919; per boat, according to size or type, 1932; length, 1944)	...	1–4	...	10–200	5–200	...	...	...	...	...	...
Coin-operated devices (per unit, per year)											
Amusement	...	...	...	...	10	10	10	10	...	...	...
Gambling	...	...	...	...	100	250	250	250	250	250	250
Narcotics											
Opium sold (per ounce)	...	0.01	0.01	0.01	0.01	0.01	0.01	0.01	0.01	...	...
Opium for smoking (per pound)	...	300	300	300	300	300	300	300	300	...	...
Importers of opium (per year)	...	24	24	24	24	24	24	24	24	...	...
Marihuana (per ounce)[e]	...	...	...	...	1	1	1	1	1	...	...
Marihuana, authorized users (per year)	...	...	...	...	24	24	24	24	24	...	...

Interest equalization tax								
Stock (percent of actual value)	...	...	...	...	...	15	11.25	11.25	...
Bonds and loans with maturity of 1 year or longer (percent of actual value according to period remaining to maturity)	...	...	...	...	...	2.75–15	0.79–11.25	0.79–11.25	...

Sources: 1913–63, Tax Foundation, *Federal Non-Income Taxes: An Examination of Selected Revenue Sources* (New York, 1965), pp. 23–26, supplemented by data from U.S. Treasury Department, *Annual Report of the Secretary of the Treasury on the State of the Finances for the Fiscal Year Ended June 30, 1940*, pp. 484–511; *1950*, pp. 260–67; and *1962*, pp. 380–88, and relevant public laws; other years, relevant public laws enacted after 1963.

a. Bows and arrows were made subject to tax effective in 1975.
b. Tax levied at manufacturers' level.
c. Tax levied on teletypewriter service only.
d. Admission charges below specified amounts, which changed over the years, were usually exempt from the tax.
e. This tax applied to persons who had already paid the required taxes on importers, users, or producers of marihuana. A tax of $100 per ounce applied to other persons selling marihuana.

Table A-7. History of Social Security and Railroad Retirement Tax Rates

Year	Maximum taxable earnings[a] (dollars)	Tax rate (percent) Employer	Employee	Self-employed
		Old age, survivors, disability, and health insurance		
1937–49	3,000	1.0	1.0	b
1950	3,000	1.5	1.5	b
1951–53	3,600	1.5	1.5	2.25
1954	3,600	2.0	2.0	3.0
1955–56	4,200	2.0	2.0	3.0
1957–58	4,200	2.25	2.25	3.375
1959	4,800	2.5	2.5	3.75
1960–61	4,800	3.0	3.0	4.5
1962	4,800	3.125	3.125	4.7
1963–65	4,800	3.625	3.625	5.4
1966	6,600	4.2	4.2	6.15
1967	6,600	4.4	4.4	6.4
1968	7,800	4.4	4.4	6.4
1969–70	7,800	4.8	4.8	6.9
1971	7,800	5.2	5.2	7.5
1972	9,000	5.2	5.2	7.5
1973	10,800	5.85	5.85	8.0
1974	13,200	5.85	5.85	7.9
1975	14,100	5.85	5.85	7.9
1976	15,300	5.85	5.85	7.9
1977	16,500	5.85	5.85	7.9
		Railroad retirement, survivors, disability, and health insurance		
1937–39	300	2.75	2.75	...
1940–42	300	3.00	3.00	...
1943–45	300	3.25	3.25	...
1946	300	3.50	3.50	...
1947–48	300	5.75	5.75	...
1949–51	300	6.00	6.00	...
1952–June 30, 1954	300	6.25	6.25	...
July 1, 1954–May 31, 1959	350	6.25	6.25	...
June 1, 1959–61	400	6.75	6.75	...
1962–Oct. 31, 1963	400	7.25	7.25	...
Nov. 1, 1963–64	450	7.25	7.25	...
1965–Sept. 30, 1965	450	8.125	8.125	...
Oct. 1, 1965–Dec. 31, 1965	450	7.125	7.125	...
1966	550	7.95	7.95	...
1967	550	8.65	8.65	...

Table A-7 (*continued*)

Year	Maximum taxable earnings[a] (*dollars*)	Tax rate (*percent*) Employer	Employee	Self-employed
1968	650	8.90	8.90	...
1969–70	650	9.55	9.55	...
1971	650	9.95	9.95	...
1972	750	9.95	9.95	...
1973–Sept. 30, 1973	900	10.60	10.60	...
Oct. 1, 1973–Dec. 31, 1973	900	15.35	5.85	...
1974	1,100	15.35	5.85	...
1975	1,175	15.35	5.85	...
1976	1,275	15.35	5.85	...
1977	1,375	15.35	5.85	...

Sources: OASDHI, *Social Security Bulletin, Annual Statistical Supplement, 1973*, p. 29, and Social Security Administration. RRSDHI, 1937–65, Marice C. Hart, "Railroad Retirement Act as Amended in 1965," *Social Security Bulletin*, vol. 29 (February 1966), pp. 27–28; 1966 and after, Railroad Retirement Board.

a. Maximum taxable wage is in dollars per year for OASDHI and in dollars per month for RRSDHI.

b. Not covered by the program until January 1, 1951.

312   *Federal Tax Policy*

Table A-8. History of Unemployment Insurance Tax Rates

Year	Covered wages[a] (dollars)	Statutory range of rates[b] (percent)	Actual rate paid[c] (percent)
		Federal unemployment insurance[d]	
1936	All wages	...	1.0
1937	All wages	...	2.0
1938	All wages	...	3.0
1939–60	3,000	...	3.0
1961	3,000	...	3.1
1962	3,000	...	3.5
1963	3,000	...	3.35
1964–69	3,000	...	3.1
1970–71	3,000	...	3.2
1972	4,200	...	3.2
1973	4,200	...	3.28
1974–76	4,200	...	3.2
1977	4,200	...	3.4
1978	6,000	...	3.4
		Railroad unemployment insurance	
July 1, 1939–47	300	3.0	3.0
1948–June 30, 1954	300	0.5–3.0	0.5
July 1, 1954–Dec. 31, 1955	350	0.5–3.0	0.5
1956	350	0.5–3.0	1.5
1957	350	0.5–3.0	2.0
1958	350	0.5–3.0	2.5
Jan. 1, 1959–May 31, 1959	350	0.5–3.0	3.0
June 1, 1959–Dec. 31, 1961	400	1.5–3.75	3.75
1962–75	400	1.5–4.0	4.0
1976	400	0.5–8.0	5.5
1977	400	0.5–8.0	e

Sources: Same as table A-1, supplemented with data from *Annual Report of the Secretary of the Treasury on the State of the Finances for the Fiscal Year ended June 30, 1940*, pp. 522–23; *1950*, pp. 270–71; and *1962*, pp. 392–93; and from the Railroad Retirement Board and the U.S. Treasury Department.

a. Covered wages are in dollars per year for federal unemployment insurance and dollars per month for railroad unemployment insurance.

b. For federal unemployment insurance, employers are taxed by the states on the basis of an experience rating determined by past unemployment records. For railroad unemployment insurance, the rate paid each year is determined by a sliding scale and is fixed annually in accordance with the balance in the railroad unemployment insurance account on September 30 of the preceding year.

c. For federal unemployment insurance, credit up to 90 percent of the tax is allowed for contributions paid into a state unemployment fund. Since 1961 credits up to 90 percent have been computed as if the tax rate were 3 percent. All employers are permitted to take the maximum credit allowed against the federal unemployment tax, even though they may actually pay a lower rate because of a good experience rating.

d. Applicable to employers of eight persons or more between 1936 and 1956, to employers of four or more from 1956 through 1971, and to employers of one or more in 1972 and later years.

e. Rate expected to exceed 5.5 percent, but exact percentage not yet determined.

Table A-9. Federal Estate Tax Rates and Rates of the State Tax Credit since 1942
Estates in thousands of dollars; rates in percent

	Basic schedule[a]		Schedule for computing state tax credit	
Taxable estate	1942–76	1977 and later years	Taxable estate	1942 and later years[b]
0–5	3 ⎫	18	0–40	0.0
5–10	7 ⎭		40–90	0.8
10–20	11	20	90–140	1.6
			140–240	2.4
20–30	14 ⎫	22	240–440	3.2
30–40	18 ⎭		440–640	4.0
40–50	22 ⎫	24	640–840	4.8
50–60	25 ⎭		840–1,040	5.6
60–80	28	⎧ 26	1,040–1,540	6.4
80–100		⎩ 28	1,540–2,040	7.2
100–150	30	⎧ 30	2,040–2,540	8.0
150–250		⎩ 32	2,540–3,040	8.8
250–500	32	34	3,040–3,540	9.6
500–750	35	37	3,540–4,040	10.4
750–1,000	37	39	4,040–5,040	11.2
1,000–1,250	39	41	5,040–6,040	12.0
1,250–1,500	42	43	6,040–7,040	12.8
1,500–2,000	45	45	7,040–8,040	13.6
2,000–2,500	49	49	8,040–9,040	14.4
2,500–3,000	53	53	9,040–10,040	15.2
3,000–3,500	56	57		
3,500–4,000	59	61	10,040 and over	16.0
4,000–4,500	63	⎧ 65		
4,500–5,000		⎩ 69		
5,000–6,000	67 ⎫			
6,000–7,000	70 ⎪			
7,000–8,000	73 ⎬	70		
8,000–10,000	76 ⎪			
10,000 and over	77 ⎭			

Sources: Revenue Act of 1941; Tax Reform Act of 1976.
a. Before credit for state taxes.
b. Rates in effect in 1926.

Table A-10. History of Estate and Gift Tax Rates

Revenue Act	Date of death	Tax rates (percent) Estates	Tax rates (percent) Gifts	Bracket subject to Minimum rate (thousands of dollars)	Bracket subject to Maximum rate (thousands of dollars)
1916	Sept. 9, 1916, to March 2, 1917	1.0–10.0	...	0–50	5,000 and over
1917[a]	March 3, 1917, to Oct. 3, 1917	1.5–15.0	...	0–50	5,000 and over
1917[b]	Oct. 4, 1917, to Feb. 23, 1919	2.0–25.0	...	0–50	10,000 and over
1918	Feb. 24, 1919, to Feb. 25, 1926	1.0–25.0	1.0–25.0[c]	0–50	10,000 and over
1926	Feb. 26, 1926, to June 5, 1932	1.0–20.0	...	0–50	10,000 and over
1932	June 6, 1932, to May 10, 1934	1.0–45.0	0.75–33.5	0–10	10,000 and over
1934	May 11, 1934, to July 29, 1935	1.0–60.0	0.75–45.0	0–10	10,000 and over
1935	July 30, 1935, to June 24, 1940	2.0–70.0	1.55–52.5	0–10	50,000 and over
1940	June 25, 1940, to Sept. 19, 1941	2.2–77.0[d]	1.65–57.75[d]	0–10	50,000 and over
1941	Sept. 20, 1941, to Dec. 31, 1976	3.0–77.0	2.25–57.75	0–5	10,000 and over
1976	Jan. 1, 1977, and later years	18.0–70.0[e]	18.0–70.0[e]	0–10	5,000 and over

Source: Same as table A-1.
a. Revenue Act of 1917.
b. War Revenue Act of 1917.
c. In effect June 2, 1924, to December 31, 1925.
d. Includes defense tax equal to 10 percent of tax liability.
e. Gift tax rates are the same as the estate tax rates.

Table A-11. History of Estate and Gift Tax Exemptions and Exclusions

Dollars

	Estate tax		Gift tax	
Revenue Act	*Specific exemption*[a]	*Insurance exclusion*	*Specific exemption*[b]	*Annual exclusion per donee*
1916	50,000	...	c	c
1918	50,000	40,000	c	c
1924	50,000	40,000	50,000	500
1926	100,000	40,000	c	c
1932	50,000	40,000	50,000	5,000
1935	40,000	40,000	40,000	5,000
1938	40,000	40,000	40,000	4,000
1942	60,000	...	30,000	3,000
1976	175,625[d]	...	175,625[d]	3,000

Source: Same as table A-1.

a. Specific exemption granted to estates of nonresident citizens dying after May 11, 1934, on the same basis as resident decedents. No exemptions granted to estates of resident aliens until October 21, 1942, when a $2,000 exemption was made available.

b. Under the Revenue Act of 1924, exemption allowed each calendar year. Under the 1932 and later acts, specific exemption allowed only once.

c. No gift tax.

d. The Tax Reform Act of 1976 unified the estate and gift taxes and provided a unified credit in lieu of exemptions. The credit translates into the amount of exemption shown in the table. The credit increases from 1977 to 1981 as follows: 1977, $30,000; 1978, $34,000; 1979, $38,000; 1980, $42,500; 1981 and later years, $47,000. These credits are equivalent to the following amounts of exemptions, respectively: 1977, $120,667; 1978, $134,000; 1979, $147,333; 1980, $161,563; 1981, $175,625.

Tax Bases of the Major Federal Taxes

THE CONCEPTS of taxable income for both the individual and the corporation income taxes as defined by the Internal Revenue Code differ substantially from the national income aggregates, which are widely used for purposes of economic analysis. This appendix derives the tax bases of the two income taxes and compares them with the official estimates of personal income and corporate profits incorporated in the national income accounts. It also presents the latest distributions by rate brackets of the tax bases of the income and estate and gift taxes.

The Individual Income Tax

Among the various tax concepts, *adjusted gross income* most nearly resembles personal income. Total personal income exceeds the aggregate of adjusted gross incomes reported on tax returns by a substantial amount each year. A large portion of the disparity can be explained by differences in definition. The individual income tax base is derived below in two steps: first, aggregate adjusted gross income of all people in the United States is estimated from personal income; second, personal exemptions and deductions are subtracted from adjusted gross income to obtain taxable income.

Relation between Personal Income and Adjusted Gross Income

Table B-1 summarizes the conceptual differences between personal income and adjusted gross income for calendar year 1974, the latest year for which such estimates are available. The differences are, first, items of income that are included in personal income but not in adjusted gross income (for example, transfer payments, practically all income in kind, tax-exempt interest), amounting to $285.0 billion; and second, income that is included in adjusted gross income but not in personal income (primarily the social security taxes paid by employers and capital gains), amounting to $87.1 billion. When these differences are taken into account, the 1974 personal income of $1,153.3 billion corresponded to an adjusted gross income of $955.4 billion.

The relation between personal income and adjusted gross income has been fairly stable in recent years. Since 1947 the difference between personal and adjusted gross income has risen gradually as transfer payments have increased. Beginning in 1970 the difference has been about 16 to 17 percent of personal income (table B-2).

If all income recipients were required to file returns and everybody reported income accurately, the total adjusted income on tax returns would correspond closely to the amounts shown in table B-2. Since neither of these conditions holds, adjusted gross incomes reported on tax returns are lower than the aggregate for all recipients. As table B-3 indicates, this gap has been declining as a percentage of total adjusted gross income; by 1974 the figure was down to 5.2 percent. The decline was very sharp during the Second World War, when exemptions and filing requirements were lowered drastically, but it has continued—though at a much slower rate and with some interruptions—throughout the 1950s, 1960s, and early 1970s, as the rise in incomes pushed more and more people above the filing requirement levels.

In 1974 the gross difference between personal income and adjusted gross income reported on tax returns was $247.2 billion (see tables B-2 and B-3). About 80 percent of this difference—or $197.8 billion—is explained by conceptual differences, and only $49.4 billion did not appear on tax returns. But this $49.4 billion cannot be regarded as a measure of underreporting. Included in this figure is the income received by people who were not required to file returns, the exact amount of which is unknown. Moreover, a larger number of nontaxable people in such low-paid occupations as domestic service and farming do not bother to file even though the law requires them to do so. In view of the magnitudes involved, the portion of the total gap between personal income and adjusted gross income that remains unexplained is relatively small. Even if as much as two-thirds of the $49.4 billion was due to underreporting, the degree of underreporting was only about 3 percent of estimated total adjusted gross income.

The Individual Income Tax Base

The steps in the derivation of the individual income tax base for the years 1947–74 are shown in table B-4. In 1974, $906.1 billion of adjusted gross income was reported on individual income tax returns. Nontaxable individuals reported $25.9 billion; those who were taxable reported $880.2 billion. The personal exemptions of taxable individuals amounted to $136.6 billion, and their deductions amounted to $171.4 billion. Subtracting these two items from adjusted gross income leaves taxable income of $572.4 billion. To this must be added the small amount of taxable income—about $1.2 billion—of individuals whose tax liabilities were wiped out by the retirement income and other credits. Thus the tax base amounted to $573.7 billion in 1974.

Table B-5 compares the tax base with personal income since the end of World War II. From 39.7 percent of personal income in 1947, taxable income rose to 52.1 percent in 1969 and has remained close to 50 percent since then.

Distribution of Taxable Individual Income

An estimated distribution of taxable income by rate brackets is shown in table B-6 for calendar year 1973. Only a small proportion of taxable income is subject to the very high rates. Of the total taxable income of $508.6 billion, $317.2 billion, or 62.4 percent, was subject to the first six bracket rates of 14 to 19 percent, and $18.2 billion, or 3.6 percent, was subject to rates of 50 percent or more.

The Corporation Income Tax

Table B-7 gives a detailed reconciliation for calendar year 1971 of three concepts of corporate profits: *profits before taxes* as defined in the national income accounts; *net profits* of all corporations as tabulated from federal corporation income tax returns; and *taxable income* of corporations.

Relation between Profits before Tax and Taxable Income

The major differences between the national income definition of profits before tax and net profits reported on tax returns are accounted for by differences in coverage and in definition of income. For example, profits before taxes include the income of government financial institutions and adjustments of the profits of insurance carriers and mutual financial intermediaries for national income purposes; on the other hand, they exclude dividends received from corporations and net capital gains, include estimated profits resulting from audit, and do not allow for the deductions for depletion, state corporation income taxes, and adjustment for bad debts. In 1971 corporate profits under the national income definition were $82.0 billion, and net profits reported on tax returns amounted to $81.9 billion. As shown in table B-7, differences in coverage and in definition of the two profit concepts offset one another (amounting to +$5.7 billion and −$5.7 billion respectively), leaving net profits on tax returns at $81.9 billion.

To arrive at taxable income, the losses of deficit corporations must be added back to reported net profits, and the nontaxable components of reported net profits must be eliminated. After these and other minor adjustments, corporate taxable income in 1971 was $83.2 billion, or $1.4 billion higher than reported net profits.

A comparison of the three income concepts for the years 1958–73 is given in table B-8.

Distribution of Taxable Corporate Income

Unlike the individual income tax, most of the corporation income tax base is concentrated in the top rate bracket. This reflects the great importance of large corporations in the corporate sector. For calendar year 1971 taxable corporate income amounted to $85.9 billion, of which $3.6 billion was subject to the 30 percent alternative tax on long-term capital gains and $2.8 billion was subject to the 10 percent minimum tax on preference income, leaving $79.6 billion subject to the normal tax and surtax rates. Only $8.9 billion, or 11 percent, of the latter amount was subject to the 22 percent corporation income tax rate, and the remaining $70.7 billion, or 89 percent, was subject to the 48 percent rate (table B-9).

Estate and Gift Taxes

In 1973, 175,000 estate tax returns were filed, of which 121,000 were taxable. The total wealth subject to tax amounted to $15.8 billion.

The decedents represented on the 1973 taxable estate tax returns were 6.5 percent of all decedents twenty or over in that year (table B-10). These returns showed gross estates of $33.3 billion; debts, mortgages, and policy loans against life insurance amounted to $4.2 billion, leaving *economic* estates of $29.1 billion. The $15.8 billion of taxable estates thus accounted for somewhat less than half the wealth left by decedents subject to estate tax (table B-11). Most of the tax base is concentrated in the lower rate brackets. In 1973, 40 percent was subject to rates below 30 percent, 52 percent to rates between 30 percent and 50 percent, and only 8 percent to rates of 50 percent or more (table B-12).

The latest data tabulated from gift tax returns are for gifts made in 1966, and the latest distribution of gifts by tax rate brackets is for 1963. Total gifts on taxable returns in 1966 amounted to $2.4 billion. After allowing for deductions and exclusions, $1.5 billion, or 61 percent, was taxable (table B-13). About 80 percent of the 1963 gift tax base was subject to rates below 30 percent; 15 percent to rates of 30 to 50 percent; and 5 percent to rates of 50 percent or more (table B-14).

Table B-1. Derivation of Adjusted Gross Income from Personal Income, 1974

Billions of dollars

Income and adjustment items	Amount
1. Personal income	1,153.3
2. Portion of personal income not included in adjusted gross income	285.0
a. Transfer payments (except military retirement pay)	139.1
b. Other labor income (except fees)	54.6
c. Imputed income	51.3
d. Other income received by nonindividuals	9.1
(1) Property income retained by fiduciaries	5.6
(2) Property income received by nonprofit institutions	3.5
e. Differences in accounting treatment	11.9
(1) Gain on sale of livestock, timber, and real estate	3.2
(2) Excess of interest accrued over interest paid on U.S. savings bonds	1.6
(3) Noncorporate nonfarm inventory valuation adjustment	−3.6
(4) Depletion and oil well drilling adjustment	1.1
(5) Bad debt adjustment	1.3
(6) Change in farm inventories (in excess of tax return data)	−1.4
(7) Excess of residential and farm tax depreciation over Bureau of Economic Analysis depreciation	9.8
f. Other excluded or exempt income	18.9
(1) Excluded business expenses	8.9
(2) Excluded sick pay	1.7
(3) Excluded moving expenses	1.6
(4) Excluded contributions to retirement plans by self-employed	0.8
(5) Excluded dividends	1.4
(6) Tax-exempt military pay and allowances	2.8
(7) Tax-exempt interest income	1.7
(8) Tax-exempt dividend distributions	0.0
3. Portion of adjusted gross income not included in personal income	87.1
a. Personal contributions for social insurance	47.6
b. Net gain from sale of capital assets	13.2
c. Annuities and pensions reported on tax returns	17.1
d. Capital consumption adjustment	4.6
e. Special assessments	0.8
f. "Other income"	3.9
4. Total adjustment for conceptual differences (line 2 minus line 3)	197.8
5. Estimated adjusted gross income of taxable and nontaxable individuals (line 1 minus line 4)	955.4

Source: U.S. Department of Commerce, Bureau of Economic Analysis. Figures are rounded.

Federal Tax Policy

Table B-2. Personal Income and Total Adjusted Gross Income, 1947–74
Billions of dollars unless otherwise specified

			Difference	
Year	*Personal income*	*Total adjusted gross income*	*Amount*	*Percent of personal income*
1947	189.8	172.7	17.1	9.0
1948	208.5	186.5	22.0	10.6
1949	205.6	183.9	21.8	10.6
1950	226.1	202.2	23.9	10.6
1951	253.7	228.6	25.1	9.9
1952	270.4	241.0	29.4	10.9
1953	286.1	255.7	30.5	10.7
1954	288.2	253.8	34.4	11.9
1955	308.8	273.6	35.1	11.4
1956	330.9	293.7	37.2	11.3
1957	349.3	306.1	43.2	12.4
1958	359.3	310.5	48.8	13.6
1959	382.1	332.9	49.2	12.9
1960	399.7	345.2	54.5	13.6
1961	415.0	357.9	57.0	13.7
1962	440.7	377.2	63.6	14.4
1963	463.1	396.9	66.2	14.3
1964	495.7	429.2	66.5	13.4
1965	537.0	464.5	72.5	13.5
1966	584.9	506.7	78.1	13.4
1967	626.6	539.2	87.5	14.0
1968	685.2	593.1	92.1	13.4
1969	745.8	641.9	104.0	13.9
1970	801.3	673.9	127.4	15.9
1971	859.1	715.4	143.7	16.7
1972	942.5	788.3	154.3	16.4
1973	1,052.4	881.8	170.7	16.2
1974	1,153.3	955.4	197.8	17.2

Source: Bureau of Economic Analysis. Figures are rounded.

Table B-3. Total Adjusted Gross Income and Adjusted Gross Income Reported on Tax Returns, 1947–74

Billions of dollars unless otherwise specified

Year	Adjusted gross income		Difference	
	Total U.S.	*Reported on tax returns*	*Amount*	*Percent of total U.S.*
1947	172.7	149.7	23.0	13.3
1948	186.5	163.6	22.9	12.3
1949	183.9	160.6	23.3	12.6
1950	202.2	179.1	23.1	11.4
1951	228.6	202.4	26.2	11.5
1952	241.0	215.3	25.7	10.7
1953	255.7	228.7	27.0	10.5
1954	253.8	229.2	24.6	9.7
1955	273.6	248.5	25.1	9.2
1956	293.7	267.8	25.9	8.8
1957	306.1	280.4	25.7	8.4
1958	310.5	281.2	29.3	9.4
1959	332.9	305.1	27.8	8.4
1960	345.2	315.5	29.7	8.6
1961	357.9	329.9	28.0	7.8
1962	377.2	348.7	28.5	7.5
1963	396.9	368.8	28.1	7.1
1964	429.2	396.7	32.5	7.6
1965	464.5	429.2	35.3	7.6
1966	506.7	468.ᵉ	38.2	7.5
1967	539.2	504.8	34.4	6.4
1968	593.1	554.4	38.7	6.5
1969	641.9	603.5	38.3	6.0
1970	673.9	631.7	42.2	6.3
1971	715.4	673.6	41.8	5.8
1972	788.3	746.0	42.3	5.4
1973	881.8	827.1	54.6	6.2
1974	955.4	906.1ᵃ	49.4	5.2

Source: Total adjusted gross income, table B-2; adjusted gross income reported on tax returns, *Statistics of Income, Individual Income Tax Returns.* Figures are rounded.
a. Preliminary.

Table B-4. Derivation of the Individual Income Tax Base, 1947–74
Billions of dollars

Year	Total adjusted gross income	Deduct: nonreported adjusted gross income	Equals: adjusted gross income reported on individual returns[a]	Deduct: adjusted gross income reported on nontaxable returns[a]	Equals: adjusted gross income reported on taxable returns[a]	Deduct: exemptions on taxable returns	Deduct: deductions on taxable returns	Equals: taxable income on taxable returns	Add: taxable income on nontaxable returns[b]	Equals: total taxable income of individuals
1947	172.7	23.0	149.7	14.4	135.3	44.3	15.6	75.4	...	75.4
1948	186.5	22.9	163.6	21.5	142.1	50.9	16.4	74.8	...	74.8
1949	183.9	23.3	160.6	22.0	138.6	50.1	16.8	71.7	...	71.7
1950	202.2	23.1	179.1	20.6	158.5	55.2	19.0	84.3	...	84.3
1951	228.6	26.2	202.4	19.2	183.2	61.4	22.6	99.2	...	99.2
1952	241.0	25.7	215.3	18.7	196.6	64.5	24.9	107.2	...	107.2
1953	255.7	27.0	228.7	18.2	210.5	68.9	27.3	114.3	...	114.3
1954	253.8	24.6	229.2	19.5	209.7	67.0	27.5	115.2	0.1	115.3
1955	273.6	25.1	248.5	18.9	229.6	71.2	30.5	127.9	0.1	128.0
1956	293.7	25.9	267.8	18.2	249.6	74.6	33.6	141.4	0.1	141.5
1957	306.1	25.7	280.4	18.2	262.2	76.8	36.2	149.2	0.2	149.4
1958	310.5	29.3	281.2	19.0	262.2	75.8	37.2	149.2	0.2	149.3
1959	332.9	27.8	305.1	17.3	287.8	79.7	41.7	166.4	0.2	166.5
1960	345.2	29.7	315.5	18.3	297.2	81.2	44.5	171.5	0.2	171.6
1961	357.9	28.0	329.9	18.6	311.3	82.5	47.2	181.6	0.1	181.8
1962	377.2	28.5	348.7	18.1	330.6	85.1	50.5	195.0	0.4	195.3
1963	396.9	28.1	368.8	18.4	350.4	87.4	54.5	208.5	0.5	209.1
1964	429.2	32.5	396.7	20.7	376.0	88.3	58.4	229.3	0.6	229.9

Year									
1965	464.5	35.3	429.2	19.9	409.3	91.9	63.1	254.3	0.7	255.1
1966	506.7	38.2	468.5	18.3	450.2	96.2	68.3	285.7	0.8	286.3
1967	539.2	34.4	504.8	17.4	487.4	99.1	74.0	314.3	0.8	315.1
1968	593.1	38.7	554.4	16.1	538.3	102.6	83.7	352.0	0.8	352.8
1969	641.9	38.3	603.5	15.3	588.2	106.3	93.7	388.2	0.7	388.8
1970	673.9	42.2	631.7	21.4	610.3	107.0	102.6	400.9[c]	0.3	401.2
1971	715.4	41.8	673.6	22.4	651.3	115.6	122.4	413.4[c]	0.6	414.0
1972	788.3	42.3	746.0	28.6	717.4	128.2	142.8	446.7[c]	1.0	447.6
1973	881.8	54.6	827.1	27.4	799.7	132.4	156.9	510.6[c]	1.3	511.9
1974[d]	955.4	49.4	906.1	25.9	880.2	136.6	171.4	572.4[c]	1.2	573.7

Sources: First three columns, table B-3; other data, *Statistics of Income, Individual Income Tax Returns*. Figures are rounded.

a. Adjusted gross income less deficit.

b. Taxable income of persons whose tax liability was completely offset by tax credits.

c. Taxable income diverges from adjusted gross income minus exemptions and deductions because returns with minimum tax only are included in taxable returns, but for some of these returns, when exemptions and deductions are subtracted from AGI, the result is a negative number.

d. Preliminary.

Federal Tax Policy

Table B-5. Personal Income, Taxable Income, and Individual Income Tax, 1947–74
Billions of dollars unless otherwise specified

Year	Personal income	Taxable income		Individual income tax		
		Amount	Percent of personal income	Amount	Percent of Personal income	Percent of Taxable income
1947	189.8	75.4	39.7	18.1	9.5	24.0
1948	208.5	74.8	35.9	15.4	7.4	20.6
1949	205.6	71.7	34.9	14.5	7.1	20.2
1950	226.1	84.3	37.3	18.4	8.1	21.8
1951	253.7	99.2	39.1	24.2	9.5	24.4
1952	270.4	107.2	39.6	27.8	10.3	25.9
1953	286.1	114.3	40.0	29.4	10.3	25.7
1954	288.2	115.3	40.0	26.7	9.3	23.2
1955	308.8	128.0	41.5	29.6	9.6	23.1
1956	330.9	141.5	42.8	32.7	9.9	23.1
1957	349.3	149.4	42.8	34.4	9.8	23.0
1958	359.3	149.3	41.6	34.3	9.5	23.0
1959	382.1	166.5	43.6	38.6	10.1	23.2
1960	399.7	171.6	42.9	39.5	9.9	23.0
1961	415.0	181.8	43.8	42.2	10.2	23.2
1962	440.7	195.3	44.3	44.9	10.2	23.0
1963	463.1	209.1	45.2	48.2	10.4	23.1
1964	495.7	229.9	46.4	47.2	9.5	20.5
1965	537.0	255.1	47.5	49.6	9.2	19.4
1966	584.9	286.3	48.9	56.1	9.6	19.6
1967	626.6	315.1	50.3	63.0	10.1	20.0
1968	685.2	352.8	51.5	76.7	11.2	21.7
1969	745.8	388.8	52.1	86.6	11.6	22.3
1970	801.3	401.2	50.1	83.9	10.5	20.9
1971	859.1	414.0	48.2	85.4	9.9	20.6
1972	942.5	447.6	47.5	93.6	9.9	20.9
1973	1,052.4	511.9	48.6	108.1	10.3	21.1
1974	1,153.3	573.7[a]	49.7[a]	123.7[a]	10.7[a]	21.6[a]

Sources: Personal income, see table B-2; tax data, *Statistics of Income, Individual Income Tax Returns.*
a. Preliminary.

Table B-6. Distribution of Taxable Income and Individual Income Tax, by Rate Bracket, 1973ᵃ

Amounts in millions of dollars

Rate (percent)	Amount		Percentage distribution	
	Taxable income	Tax	Taxable income	Tax
14	52,342	7,328	10.29	6.70
15	45,874	6,881	9.02	6.29
16	45,955	7,353	9.04	6.72
17	39,961	6,793	7.86	6.21
18	4,412	794	0.87	0.73
19	128,609	24,436	25.29	22.34
21	13,108	2,753	2.58	2.52
22	61,692	13,572	12.13	12.41
23	752	173	0.15	0.16
24	7,738	1,857	1.52	1.70
25	35,929	8,982	7.06	8.21
27	2,547	688	0.50	0.63
28	16,838	4,715	3.31	4.31
29	1,376	399	0.27	0.36
31	1,041	323	0.20	0.30
32	9,858	3,154	1.94	2.88
34	658	224	0.13	0.20
35	79	28	0.02	0.03
36	6,983	2,514	1.37	2.30
38	435	165	0.09	0.15
39	4,595	1,792	0.90	1.64
40	553	221	0.11	0.20
41	42	17	0.01	0.02
42	3,554	1,493	0.70	1.36
45	3,272	1,472	0.64	1.35
48	2,171	1,042	0.43	0.95
50	3,530	1,765	0.69	1.61
51	16	8	*	0.01
52	22	12	*	0.01
53	1,968	1,043	0.39	0.95
55	1,411	776	0.28	0.71
56	6	4	*	*
58	846	491	0.17	0.45
59	11	6	*	0.01
60	731	438	0.14	0.40
61	9	5	*	*
62	866	537	0.17	0.49
63	9	6	*	0.01
64	611	391	0.12	0.36
66	449	296	0.09	0.27

Table B-6 (*continued*)

Rate (*percent*)	Amount		Percentage distribution	
	Taxable income	*Tax*	*Taxable income*	*Tax*
67	10	7	*	0.01
68	342	232	0.07	0.21
69	270	186	0.05	0.17
70	2,472	1,731	0.49	1.58
Subtotal	503,952	107,090	99.09	97.89
50[b]	870	435	0.17	0.40
50[c]	3,739	1,870	0.74	1.71
Total	508,562	109,395	100.00	100.00

Source: *Statistics of Income—1973, Individual Income Tax Returns*, table 3.13. Totals and percentages are derived from unrounded data.
* 0.005 percent or less.
a. Includes all returns with income subject to tax except returns with capital gains tax only.
b. Alternative capital gains tax rate.
c. Fifty percent maximum tax rate.

Table B-7. Reconciliation of Corporation Profits before Taxes, Net Profits Reported on Tax Returns, and Taxable Income, 1971
Billions of dollars

Income and adjustment items	Amount
Profits before taxes, national income definition[a]	82.0
Differences in coverage	
Income of Federal Reserve banks, federal home loan banks, and federal land banks	−3.4
Adjustment for insurance carriers and mutual financial intermediaries	1.5
Corporate income from equities in foreign corporations and branches	12.2
Total income received from equities in foreign corporations (including individuals), net of corresponding outflows	−4.6
Subtotal	5.7
Differences in definition	
Dividends received from domestic corporations	5.5
Net capital gains from sales of property	7.6
Costs of trading or issuing corporate securities	1.7
Income disclosed by audit	−7.6
Depletion, drilling costs in excess of depreciation, and oil well bonus payments written off	−4.8
State corporation income taxes	−4.2
Bad debt adjustment	−3.8
Subtotal	−5.7
Equals: Net profits reported on tax returns, all corporations	81.9
Adjustments to compute taxable income	
Losses of corporations with no net income	17.0
Constructive taxable income from related foreign corporations	2.0
Wholly tax exempt interest	−4.2
Dividends received deduction	−3.2
Net operating loss deduction	−3.5
Western hemisphere trade deduction	−0.3
Taxable income of Subchapter S corporations	−3.4
Regulated investment company income	−2.9
Subtotal	1.4
Equals: Taxable income	83.2

Sources: Worksheets of the Bureau of Economic Analysis, and *Statistics of Income—1971, Corporation Income Tax Returns,* pp. 16, 18, 108–09. Figures are rounded.
a. Without inventory valuation and capital consumption adjustment.

Table B-8. Corporation Profits before Taxes, Net Profits, and Taxable Income, 1958–73
Billions of dollars

Year	Profits before taxes,[a] national income definition	Net profits reported on tax returns[b]	Taxable income
1958	41.1	39.2	39.3
1959	51.6	47.7	47.6
1960	48.5	44.5	47.2
1961	48.6	47.0	47.9
1962	53.6	50.8	51.7
1963	57.7	55.7	54.3
1964	64.7	63.1	60.4
1965	75.2	74.7	70.8
1966	80.7	81.3	77.1
1967	77.3	79.3	74.8
1968	85.6	87.5	81.4
1969	83.4	82.1	81.2
1970	71.5	68.0	72.4
1971	82.0	81.9	83.2
1972	96.2	99.8[c]	94.9[c]
1973	115.8	122.1[c]	114.3[c]

Sources: Profits before taxes, Bureau of Economic Analysis. Reported net profits and taxable income, *Statistics of Income, Corporation Income Tax Returns.*
a. Without inventory valuation and capital consumption adjustment.
b. Includes corporations with and without net income. Beginning in 1963, reported net profits are designated "receipts less deductions" in *Statistics of Income.*
c. Preliminary.

Table B-9. **Distribution of Corporation Taxable Income, by Rate Bracket, 1971**

Millions of dollars unless otherwise specified

Taxable income bracket	Tax rate (percent)	Number of corporations	Taxable income	Tax
		Amount		
Normal tax and surtax				
Under $25,000	22[a]	595,995	8,855	1,948[b]
$25,000 and over	48[a]	183,367	70,735	33,953[b]
Subtotal	...	779,362	79,591	36,089[c]
Add: Long-term capital gains subject to alternative tax	30[d]	...	3,565	1,053
Add: Tax on preference income	...	...	2,790	279
Add: Tax from recomputing prior year investment credit	...	...	...	88
Total before credits	...	...	85,946	37,508
Less: Foreign tax credit	...	...	...	5,656
Less: Investment credit	...	...	...	1,634
Total after credits	35.2[e]	779,362	85,946	30,218
		Percentage distribution		
Normal tax and surtax				
Under $25,000	...	76	11	5
$25,000 and over	...	24	89	95
Total	...	100	100	100

Source: *Statistics of Income—1971, Corporation Income Tax Returns*, pp. 122–24. Figures are rounded.

a. Statutory rate.

b. Taxes in the two brackets do not add to the total because net income classes in the *Statistics of Income* tabulation, from which the distribution was calculated, do not correspond exactly to the normal tax and surtax brackets.

c. Derived by subtracting from total before credits the sum of the additional and alternative taxes.

d. The alternative tax rate is 30 percent on net long-term capital gains over net short-term capital gains, except for gains from certain binding contracts, distributions, and installment sales, which are taxed at the rate of 25 percent.

e. Computed effective rate on taxable income.

Table B-10. Number of Taxable Estate Tax Returns Filed as a Percentage of Deaths, Selected Years, 1939–73

Year	Deaths (adults[a])	Taxable estate tax returns filed	
		Number[b]	Percent of deaths
1939	1,204,080	12,720	1.06
1940	1,235,484	12,907	1.04
1941	1,215,627	13,336	1.10
1942	1,209,661	13,493	1.12
1943	1,275,400	12,726	1.00
1944	1,237,508	12,154	0.98
1945	1,238,360	13,869	1.12
1947	1,277,852	18,232	1.43
1948	1,284,535	19,742	1.54
1949	1,284,196	17,469	1.36
1950	1,303,171	17,411	1.34
1951	1,328,809	18,941	1.43
1954	1,331,498	24,997	1.88
1955	1,378,588	25,143	1.82
1957	1,475,320	32,131	2.18
1959	1,498,549	38,515	2.57
1961	1,548,061	45,439	2.94
1963	1,663,115	55,207	3.32
1966	1,727,240	67,404[c]	3.90
1970	1,796,940	93,424[c]	5.20
1973	1,867,689	120,761[c]	6.47

Sources: Deaths, U.S. Department of Health, Education, and Welfare, Division of Vital Statistics. Taxable estate returns, *Statistics of Income, Estate Tax Returns.*
a. Aged twenty and over.
b. Citizens and resident aliens.
c. Not strictly comparable with 1939–63 data. For 1966 and later years, the estate tax after credits was the basis for determining taxable returns. For prior years, the basis was the estate tax before credits.

Table B-11. Number of Taxable Estate Tax Returns, Gross and Economic Estate, and Estate Tax before and after Credits, Selected Years, 1939–73

Millions of dollars

Year[a]	Number of taxable returns	Gross estate on taxable returns	Economic estate[b] on taxable returns	Taxable estate[c]	Estate tax Before credits	Estate tax After credits
1939	12,720	2,564	2,390	1,538	330	277
1940	12,907	2,448	2,295	1,479	296	250
1941	13,336	2,578	2,410	1,561	346	292
1942	13,493	2,550	2,373	1,525	354	308
1943	12,726	2,452	2,284	1,397	398	362
1944	12,154	2,720	2,551	1,509	452	405
1945	13,869	3,246	3,081	1,900	596	531
1947	18,232	3,993	3,804	2,319	694	622
1948	19,742	4,445	4,224	2,585	799	715
1949	17,469	4,272	4,059	2,107	635	567
1950	17,411	4,126	3,919	1,917	534	484
1951	18,941	4,656	n.a.	2,189	644	577
1954	24,997	6,288	6,007	2,969	869	779
1955	25,143	6,387	6,109	2,991	872	778
1957	32,131	8,904	n.a.	4,342	1,353	1,177
1959	38,515	9,996	9,540	4,651	1,346	1,186
1961	45,439	12,733	12,213	6,014	1,847	1,619
1963	55,207	14,714	14,059	7,071	2,087	1,841
1966	67,404[d]	19,227[d]	17,974[d]	9,160	2,755	2,414
1970	93,424[d]	25,585[d]	22,140[d]	11,662	3,413	3,000
1973	120,761[d]	33,294[d]	29,066[d]	15,815	4,720	4,153

Sources: 1939–51, *Statistics of Income, Part 1*; 1954–66, *Statistics of Income, Fiduciary, Gift, and Estate Tax Returns*; 1970–73, *Statistics of Income, Estate Tax Returns*. Data are for estate tax returns of citizens and resident aliens.

n.a. Not available.

a. Returns are classified by year in which they were filed.

b. Economic estate is gross estate reduced by the amount of debt (including mortgages and loans against life insurance policies).

c. Before 1953 "taxable estate" was labeled "net estate" in *Statistics of Income*.

d. Not strictly comparable with prior years. For 1966–73 estate tax after credits was the basis for determining taxable returns. For earlier years the basis was estate tax before credits.

334   *Federal Tax Policy*

Table B-12. Distribution of Taxable Estates, by Rate Bracket, 1973

Estate tax rate (percent)	Amount (millions of dollars)		Percentage distribution	
	Taxable estate	Tax[a]	Taxable estate	Tax
3	582	17	3.7	0.4
7	532	37	3.4	0.8
11	938	103	5.9	2.2
14	800	112	5.0	2.4
18	691	124	4.4	2.6
22	606	133	3.8	2.8
25	536	134	3.4	2.8
28	1,647	461	10.4	9.8
30	3,133	940	19.8	19.9
32	2,093	670	13.2	14.2
35	1,013	354	6.4	7.5
37	615	228	3.9	4.8
39	430	168	2.7	3.5
42	316	133	2.0	2.8
45	430	194	2.7	4.1
49	288	141	1.8	3.0
53	203	108	1.3	2.3
56	149	83	0.9	1.8
59	115	68	0.7	1.4
63	167	105	1.1	2.2
67	116	78	0.7	1.6
70	82	57	0.5	1.2
73	58	42	0.4	0.9
76	78	59	0.5	1.3
77	232	179	1.5	3.8
Total	15,850	4,729	100.0	100.0

Source: *Statistics of Income—1972, Estate Tax Returns*, table 12. Totals and percentages are derived from unrounded data.
a. Tax before credits.

Table B-13. Number of Taxable Gift Tax Returns, Total Gifts, Taxable Gifts, and Gift Tax, Selected Years, 1939–66

Millions of dollars

Year[a]	Number of taxable returns	Total gifts on taxable returns	Taxable gifts (current year)	Gift tax (current year)
1939	3,929	220	132	19
1940	4,930	347	226	34
1941	8,940	714	484	70
1942	4,380	222	121	25
1943	4,656	209	124	30
1944	4,979	276	148	38
1945	5,540	289	170	37
1946	6,808	426	265	62
1947	6,822	439	257	64
1948	6,559	391	209	45
1949	6,114	340	178	36
1950	8,366	596	338	78
1951	8,360	516	304	67
1953	8,464	489	258	56
1957	14,736	923	518	113
1959	15,793	928	478	105
1961	17,936	1,219	657	158
1963	20,598	1,402	790	183
1966	29,547	2,373	1,455	413

Sources: 1939–53, *Statistics of Income, Part 1*; 1957–66, *Statistics of Income, Fiduciary, Gift, and Estate Tax Returns*.

a. Returns are classified by year in which they were filed. Data after 1966 are not published.

Table B-14. Distribution of Taxable Gifts, by Rate Bracket, 1963[a]

Rate (percent)	Amount (thousands of dollars) — Taxable gifts	Tax	Percentage distribution — Taxable gifts	Tax
2¼	39,386	887	5.0	0.5
5¼	31,671	1,664	4.0	0.9
8¼	50,371	4,155	6.4	2.3
10½	38,513	4,044	4.9	2.2
13½	31,136	4,203	3.9	2.3
16½	26,129	4,311	3.3	2.4
18¾	22,415	4,203	2.8	2.3
21	65,366	13,727	8.3	7.5
22½	122,698	27,607	15.5	15.1
24	91,880	22,051	11.6	12.0
26¼	51,861	13,614	6.6	7.4
27¾	33,964	9,425	4.3	5.1
29¼	25,701	7,518	3.3	4.1
31½	22,590	7,116	2.9	3.9
33¾	32,195	10,866	4.1	5.9
36¾	19,780	7,269	2.5	4.0
39¾	15,015	5,968	1.9	3.3
42	10,072	4,230	1.3	2.3
44¼	6,641	2,939	0.8	1.6
47¼	14,671	6,932	1.9	3.8
50¼	11,510	5,784	1.5	3.2
52½	8,479	4,452	1.1	2.4
54¾	4,703	2,575	0.6	1.4
57	2,939	1,675	0.4	0.9
57¾	10,623	6,135	1.3	3.3
Total	790,311	183,351	100.0	100.0

Source: *Statistics of Income, Fiduciary, Gift, and Estate Tax Returns, 1962.* Figures are rounded.
a. The year 1963 is the latest for which a distribution of taxable gifts by rate brackets is available.

Statistical Tables

Table C-1. Federal Receipts, Expenditures, and Surpluses or Deficits, under the Official and National Income Accounts Budget Concepts, Fiscal Years 1954–76

Billions of dollars

Fiscal year	Official (unified) federal budget[a]			National income accounts budget[a]		
	Receipts	Expenditures	Surplus(+) or deficit (−)	Receipts	Expenditures	Surplus(+) or deficit (−)
1954	69.7	70.9	−1.2	65.8	74.3	−8.5
1955	65.5	68.5	−3.0	67.4	67.2	+0.2
1956	74.5	70.5	+4.1	76.3	70.0	+6.3
1957	80.0	76.7	+3.2	81.0	76.0	+5.0
1958	79.6	82.6	−2.9	78.1	82.8	−4.7
1959	79.2	92.1	−12.9	85.4	91.2	−5.8
1960	92.5	92.2	+0.3	94.8	91.3	+3.5
1961	94.4	97.8	−3.4	95.0	98.1	−3.1
1962	99.7	106.8	−7.1	104.0	106.2	−2.2
1963	106.6	111.3	−4.8	110.0	111.7	−1.7
1964	112.7	118.6	−5.9	115.6	117.2	−1.6
1965	116.8	118.4	−1.6	120.0	118.5	+1.5
1966	130.9	134.7	−3.8	132.7	132.7	0.0
1967	149.6	158.3	−8.7	146.0	154.9	−8.9
1968	153.7	178.8	−25.2	160.0	172.2	−12.2
1969	187.8	184.5	+3.2	190.1	184.7	+5.4
1970	193.7	196.6	−2.8	194.9	195.6	−0.7
1971	188.4	211.4	−23.0	192.5	212.7	−20.2
1972	208.6	231.9	−23.2	213.5	232.9	−19.4
1973	232.2	246.5	−14.3	240.5	256.2	−15.7
1974	264.9	268.4	−3.5	271.9	278.9	−7.0
1975	281.0	324.6	−43.6	283.2	329.5	−46.3
1976	300.0	365.6	−65.6	307.4[b]	378.7[b]	−71.3[b]

Sources: *The Budget of the United States Government*, various years. Figures are rounded.
a. For an explanation of the differences between the two budget concepts, see p. 16.
b. Estimated.

Table C-2. Full Employment Receipts, Expenditures, and Surpluses or Deficits, under the Official and National Income Accounts Budget Concepts, Fiscal Years 1953–75

Billions of dollars

Fiscal year	Official (unified) federal budget			National income accounts budget[a]		
	Receipts	Expenditures	Surplus(+) or deficit (−)	Receipts	Expenditures	Surplus(+) or deficit (−)
1953	...	...	...	68.2	75.6	−7.4
1954	...	...	...	67.9	74.3	−6.4
1955	...	...	...	68.8	67.7	+1.1
1956	...	...	...	74.7	69.8	+4.9
1957	...	...	...	82.5	76.1	+6.4
1958	...	...	...	87.1	81.6	+5.5
1959	...	...	...	91.6	89.8	+1.8
1960	99.9	91.4	+8.5	101.2	90.7	+10.5
1961	106.9	96.2	+10.7	108.1	96.0	+12.1
1962	109.2	105.9	+3.3	112.3	105.4	+6.9
1963	115.7	110.0	+5.7	120.1	111.0	+9.1
1964	120.7	118.0	+2.7	122.3	116.4	+5.9
1965	120.8	118.0	+2.8	124.4	118.1	+6.3
1966	128.6	134.8	−6.2	132.1	133.0	−0.9
1967	147.7	158.4	−10.7	148.2	155.0	−6.8
1968	153.6	178.9	−25.3	163.0	172.2	−9.2
1969	184.6	185.0	−0.4	191.6	185.0	+6.6
1970	199.1	196.1	+3.0	205.0	195.9	+9.1
1971	213.4	209.2	+4.2	213.0	210.2	+2.8
1972	223.5	228.9	−5.4	226.8	229.7	−3.0
1973	244.0	245.0	−1.0	250.4	254.2	−3.7
1974	282.2	267.3	+14.9	292.4	276.2	+16.2
1975	323.0	317.1	+5.9	333.1	323.3	+9.8

Sources: Office of Management and Budget and Council of Economic Advisers.
a. Average of quarterly data.

Table C-3. Relation of Federal, State, and Local Government Receipts to Gross National Product, 1946–75[a]

National income accounts basis

| | | Receipts of federal, state, and local governments | | | | | |
| | Gross national product (billions of dollars) | Amount (billions of dollars) | | | Percent of gross national product | | |
Year		Total	Federal	State and local[b]	Total	Federal	State and local[b]
1946	209.6	51.0	39.1	11.9	24.3	18.7	5.7
1947	232.8	56.9	43.2	13.7	24.5	18.6	5.9
1948	259.1	58.9	43.2	15.7	22.7	16.7	6.1
1949	258.0	55.9	38.7	17.2	21.7	15.0	6.7
1950	286.2	69.0	50.0	19.0	24.1	17.5	6.6
1951	330.2	85.2	64.3	21.0	25.8	19.5	6.3
1952	347.2	90.1	67.3	22.8	26.0	19.4	6.6
1953	366.1	94.6	70.0	24.6	25.8	19.1	6.7
1954	366.3	89.9	63.7	26.1	24.5	17.4	7.1
1955	399.3	101.1	72.6	28.5	25.3	18.2	7.1
1956	420.7	109.6	78.0	31.7	26.1	18.5	7.5
1957	442.8	116.2	81.9	34.3	26.2	18.5	7.7
1958	448.9	115.0	78.7	36.3	25.6	17.5	8.1
1959	486.5	129.4	89.8	39.6	26.6	18.5	8.1
1960	506.0	139.5	96.1	43.4	27.6	19.0	8.6
1961	523.3	144.8	98.1	46.8	27.7	18.7	8.9
1962	563.8	156.7	106.2	50.5	27.8	18.8	9.0
1963	594.7	168.5	114.4	54.1	28.3	19.2	9.1
1964	635.7	174.0	114.9	59.1	27.4	18.1	9.3
1965	688.1	188.3	124.3	64.0	27.4	18.1	9.3
1966	753.0	212.3	141.8	70.4	28.2	18.8	9.4
1967	796.3	228.2	150.5	77.7	28.7	18.9	9.8
1968	868.5	263.4	174.7	88.7	30.3	20.1	10.2
1969	935.5	296.3	197.0	99.3	31.7	21.1	10.6
1970	982.4	302.6	192.1	110.5	30.8	19.5	11.2
1971	1,063.4	322.2	198.6	123.6	30.3	18.7	11.6
1972	1,171.1	367.4	227.5	139.9	31.4	19.4	11.9
1973	1,306.6	411.2	258.3	152.9	31.5	19.8	11.7
1974	1,413.2	454.6	288.2	166.4	32.2	20.4	11.8
1975	1,516.3	466.4	286.5	179.9	30.8	18.9	11.9

Sources: Department of Commerce, Bureau of Economic Analysis. Figures are rounded.

a. The receipts in this table are on the national income accounts basis of the Department of Commerce and therefore differ from the official unified budget receipts as defined in the budget message. In this table, receipts of trust funds and taxes other than corporation taxes are on a cash basis, but, unlike the unified budget, corporation taxes are on an accrual basis.

b. State and local receipts have been adjusted to exclude federal grants-in-aid.

340 Federal Tax Policy

Table C-4. Federal Budget Receipts, by Source, Fiscal Years 1954-76[a]

Fiscal year	Total	In- dividual	Corpo- ration	Excise	Estate and gift	Em- ploy- ment[b]	Cus- toms	Other[c]
					Taxes			
			Amount (millions of dollars)					
1954	69,719	29,545	21,103	9,946	934	7,210	542	438
1955	65,469	28,749	17,862	9,131	924	7,866	585	352
1956	74,547	32,190	20,881	9,930	1,161	9,323	682	381
1957	79,990	35,656	21,167	10,534	1,365	9,997	735	536
1958	79,636	34,737	20,074	10,638	1,393	11,239	782	773
1959	79,249	36,776	17,309	10,578	1,333	11,722	925	605
1960	92,492	40,741	21,494	11,676	1,606	14,683	1,105	1,187
1961	94,389	41,338	20,954	11,860	1,896	16,438	982	919
1962	99,676	45,571	20,523	12,534	2,016	17,046	1,142	843
1963	106,560	47,588	21,579	13,194	2,167	19,804	1,205	1,023
1964	112,662	48,697	23,493	13,731	2,394	22,012	1,252	1,084
1965	116,833	48,792	25,461	14,570	2,716	22,258	1,442	1,594
1966	130,856	55,446	30,073	13,062	3,066	25,567	1,767	1,875
1967	149,552	61,526	33,971	13,719	2,978	33,349	1,901	2,108
1968	153,671	68,726	28,665	14,079	3,051	34,622	2,038	2,491
1969	187,784	87,249	36,678	15,222	3,491	39,918	2,319	2,908
1970	193,743	90,412	32,829	15,705	3,644	45,298	2,430	3,424
1971	188,392	86,230	26,785	16,614	3,735	48,578	2,591	3,858
1972	208,649	94,737	32,166	15,477	5,436	53,914	3,287	3,633
1973	232,225	103,246	36,153	16,260	4,917	64,542	3,188	3,921
1974	264,932	118,952	38,620	16,844	5,035	76,780	3,334	5,369
1975	280,997	122,386	40,621	16,551	4,611	86,441	3,676	6,711
1976	300,005	131,603	41,409	16,963	5,216	92,714	4,074	8,026
			Percent of total					
1954	100	42.4	30.3	14.3	1.3	10.3	0.8	0.6
1955	100	43.9	27.3	13.9	1.4	12.0	0.9	0.5
1956	100	43.2	28.0	13.3	1.6	12.5	0.9	0.5
1957	100	44.6	26.5	13.2	1.7	12.5	0.9	0.7
1958	100	43.6	25.2	13.4	1.7	14.1	1.0	1.0
1959	100	46.4	21.8	13.3	1.7	14.8	1.2	0.8
1960	100	44.0	23.2	12.6	1.7	15.9	1.2	1.3
1961	100	43.8	22.2	12.6	2.0	17.4	1.0	1.0
1962	100	45.7	20.6	12.6	2.0	17.1	1.1	0.8
1963	100	44.7	20.3	12.4	2.0	18.6	1.1	1.0
1964	100	43.2	20.9	12.2	2.1	19.5	1.1	1.0

Table C-4 (*continued*)

Fiscal year	Total	In- dividual	Corpo- ration	Excise	Estate and gift	Em- ploy- ment[b]	Cus- toms	Other[c]
						Taxes		
1965	100	41.8	21.8	12.5	2.3	19.1	1.2	1.4
1966	100	42.4	23.0	10.0	2.3	19.5	1.4	1.4
1967	100	41.1	22.7	9.2	2.0	22.3	1.3	1.4
1968	100	44.7	18.7	9.2	2.0	22.5	1.3	1.6
1969	100	46.5	19.5	8.1	1.9	21.3	1.2	1.5
1970	100	46.7	16.9	8.1	1.9	23.4	1.3	1.8
1971	100	45.8	14.2	8.8	2.0	25.8	1.4	2.0
1972	100	45.4	15.4	7.4	2.6	25.8	1.6	1.7
1973	100	44.5	15.6	7.0	2.1	27.8	1.4	1.7
1974	100	44.9	14.6	6.4	1.9	29.0	1.3	2.0
1975	100	43.6	14.5	5.9	1.6	30.8	1.3	2.4
1976	100	43.9	13.8	5.7	1.7	30.9	1.4	2.7

Sources: 1954–60, *Statistical Appendix to Annual Report of the Secretary of the Treasury on the State of the Finances for the Fiscal Year Ended June 30, 1969*, pp. 14, 17; 1961–75, *Treasury Bulletin* (August 1970), pp. 2–3, and ibid. (November 1975), pp. 3–4; 1976, Department of the Treasury. Figures are rounded.

a. Receipts in this table are on the official unified budget basis and are net after refunds. For 1954–56, breakdowns for tax refunds for individual, corporation, excise, and estate and gift taxes are based on data from the consolidated cash budget statement in *The Budget of the United States Government for the Fiscal Year Ending June 30, 1965*, p. 462.

b. Includes payroll taxes for social security and unemployment insurance, employee contributions for federal retirement, and contributions for supplementary medical insurance.

c. Includes deposits of earnings by Federal Reserve banks and miscellaneous receipts.

Table C-5. Tax Revenues as a Percentage of Gross National Product and Distribution of Tax Revenues, by Source, Selected Countries, 1973[a]

Tax source	United States	Can-ada	Japan	Aus-tralia	Aus-tria	Bel-gium	Den-mark	France	Ger-many	Italy	Nether-lands	Nor-way	Swe-den	Swit-zer-land	United King-dom
Percent of gross national product															
Individual income	9.3	11.5	6.1	9.0	8.2	10.2	22.6	4.0	10.9	3.6	12.1	12.4	17.6	8.9	10.8
Corporate income	3.2	4.1	4.7[b]	3.6	1.3	3.0	1.4	2.2	1.9	2.1	3.0	1.0	1.9	2.0	2.5
Payroll	6.1	3.0	4.1	1.0	12.3	11.0	2.3	15.5	13.1	12.0	16.0	13.4	10.6	7.2	5.7
Goods and services[c]	5.3	12.0	6.3[b]	8.2	14.2	12.1	15.8	14.3	10.5	11.1	11.7	18.0	13.1	6.6	9.5
Property	3.6	3.2	1.1	1.4	0.6[d]	0.0	1.8[d]	0.7	0.8[d]	0.3	0.7[d]	0.9[d]	0.2[d]	1.5[d]	3.7
Inheritances and gifts	0.5	0.1	0.3	0.5	0.1	0.3	0.2	0.2	0.1	0.1	0.2	0.1	0.1	0.2	0.6
Total tax revenue	28.0	33.9	22.6	23.8	36.6	36.6	44.1	36.9	37.3	29.2	43.8	45.9	43.5	26.4	32.8
Distribution by source															
Individual income	33.2	33.9	26.8	38.0	22.3	28.0	51.2	10.9	29.2	12.3	27.6	27.0	40.4	33.6	33.1
Corporate income	11.4	12.0	20.9[b]	15.0	3.6	8.2	3.2	6.1	5.1	7.0	6.8	2.3	4.3	7.5	7.7
Payroll	21.9	8.9	18.3	4.4	33.5	30.0	5.3	41.9	35.3	41.2	36.6	29.3	24.3	27.3	17.4
Goods and services[c]	19.0	35.3	27.8[b]	34.6	38.7	33.0	35.9	38.7	28.1	38.0	26.8	39.2	30.2	25.1	28.9
Property	12.7	9.5	5.0	5.7	1.7	0.0	4.1	1.8	2.2	0.9	1.7	2.0	0.6	5.6	11.2
Inheritances and gifts	1.7	0.4	1.2	2.2	0.1	0.8	0.4	0.6	0.1	0.5	0.5	0.2	0.3	0.9	1.8
Total tax revenue	100.0	100.0	100.0	100.0	100.0	100.0	100.0	100.0	100.0	100.0	100.0	100.0	100.0	100.0	100.0

Source: Organisation for Economic Co-operation and Development, *Revenue Statistics of OECD Member Countries, 1965–1973* (Paris: OECD, 1975). Figures are rounded.
a. Includes national and local taxes.
b. The Japanese enterprise tax levied by the prefectural governments is included in the corporate income tax and excluded from the tax on goods and services.
c. Includes sales, value added, and excise taxes, taxes on imports and exports, taxes on transfers of property and securities, other transaction taxes paid by enterprises, and miscellaneous other taxes.
d. Includes net wealth taxes.

Table C-6. Number and Amount of Standard and Itemized Deductions, Taxable and Nontaxable Federal Individual Income Tax Returns, 1944–74

Year	Total number of returns (millions)	Standard deduction		Itemized deductions		Total deductions	
		Number[a] (millions)	Amount (billions of dollars)	Number[a] (millions)	Amount (billions of dollars)	Amount (billions of dollars)	Percent of adjusted gross income
1944	47.1	38.7	8.0	8.4	4.8	12.8	11.0
1945	49.9	41.5	8.1	8.5	5.5	13.6	11.3
1946	52.8	44.1	8.9	8.8	6.3	15.2	11.3
1947	55.1	44.7	9.8	10.4	7.8	17.6	11.8
1948	52.1	43.2	11.5	8.8	7.9	19.4	11.9
1949	51.8	42.1	11.1	9.7	8.8	19.9	12.4
1950	53.1	42.7	12.0	10.3	9.9	21.9	12.2
1951	55.4	43.9	13.3	11.6	11.9	25.2	12.5
1952	56.5	43.7	13.7	12.8	13.6	27.3	12.7
1953	57.8	43.4	14.2	14.4	15.6	29.8	13.0
1954	56.7	41.0	13.3	15.7	17.4	30.7	13.4
1955	58.3	41.4	13.6	16.9	20.0	33.6	13.5
1956	59.2	40.7	13.8	18.5	22.6	36.4	13.6
1957	59.8	39.7	13.8	20.2	25.7	39.5	14.1
1958	59.1	38.3	13.2	20.8	27.5	40.7	14.5
1959	60.3	37.8	13.4	22.5	32.0	45.4	14.9
1960	61.0	36.9	13.1	24.1	35.3	48.4	15.3
1961	61.5	36.2	12.9	25.3	38.4	51.3	15.6
1962	62.7	36.3	13.1	26.5	41.7	54.8	15.7
1963	63.9	35.8	13.1	28.2	46.1	59.2	16.1
1964	65.4	38.5	20.2	26.9	46.8	67.0	16.9
1965	67.6	39.7	20.6	27.9	50.7	71.4	16.6
1966	70.2	41.6	21.8	28.6	54.6	76.4	16.3
1967	71.7	41.9	22.1	29.8	59.6	81.7	16.2
1968	73.7	41.7	22.1	32.0	69.2	91.3	16.4
1969	75.8	40.9	21.6	34.9	80.2	101.8	16.8
1970	74.3	38.8	32.4	35.4	88.2	120.5	19.0
1971	74.6	43.9	48.1	30.7	91.9	139.9	20.7
1972	77.6	50.6	69.8	27.0	96.7	166.4	22.2
1973	80.7	52.6	73.6	28.0	107.0	180.6	21.7
1974[b]	83.3	53.6	75.8	29.7	119.7	195.5	21.6

Sources: *Statistics of Income, Individual Income Tax Returns.* Amount of standard deduction for 1944–57 estimated by author on the basis of the distribution of the number of tax returns by income classes and marital status in *Statistics of Income,* and for 1958–74 obtained directly from *Statistics of Income.* Figures are rounded.

a. Returns with standard deduction, 1955–74, include a small number with no adjusted gross income and no deductions. For 1944–54, returns with no adjusted gross income are included in the number of returns with itemized deductions.

b. Preliminary.

Table C-7. Federal Individual Income Tax Liabilities, Prepayments, and Final Balances of Tax Due and Overpayments, 1944–73

Billions of dollars

	Tax liabilities			Prepayments		Final balances	
Year	Total	Income tax	Self-employ-ment tax	With-holdingª	Declara-tion pay-mentsᵇ	Tax due	Over-pay-ments
1944	16.2	16.2	...	9.6	5.5	2.4	1.4
1945	17.1	17.1	...	10.5	6.0	2.4	1.8
1946	16.1	16.1	...	9.2	6.0	2.7	1.9
1947	18.1	18.1	...	11.2	5.8	3.0	2.0
1948	15.4	15.4	...	10.6	5.3	2.2	2.7
1949	14.5	14.5	...	9.6	4.7	2.1	2.0
1950	18.4	18.4	...	11.8	5.6	3.1	2.1
1951	24.4	24.2	0.2	16.6	6.6	3.7	2.5
1952	28.0	27.8	0.2	20.3	7.1	3.6	2.9
1953	29.7	29.4	0.2	22.6	7.0	3.4	3.3
1954	27.0	26.7	0.3	20.5	7.2	3.0	3.7
1955	30.1	29.6	0.5	22.7	7.2	3.8	3.6
1956	33.3	32.7	0.5	25.2	7.9	4.1	4.0
1957	35.0	34.4	0.6	27.4	8.2	3.9	4.5
1958	34.9	34.3	0.6	27.6	8.0	4.1	4.8
1959	39.3	38.6	0.7	30.8	8.6	5.1	5.1
1960	40.3	39.5	0.8	32.7	8.6	4.7	5.7
1961	43.1	42.2	0.8	34.4	9.0	5.7	6.0
1962	45.8	44.9	0.9	37.4	9.3	5.6	6.6
1963	49.2	48.2	1.0	40.2	9.7	6.3	6.9
1964	48.2	47.2	1.0	36.9	10.1	7.1	5.9
1965	50.6	49.6	1.1	39.3	10.7	7.5	6.8
1966	57.6	56.1	1.5	46.9	11.8	7.6	8.6
1967	64.5	63.0	1.6	53.1	13.1	8.4	10.2
1968	78.4	76.7	1.7	62.9	16.0	10.6	11.0
1969	88.5	86.6	1.9	75.2	17.5	10.5	14.6
1970	85.8	83.9	1.8	76.1	16.7	8.7	15.7
1971	87.5	85.4	2.0	75.9	17.5	9.5	15.4
1972	95.9	93.6	2.3	91.2	18.4	9.9	23.5
1973	111.2	108.2	3.0	103.6	19.6	12.8	24.9

Source: *Statistics of Income, Individual Income Tax Returns.* Figures are rounded.
a. Includes excess social security taxes withheld.
b. Includes payments with requests for extension of filing time, credit for gasoline, fuel, and oil, and other tax payments or credits.

Table C-8. Number of Federal Individual Income Tax Returns by Type of Final Settlement, 1944–73

Millions

Year	Total number of returns	Returns with		No over-payments or balances due
		Tax due	*Overpayments*	
1944	47.1	22.6	22.9	1.6
1945	49.9	14.5	33.5	1.9
1946	52.8	13.6	34.4	4.8
1947	55.1	15.3	33.0	6.7
1948	52.1	8.1	38.4	5.6
1949	51.8	13.8	30.2	7.9
1950	53.1	14.3	32.0	6.8
1951	55.4	18.6	31.0	5.8
1952	56.5	19.3	32.1	5.1
1953	57.8	19.0	32.7	6.2
1954	56.7	16.6	35.2	5.0
1955	58.3	18.7	35.4	4.2
1956	59.2	19.4	36.1	3.7
1957	59.8	18.6	37.6	3.6
1958	59.1	18.1	37.4	3.6
1959	60.3	19.1	38.4	2.8
1960	61.0	18.1	39.4	3.5
1961	61.5	18.6	40.0	2.9
1962	62.7	18.7	40.9	3.1
1963	63.9	19.3	41.4	3.3
1964	65.4	22.5	39.3	3.5
1965	67.6	20.0	44.3	3.2
1966	70.2	17.8	49.4	3.0
1967	71.7	17.5	51.2	3.0
1968	73.7	20.3	50.6	2.8
1969	75.8	17.9	54.9	3.0
1970	74.3	16.5	55.3	2.5
1971	74.6	17.0	55.3	2.4
1972	77.6	11.9	63.3	2.3
1973	80.7	14.2	64.2	2.2

Source: *Statistics of Income, Individual Income Tax Returns.* Figures are rounded.

Table C-9. Distribution of Taxable Federal Individual Income Tax Returns and Tax Liabilities, 1950 and 1974

Adjusted gross income class (dollars)	Taxable returns		Tax liabilities	
	Number (thousands)	Percent of total	Amount (millions of dollars)	Percent of total
1950				
Under 3,000	16,285	42.6	2,189	11.9
3,000–5,000	14,409	37.7	4,221	23.0
5,000–10,000	6,115	16.0	3,984	21.7
10,000–25,000	1,075	2.8	2,531	13.8
25,000–50,000	220	0.6	1,888	10.3
50,000–100,000	63	0.2	1,517	8.3
100,000 and over	20	0.1	2,045	11.1
Total	38,187	100.0	18,375	100.0
1974				
Under 3,000[a]	3,535	5.3	238	0.2
3,000–5,000	8,175	12.2	2,007	1.6
5,000–10,000	19,740	29.4	13,646	11.0
10,000–25,000	30,482	45.3	59,264	47.9
25,000–50,000	4,451	6.6	24,995	20.2
50,000–100,000	698	1.0	12,228	9.9
100,000 and over	166	0.2	11,312	9.1
Total	67,248	100.0	123,690	100.0

Sources: *Statistics of Income, Individual. Income Tax Returns.* Figures are rounded.
a. Includes a small number of returns with no adjusted gross income.

Table C-10. Federal Individual Income Tax Liabilities before Credit and Tax Saving for Single Persons, Heads of Households, and Married Couples Filing Joint Returns, and Basic Rate Schedule, by Taxable Income, 1977 Rates

Dollars

Taxable income	Basic (married, separate returns)	Tax liability			Tax saving over basic rate			Tax saving as percent of basic rate		
		Single	Head of house-hold	Married, joint return	Single	Head of house-hold	Married, joint return	Single	Head of house-hold	Married, joint return
500	70	70	70	70	0	0	0	0	0	0
1,000	145	145	140	140	0	5	5	0	3.5	3.5
1,500	225	225	220	215	0	5	10	0	2.2	4.4
2,000	310	310	300	290	0	10	20	0	3.2	6.5
3,000	500	500	480	450	0	20	50	0	4.0	10.0
4,000	690	690	660	620	0	30	70	0	4.4	10.1
6,000	1,130	1,110	1,040	1,000	20	90	130	1.8	8.0	11.5
8,000	1,630	1,590	1,480	1,380	40	150	250	2.5	9.2	15.3
10,000	2,190	2,090	1,940	1,820	100	250	370	4.6	11.4	16.9
12,000	2,830	2,630	2,440	2,260	200	390	570	7.1	13.8	20.1
14,000	3,550	3,210	2,980	2,760	340	570	790	9.6	16.1	22.3
16,000	4,330	3,830	3,540	3,260	500	790	1,070	11.5	18.2	24.7
18,000	5,170	4,510	4,160	3,820	660	1,010	1,350	12.8	19.5	26.1
20,000	6,070	5,230	4,800	4,380	840	1,270	1,690	13.8	20.9	27.8
22,000	7,030	5,990	5,500	5,020	1,040	1,530	2,010	14.8	21.8	28.6
24,000	8,030	6,790	6,220	5,660	1,240	1,810	2,370	15.4	22.5	29.5
26,000	9,030	7,590	6,980	6,380	1,440	2,050	2,650	15.9	22.7	29.3
28,000	10,090	8,490	7,800	7,100	1,600	2,290	2,990	15.9	22.7	29.6
32,000	12,210	10,290	9,480	8,660	1,920	2,730	3,550	15.7	22.4	29.1
36,000	14,410	12,290	11,280	10,340	2,120	3,130	4,070	14.7	21.7	28.2
38,000	15,510	13,290	12,240	11,240	2,220	3,270	4,270	14.3	21.1	27.5

Table C-10 (continued)

Taxable income	Basic (married, separate returns)	Tax liability			Tax saving over basic rate			Tax saving as percent of basic rate		
		Single	Head of household	Married, joint return	Single	Head of household	Married, joint return	Single	Head of household	Married, joint return
40,000	16,670	14,390	13,260	12,140	2,280	3,410	4,530	13.7	20.5	27.2
44,000	18,990	16,590	15,340	14,060	2,400	3,650	4,930	12.6	19.2	26.0
50,000	22,590	20,190	18,640	17,060	2,400	3,950	5,530	10.6	17.5	24.5
52,000	23,830	21,430	19,760	18,060	2,400	4,070	5,770	10.1	17.1	24.2
60,000	28,790	26,390	24,400	22,300	2,400	4,390	6,490	8.3	15.2	22.5
64,000	31,350	28,950	26,720	24,420	2,400	4,630	6,930	7.7	14.8	22.1
70,000	35,190	32,790	30,260	27,720	2,400	4,930	7,470	6.8	14.0	21.2
76,000	39,150	36,750	33,920	31,020	2,400	5,230	8,130	6.1	13.4	20.8
80,000	41,790	39,390	36,400	33,340	2,400	5,390	8,450	5.7	12.9	20.2
88,000	47,230	44,830	41,440	37,980	2,400	5,790	9,250	5.1	12.3	19.6
90,000	48,590	46,190	42,720	39,180	2,400	5,870	9,410	4.9	12.1	19.4
100,000	55,490	53,090	49,120	45,180	2,400	6,370	10,310	4.3	11.5	18.6
120,000	69,490	67,090	62,320	57,580	2,400	7,170	11,910	3.5	10.3	17.1
140,000	83,490	81,090	75,720	70,380	2,400	7,770	13,110	2.9	9.3	15.7
150,000	90,490	88,090	82,520	76,980	2,400	7,970	13,510	2.7	8.8	14.9
160,000	97,490	95,090	89,320	83,580	2,400	8,170	13,910	2.5	8.4	14.3
180,000	111,490	109,090	103,120	97,180	2,400	8,370	14,310	2.2	7.5	12.8
200,000	125,490	123,090	117,120	110,980	2,400	8,370	14,510	1.9	6.7	11.6
300,000	195,490	193,090	187,120	180,980	2,400	8,370	14,510	1.2	4.3	7.4
400,000	265,490	263,090	257,120	250,980	2,400	8,370	14,510	0.9	3.2	5.5
1,000,000	685,490	683,090	677,120	670,980	2,400	8,370	14,510	0.4	1.2	2.1

Source: Computed from table 4-2. Tax liabilities are before the deduction of the $35 per capita credit or 2 percent of taxable income up to $180, whichever is higher.

Table C-11. Influence of Various Provisions on Effective Rates of Federal Individual Income Tax, 1976

Percent

Total income class[a] (dollars)	Nominal tax rate[b]	Reduction due to							Actual tax rate[g]
		Personal exemptions	Deduc-tions[c]	Tax preference items[d]	Capital gains[e]	Maximum tax[f]	Income splitting	Earned income credit	
0–600	14.0	14.0	...	...	...	...	...	0.6	−0.6
600–1,000	14.4	14.4	...	...	...	...	...	0.4	−0.4
1,000–1,500	14.8	12.6	2.1	...	...	...	...	0.4	−0.4
1,500–2,000	15.3	10.4	4.9	...	...	...	...	1.0	−1.0
2,000–2,500	15.8	9.3	6.6	...	...	...	...	0.4	−0.4
2,500–3,000	16.4	9.3	6.8	...	...	...	...	1.3	−0.9
3,000–3,500	16.8	8.8	6.5	...	...	...	*	1.5	0.0
3,500–4,000	17.1	8.4	6.1	...	*	...	*	1.4	1.2
4,000–4,500	17.5	8.8	5.8	...	*	...	0.2	1.9	0.8
4,500–5,000	17.9	8.2	5.9	...	0.1	...	0.1	1.3	2.4
5,000–6,000	18.5	7.6	5.8	...	0.1	...	0.2	0.9	4.0
6,000–7,000	19.3	7.9	5.6	...	*	...	0.3	0.7	4.8
7,000–8,000	20.0	7.7	5.3	...	0.1	...	0.4	0.2	6.3
8,000–9,000	20.7	7.4	5.4	...	*	...	0.6	*	7.3
9,000–10,000	21.4	6.8	5.3	...	*	...	0.6	...	8.6
10,000–11,000	22.2	7.6	5.3	...	0.1	...	0.9	...	8.3
11,000–12,000	23.1	7.8	5.7	...	0.1	...	1.0	...	8.4
12,000–13,000	24.0	7.6	5.8	...	0.1	...	1.4	...	9.1

Table C-11 (continued)

Total income class[a] (dollars)	Nominal tax rate[b]	Reduction due to							Actual tax rate[g]
		Personal exemptions	Deduc- tions[c]	Tax preference items[d]	Capital gains[e]	Maximum tax[f]	Income splitting	Earned income credit	
13,000–15,000	25.3	7.4	6.1	…	0.1	…	1.7	…	9.9
15,000–20,000	28.1	7.0	7.1	…	0.2	…	2.6	…	11.2
20,000–25,000	32.1	6.5	7.9	…	0.2	…	4.2	…	13.2
25,000–50,000	38.1	5.2	9.0	…	0.8	*	6.5	…	16.5
50,000–75,000	47.7	3.4	11.0	*	1.5	0.7	7.3	…	23.9
75,000–100,000	52.9	2.5	11.4	0.2	3.2	1.2	6.5	…	27.9
100,000–150,000	57.4	1.9	12.0	0.8	4.6	1.9	5.7	…	30.5
150,000–200,000	61.2	1.3	13.3	1.0	6.4	2.3	4.6	…	32.2
200,000–500,000	64.5	0.8	14.3	2.3	9.4	2.0	3.1	…	32.7
500,000–1,000,000	67.5	0.3	16.1	2.4	14.6	1.3	1.6	…	31.2
1,000,000 and over	69.1	0.1	18.0	1.9	19.5	0.6	1.1	…	27.9
Total	30.6	6.4	7.5	0.1	0.7	0.1	3.2	0.1	12.4

Source: Brookings 1972 tax file projected to 1976. Figures are rounded.
* 0.05 percent or less.

a. Total income is the sum of adjusted gross income, excludable sick pay, excludable dividends, excludable moving expenses, and tax preference items as defined in the Tax Reform Act of 1969, including excluded net long-term capital gains.

b. Rate schedule for married couples filing separate returns applied to total income.

c. Standard and itemized deductions plus dividend, sick pay, and moving expense exclusions.

d. Special calculation for tax preference items, except excluded net long-term capital gains. The net effect of this category was calculated by eliminating the minimum tax on preference items and including these items in total income to be taxed at the regular rates.

e. Combined effect of the alternative tax calculation for taxpayers with capital gains and excluded net long-term capital gains.

f. Effect of maximum marginal tax rate of 50 percent on earned taxable income.

g. Includes reductions for retirement and foreign tax credits, which are not shown separately.

Table C-12. Itemized Deductions as a Percentage of Adjusted Gross Income,
by Adjusted Gross Income Class, Taxable and Nontaxable
Federal Individual Income Tax Returns, 1974

Adjusted gross income class (dollars)	Total	Contri-butions	Interest	Taxes	Medical and dental	Other
Under 1,000	456.6	30.3	97.3	88.8	200.4	39.9
1,000–2,000	133.2	9.2	24.3	48.5	28.1	23.1
2,000–3,000	80.2	8.5	17.5	22.7	25.8	5.7
3,000–4,000	62.6	7.4	12.9	17.4	21.2	3.8
4,000–5,000	50.8	5.4	9.3	13.2	17.5	5.4
5,000–6,000	42.5	4.9	10.5	11.4	11.2	4.4
6,000–7,000	37.5	4.5	9.4	10.6	9.0	4.0
7,000–8,000	34.9	3.7	9.9	10.2	7.7	3.5
8,000–9,000	30.7	3.4	8.8	9.1	6.0	3.3
9,000–10,000	27.9	3.1	8.5	8.3	4.6	3.5
10,000–15,000	25.2	2.7	8.5	8.1	3.1	2.9
15,000–20,000	21.5	2.3	7.4	7.8	1.7	2.3
20,000–25,000	19.4	2.3	6.3	7.7	1.3	1.8
25,000–30,000	18.8	2.3	5.9	7.8	1.1	1.7
30,000–50,000	18.3	2.4	5.3	7.8	1.0	1.8
50,000–100,000	17.5	3.0	4.7	7.5	0.6	1.7
100,000–200,000	18.3	3.8	5.0	7.1	0.4	2.1
200,000–500,000	21.1	5.9	5.6	6.8	0.3	2.5
500,000–1,000,000	25.1	8.8	6.4	6.8	0.1	3.0
1,000,000 and over	25.0	11.7	5.2	5.8	*	2.3
All returns	21.9	2.7	6.8	8.0	2.1	2.3

Source: *Preliminary Report, Statistics of Income—1974, Individual Income Tax Returns*, pp. 20–21. Figures are rounded.
* 0.05 or less.

Table C-13. Estimated Revenue from Capital Gains and Income Taxation, 1948–73
Billions of dollars unless otherwise specified

Calendar year of liability	Individuals and fiduciaries			Corporations			Individuals, fiduciaries, and corporations		
	Total income taxes	Estimated tax on capital gains and losses		Total income and excess profits taxes	Estimated tax on capital gains and losses		Total income and excess profits taxes	Estimated tax on capital gains and losses	
		Amount	Percent of total tax		Amount	Percent of total tax		Amount	Percent of total tax
1948	15.6	0.6	3.8	11.6	0.2	1.7	27.2	0.8	2.9
1949	14.7	0.4	2.7	9.5	0.2	2.1	24.2	0.6	2.5
1950	18.5	0.9	4.9	16.8	0.3	1.8	35.3	1.2	3.4
1951	24.4	0.9	3.7	21.5	0.3	1.4	45.9	1.2	2.6
1952	28.0	0.8	2.9	19.1ᵃ	0.3	1.6	47.1	1.1	2.3
1953	29.7	0.7	2.4	19.3	0.3	1.6	49.0	1.0	2.0
1954	26.9	1.1	4.1	16.2	0.5	3.1	43.1	1.6	3.7
1955	29.9	1.6	5.4	20.7	0.5	2.4	50.6	2.1	4.2
1956	33.1	1.5	4.5	20.4	0.5	2.5	53.5	2.0	3.7
1957	34.8	1.2	3.4	19.5	0.4	2.1	54.3	1.6	2.9
1958	34.6	1.4	4.0	17.7	0.6	3.4	52.3	2.0	3.8
1959	39.0	2.3	5.9	21.3	0.4	1.9	60.3	2.7	4.5

1960	39.8	1.9	4.8	20.7	0.6	2.9	60.5	2.5	4.1
1961	42.6	2.9	6.8	20.7	0.8	3.9	63.3	3.7	5.8
1962	45.3	2.1	4.6	21.5	0.7	3.3	66.8	2.8	4.2
1963	48.7	2.3	4.7	23.3	0.7	3.0	72.0	3.0	4.2
1964	47.8	2.7	5.6	24.3	0.7	2.9	72.1	3.4	4.7
1965	50.2	3.4	6.8	27.4	0.8	2.9	77.6	4.2	5.4
1966	56.8	3.4	6.0	29.5	0.9	3.1	86.3	4.3	5.0
1967	63.8	5.0	7.8	28.1	1.0	3.6	91.9	6.0	6.5
1968	77.6	7.2	9.3	33.6	1.3	3.9	111.2	8.5	7.6
1969	87.4	4.8[b]	5.5	33.5	1.4	4.2	120.9	6.2	5.1
1970	84.4	2.3	2.7	27.9	1.1	3.9	112.3	3.4	3.0
1971	85.9	3.8[b]	4.4	30.2	1.3	4.3	116.1	5.1	4.4
1972	94.3	5.3	5.6	33.5	1.8[b]	5.4	127.8	7.1	5.6
1973	108.9	5.0[b]	4.6	38.6	2.0[b]	5.2	147.5	7.0	4.7

Sources: Capital gains tax for individuals and fiduciaries, 1948–68, Department of the Treasury, Office of Tax Analysis; 1969–73, Brookings tax files for 1970 and 1972. Capital gains tax for corporations, 1948–67, Office of Tax Analysis; 1968–73, *Statistics of Income, Corporation Income Tax Returns*. The actual revenue figures are as reported in *Statistics of Income*, except for fiduciaries in 1969, which is an interpolated figure, and 1971–73, which are derived from fiscal year data.

a. Includes the foreign tax credit, which is not separately available for 1952.

b. Estimates based on incomplete data.

Table C-14. Estimated Federal Tax Expenditures,[a] by Budget Function, Fiscal Years 1976 and 1977

Millions of dollars

Budget function and tax provision	Amount of tax expenditure	
	1976	1977
National defense	**730**	**740**
Exclusion of benefits and allowances to armed forces personnel	650	650
Exclusion of military disability pensions	80	90
International affairs	**2,115**	**2,050**
Exclusion of income earned abroad by U.S. citizens	145	160
Exclusion of gross-up on dividends of less developed countries' corporations	55	55
Deferral of income of domestic international sales corporations	1,340	1,420
Deferral of income of controlled foreign corporations	525	365
Special rate for western hemisphere trade corporations	50	50
Agriculture	**1,390**	**1,535**
Expensing of certain capital outlays	460	475
Capital gains treatment of certain income	520	605
Deductibility of noncash patronage dividends and other income of cooperatives	410	455
Natural resources, environment, and energy	**2,840**	**3,190**
Exclusion of interest on state and local government pollution control bonds	160	245
Expensing of exploration and development costs	805	1,035
Excess of percentage over cost depletion	1,580	1,595
Pollution control, 5-year amortization	20	15
Capital gains treatment of royalties on coal and iron ore	60	70
Capital gains treatment of certain timber income	215	230
Commerce and transportation	**44,245**	**47,855**
Exemption of credit unions	125	135
Corporation surtax exemption	5,015	6,185
Deferral of tax on shipping companies	105	130
Railroad rolling stock, 5-year amortization	30	10
Financial institutions, excess bad debt reserves	815	570
Deductibility of nonbusiness state gasoline taxes	575	600
Depreciation on rental housing in excess of straight line	550	580
Depreciation on buildings (other than rental housing) in excess of straight line	490	495
Expensing of research and development expenditures	660	695
Capital gains, corporate (other than farming and timber)	760	900
Investment credit	8,260	9,115
Asset depreciation range	1,590	1,805
Dividend exclusion	335	350
Capital gains, individual (other than farming and timber)	5,455	6,225

Table C-14 (*continued*)

Budget function and tax provision	Amount of tax expenditure	
	1976	*1977*
Capital gains at death	6,720	7,280
Deferral of capital gains on home sales	845	890
Deductibility of mortgage interest on owner-occupied homes	4,545	4,710
Deductibility of property tax on owner-occupied homes	3,690	3,825
Deductibility of interest on consumer credit	1,040	1,075
Exclusion of interest on state and local industrial development bonds	225	285
Excess first-year depreciation	225	260
Expensing of contruction period interest and taxes	1,565	1,635
Credit for purchase of new home	625	100
Community and regional development:		
housing rehabilitation, 5-year amortization	**90**	**65**
Education, manpower, and social services	**5,193**	**5,626**
Exclusion of scholarships and fellowships	210	220
Parental personal exemptions for students aged 19 and over	690	715
Deductibility of contributions to educational institutions	665	780
Deductibility of charitable contributions (various social services)	3,283	3,476
Deductibility of child and dependent care expenses	330	420
Child care facilities, 5-year amortization	5	5
Credit for employing recipients of aid to families with dependent children and public assistance recipients under work incentive program	10	10
Health	**6,617**	**7,324**
Exclusion of employers' contributions to medical insurance premiums and medical care	3,665	4,225
Deductibility of medical expenses	2,020	2,095
Deductibility of charitable contributions	932	1,004
Income security	**22,755**	**24,435**
Exclusion of social security benefits		
Disability insurance benefits	315	370
Old age and survivors insurance benefits for aged	3,045	3,525
Benefits for dependents and survivors	495	565
Exclusion of railroad retirement system benefits	185	200
Exclusion of unemployment insurance benefits	3,305	2,855
Exclusion of workmen's compensation benefits	555	640
Exclusion of public assistance benefits	115	130
Exclusion of special benefits for disabled coal miners	50	50
Exclusion of sick pay	330	350
Net exclusion of pension contributions and earnings		
Employer plans	5,745	6,475
Plans for self-employed and others	770	965

Table C-14 (*continued*)

Budget function and tax provision	Amount of tax expenditure	
	1976	*1977*
Exclusion of other employee benefits		
Premiums on group term life insurance	805	895
Premiums on accident and accidental death insurance	55	60
Income of trusts to finance supplementary unemployment benefits	5	5
Meals and lodging	285	305
Exclusion of capital gains on home sales if 65 or over	45	50
Excess of percentage standard deduction over minimum standard deduction	1,465	1,560
Additional exemption for the blind	20	25
Additional exemption for 65 or over	1,155	1,220
Retirement income credit	120	110
Earned income credit, nonrefundable portion	290	280
Earned income credit, refundable portion	1,165	1,110
Exclusion of interest on life insurance savings	1,695	1,855
Deductibility of casualty losses	300	330
Maximum tax on earned income	440	505
Veterans' benefits and services	**950**	**905**
Exclusion of veterans' disability compensation	590	595
Exclusion of veterans' pensions	30	30
Exclusion of GI bill benefits	330	280
General government: credits and deductions for political contributions	**40**	**65**
Revenue sharing and general purpose fiscal assistance	**10,915**	**11,505**
Exclusion of interest on general purpose state and local debt	4,170	4,540
Exclusion of income earned in U.S. possessions	240	285
Deductibility of nonbusiness state and local taxes (other than on owner-occupied homes and gasoline)	6,505	6,680
Interest: deferral of interest on savings bonds	**605**	**685**
Total, all tax expenditures[b]	**98,485**	**105,980**

Source: Congressional Budget Office.

a. Tax expenditures are defined in the Congressional Budget and Impoundment Control Act of 1974 as "revenue losses attributable to provisions of the Federal tax laws which allow a special exclusion, exemption, or deduction from gross income or which provide a special credit, a preferential rate of tax, or a deferral of tax liability."

b. The totals are the mathematical sums of the columns. Individual estimates in this table are based on the assumption that no other changes are made in the tax law. Consequently the aggregate revenue effect will not equal the sum of the revenue effects of the individual items shown.

Table C-15. Estimated Federal Budget Outlays and Tax Expenditures,[a] by Budget Function, Fiscal Years 1976 and 1977

Millions of dollars unless otherwise specified

Budget function	Total budget outlays		Tax expenditures		Tax expenditures as percent of budget outlays	
	1976	1977	1976	1977	1976	1977
National defense	90,216	101,129	730	740	0.8	0.7
International affairs	4,462	6,824	2,115	2,050	47.4	30.0
General science, space, and technology	4,197	4,507	0	0	...	...
Natural resources, environment, and energy	11,674	13,772	2,840	3,190	24.3	23.2
Agriculture	1,994	1,729	1,390	1,535	69.7	88.8
Commerce and transportation	17,239	16,498	44,245	47,855	256.7	290.1
Community and regional development	5,023	5,532	90	65	1.8	1.2
Education, training, employment, and social services	17,678	16,615	5,193	5,626	29.4	33.9
Health	33,601	34,393	6,617	7,324	19.7	21.3
Income security	126,896	137,115	22,755	24,435	17.9	17.8
Veterans' benefits and services	18,444	17,196	950	905	5.2	5.3
Law enforcement and justice	3,325	3,426	0	0	...	...
Interest	35,500	41,297	605	685	1.7	1.7
General government	2,951	3,433	40	65	1.4	1.9
Revenue sharing and general purpose assistance	7,114	7,351	10,915	11,505	153.4	156.5
Total (excluding undistributed offsetting receipts)	380,314	410,817	98,485[b]	105,980[b]	25.9[b]	25.8[b]

Sources: Budget outlays, 1976, Department of the Treasury; 1977, *The Budget of the United States Government, Fiscal Year 1977*, pp. 360–64. Tax expenditures, table C-14.
a. For definition of tax expenditures, see table C-14, note a.
b. The totals are the mathematical sums of the columns. Individual estimates in this table are based on the assumption that no other changes are made in the tax law. Consequently the aggregate revenue effect will not equal the sum of the revenue effects of the individual items shown.

Table C-16. Schedule of Transition to the Current Payment System for Corporations
Percentage of tax liability due in each installment

Income year	Income year April	June	Sep-tem-ber	De-cem-ber	Following year March	June	Sep-tem-ber	De-cem-ber	Total
1949	...	...	...	...	25	25	25	25	100
1950	...	...	...	...	30	30	20	20	100
1951	...	...	...	...	35	35	15	15	100
1952	...	...	...	...	40	40	10	10	100
1953	...	...	...	...	45	45	5	5	100
1954	...	...	...	...	50	50	...	...	100
1955a	...	...	5	5	45	45	...	...	100
1956a	...	...	10	10	40	40	...	...	100
1957a	...	...	15	15	35	35	...	...	100
1958a	...	...	20	20	30	30	...	...	100
1959a	...	...	25	25	25	25	...	...	100
1960a	...	...	25	25	25	25	...	...	100
1961a	...	...	25	25	25	25	...	...	100
1962a	...	...	25	25	25	25	...	...	100
1963a	...	...	25	25	25	25	...	...	100
1964a	1	1	25	25	24	24	...	...	100
1965a	4	4	25	25	21	21	...	...	100
1966a	12	12	25	25	13	13	...	...	100
1967a and later yearsb	25	25	25	25	...	...	...	...	100

Sources: Same as table A-1.
a. Applicable only to tax liability in excess of $100,000. The first $100,000 of a corporation's tax liability was paid in equal installments in March and June of the following year.
b. Beginning in 1968, the $100,000 exclusion was reduced to $5,500. A transitional exemption was provided for 1968–71 (80 percent in 1968, 60 percent in 1969, 40 percent in 1970, and 20 percent in 1971). A second transitional period began in 1972 that put corporations on a completely current basis in 1977.

Table C-17. Selected Ratios Relating to the Corporate Sector, 1929–75

Year	National income originating in corporate business as percent of income originating in business (1)	Gross domestic corporate product as percent of gross business domestic product (2)	Gross corporate saving as percent of gross national product (3)	Property income as percent of gross corporate product less indirect taxes[a] (4)	Dividends as percent of domestic corporate cash flow, nonfinancial corporations[b] (5)
1929	58.1	56.1	7.2	31.8	45.6
1930	57.9	56.8	5.5	29.0	77.3
1931	55.3	53.5	2.4	23.7	118.8
1932	52.6	51.7	−0.3	18.5	218.2
1933	52.8	52.5	0.1	17.4	52.6
1934	57.2	56.2	3.1	24.5	46.9
1935	56.0	56.0	4.4	26.8	43.9
1936	59.1	56.8	4.0	28.6	55.3
1937	59.3	58.1	4.7	27.3	54.4
1938	57.3	56.0	5.2	25.7	47.3
1939	59.0	57.1	5.3	26.7	39.3
1940	61.1	59.1	6.8	30.3	36.7
1941	62.3	60.6	6.0	32.6	30.3
1942	61.9	61.3	6.1	32.9	27.3
1943	62.8	62.4	5.8	31.9	26.5
1944	62.3	60.4	5.8	30.8	26.9
1945	59.0	57.2	4.8	28.5	30.2
1946	56.2	56.3	4.5	24.8	28.3
1947	60.2	59.1	5.9	27.0	24.5
1948	61.0	60.5	7.9	29.7	24.3
1949	61.3	60.1	8.3	29.4	27.8
1950	62.7	61.2	6.9	31.0	26.1
1951	63.5	61.4	6.6	30.5	27.9
1952	63.4	61.6	6.8	28.4	28.6
1953	64.6	62.5	6.5	27.1	27.2
1954	64.0	61.9	7.1	27.4	26.4
1955	65.8	63.7	8.0	29.6	24.2
1956	66.2	64.8	7.6	27.8	25.1
1957	66.1	64.6	7.5	27.3	25.3
1958	64.4	63.0	7.3	26.6	26.2
1959	66.6	65.1	8.0	28.2	23.8
1960	67.0	65.8	7.6	26.9	25.6
1961	66.9	65.6	7.5	26.7	25.6
1962	68.1	66.4	8.1	27.4	24.1
1963	68.7	67.0	8.1	27.8	24.7
1964	69.3	67.9	8.4	28.1	23.8

Table C-17 (*continued*)

Year	National income originating in corporate business as percent of income originating in business (1)	Gross domestic corporate product as percent of gross business domestic product (2)	Gross corporate saving as percent of gross national product (3)	Property income as percent of gross corporate product less indirect taxes[a] (4)	Dividends as percent of domestic corporate cash flow, nonfinancial corporations[b] (5)
1965	70.0	68.7	8.8	29.0	23.4
1966	70.8	69.3	8.8	28.8	22.8
1967	71.1	69.6	8.4	27.6	23.4
1968	72.1	70.6	7.9	27.4	24.4
1969	72.8	71.4	7.3	25.7	24.0
1970	72.7	71.2	6.7	24.1	24.1
1971	72.8	71.1	7.3	24.9	21.7
1972	73.3	71.6	9.6	25.3	20.1
1973	72.8	71.3	8.9	24.1	19.3
1974	73.3	71.2	7.6	22.3	22.1
1975	73.2	71.3	9.2	24.4	20.6

Sources: Department of Commerce, Bureau of Economic Analysis.

a. Property income includes corporate profits before taxes with inventory valuation and capital consumption adjustments, capital consumption allowances with capital consumption adjustment, and net interest.

b. Cash flow is net corporate profits after taxes plus corporate capital consumption allowances before capital consumption adjustment.

Table C-18. Rates of Return before and after Federal Income Tax, Manufacturing Corporations, 1927–41, 1948–61, and 1964–71

Percent

Year	Rate of return				Debt–capital ratio[d]	General corporation income tax rate
	On equity capital[a]		On total capital[b]			
	Before tax	After tax[c]	Before tax	After tax[c]		
1927	7.5	6.5	7.6	6.7	15.1	13.5
1928	9.1	8.0	9.0	8.0	15.6	12.0
1929	9.9	8.8	9.6	8.7	14.9	11.0
1930	2.1	1.5	2.9	2.4	15.3	12.0
1931	−1.6	−2.0	−0.4	−0.6	15.4	12.0
1932	−3.9	−4.2	−2.3	−2.5	15.5	13.75
1933	0.5	0.0	1.3	0.9	15.5	13.75
1934	2.4	1.8	2.8	2.3	13.7	13.75
1935	4.8	3.9	4.9	4.1	14.9	13.75
1936	9.5	8.0	8.8	7.5	14.2	15.0
1937	9.2	7.6	8.6	7.3	15.4	15.0
1938	3.9	3.0	3.9	3.2	15.4	19.0
1939	8.5	7.0	7.9	6.6	14.9	19.0
1940	12.2	8.7	11.1	8.1	14.4	24.0
1941	22.3	11.7	19.6	10.6	14.9	31.0
1948	22.4	14.0	19.5	12.4	15.7	38.0
1949	16.4	10.1	14.5	9.2	14.7	38.0
1950	25.4	14.3	22.2	12.8	14.8	42.0
1951	24.5	10.9	21.2	9.8	17.3	50.75
1952	18.9	8.3	16.2	7.5	19.2	52.0
1953	19.1	8.5	16.2	7.6	19.1	52.0
1954	15.6	7.9	13.4	7.2	18.9	52.0
1955	20.6	10.8	17.6	9.5	18.2	52.0
1956	18.2	9.6	15.5	8.5	20.0	52.0
1957	15.9	7.8	13.6	7.2	20.5	52.0
1958	12.2	6.4	10.7	6.1	20.4	52.0
1959	15.8	8.4	13.6	7.7	20.4	52.0
1960	13.4	7.0	11.7	6.6	20.6	52.0
1961	13.0	7.0	11.4	6.6	20.6	52.0
1964	16.4	9.8	14.1	8.9	22.3	50.0
1965	18.9	11.6	15.8	10.2	23.9	48.0
1966	19.5	12.1	16.1	10.5	26.6	48.0
1967	16.5	10.3	13.7	9.2	27.7	48.0
1968	16.9	9.8	13.9	8.9	29.9	52.8
1969	14.5	8.3	12.3	8.0	32.1	52.8
1970	10.5	6.2	9.8	6.9	34.5	49.2
1971	12.3	7.6	10.6	7.5	34.3	48.0

Sources: 1935–58, Marian Krzyzaniak and Richard A. Musgrave, *The Shifting of the Corporation Income Tax* (Johns Hopkins Press, 1963), p. 73; other years, *Statistics of Income, Corporation Income Tax Returns*.

a. Equity capital is average of book value of stock and undistributed surplus at the beginning and end of the year.

b. Profits plus interest paid as percentage of average equity capital plus debt capital at the beginning and end of the year.

c. For 1927–49, 1952, and 1957, no allowances have been made for the foreign tax credit. The rates of return are therefore slightly understated, probably by 0.3 percentage point or less.

d. End of year.

Table C-19. Sources and Uses of Funds, Nonfarm Nonfinancial Corporate Business, 1960, 1965, 1970, 1975

Source or use of funds	Amount (billions of dollars)				Percentage distribution			
	1960	1965	1970	1975	1960	1965	1970	1975
Source								
Internal	34.4	56.6	58.7	105.3	72.6	61.9	57.0	71.5
Undistributed profits	10.0	23.1	9.7	33.6	21.1	25.3	9.4	22.8
Corporate inventory valuation adjustment	0.2	-1.7	-3.6	-17.1	0.4	-1.9	-3.5	-11.6
Capital consumption allowances	24.2	35.2	52.7	88.8	51.1	38.5	51.2	60.3
External	12.9	34.8	44.2	42.0	27.2	38.1	43.0	28.5
Stocks	1.5	-0.1	5.7	9.5	3.2	-0.1	5.5	6.4
Bonds	3.5	5.4	19.8	29.6	7.4	5.9	19.2	20.1
Mortgages	2.5	3.9	5.2	8.5	5.3	4.3	5.1	5.8
Bank loans[a]	2.2	10.6	5.6	-12.7	4.6	11.6	5.4	-8.6
Other loans	2.2	0.6	3.3	-0.8	4.6	0.7	3.2	-0.5
Trade debt	3.1	12.1	7.4	11.2	6.5	13.2	7.2	7.6
Profits tax liability	-2.2	2.2	-3.7	-4.2	-4.6	2.4	-3.6	-2.9
Other liabilities	0.1	0.1	1.0	0.9	0.2	0.1	1.0	0.6
Sources, total	47.4	91.4	102.9	147.3	100.0	100.0	100.0	100.0

Use								
Purchases of physical assets	38.7	62.3	82.0	98.8	93.5	75.5	86.3	73.0
Nonresidential fixed investment	34.6	52.3	73.2	108.9	83.6	63.4	77.1	80.5
Residential structures	1.1	2.0	3.8	3.5	2.7	2.4	4.0	2.6
Change in business inventories	3.0	7.9	5.0	-13.6	7.2	9.6	5.3	-10.1
Increase in financial assets	2.6	20.2	12.9	36.5	6.3	24.5	13.6	27.0
Liquid assets	-4.1	2.6	-0.4	18.4	-9.9	3.2	-0.4	13.6
Demand deposits and currency	-1.8	0.3	0.9	2.0	-4.3	0.4	0.9	1.5
Time deposits	2.4	2.3	1.7	-3.7	5.8	2.8	1.8	-2.7
U.S. government securities	-6.0	-2.5	0.5	16.1	-14.5	-3.0	0.5	11.9
Commercial paper	1.6	0.5	0.5	1.8	3.9	0.6	0.5	1.3
State and local obligations	-0.3	0.9	-0.6	-0.2	-0.7	1.1	-0.6	-0.1
Security repurchase agreement	0.0	1.1	-3.4	2.2	0.0	1.3	-3.6	1.6
Consumer credit	0.4	0.2	0.7	1.1	1.0	0.2	0.7	0.8
Trade credit	4.0	14.0	8.4	9.7	9.7	17.0	8.8	7.2
Other financial assets	2.3	3.4	4.2	7.4	5.6	4.1	4.4	5.5
Uses, total	41.4	82.5	95.0	135.3	100.0	100.0	100.0	100.0
Discrepancy (sources less uses)	6.0	8.9	8.0	12.0	...	...	...	...

Source: Board of Governors of the Federal Reserve System. Figures are rounded.

a. Not elsewhere classified.

                                                  Federal Tax Policy

Table C-20. Assets of Selected Federal Trust Funds, Fiscal Years 1937–76
Billions of dollars

June 30	Old age and survivors insurance	Disability insurance	Hospital insurance	Supplementary medical insurance	Unemployment insurance	Railroad retirement
1937	0.3	...	...	...	0.3	*
1938	0.8	...	...	...	0.9	0.1
1939	1.2	...	...	...	1.3	0.1
1940	1.7	...	...	...	1.7	0.1
1941	2.4	...	...	...	2.3	0.1
1942	3.2	...	...	...	3.2	0.1
1943	4.3	...	...	...	4.4	0.2
1944	5.4	...	...	...	5.9	0.3
1945	6.6	...	...	...	7.3	0.5
1946	7.6	...	...	...	7.4	0.7
1947	8.8	...	...	...	7.9	0.8
1948	10.0	...	...	...	8.3	1.4
1949	11.3	...	...	...	8.2	1.8
1950	12.9	...	...	...	7.4	2.2
1951	14.7	...	...	...	8.1	2.5
1952	16.6	...	...	...	8.7	2.9
1953	18.4	...	...	...	9.2	3.2
1954	20.0	...	...	...	9.0	3.4
1955	21.1	...	...	...	8.5	3.5
1956	22.6	...	...	...	8.8	3.7
1957	23.0	0.3	...	...	9.1	3.7
1958	22.8	1.1	...	...	7.8	3.7
1959	21.5	1.7	...	...	6.7	3.6
1960	20.8	2.2	...	...	6.7	3.9
1961	20.9	2.5	...	...	5.8	3.8
1962	19.7	2.5	...	...	5.8	3.8
1963	19.0	2.4	...	...	6.3	3.8
1964	19.7	2.3	...	...	6.9	3.9
1965	20.2	2.0	...	...	7.9	4.0
1966	19.9	1.7	0.9	...	9.3	4.2
1967	23.5	2.0	1.3	0.5	10.6	4.5
1968	25.5	2.6	1.4	0.3	11.6	4.6
1969	28.2	3.7	2.0	0.4	12.7	4.7
1970	32.6	5.1	2.7	0.1	13.1	4.9
1971	34.3	6.4	3.1	0.3	11.3	4.9
1972	36.4	7.4	2.9	0.5	9.8	4.8
1973	36.4	7.9	4.4	0.7	11.1	4.6
1974	37.9	8.3	7.9	1.3	12.4	4.6
1975	40.0	8.2	9.9	1.4	7.2	4.3
1976ᵃ	45.2ᵇ	ᵇ	12.4ᶜ	ᶜ	5.6	4.1

Sources: *Treasury Bulletin* (August 1944, 1952, 1961, 1970, and November 1975); *Special Analyses, Budget of the United States Government, Fiscal Year 1977*, p. 43.
* Less than $50 million.
a. Estimated.
b. Disability insurance is included in old age and survivors insurance.
c. Supplementary medical insurance is included in hospital insurance.

Table C-21. Number of Estate Tax Returns, Value of Estates, and Amount of Tax, by Size of Gross Estate, 1973[a]

Millions of dollars unless otherwise specified

Size of gross estate (dollars)	Number of returns	Gross estate	Estate tax before state tax credit[b]	State death tax credit	Estate tax after credit
60,000–100,000	64,966	5,133	35	*	35
100,000–150,000	45,942	5,592	160	2	158
150,000–200,000	21,476	3,695	215	5	210
200,000–300,000	18,918	4,577	421	17	404
300,000–500,000	12,283	4,667	598	36	562
500,000–1,000,000	7,286	4,952	802	67	734
1,000,000–2,000,000[c]	2,662	3,745	699	79	620
2,000,000–3,000,000	652	1,571	363	49	314
3,000,000–5,000,000	405	1,534	384	56	328
5,000,000–10,000,000	220	1,505	433	70	363
10,000,000 and over	89	1,900	521	94	426
Total	174,899	38,869	4,630	477	4,153

Source: *Statistics of Income—1972, Estate Tax Returns*, table 1. Figures are rounded.

* $500,000 or less.

a. Returns are classified by the year in which they were filed.

b. Estate tax after credit for federal gift taxes, foreign death taxes, and estate tax on prior transfers, but before state death taxes.

c. The $1,000,000–$2,000,000 gross estate class contains data for 93 nontaxable returns of $1,000,000 and over for which a more detailed breakdown by size of gross estate is not available. The gross estate for the 93 returns was $241 million.

Table C-22. Number of Gift Tax Returns, and Amounts of Gifts and Gift Tax, by Size of Total Gifts before Splitting, 1966[a]

Millions of dollars unless otherwise specified

Size of total gifts before splitting (dollars)	Number of returns	Total gifts[b]	Taxable gifts			Gift tax, current year
			Current year	Prior years	All years	
Taxable returns	**29,547**	**2,373**	**1,455**	**2,949**	**4,404**	**413**
No total gifts before splitting[c]	4,615	...	198	287	485	47
Under 10,000	3,199	19	21	171	192	4
10,000–20,000	3,897	57	45	264	309	15
20,000–30,000	2,970	73	27	157	184	3
30,000–40,000	2,870	100	34	134	168	5
40,000–50,000	2,394	106	34	100	134	4
50,000–100,000	5,613	393	147	304	451	20
100,000–500,000	3,462	638	365	649	1,014	79
500,000–1,000,000	291	202	126	227	353	34
1,000,000–2,000,000	144	198	120	173	293	36
2,000,000–3,000,000	40	95	51	89	140	18
3,000,000–5,000,000	25	98	48	64	112	18
5,000–000–10,000,000	16	103	50	28	78	20
10,000,000 and over	10	292	189	301	490	109
Nontaxable returns	**83,249**	**1,589**	...	**1,026**[d]	**1,026**[d]	...
Total, all returns	**112,796**	**3,962**	**1,455**	**3,975**	**5,430**	**413**

Source: *Statistics of Income, Fiduciary, Gift, and Estate Tax Returns, 1965*, pp. 41, 50–51. Figures are rounded.

a. Returns are classified by the year in which they were filed. Data after 1966 are not published.

b. Total gifts are before splitting provision for gifts by and between husband and wife.

c. Taxed on spouse's gifts, under gift splitting provisions.

d. Returns were nontaxable for current year gifts but taxable for prior year gifts.

**Table C-23. General Expenditure of State and Local Governments,
by Major Function, Fiscal Years 1964 and 1974**

Millions of dollars unless otherwise specified

				Increase 1964–74	
	Amount			Percentage distribution of increase	Percentage increase
Function	*1964*	*1974*	*Amount*	*increase*	*increase*
	Total state and local				
Total general expenditure[a]	69,302	198,618	129,316	100.0	186.6
Education	26,533	75,833	49,300	38.1	185.8
Highways	11,664	19,946	8,282	6.4	71.0
Public welfare	5,766	24,745	18,979	14.7	329.2
Health and hospitals	4,910	15,945	11,035	8.5	224.7
Police and fire	3,588	10,326	6,738	5.2	187.8
Natural resources	1,835	3,661	1,826	1.4	99.5
Sewerage and other sanitation	2,267	5,995	3,728	2.9	164.4
Housing and urban renewal	1,142	3,461	2,319	1.8	203.1
General control and financial administration	2,567	7,536	4,969	3.8	193.6
Interest on debt	2,356	7,666	5,310	4.1	225.4
Other	6,674	23,504	16,830	13.0	252.2
	State				
Total general expenditure[a,b]	24,275	73,950	49,675	100.0	204.6
Education	5,711	19,753	14,042	28.3	245.9
Highways	7,850	12,636	4,786	9.6	61.0
Public welfare	2,796	15,169	12,373	24.9	442.5
Health and hospitals	2,464	7,495	5,031	10.1	204.2
Police	315	1,145	830	1.7	263.5
Natural resources	1,185	2,917	1,732	3.5	146.2
Housing and urban renewal	17	382	365	0.7	2,147.1
General control and financial administration	871	2,799	1,928	3.9	221.4
Interest on debt	765	2,863	2,098	4.2	274.2
Other	2,301	8,791	6,490	13.1	282.1

Table C-23 (*continued*)

| | Amount | | Increase 1964–74 | | |
Function	1964	1974	Amount	Percent-age distri-bution of increase	Percent-age increase
			Local		
Total general expenditure[a,b]	45,027	124,668	79,641	100.0	176.9
Education	20,822	56,080	35,258	44.3	169.3
Highways	3,814	7,310	3,496	4.4	91.7
Public welfare	2,970	9,576	6,606	8.3	222.4
Health and hospitals	2,446	8,451	6,005	7.5	245.5
Police and fire	3,273	9,181	5,908	7.4	180.5
Natural resources	650	744	94	0.1	14.5
Sewerage and other sanitation	2,267	5,995	3,728	4.7	164.4
Housing and urban renewal	1,125	3,079	1,954	2.5	173.7
General control and financial adminis-tration	1,697	4,737	3,040	3.8	179.1
Interest on debt	1,590	4,803	3,213	4.0	202.1
Other	4,373	14,712	10,339	13.0	236.4

Sources: Bureau of the Census, *Governmental Finances in 1963–64*, p. 25; *Governmental Finances in 1973–74*, p. 23. Figures are rounded.

a. Excludes insurance trust, utility, and liquor store expenditures. Includes federal grants-in-aid.

b. Grants-in-aid are shown according to final spending level.

Table C-24. General Revenue of State and Local Governments, by Source, Fiscal Years 1964 and 1974

Millions of dollars unless otherwise specified

Source	Amount 1964	Amount 1974	Increase 1964–74 Amount	Percentage distribution of total increase	Percentage distribution of revenue from own sources
Total state and local					
General revenue[a]	68,443	207,730	139,287	100.0	...
Revenue from federal government[b]	10,002	41,831	31,829	22.9	...
General revenue from own sources	58,440	165,899	107,459	77.1	100.0
Taxes	47,785	130,722	82,937	59.5	77.2
Property	21,241	47,754	26,513	19.0	24.7
Sales and gross receipts	15,762	46,098	30,336	21.8	28.2
Individual income	3,791	19,491	15,700	11.3	14.6
Corporation income	1,695	6,015	4,320	3.1	4.0
Other	5,295	11,364	6,069	4.4	5.6
Charges and miscellaneous	10,655	35,177	24,522	17.6	22.8
State					
General revenue[c]	37,648	122,327	84,679	100.0	...
Revenue from federal government[b]	9,046	31,632	22,586	26.7	...
Revenue from local governments	417	1,538	1,121	1.3	...
General revenue from own sources	28,184	89,157	60,973	72.0	100.0
Taxes	24,243	74,207	49,964	59.0	81.9
Property	722	1,301	579	0.7	0.9
Sales and gross receipts	13,957	40,556	26,599	31.4	43.6
Individual income	3,415	17,078	13,663	16.1	22.4
Corporation income	1,695	6,015	4,320	5.1	7.1
Other	4,454	9,257	4,803	5.7	7.9
Charges and miscellaneous	3,942	14,950	11,008	13.0	18.1
Local					
General revenue[d]	44,084	131,494	87,410	100.0	...
Revenue from federal government[b]	956	10,199	9,243	10.6	...
Revenue from state governments	12,873	44,553	31,680	36.2	...

Table C-24 (*continued*)

Source	Amount		Increase 1964–74		
				Percentage distribution of total	Percentage distribution of revenue from own
	1964	1974	Amount	increase	sources
General revenue from own sources	30,256	76,742	46,486	53.2	100.0
Taxes	23,542	56,515	32,973	37.7	70.9
Property	20,519	46,452	25,933	29.7	55.8
Sales and gross receipts	1,806	5,542	3,736	4.3	8.0
Individual income	376	2,413	2,037	2.3	4.4
Other	841	2,108	1,267	1.4	2.7
Charges and miscellaneous	6,714	20,227	13,513	15.5	29.1

Sources: Same as table C-23 (pp. 22 and 20, respectively, of the sources). Figures are rounded.

a. Excludes insurance trust, liquor store, and utility revenues. Total state and local general revenue does not equal the sum of state general revenue and local general revenue because duplicative transactions between state and local governments are excluded.

b. Includes grants-in-aid, shared taxes, payments for services performed on a reimbursement or cost-sharing basis, and payments in lieu of taxes. Excludes loans and commodities or other aids in kind.

c. Excludes insurance trust and liquor store revenues.

d. Excludes insurance trust, liquor store, and utility revenues.

Table C-25. State and Local Government Debt, Fiscal Years 1959–74

End of fiscal year	Debt outstanding	
	Amount (millions of dollars)	Index (1959 = 100)
1959	64,110	100.0
1960	69,955	109.1
1961	75,023	117.0
1962	81,278	126.8
1963	85,056	132.7
1964	92,222	143.8
1965	99,512	155.2
1966	107,051	167.0
1967	113,659	177.3
1968	121,158	189.0
1969	133,548	208.3
1970	143,570	223.9
1971	158,827	247.7
1972	174,502	272.2
1973	188,485	294.0
1974	206,616	322.3
1975	221,224	345.1

Sources: *Governmental Finances*, annual issues.

Table C-26. Major Tax Sources Used by the States, January 1, 1977

Tax	States using tax
Sales	Forty-five states and the District of Columbia; exceptions are Alaska, Delaware, Montana, New Hampshire, Oregon
Individual income	Forty-one states and the District of Columbia; exceptions are Connecticut, Florida, Nevada, New Hampshire, South Dakota, Tennessee, Texas, Washington, Wyoming
Corporation income	Forty-five states and the District of Columbia; exceptions are Nevada, South Dakota, Texas, Washington, Wyoming
Estate and inheritance tax[a]	Forty-nine states and the District of Columbia; exception is Nevada
Motor fuel	All fifty states and the District of Columbia
Cigarette	All fifty states and the District of Columbia
Alcoholic beverage	All fifty states and the District of Columbia

Source: Advisory Commission on Intergovernmental Relations.

a. Sixteen states also impose a gift tax: California, Colorado, Delaware, Louisiana, Minnesota, New York, North Carolina, Oklahoma, Oregon, Rhode Island, South Carolina, Tennessee, Vermont, Virginia, Washington, Wisconsin.

Table C-27. Marginal Burden of State Individual and Corporation Income Taxes before and after Allowing for Federal and State Deductibility, July 1, 1975

Percent

State	Individual income tax					Corporation income tax	
	Range of state's nominal rates	Highest marginal state tax burden[a]		Marginal burden of state tax in		State's highest nominal rate	Marginal burden of state tax in highest federal tax bracket
		Taxable income class (thousands of dollars)	As percent of taxable income	Lowest federal tax bracket	Highest federal tax bracket		
Alabama[b]	1.5–5.0	5–8	3.3	1.1	0.5	5.0	1.4
Alaska[c]	3.0–14.5	44–52	4.8	2.6	4.4[d]	9.4	4.9
Arizona[e]	2.0–8.0	12–16	4.2	1.4	0.7	10.5	2.7
Arkansas[c]	1.0–7.0	15–16	4.5	0.9	2.1	6.0	3.1
California[e]	1.0–11.0	31–32	6.7	0.9	3.3	9.0	4.7
Colorado[b]	3.0–8.0	10–12	5.0	2.2	0.8	5.0	2.6[c]
Connecticut[f]	...	...	...	...	...	10.0	4.7
Delaware[e,g]	1.6–19.8	50–52	7.7	1.0	5.9	7.2	3.7
Florida[c]	...	...	...	...	...	5.0	2.6
Georgia[c]	1.0–6.0	10–12	4.7	0.9	1.8	6.0	3.1
Hawaii[f]	2.25–11.0	10–12	6.1	1.9	3.0	6.35	3.1
Idaho[e]	2.0–7.5	10–12	5.8	1.7	2.2	6.5	3.4
Illinois[e]	2.5	0–1	2.2	2.2	0.8	4.0	2.1
Indiana[e]	2.0	0–1	1.7	1.7	0.6	5.5	2.9
Iowa[b]	0.75–7.0	9–12	4.3	0.6	0.7	10.0	2.8
Kansas[b]	2.0–6.5	14–16	3.7	1.5	0.6	6.8	3.5[c]
Kentucky[b]	2.0–6.0	8–12	3.7	1.5	0.6	5.8	3.0[e]
Louisiana[b]	2.0–6.0	20–24	1.9	1.5	0.6	4.0	1.1
Maine[e]	1.0–6.0	20–24	2.7	0.9	1.8	7.0	3.6
Maryland[e]	2.0–5.0	3–4	4.2	1.7	1.5	7.0	3.6
Massachusetts[e]	5.0	0–1	4.3	4.3	1.5	8.6	4.4
Michigan[e]	3.9	0–1	3.4	3.4	1.2	7.8	4.1
Minnesota[b]	1.6–15.0	12.5–16	8.2	1.2	1.5	12.0	6.2[c]
Mississippi[e]	3.0–4.0	5–8	3.2	2.6	1.2	4.0	2.1
Missouri[b]	1.5–6.0	9–12	3.7	1.1	0.6	5.0	1.4

Montana[b]	2.2–12.1	14–16	5.7	1.6	1.2	6.75	3.5[o]
Nebraska[f]	1.68–8.4[h]	40–44	2.8	1.4	2.3	3.3	1.7
New Hampshire[e]	...	...	...	...	...	7.0	3.6
New Jersey[e,i]	2.0–2.5	0–1	1.7	1.7	0.8	5.5	2.9
New Mexico[f]	0.9–9.0	40–44	3.8	0.8	2.5	5.0	2.5
New York[e]	2.05–15.38	25–28	9.8	1.8	4.6	9.0	4.7
North Carolina[e]	3.0–7.0	10–12	5.5	2.6	2.1	6.0	3.1
North Dakota[b]	0.75–7.5	8–12	4.6	0.6	0.7	6.0	1.7
Ohio[e]	0.5–3.5	20–24	2.0	0.4	1.0	8.0	4.2
Oklahoma[e,j]	0.5–6.0	15–16	4.2	0.3	1.7	4.0	2.0[f]
Oregon[c,k]	4.0–10.0	20–24	6.8	2.6	3.0	6.0	3.1
Pennsylvania[e]	2.0	0–1	1.7	1.7	0.6	9.5	4.5[f]
Rhode Island[e]	2.38–11.9[l]	44–52	4.2	2.0	3.6	8.0	4.2
South Carolina[e,m]	2.0–7.0	10–12	5.5	1.5	2.1	6.0	3.1
Tennessee[f]	...	...	...	...	...	6.0	2.9
Utah[b]	3.0–8.0	7.5–8	5.3	2.2	0.8	6.0	1.7
Vermont[f]	3.81–19.07[n]	40–44	6.0	3.2	4.8	7.5	3.6
Virginia[e]	2.0–5.75	12–16	4.3	1.7	1.7	6.0	3.1
West Virginia[e]	2.1–9.6	40–44	3.1	1.8	2.9[d]	6.0	3.1
Wisconsin[f]	3.1–11.4	14–16	7.7	2.6	3.1	7.9	2.1[e,o]
District of Columbia[e]	2.0–10.0	17–20	6.5	1.7	3.0	8.0	4.2

Source: Basic data are from Advisory Commission on Intergovernmental Relations, *Federal-State-Local Finances: Significant Features of Fiscal Federalism* (1974–75 edition), tables 16 and 23.

a. The marginal state tax burden is defined as the percent of an additional dollar of income that is taken in taxes as a result of the state income tax, using rates for married couples filing joint returns. Federal and state taxable income are assumed to be equal.

b. State tax deductible against federal tax and federal tax deductible against state tax.

c. State tax deductible against federal tax.

d. The state tax includes several rates within the highest federal tax bracket. This number is for the highest state bracket.

e. State tax deductible against federal tax, federal tax deductible against state tax, and state tax deductible against state tax.

f. State tax deductible against federal tax and state tax deductible against state tax.

g. Federal deductibility limited to $600 for joint returns.

h. State tax is 12 percent of federal liabilities.

i. New Jersey had no income tax in 1975. These rates are those in a law passed in July 1976.

j. Federal income tax deductibility limited to $500, plus 5 percent of taxes in excess of $500 up to a $1,700 maximum. This table assumes deductibility only up to the point where federal taxes equal $500.

k. Federal deductibility limited to $5,000.

l. State tax is 17 percent of federal liabilities.

m. Federal deductibility limited to $500 per taxpayer ($1,000 for joint returns).

n. State tax is 25 percent of federal liabilities, plus a 9 percent surcharge.

o. Deductibility of federal corporation income taxes limited to 10 percent of corporate net income before federal tax.

Bibliographical Notes

Chapter 1. Introduction

Among standard textbooks in public finance devoting considerable space to federal taxation are the following: John F. Due and Ann F. Friedlaender, *Government Finance: Economics of the Public Sector,* 5th ed. (Richard D. Irwin, 1973); James M. Buchanan and Marilyn R. Flowers, *The Public Finances: An Introductory Textbook,* 4th ed. (Richard D. Irwin, 1975); Richard A. Musgrave and Peggy B. Musgrave, *Public Finance in Theory and Practice,* 2d ed. (McGraw-Hill, 1976).

The most authoritative advanced books are by Richard A. Musgrave, *The Theory of Public Finance* (McGraw-Hill, 1959); Carl S. Shoup, *Public Finance* (Aldine, 1969); Alan S. Blinder and others, *The Economics of Public Finance* (Brookings Institution, 1974); and Arnold C. Harberger, *Taxation and Welfare* (Little, Brown, 1974).

Outstanding articles in the history of taxation are reprinted in Richard A. Musgrave and Alan T. Peacock, eds., *Classics in the Theory of Public Finance* (Macmillan, 1958); and in Richard A. Musgrave and Carl S. Shoup, eds., *Readings in the Economics of Taxation* (Richard D. Irwin, 1959).

The articles on "Taxation," in the *International Encyclopedia of the Social Sciences* (Macmillan and Free Press, 1968), vol. 15, pp. 521–60, give a general overview of the objectives of taxation and analyses of the major taxes now in use in the United States and other countries. Reviews of the literature on the incidence and economic effects of taxation are provided by Peter Mieszkowski, "Tax Incidence Theory: The Effects of Taxes on the Distribution of Income," *Journal of Economic Literature,* vol. 7 (December 1969), pp. 1103–24; and by George F. Break, "The Incidence and Economic Effects of Taxation," in *The Economics of Public Finance* (cited above).

For a competent and imaginative analysis of the requirements of a modern tax system, see the Canadian *Report of the Royal Commission on Taxation* (Carter Commission), 6 vols., and the accompanying *Studies of the Royal Commission on Taxation,* 30 vols. (Ottawa: Queen's Printer, 1966 and 1967).

Methods used to estimate the distribution of federal, state, and local tax burdens by income classes are described in detail by Joseph A. Pechman and Benjamin A. Okner, *Who Bears the Tax Burden?* (Brookings Institution, 1974).

Chapter 2. Taxes and Economic Policy

Methods of assessing the economic impact of the government budget are evaluated by Joergen Lotz, "Techniques of Measuring the Effects of Fiscal Policy," in Organisation for Economic Co-operation and Development, *OECD Economic Outlook, Occasional Studies* (Paris: OECD, July 1971). Wilfred Lewis, Jr., in *Federal Fiscal Policy in the Postwar Recessions* (Brookings Institution, 1962), measures the quantitative impact of the automatic stabilizers and discretionary actions taken during the recessions and recoveries after the Second World War.

The various budget concepts in use by the federal government and a proposed revision of the budget, which was later adopted as the official unified budget, are discussed in *Report of the President's Commission on Budget Concepts* and *Staff Papers and Other Materials Reviewed by the President's Commission* (Government Printing Office, 1967). The economic implications of various budget concepts are analyzed in Wilfred Lewis, Jr., ed., *Budget Concepts for Economic Analysis* (Brookings Institution, 1968).

The concept of the full employment surplus and the role of tax policy in economic decisions are lucidly presented in *Economic Report of the President, January 1962,* pp. 70–84. The concept is integrated into the analysis of saving and investment in *Economic Report of the President, January 1966,* pp. 42–44. For an able defense of the full employment budget and an analysis of the problems of interpretation during inflationary periods, see Arthur M. Okun and Nancy H. Teeters, "The Full Employment Surplus Revisited," *Brookings Papers on Economic Activity, 1:1970,* pp. 77–110. Also worth reading are the rationale for the 1964 tax cut in *Economic Report of the President, January 1963,* pp. 66–83, and Walter W.

Heller, *New Dimensions of Political Economy* (Harvard University Press, 1966); and the discussion of the Employment Act on its twentieth anniversary in *Economic Report of the President, January 1966,* pp. 170–86.

The budget policy of the Committee for Economic Development was first presented in *Taxes and the Budget: A Program for Prosperity in a Free Economy,* A Statement on National Policy by the Research and Policy Committee (CED, 1947). A shorter version of the policy is given in the CED's pamphlet *The Stabilizing Budget Policy: What It Is and How It Works* (CED, 1950). For a discussion and critique of this policy, see Walter W. Heller, "CED's Stabilizing Budget Policy after Ten Years," *American Economic Review,* vol. 47 (September 1957), pp. 634–51 (reprinted in *Readings in Business Cycles* [Richard D. Irwin, 1965], pp. 696–712).

Much has been written about fiscal policy and its impact on economic growth and stability. For a sample of the best in this literature, see Paul A. Samuelson, "Principles and Rules in Modern Fiscal Policy: A Neo-Classical Reformulation," *Money, Trade, and Economic Growth: In Honor of John Henry Williams* (Macmillan, 1951), pp. 157–76; Herbert Stein and Edward F. Denison, "High Employment and Growth in the American Economy," *Goals for Americans: The Report of the President's Commission on National Goals* (Prentice-Hall, 1960), pp. 163–90; *Foreign Tax Policies and Economic Growth,* A Conference Report of the National Bureau of Economic Research and the Brookings Institution (Columbia University Press, 1966); Albert Ando, E. Cary Brown, and Ann F. Friedlaender, *Studies in Economic Stabilization* (Brookings Institution, 1968); Walter W. Heller and others, *Fiscal Policy for a Balanced Economy* (Organisation for Economic Co-operation and Development, 1968); Milton Friedman and Walter W. Heller, *Monetary vs. Fiscal Policy* (Norton, 1969); Arthur M. Okun, *The Political Economy of Prosperity* (Brookings Institution, 1970); and Alan S. Blinder and Robert M. Solow, "Analytical Foundations of Fiscal Policy," in *The Economics of Public Finance* (cited above for chapter 1), pp. 3–115.

The issues raised by wage-price or incomes policies to help reconcile full employment with price stability are presented in George P. Shultz and Robert Z. Aliber, eds., *Guidelines, Informal Controls, and the Market Place* (University of Chicago Press, 1966), and John Sheahan, *The Wage-Price Guideposts* (Brookings Institution, 1967). The history of wage-price policy in the United States since the end of the Second World War is reviewed and appraised in Craufurd D. Goodwin, ed., *Exhortation and Controls: The Search for a Wage-Price Policy, 1945–1971* (Brookings Institution, 1975). The experience with the 1971–73 controls in the United States is analyzed by Arnold R. Weber, *In Pursuit of Price Sta-*

bility: The Wage-Price Freeze of 1971 (Brookings Institution, 1973); and Robert F. Lanzillotti, Mary T. Hamilton, and R. Blaine Roberts, *Phase II in Review: The Price Commission Experience* (Brookings Institution, 1975).

The basic empirical work on the relation between unemployment, wages, and prices in the United States was done by George L. Perry, *Unemployment, Money Wage Rates, and Inflation* (M.I.T. Press, 1966). For an excellent analysis of the costs of inflation and the difficulties of slowing it down, see Arthur M. Okun, "Inflation: Its Mechanics and Welfare Costs," *Brookings Papers on Economic Activity, 2:1975,* pp. 351–90.

For a discussion of national debt policy, see Marshall A. Robinson, *The National Debt Ceiling* (Brookings Institution, 1959). Different views on the "burden" of the national debt are summarized in James M. Ferguson, ed., *Public Debt and Future Generations* (University of North Carolina Press, 1964).

Criteria for evaluating government expenditures are discussed in Francis M. Bator, *The Question of Government Spending* (Harper, 1960); Robert Dorfman, ed., *Measuring Benefits of Government Investments* (Brookings Institution, 1965); and Samuel B. Chase, Jr., ed., *Problems in Public Expenditure Analysis* (Brookings Institution, 1968). The methods of evaluating government expenditures are discussed critically in Charles L. Schultze, *The Politics and Economics of Public Spending* (Brookings Institution, 1968); and Peter O. Steiner, "Public Expenditure Budgeting," in Blinder and others, *The Economics of Public Finance* (cited above for chapter 1), pp. 241–357. The annual volumes *Setting National Priorities* published by the Brookings Institution provide an analysis of the choices in the federal budget.

Chapter 3. The Tax Legislative Process

The standard work on the tax legislative process is Roy Blough, *The Federal Taxing Process* (Prentice-Hall, 1952). In addition to the discussion of legislative procedures, this book examines in detail the interest and pressure groups involved in tax legislation and also reviews considerations relating to the level and distribution of taxes. The political cross-currents that influence the tax decisionmaking process are analyzed in Edward S. Flash, Jr., *Economic Advice and Presidential Leadership: The Council of Economic Advisers* (Columbia University Press, 1965), chap. 5; Ira Sharkansky, *The Politics of Taxing and Spending* (Bobbs-Merrill, 1969); and John F. Manley, *The Politics of Finance: The House Committee on Ways and Means* (Little, Brown, 1970).

The reader will obtain some insight into the intricacies of the legislative process by reviewing the tax messages, hearings, and reports by the House Ways and Means Committee and the Senate Finance Committee relating to any one of the major tax bills listed in table 3-1.

The congressional method of conducting responsible and thorough reviews of federal tax issues is best illustrated by the 1955 and 1972–74 inquiries of the Joint Economic Committee and the 1959 and 1975 inquiries of the House Ways and Means Committee. In each case, a set of papers by leading experts was first published, and hearings or discussions on these papers were later held to permit the committee members to interrogate the experts. See the following publications: Joint Committee on the Economic Report, *Federal Tax Policy for Economic Growth and Stability*, 84:1 (Government Printing Office, 1955 and 1956), 2 vols. (Papers and Hearings); House Ways and Means Committee, *Tax Revision Compendium,* Compendium of Papers on Broadening the Tax Base (GPO, 1959), 3 vols., and *Income Tax Revision,* Panel Discussions, 86:1 (GPO, 1960); Joint Economic Committee, *The Economics of Federal Subsidy Programs,* 92:2 (GPO, 1972) and 93:1 and 2 (GPO, 1973 and 1974), 9 vols. (Papers and Hearings); House Ways and Means Committee, *Tax Reform (Invited Panelists),* Panel Discussions, and *Tax Reform (Administration and Public Witnesses),* Public Hearings, 5 vols., 94:1 (GPO, 1975).

Federal excise taxes were evaluated in a series of papers by some of the nation's leading tax experts in House Ways and Means Committee, *Excise Tax Compendium* (GPO, 1964); panel discussions on June 15 and 16, 1964, were published in *Federal Excise Tax Structure*, 88:2 (GPO, 1964), part 2, and subsequent hearings were published in parts 3–6. These papers and hearings were influential in the preparation of the Excise Tax Reduction Act of 1965.

Chapter 4. The Individual Income Tax

The most authoritative treatise on this tax is Richard Goode, *The Individual Income Tax,* rev. ed. (Brookings Institution, 1976). A scholarly analysis of the arguments for and against progression will be found in Walter J. Blum and Harry Kalven, Jr., *The Uneasy Case for Progressive Taxation* (University of Chicago Press, 1953); a review of the issues is given in Charles O. Galvin and Boris I. Bittker, *The Income Tax: How Progressive Should It Be?* (American Enterprise Institute for Public Policy Research, 1969). The reader may also wish to consult the following classics: Henry C. Simons, *Personal Income Taxation* (University of Chicago Press, 1938); and William Vickrey, *Agenda for Progressive Taxation* (Ronald Press, 1947).

Empirical analyses of the impact of income taxation on economic incentives, based on interviews with individual taxpayers, are J. Keith Butters, Lawrence E. Thompson, and Lynn L. Bollinger, *Effects of Taxation: Investments by Individuals* (Harvard University, Graduate School of Business Administration, 1953); George F. Break, "Income Taxes and Incentives to Work: An Empirical Study," *American Economic Review,* vol. 47 (September 1957), pp. 529–49; Robin Barlow, Harvey E. Brazer, and James N. Morgan, *Economic Behavior of the Affluent* (Brookings Institution, 1966); Daniel M. Holland, "The Effect of Taxation on Effort: Some Results for Business Executives," in National Tax Association, *Proceedings of the Sixty-second Annual Conference on Taxation* (1970), pp. 428–517; and Donald B. Fields and W. T. Stanbury, "Incentives, Disincentives and the Income Tax: Further Empirical Evidence," *Public Finance,* vol. 25, no. 3 (1970), pp. 381–415, and "Income Taxes and Incentives to Work: Some Additional Empirical Evidence," *American Economic Review,* vol. 61 (June 1971), pp. 435–43. For a summary of econometric analyses of the relation between wages and work effort, see Glen G. Cain and Harold W. Watts, eds., *Income Maintenance and Labor Supply: Econometric Studies* (Rand McNally for Markham, 1973).

Estimates of the built-in flexibility of the individual income tax are given by Joseph A. Pechman, "Responsiveness of the Federal Individual Income Tax to Changes in Income," *Brookings Papers on Economic Activity, 2:1973,* pp. 385–421.

The usefulness of the concept of a comprehensive income tax is discussed in detail by Boris I. Bittker, Charles O. Galvin, Richard A. Musgrave, and Joseph A. Pechman in *A Comprehensive Income Tax Base? A Debate* (Federal Tax Press, 1968). Quantitative measures of the erosion of the individual income tax base are provided by Joseph A. Pechman and Benjamin A. Okner, "Individual Income Tax Erosion by Income Classes," in *The Economics of Federal Subsidy Programs* (cited above for chapter 3), pt. 1, pp. 13–40 (Brookings Reprint 230); and in Commission to Revise the Tax Structure, *Reforming the Federal Tax Structure* (Fund for Public Policy Research, 1973).

The concept of "tax expenditures" was first proposed by Bernard Wolfman, "Federal Tax Policy and the Support of Science," *University of Pennsylvania Law Review,* vol. 114 (December 1965), pp. 171–86. A detailed exposition of the rationale of tax expenditures is provided by Stanley S. Surrey, *Pathways to Tax Reform: The Concept of Tax Expenditures* (Harvard University Press, 1973). Official estimates of tax expenditures are given annually in *Special Analyses, Budget of the United States Government,* and in the annual report of the Congressional Budget Office (the latest report is *Budget Options for Fiscal Year 1977,* GPO, 1976).

Estimates of the incentive effects of the charitable deduction are provided by Martin Feldstein, "The Income Tax and Charitable Contributions: Part I—Aggregate and Distributional Effects; Part II—The Impact on Religious, Educational and Other Organizations," *National Tax Journal,* vol. 28 (March and June 1975), pp. 81–100, 209–26.

Five books for the general reader on income tax reform are Louis Eisenstein, *The Ideologies of Taxation* (Ronald Press, 1961); Dan Throop Smith, *Federal Tax Reform* (McGraw-Hill, 1961); Philip M. Stern, *The Rape of the Taxpayer* (Random House, 1973); George F. Break and Joseph A. Pechman, *Federal Tax Reform: The Impossible Dream?* (Brookings Institution, 1975); Robert M. Brandon, Jonathan Rowe, and Thomas H. Stanton, *Tax Politics* (Pantheon, 1976).

The major structural features of the individual income tax are discussed in detail in the following sources: Lawrence H. Seltzer, *The Nature and Tax Treatment of Capital Gains and Losses* (National Bureau of Economic Research, 1951); C. Harry Kahn, *Personal Deductions in the Federal Income Tax* (Princeton University Press for the NBER, 1960); Michael E. Levy, *Income Tax Exemptions* (Amsterdam: North-Holland, 1960); Harold M. Groves, *Federal Tax Treatment of the Family* (Brookings Institution, 1963); David J. Ott and Allan H. Meltzer, *Federal Tax Treatment of State and Local Securities* (Brookings Institution, 1963); Martin David, *Alternative Approaches to Capital Gains Taxation* (Brookings Institution, 1968); C. Harry Kahn, *Employee Compensation Under the Income Tax* (Columbia University Press for the NBER, 1968); Lawrence H. Seltzer, *The Personal Exemptions in the Income Tax* (Columbia University Press for the NBER, 1968); Richard E. Slitor, *The Federal Income Tax in Relation to Housing,* prepared for the National Commission on Urban Problems, Research Report 5 (GPO, 1968); Arnold C. Harberger and Martin J. Bailey, eds., *The Taxation of Income from Capital* (Brookings Institution, 1969); William D. Andrews, "Personal Deductions in an Ideal Income Tax," *Harvard Law Review,* vol. 86 (December 1972), pp. 309–85; Emil M. Sunley, Jr., "The Maximum Tax on Earned Income," *National Tax Journal,* vol. 27 (December 1974), pp. 543–52; and Boris I. Bittker, "Federal Income Taxation and the Family," *Stanford Law Review,* vol. 27 (July 1975), pp. 1389–1463. A comparison of the effects of the individual income tax and an expenditure tax on economic growth is provided by Robert E. Hall, "Consumption Taxes versus Income Taxes: Implications for Economic Growth," in National Tax Association, *Proceedings of the Sixty-first Annual Conference on Taxation* (1969), pp. 125–45.

Negative taxation in the form suggested in the text was first discussed by Milton Friedman in *Capitalism and Freedom* (University of Chicago

Press, 1962), pp. 191–94. The philosophy and mechanics of negative taxation are analyzed in detail in Christopher Green, *Negative Taxes and the Poverty Problem* (Brookings Institution, 1967), and James Tobin, Joseph A. Pechman, and Peter M. Mieszkowski, "Is A Negative Income Tax Practical?" *Yale Law Journal,* vol. 77 (November 1967), pp. 1–27. The President's Commission on Income Maintenance Programs recommended a negative income tax for the United States in its report *Poverty Amid Plenty: The American Paradox* (GPO, 1969); background materials prepared for the Commission are assembled in *Background Papers* (GPO, 1970), and *Technical Studies* (GPO, 1970). President Nixon's family assistance plan is described in detail in Senate Finance Committee, *H.R. 16311, The Family Assistance Act of 1970,* Revised and Resubmitted to the Senate Committee on Finance by the Administration, 91:2 (GPO, 1970.) An analysis of the first social experiment in negative income taxation is given in Joseph A. Pechman and P. Michael Timpane, eds., *Work Incentives and Income Guarantees: The New Jersey Negative Income Tax Experiment* (Brookings Institution, 1975).

For analyses of the effects of inflation on the personal income tax, see Thelma Liesner and Mervyn A. King, eds., *Indexing for Inflation* (London: Heinemann Educational Books, 1975); Henry J. Aaron, ed., *Inflation and the Income Tax* (Brookings Institution, 1976); and Organisation for Economic Co-operation and Development, *The Adjustment of Personal Income Tax Systems for Inflation* (Paris: OECD, 1976).

Chapter 5. The Corporation Income Tax

Richard Goode's classic, *The Corporation Income Tax* (Wiley, 1951), provides a thorough analysis and appraisal of the role of the corporation income tax. A discussion of the merits of this tax in comparison with other taxes is given in a symposium volume of the Tax Institute of America, *Alternatives to Present Federal Taxes* (Tax Institute, 1964).

For differing viewpoints on the incidence of the corporation income tax, see Arnold C. Harberger, "The Incidence of the Corporation Income Tax," *Journal of Political Economy,* vol. 70 (June 1962), pp. 215–40; Marian Krzyzaniak and Richard A. Musgrave, *The Shifting of the Corporation Income Tax* (Johns Hopkins Press, 1963); Challis A. Hall, Jr., "Direct Shifting of the Corporation Income Tax in Manufacturing," *American Economic Review,* vol. 54 (May 1964), pp. 258–71; Marian Krzyzaniak, ed., *Effects of Corporation Income Tax* (Wayne State University Press, 1966); Robert J. Gordon, "The Incidence of the Corporation Income Tax in U.S. Manufacturing, 1925–62," *American Economic Review,* vol. 57 (September 1967), pp. 731–58; Peter Mieszkowski, "Tax

Incidence Theory: The Effects of Taxes on the Distribution of Income"
(cited above for chapter 1); Martin Feldstein, "Tax Incidence in a Growing Economy with Variable Factor Supply," *Quarterly Journal of Economics,* vol. 88 (November 1974), pp. 551–73; John B. Shoven and John
Whalley, "A General Equilibrium Calculation of the Effects of Differential
Taxation of Income from Capital in the U.S.," *Journal of Public Economics,* vol. 1 (November 1972), pp. 281–321; and Joseph E. Stiglitz,
"The Corporation Tax," *Journal of Public Economics,* vol. 5 (April–May
1976), pp. 303–11.

The treatment of dividends under the income taxes has been investi-
gated thoroughly in two books by Daniel M. Holland: *The Income-Tax
Burden on Stockholders* (Princeton University Press for the National
Bureau of Economic Research, 1958), and *Dividends Under the Income
Tax* (Princeton University Press for the NBER, 1962). Methods of integrating the corporation and individual income taxes are analyzed in detail
by Charles E. McLure, Jr., "Integration of the Personal and Corporate
Income Taxes: The Missing Element in Recent Tax Reform Proposals,"
Harvard Law Review, vol. 88 (January 1975), pp. 532–82. For a recent
analysis, see George F. Break and Joseph A. Pechman, "Relationship Between the Corporation and Individual Income Taxes," *National Tax
Journal,* vol. 28 (September 1975), pp. 341–52. For what other countries
do, see Organisation for Economic Co-operation and Development, *Company Tax Systems in OECD Member Countries* (Paris: OECD, 1973).

The influence of federal taxation on corporate financial policy is appraised in Dan Throop Smith, *Effects of Taxation: Corporate Financial
Policy* (Harvard University, Graduate School of Business Administration, 1952). John A. Brittain, in *Corporate Dividend Policy* (Brookings
Institution, 1966), measures the impact of the income taxes on the
dividend payout policy of corporations.

The basic articles on the incentive effects of depreciation are by E. Cary
Brown, "Business-Income Taxation and Investment Incentives," in Lloyd
A. Metzler and others, *Income, Employment and Public Policy: Essays in
Honor of Alvin H. Hansen* (Norton, 1948); and Paul A. Samuelson,
"Tax Deductibility of Economic Depreciation to Insure Invariant Valua-
tions," *Journal of Political Economy,* vol. 72 (December 1964), pp.
604–06. Other useful articles on depreciation and the investment credit are
Samuel B. Chase, Jr., "Tax Credits for Investment Spending," *National
Tax Journal,* vol. 15 (March 1962), pp. 32–52; Melvin White and Anne
White, "Tax Neutrality of Instantaneous versus Economic Depreciation,"
in Richard M. Bird and John G. Head, eds., *Modern Fiscal Issues: Essays
in Honor of Carl S. Shoup* (University of Toronto Press, 1972), pp.
105–16; and Emil M. Sunley, Jr., "Towards a More Neutral Investment
Tax Credit," *National Tax Journal,* vol. 26 (June 1973), pp. 209–20.

The need for liberalized depreciation policies in taxation (before the adoption of these policies in recent years) was presented by George W. Terborgh in *Realistic Depreciation Policy* (Machinery and Allied Products Institute, 1954). Terborgh has also provided a succinct summary of the effects of the investment credit and depreciation changes in 1962 on rates of return in *Incentive Value of the Investment Credit, the Guideline Depreciation System, and the Corporate Rate Reduction* (MAPI, 1964). Measures of the impact on investment of accelerated depreciation and the investment credit are provided in Gary Fromm, ed., *Tax Incentives and Capital Spending* (Brookings Institution, 1971). For a survey of the literature on the factors influencing investment behavior, see Dale W. Jorgenson, "Econometric Studies of Investment Behavior: A Survey," *Journal of Economic Literature,* vol. 9 (December 1971), pp. 1111–47.

Other structural features of the corporation income tax are discussed in Stephen L. McDonald, *Federal Tax Treatment of Income from Oil and Gas* (Brookings Institution, 1963); Lawrence B. Krause and Kenneth W. Dam, *Federal Tax Treatment of Foreign Income* (Brookings Institution, 1964); Peggy B. Musgrave, *United States Taxation of Foreign Investment Income* (Harvard Law School, International Tax Program, 1969); Peggy B. Musgrave, *Direct Investment Abroad and the Multinationals: Effects on the United States Economy,* prepared for the Subcommittee on Multinational Corporations of the Senate Committee on Foreign Relations, 94:1 (Government Printing Office, 1975); *Treasury Department Report on Private Foundations, February 2, 1965,* Senate Finance Committee Print, 89:1 (GPO, 1965). The effect of the corporation income tax on export prices is analyzed by Robert Z. Aliber and Herbert Stein in "The Price of U.S. Exports and the Mix of U.S. Direct and Indirect Taxes," *American Economic Review,* vol. 54 (September 1964), pp. 703–10. A report of the National Bureau of Economic Research and the Brookings Institution, *The Role of Direct and Indirect Taxes in the Federal Revenue System* (Princeton University Press, 1964), discusses the effect of various taxes on the balance of payments under a system of federal exchange rates.

Inflation accounting for business income is analyzed in detail in Liesner and King, eds., *Indexing for Inflation* (cited above for chapter 4); *Inflation Accounting,* Report of the Inflation Accounting Committee, Cmnd. 6225 (London: Her Majesty's Stationery Office, 1975); William Fellner, Kenneth W. Clarkson, and John H. Moore, *Correcting Taxes for Inflation* (American Enterprise Institute for Public Policy Research, 1975); and Aaron, ed., *Inflation and the Income Tax* (cited above for chapter 4). Estimates of business profits adjusted for inflation are given by John B. Shoven and Jeremy I. Bulow, "Inflation Accounting and Nonfinancial Corporate Profits: Financial Assets and Liabilities," *Brookings Papers on Economic Activity, 1:1976,* pp. 15–57.

Chapter 6. Consumption Taxes

There are excellent treatises on the major general consumption taxes. John F. Due, in *Sales Taxation* (University of Illinois Press, 1957), discusses the role of consumption taxes in the tax structure and evaluates the different forms and features of sales and value added taxes, taking the experience of various countries into account. A brilliant defense of, and plea for, the adoption of a graduated expenditure tax may be found in Nicholas Kaldor, *An Expenditure Tax* (London: Allen and Unwin, 1955). The administrative and compliance problems of an expenditure tax are examined in Advisory Commission on Intergovernmental Relations, *The Expenditure Tax: Concept, Administration and Possible Applications* (Government Printing Office, 1974). The most recent defense of the expenditure tax is by William D. Andrews, "A Consumption-Type or Cash Flow Personal Income Tax," *Harvard Law Review*, vol. 87 (April 1974), pp. 1113–88. For a critique of this view and a rebuttal, see Alvin C. Warren, Jr., "Fairness and a Consumption-Type or Cash Flow Personal Income Tax," and William D. Andrews, "A Reply to Professor Warren," both in *Harvard Law Review,* vol. 88 (March 1975), pp. 931–58.

The value added tax is explored by Clara K. Sullivan in *The Tax on Value Added* (Columbia University Press, 1965); and Advisory Commission on Intergovernmental Relations, *The Value-Added Tax and Alternative Sources of Revenue* (GPO, 1973). Daniel C. Morgan, Jr., discusses the sales tax in *Retail Sales Tax: An Appraisal of New Issues* (University of Wisconsin Press, 1964).

The relative merits of income and consumption taxes are examined in detail in *The Role of Direct and Indirect Taxes in the Federal Revenue System* (cited above for chapter 5); and Richard A. Musgrave, ed., *Broad-Based Taxes: New Options and Sources* (Johns Hopkins University Press, 1973). For an evaluation of the federal excise tax structure, see the *Excise Tax Compendium* (cited above for chapter 3).

The use of taxation to control pollution is explained by Allen V. Kneese and Charles L. Schultze, *Pollution, Prices, and Public Policy* (Brookings Institution, 1975).

Chapter 7. Payroll Taxes

The literature on payroll taxes is an outgrowth of discussions on financing the social security system. One of the earliest analyses of payroll taxation is contained in Seymour E. Harris, *Economics of Social*

Security (McGraw-Hill, 1941); part 2 of this volume is devoted to the incidence of payroll taxes. For a comprehensive analysis, see Joseph A. Pechman, Henry J. Aaron, and Michael K. Taussig, *Social Security: Perspectives for Reform* (Brookings Institution, 1968), chap. 8. For an analysis of the economic and distributional effects of payroll taxes, see John A. Brittain, *The Payroll Tax for Social Security* (Brookings Institution, 1972).

The reader may also wish to refer to John J. Carroll, *Alternative Methods of Financing Old-Age, Survivors, and Disability Insurance* (University of Michigan, Institute of Public Administration, 1960); Richard A. Lester, *The Economics of Unemployment Compensation* (Princeton University, Industrial Relations Section, 1962); Margaret S. Gordon, *The Economics of Welfare Policies* (Columbia University Press, 1963); William Haber and Merrill G. Murray, *Unemployment Insurance in the American Economy* (Richard D. Irwin, 1966); William G. Bowen and others, eds., *The American System of Social Insurance: Its Philosophy, Impact, and Future Development* (McGraw-Hill, 1968); and Alicia H. Munnell, *The Future of Social Security* (Brookings Institution, 1977). Questions of financing are discussed in the reports of the Advisory Council on Social Security.

Methods of lowering the burden of payroll taxation on low-income workers are analyzed in detail in U.S. Department of Health, Education, and Welfare, Social Security Administration, Office of Research and Statistics, *Reducing Social Security Contributions for Low-Income Workers: Issues and Analysis* (Government Printing Office, 1974).

A comprehensive survey of social security systems in other countries is provided in Social Security Administration, Office of Research and Statistics, *Social Security Programs Throughout the World, 1975*, Research Report 48 (GPO, 1976).

Chapter 8. Estate and Gift Taxes

Although it is out of date now as a statement of current law, the classic account of the development of the federal estate and gift taxes in this country is still Randolph E. Paul, *Federal Estate and Gift Taxation*, 2 vols. (Little, Brown, 1942), and *1946 Supplement* (Little, Brown, 1946). A later historical review and analysis of these taxes is Louis Eisenstein, "The Rise and Decline of the Estate Tax," in *Federal Tax Policy for Economic Growth and Stability* (cited above for chapter 3), pp. 819–47 (reprinted with minor changes in *Tax Law Review*, vol. 11 [March 1956], pp. 223–59). The most recent volumes on wealth taxation are Alan A. Tait, *The Taxation of Personal Wealth* (University of Illinois Press,

1967), and C. T. Sandford, *Taxing Personal Wealth* (London: Allen and Unwin, 1971).

Robert J. Lampman provided estimates of the size distribution of wealth in the United States in *The Share of Top Wealth-Holders in National Wealth, 1922–56* (Princeton University Press for the National Bureau of Economic Research, 1962), based largely on data from federal estate tax returns. His estimates have been updated by James D. Smith and Stephen D. Franklin, "The Concentration of Personal Wealth, 1922–1969," *American Economic Review,* vol. 64 (May 1974), pp. 162–67. Estimates of the distribution of wealth are prepared periodically on the basis of estate tax returns by the Internal Revenue Service, most recently in *Statistics of Income—1972, Personal Wealth Estimated from Estate Tax Returns* (Government Printing Office, 1976).

The first estimates of the amount of gift and trust transfers were made on the basis of 1945 estate tax returns and prior gift tax returns of the same decedents. These estimates were presented by Secretary of the Treasury John W. Snyder in Exhibit 5 of his statement before the House Ways and Means Committee on February 3, 1950, and published in vol. 1 of the Hearings, *Revenue Revision of 1950,* 81:2 (GPO, 1950), pp. 75–89. More recent data on gift and trust transfers and a thorough analysis of the major structural problems in estate and gift taxation may be found in Carl S. Shoup, *Federal Estate and Gift Taxes* (Brookings Institution, 1966). The use of trusts and the methods of taxing them under the transfer taxes are explored in detail in Gerald R. Jantscher, *Trusts and Estate Taxation* (Brookings Institution, 1967). The incentive effect of the full deduction for bequests to charitable organizations is estimated by Michael J. Boskin, "Estate Taxation and Charitable Bequests," *Journal of Public Economics,* vol. 5 (January–February 1976), pp. 27–56.

Proposals for reforming the estate and gift taxes are analyzed by Jerome Kurtz and Stanley S. Surrey, "Reform of Death and Gift Taxes: The 1969 Treasury Proposals, the Criticisms, and a Rebuttal," *Columbia Law Review,* vol. 70 (December 1970), pp. 1365–1401; and David Westfall, "Revitalizing the Federal Estate and Gift Taxes," *Harvard Law Review,* vol. 83 (March 1970), pp. 986–1013.

The recommendations of the American Law Institute estate and gift tax project are contained in *Federal Estate and Gift Taxation: Recommendations Adopted by the American Law Institute and Reporters' Studies* (American Law Institute, 1969). The proposals of the Carter Commission in Canada appear in vol. 3, chap. 17, and vol. 4, chap. 21, of the *Report of the Royal Commission on Taxation* (cited above for chapter 1). A model accessions tax was worked out in detail under the direction of the American Law Institute estate and gift tax project and appears in the report cited above. A briefer description is contained in William D. Andrews, "The Accessions Tax Proposal," *Tax Law Review,* vol. 22 (May 1967), pp. 589–633. A recent analysis of this proposal is given by C. T. Sandford, J. R. M. Willis, and D. J. Ironside, *An Accessions Tax* (London: Institute for Fiscal Studies, 1973).

Chapter 9. State and Local Taxes

The best general sources on the state-local tax structure and the major issues in this area are Dick Netzer, "State-Local Finance and Intergovernmental Fiscal Relations," in Blinder and others, *Economics of Public Finance* (cited above for chapter 1), pp. 361–421; Advisory Commission on Intergovernmental Relations (ACIR), *Federal-State-Local Finances: Significant Features of Fiscal Federalism,* 1973–74 edition (Government Printing Office, 1974), and 1974–75 edition (advance release) (ACIR, 1975); ACIR, *Significant Features of Fiscal Federalism, 1976 Edition, 1. Trends* (ACIR, 1976); L. Laszlo Ecker-Racz, *It's Your Business: Local and State Finance* (National Municipal League, 1976); and James A. Maxwell and J. Richard Aronson, *Financing State and Local Governments,* 3d ed. (Brookings Institution, 1977).

There is much literature on the property tax. Jens P. Jensen, *Property Taxation in the United States* (University of Chicago Press, 1931), evaluates this tax from the vantage point of the late 1920s and early 1930s; and Dick Netzer, *Economics of the Property Tax* (Brookings Institution, 1966), analyzes the economic impact of the tax and its role in the U.S. tax system in the mid-1960s. The new view that the property tax is a tax on capital is explained by Henry J. Aaron, *Who Pays the Property Tax?* (Brookings Institution, 1975).

Recent developments in property tax administration are summarized in ACIR, *The Property Tax in a Changing Environment* (GPO, 1974). The "circuit breaker" idea is explained in ACIR, *Property Tax Circuit-Breakers: Current Status and Policy Issues* (ACIR, 1975). For a critique of circuit breakers, see Henry J. Aaron, "What Do Circuit-Breaker Laws Accomplish?" in George E. Peterson, ed., *Property Tax Reform* (John C. Lincoln Institute and Urban Institute, 1973), pp. 53–64 (Brookings Reprint 277).

Problems of land value taxation are discussed in *Building the American City,* Report of the National Commission on Urban Problems, House Document 91-34 (GPO, 1969), part 4, chap. 6. Increases in the value of real estate are estimated by Allen D. Manvel, "Trends in the Value of Real Estate and Land, 1956 to 1966," in *Three Land Research Studies,* prepared for the National Commission on Urban Problems, Research Report 12 (GPO, 1968).

Federal-state-local fiscal relations may be studied by referring to ACIR, *Measures of State and Local Fiscal Capacity and Tax Effort* (GPO, 1962); James A. Maxwell, *Tax Credits and Intergovernmental Fiscal Relations* (Brookings Institution, 1962); ACIR, *The Role of Equalization in Federal Grants* (ACIR, 1964); Richard A. Musgrave, ed., *Essays in Fiscal Federalism* (Brookings Institution, 1965); ACIR, *Fiscal Balance in the American Federal System*, 2 vols. (GPO, 1967); George F. Break, *Intergovernmental Fiscal Relations in the United States* (Brookings Institution, 1967); and Wallace E. Oates, *Fiscal Federalism* (Harcourt Brace Jovanovich, 1972).

The early literature on revenue sharing is summarized in *Revenue Sharing and Its Alternatives: What Future for Fiscal Federalism?* Hearings before the Subcommittee on Fiscal Policy of the Joint Economic Committee, 90:1 (GPO, 1967). The pros and cons of revenue sharing are discussed in Walter W. Heller and others, *Revenue Sharing and the City,* Harvey S. Perloff and Richard P. Nathan, eds. (Johns Hopkins Press, 1968), and *Financing State and Local Governments* (Federal Reserve Bank of Boston, 1970). President Nixon's revenue sharing plan is compared with a number of other variants in Murray L. Weidenbaum and Robert L. Joss, "Alternative Approaches to Revenue Sharing: A Description and Framework for Evaluation," *National Tax Journal,* vol. 23 (March 1970), pp. 2–22.

For an evaluation of the revenue sharing plan adopted by the federal government during the first years of its operation, see Richard P. Nathan, Allen D. Manvel, Susannah E. Calkins, and associates, *Monitoring Revenue Sharing* (Brookings Institution, 1975). The National Science Foundation supported a large number of studies of general revenue sharing which are summarized in *General Revenue Sharing: Research Utilization Project,* National Science Foundation, Research Applied to National Needs, 5 vols. (GPO, 1975). See also Wallace E. Oates, ed., *Financing the New Federalism: Revenue Sharing, Conditional Grants, and Taxation* (Johns Hopkins University Press, 1975).

For more specific aspects of intergovernmental relations, see ACIR, *Coordination of State and Federal Inheritance, Estate, and Gift Taxes* (ACIR, 1961), and *Federal-State Coordination of Personal Income Taxes* (ACIR, 1965); and *State Taxation of Interstate Commerce,* Report of the Special Subcommittee on State Taxation of Interstate Commerce of the House Committee on the Judiciary, vols. 1 and 2, House Report 1480, 88:2 (GPO, 1964), and vols. 3 and 4, House Reports 565 and 952, 89:1 (GPO, 1965).

Numerous official state and city tax commission reports provide excellent sources of information for and analyses of state-local tax problems. Among the best are *Report of the Governor's Minnesota Tax Study Committee, 1956* (Colwell Press, 1956); *Michigan Tax Study Staff Papers* (Lansing: State of Michigan, 1958); University of Wisconsin Tax Study Committee, *Wisconsin's State and Local Tax Burden: Impact, Incidence and Tax Revision Alternatives* (University of Wisconsin, 1959); University of Maryland, College of Business and Public Administration, *Maryland Tax Study* (University of Maryland, 1965); and City of New York, Temporary Commission on City Finances, *Toward Fiscal Strength: Overcoming New York City's Financial Dilemma,* Second Interim Report (New York City, November 1965 [available from Municipal Reference Library]); *Report of Governor's Revenue Study Committee, 1968–69* (State of Illinois, 1969); and *Report of the Connecticut State Revenue Task Force,* Submitted to the Governor and General Assembly (State of Connecticut, 1971), and *Papers,* Prepared for the Connecticut State Revenue Task Force, 6 vols. (1970). The intergovernmental problems of urban communities and methods of increasing the fiscal resources of the nation's cities are discussed in ACIR, *Urban America and the Federal System* (GPO, 1969); and ACIR, *City Financial Emergencies: The Intergovernmental Dimension* (GPO, 1973).

Appendix A. Historical Notes

Edwin R. A. Seligman, in "Income Tax," *Encyclopaedia of the Social Sciences* (Macmillan, 1932), vol. 7, pp. 626–39, traces income taxation in Europe and the United States up to the early 1930s. The reader may also wish to refer to the history of the development of progression in the British income tax in F. Shehab, *Progressive Taxation* (Oxford University Press, 1953). For histories of taxation in this country, see Sidney Ratner, *Taxation and Democracy in America* (Wiley, 1942); and Randolph Paul, *Taxation in the United States* (Little, Brown, 1954). Lewis H. Kimmel analyzes the changes in American attitudes toward government taxing, spending, and borrowing in *Federal Budget and Fiscal Policy, 1789–1958* (Brookings Institution, 1959). Herbert Stein traces the changes in attitudes toward federal budget deficits by government officials, economists, and businessmen in *The Fiscal Revolution in America* (University of Chicago Press, 1969).

The *Annual Reports of the Secretary of the Treasury on the State of the Finances* summarize the major features of tax legislation enacted each year in a section titled "Taxation Developments." Comprehensive summaries of tax rates are provided for 1913–40 in the 1940 Report (pp. 466–534); for 1940–50 in the 1950 Report (pp. 251–80); and for 1950–62 in the 1962 Report (pp. 370–402).

Index